AF754204

The Contribution of the International Tribunal for the Law of the Sea to the Rule of Law: 1996–2016

La contribution du Tribunal international du droit de la mer à l'état de droit : 1996-2016

The Contribution of the International Tribunal for the Law of the Sea to the Rule of Law: 1996–2016

La contribution du Tribunal international du droit de la mer à l'état de droit : 1996-2016

BRILL
NIJHOFF

LEIDEN | BOSTON

Cover illustration: Commemorative ceremony in the Hamburg City Hall, 7 October 2016.
Photo by Wallocha.

International Tribunal for the Law of the Sea
Tribunal international du droit de la mer
Am Internationalen Seegerichtshof 1
22609 Hamburg, Germany

Typeface for the Latin, Greek, and Cyrillic scripts: "Brill". See and download: brill.com/brill-typeface.

ISBN 978-90-04-34426-6 (hardback)
ISBN 978-90-04-35683-2 (e-book)

Copyright 2018 by International Tribunal for the Law of the Sea.
This work is published by Koninklijke Brill NV. Koninklijke Brill NV incorporates the imprints Brill, Brill Hes & De Graaf, Brill Nijhoff, Brill Rodopi, Brill Sense and Hotei Publishing.
Koninklijke Brill NV reserves the right to protect the publication against unauthorized use and to authorize dissemination by means of offprints, legitimate photocopies, microform editions, reprints, translations, and secondary information sources, such as abstracting and indexing services including databases. Requests for commercial re-use, use of parts of the publication, and/or translations must be addressed to Koninklijke Brill NV.

This book is printed on acid-free paper and produced in a sustainable manner.

Printed by Printforce, the Netherlands

Table of Contents/Table des matières

PART 2 / PARTIE 2
The Contribution of the Tribunal to the Progressive Development of International Law
La contribution du Tribunal au développement progressif du droit international

PART 3 / PARTIE 3
The Contribution of the Tribunal to the Rule of Law: The Point of View of Practitioners
La contribution du Tribunal à l'état de droit : Le point de vue des praticiens

PART 4 / PARTIE 4
Improving Working Methods in International Adjudication
L'amélioration des méthodes de travail de la justice internationale

Annexes

List of Abbreviations

Agreement on Part XI	Agreement relating to the implementation of Part XI of the United Nations Convention on the Law of the Sea
AJIL	*American Journal of International Law*
Assembly	Assembly of the International Seabed Authority
Authority	International Seabed Authority
BIICL	British Institute of International and Comparative Law
BYIL	*British Yearbook of International Law*
CJIL	*Chinese Journal of International Law*
CLCS	Commission on the Limits of the Continental Shelf
Convention	United Nations Convention on the Law of the Sea
Council	Council of the International Seabed Authority
Court	International Court of Justice
EJIL	*European Journal of International Law*
EEZ	Exclusive Economic Zone
Guidelines	Guidelines concerning the Preparation and Presentation of Cases before the Tribunal
GYBIL	*German Yearbook of International Law*
ICJ	International Court of Justice
ICLQ	*International and Comparative Law Quarterly*
IJMCL	*International Journal of Marine and Coastal Law*
ILC	International Law Commission
ILC Draft Articles [on State Responsibility]	Draft articles on Responsibility of States for internationally wrongful acts, adopted by the International Law Commission at its fifty-third session (2001)
IUU fishing	Illegal, unreported and unregulated fishing
Max Planck UNYB	*Max Planck Yearbook of United Nations Law*
MCA Convention	Convention on the Determination of the Minimal Conditions for Access and Exploitation of Marine Resources within the Maritime Areas under Jurisdiction of the Member States of the Sub-Regional Fisheries Commission
MPEIL Online	*Max Planck Encyclopaedia of International Law Online*
nm	nautical miles
PCIJ	Permanent Court of International Justice
PCA	Permanent Court of Arbitration
RIAA	*Reports of International Arbitral Awards*
Rules	Rules of the International Tribunal for the Law of the Sea

Statute	Statute of the International Tribunal for the Law of the Sea (Annex VI to the Convention)
SRFC	Sub-Regional Fisheries Commission
Tribunal	International Tribunal for the Law of the Sea
UN	United Nations Organization
UNTS	*United Nations Treaty Series*

Liste des abréviations

Accord sur la partie XI	Accord relatif à l'application de la partie XI de la Convention des Nations Unies sur le droit de mer
Assemblée	Assemblée de l'Autorité internationale des fonds marins
Autorité	Autorité internationale des fonds marins
CDI	Commission du droit international
CIJ	Cour internationale de Justice
CLPC	Commission des limites du plateau continental
Comité	Comité du Règlement et de la pratique en matière judiciaire
Conseil	Conseil de l'Autorité internationale des fonds marins
Convention	Convention des Nations Unies sur le droit de la mer
Cour	Cour internationale de Justice
CPJI	Cour permanente de Justice internationale
CSRP	Commission sous-régionale des pêches
Lignes directrices	Lignes directrices concernant la préparation et la présentation des affaires dont le Tribunal est saisi
ONU	Organisation des Nations Unies
Pêche INN	Pêche illicite, non déclarée et non réglementée
RSA	*Recueil des sentences arbitrales*
Règlement	Règlement du Tribunal international du droit de la mer
Résolution	Résolution sur la pratique interne du Tribunal en matière judicaire
Statut	Statut du Tribunal international du droit de la mer (annexe VI à la Convention)
Tribunal	Tribunal international du droit de la mer
RTNU	*Recueil des Traités des Nations Unies*
WWF	Fonds Mondial pour la Nature
ZEE	Zone économique exclusive

Introduction

On the occasion of its 20th Anniversary, the International Tribunal for the Law of the Sea held a one-and-a-half day international symposium at the premises of the Tribunal on 5 and 6 October 2016, on the theme "The contribution of the Tribunal to the Rule of Law".

The aim of the symposium was to highlight the role played by the Tribunal over the last 20 years in the system for the peaceful settlement of law of the sea related disputes, set out in Part XV of the United Nations Convention on the Law of the Sea. Approximately 180 international guest attended the symposium, which was designed for academics and legal practitioners. The symposium was organized with the financial support of the Government of Japan.

This publication reproduces the statements presented during the symposium, in the order in which they were delivered and in their original language. The question and answer sessions have not been transcribed for this volume.

This volume was financed by the Federal Foreign Office of Germany.

Philippe Gautier
Registrar

© 2018, BY INTERNATIONAL TRIBUNAL FOR THE LAW OF THE SEA | DOI 10.1163/9789004356832_002

Introduction

A l'occasion de son 20e anniversaire, le Tribunal international du droit de la mer a organisé un colloque international d'un jour et demi au siège du Tribunal les 5 et 6 octobre 2016, avec pour thème « La contribution du Tribunal à l'état de droit ».

Le colloque avait pour but de souligner le rôle joué par le Tribunal ces 20 dernières années dans le cadre du système de règlement pacifique des différends relatifs au droit de la mer, mis en place par la partie XV de la Convention des Nations Unies sur le droit de la mer. Environ 180 invités venant de différents pays ont assisté à ce colloque qui était destiné à un public d'universitaires et de praticiens du droit. Le colloque a été organisé avec le soutien financier du Gouvernement du Japon.

La publication reproduit les exposés présentés au cours du colloque, dans l'ordre dans lequel ils ont été faits et dans leur langue originale. Les séances de questions-réponses n'ont pas été retranscrites dans le volume.

Ce volume a été financé par l'Office fédéral des affaires étrangères de l'Allemagne.

Le Greffier
Philippe Gautier

© 2018, BY INTERNATIONAL TRIBUNAL FOR THE LAW OF THE SEA | DOI 10.1163/9789004356832_003

Opening Statement of the President of the Tribunal, Judge Vladimir Golitsyn

We have gathered here today to commemorate the 20th anniversary of the Tribunal. On this special occasion, we are very pleased to hold this symposium on "The contribution of the Tribunal to the rule of law". On behalf of the Tribunal, I extend a warm welcome to all participants, especially the many who have pleaded before the Tribunal over these twenty years.

This is the second event which the Tribunal is holding in celebration of its 20th anniversary. The first was a round table, which was held at UN Headquarters in New York, in June 2016, and organized with the financial support of the Korea Maritime Institute. Today's symposium has been made possible thanks to the financial contribution of the Government of Japan. On behalf of the Tribunal, I wish to express our sincere appreciation to both the Government of Japan and the Korea Maritime Institute for their generous support.

It is now twenty years since the Tribunal held its first meeting on 1 October 1996. Mr Hans Corell, the then Legal Counsel of the United Nations, who represented the Secretary-General of the United Nations on that occasion, opened that meeting of the Tribunal on what he called "a historic day". The official inauguration of the Tribunal took place a few days later, on 18 October 1996, when the newly elected judges made their solemn declarations in the City Hall of Hamburg, in the presence of Mr Boutros Boutros-Ghali, the Secretary-General of the United Nations.

The Tribunal began its work by devoting itself first to the establishment of its judicial organization and, as early as October 1997, the Tribunal already adopted three main instruments, namely: the Rules; a set of Guidelines to assist parties in presenting cases; and a Resolution on the Internal Judicial Practice of the Tribunal.

In November 1997, it received the first application instituting proceedings, which was for the prompt release of a vessel and its crew, pursuant to article 292 of the Convention. In December 1997, the Tribunal was seized of its first dispute on the merits, the *M/V "SAIGA" (No. 2)* case. The Judgment in that case was delivered 16 months after proceedings were instituted. You will agree with me that this is a remarkably short period.

The Judgment in the *M/V "SAIGA" (No. 2)* case provided an early opportunity for the Tribunal to contribute to the progressive development of international law and the law of the sea. I will therefore highlight some of the most important conclusions reached by the Tribunal in that case.

© 2018, BY INTERNATIONAL TRIBUNAL FOR THE LAW OF THE SEA | DOI 10.1163/9789004356832_004

The first contribution I wish to highlight relates to the question of "nationality of claims". In its Judgment, the Tribunal concluded that "the Convention considers a ship as a unit", and therefore that "the ship, every thing on it, and every person involved or interested in its operations are treated as an entity linked to the flag State. The nationalities of these persons are not relevant."[1] Another important aspect of this case concerns the question as to whether the existence of a "genuine link" constitutes a requirement for granting nationality to a ship. Here, with reference to article 94 of the Convention, the Tribunal stated that nothing in that article "permit[s] a State which discovers evidence indicating the absence of proper jurisdiction and control by a flag State over a ship to refuse to recognize the right of the ship to fly the flag of the flag State."[2] When assessing the force used in the arrest of the vessel *Saiga*, the Tribunal stated that "[c]onsiderations of humanity must apply in the law of the sea, as they do in other areas of international law."[3] This declaration may be seen as reading human rights law into the law of the sea, another fundamental pronouncement.

The Judgment in the *M/V "SAIGA" (No. 2)* case paved the way for the Tribunal's later jurisprudence, in which it looked further at issues of "considerations of humanity", "nationality of claims" and "genuine link".

Thus, issues of "considerations of humanity" arose, for instance, in a case on the merits concerning the arrest of the vessel M/V "Louisa". The *M/V "Virginia G"* case provided the Tribunal with the opportunity to address the issues concerning "nationality of claims" and "genuine link".

In the *M/V "Louisa"* case, which I have just mentioned, the Tribunal was confronted with the issue of the application of article 300 of the Convention on "good faith and abuse of rights" which was invoked for the first time before the Tribunal. In its findings in that case the Tribunal provided important clarifications concerning the application of this article by stating "that it is apparent from the language of article 300 of the Convention that article 300 cannot be invoked on its own. It becomes relevant only when 'the rights, jurisdiction and freedoms recognized' in the Convention are exercised in an abusive manner."[4]

---

1 *M/V "SAIGA" (No. 2) (Saint Vincent and the Grenadines* v. *Guinea), Judgment, ITLOS Reports 1999*, p. 10, at p. 48, para. 106.

2 *Ibid.*, at p. 41, para. 82.

3 *Ibid.*, at p. 62, para. 155.

4 *M/V "Louisa" (Saint Vincent and the Grenadines* v. *Kingdom of Spain), Judgment, ITLOS Reports 2013*, p. 4, *at* p. 43, para. 137; see also *M/V "Virginia G" (Panama/Guinea-Bissau), Judgment, ITLOS Reports 2014*, p. 4, at p. 109, para. 396.

In the *M/V "Virginia G"* case, which I mentioned before, the Tribunal was confronted with a legal issue which is not directly addressed in the Convention, namely the status of bunkering activities conducted in support of foreign vessels fishing in the EEZ of a coastal State. In this regard, the Tribunal provided in its Judgment what could be called a progressive interpretation of the Convention. The Tribunal concluded that "the regulation by a coastal State of bunkering of foreign vessels fishing in its exclusive economic zone is among those measures which the coastal State may take in its exclusive economic zone to conserve and manage its living resources ... under the Convention".[5]

In its initial phase, the Tribunal's case law developed mainly in relation to cases where the exercise of its jurisdiction was compulsory. I refer to the prompt release of vessels and crews and the prescription of provisional measures pending the constitution of an arbitral tribunal. With the handling of these urgent cases, the Tribunal earned a reputation for being able to administer justice in an expeditious and cost-effective manner.

As regards prompt release cases under article 292 of the Convention, the Tribunal developed a coherent jurisprudence, in particular, in applying relevant factors for determining a reasonable bond or other financial security. It also provided important clarifications on the financial nature of the bond or other financial security, the effects of the confiscation of the vessel, and the relationship between the provisions of article 292 and domestic procedures. During this symposium, judgments of the Tribunal in prompt release cases will be addressed in detail.

I am quite sure that the contribution to the progressive development of international law made by the Tribunal in its Judgments on provisional measures will also receive proper attention during the symposium. However, I would like to highlight that early decisions on provisional measures enabled the Tribunal to make an important contribution to the protection and preservation of the marine environment. This point is illustrated, among others, in the Tribunal's use of the notion of "prudence and caution"[6] in the *Southern Bluefin Tuna* cases, which, in effect, means application of the precautionary approach; and

---

5 *M/V "Virginia G" (Panama/Guinea-Bissau), Judgment, ITLOS Reports 2014*, p. 4, at p. 69, para. 217.

6 *Southern Bluefin Tuna (New Zealand* v. *Japan; Australia* v. *Japan), Provisional Measures, Order of 27 August 1999, ITLOS Reports 1999*, p. 280, at p. 296, paras. 77 and 79; see *MOX Plant (Ireland* v. *United Kingdom), Provisional Measures, Order of 3 December 2001, ITLOS Reports 2001*, p. 95, at p. 110, para. 84; *Land Reclamation in and around the Straits of Johor (Malaysia* v. *Singapore), Provisional Measures, Order of 8 October 2003, ITLOS Reports 2003*, p. 10, at p. 26, para. 99.

in the statement by the Tribunal in those cases, that "the conservation of the living resources of the sea is an element in the protection and preservation of the marine environment".[7]

In this connection I wish to point out that, while in the case of provisional measures, the measures that may be ordered by the Tribunal are "provisional" in nature, in some instances the specific measures prescribed by the Tribunal assisted the parties in reaching an amicable solution to their dispute.

The filing, in 2009, of the first maritime delimitation case constituted a landmark in the Tribunal's work. This case, which involved a dispute concerning the delimitation of maritime areas between Bangladesh and Myanmar in the Bay of Bengal, required the Tribunal to deal with unprecedented issues and provided a further opportunity for the Tribunal to contribute to the development of international law and the law of the sea. As this case will be addressed in detail during the symposium, I will refer only to some of its more important elements.

Perhaps the most remarkable feature of this case is that, for the first time in international adjudication, an international court or tribunal effected the delimitation of the continental shelf between the parties at a distance beyond 200 nm.

In that case, the Tribunal provided some important clarifications and developed innovative approaches.

On the issue of "entitlement to a continental shelf", the Tribunal observed that such entitlement "exists by the sole fact that the basis of entitlement, namely, sovereignty over the land territory, is present", and "does not require the establishment of outer limits."[8] With regard to the meaning of the notion of "natural prolongation" under article 76 of the Convention, the Tribunal found that a State's entitlement to a continental shelf beyond 200 nm should "be determined by reference to the outer edge of the continental margin"[9] and that natural prolongation should not constitute "a separate and independent criterion a coastal State must satisfy".[10]

In the *Bangladesh/Myanmar* case, the Tribunal initiated an innovative approach to dealing with the so-called grey zone in delimitation cases, establishing that, pursuant to various provisions of the Convention, in such a situation

---

7 *Southern Bluefin Tuna (New Zealand* v. *Japan), Order of 3 August 1999, ITLOS Reports 1999*, p. 280, at p. 295, para. 70.

8 *Delimitation of the maritime boundary in the Bay of Bengal (Bangladesh/Myanmar), Judgment, ITLOS Reports 2012*, p. 4, at p. 107, para. 409.

9 *Ibid.*, at p. 114, para. 437.

10 *Ibid.*, at p. 113, para. 435.

"each coastal State must exercise its rights and perform its duties with due regard to the rights and duties of the other",[11] and that "[i]t is not unusual in such cases for States to enter into agreements or cooperative arrangements to deal with problems resulting from the delimitation."[12]

In the *Bangladesh/Myanmar* case the Tribunal once again proved its ability to work efficiently as it took slightly more than two years for the Tribunal to deliver its Judgment. This is remarkably fast for such a complex delimitation case.

In 2014, a second delimitation case, the *Dispute concerning delimitation of the maritime boundary between Ghana and Côte d'Ivoire in the Atlantic Ocean*, was submitted to a special chamber of the Tribunal. Proceedings on the merits of the case are pending and it is expected that the hearing will be held in February 2017.

As to advisory jurisdiction, so far two requests have been submitted to the Tribunal.

The first request for an advisory opinion was received by the Seabed Disputes Chamber of the Tribunal in 2010. The Authority submitted three questions dealing with the responsibilities and liability of States sponsoring contractors engaged in deep seabed mining activities. In its Advisory Opinion delivered in 2011, the Chamber provided clarifications on a number of substantive matters that are crucial to the implementation of the Convention's regime on deep seabed mining.

The Chamber held that the liability of sponsoring States and that of contractors sponsored by them exist in parallel. A sponsoring State's liability arises from its failure to carry out its own responsibilities and there is no residual liability.

The Chamber clarified the meaning of key legal concepts such as the "responsibility to ensure" and the "duty of due diligence". The Chamber defined the notion of "responsibility to ensure" as "an obligation to deploy adequate means, to exercise best possible efforts, to do the utmost" and "as an obligation 'of conduct' and not 'of result'".[13] Similarly, with reference to the content of the "due diligence" obligation, the Chamber observed that "'due diligence' is a variable concept" which "may change over time as measures considered sufficiently diligent at a certain moment may become not diligent enough in light,

11 *Ibid.*, at p. 121, para. 475.

12 *Ibid.*, at p. 120, para. 472.

13 *Responsibilities and obligations of States with Respect to activities in the Area (Request for Advisory Opinion submitted to the Seabed Disputes Chamber), Advisory Opinion, 1 February 2011, ITLOS Reports 2011*, p. 10, at p. 41, para. 110.

for instance, of new scientific or technological knowledge. It may also change in relation to the risks involved in the activity."[14]

The second request for an advisory opinion was submitted to Tribunal as a whole by the Sub-Regional Fisheries Commission (SRFC), which put to the Tribunal four questions concerning IUU fishing activities in the EEZs of the seven SRFC Member States.

In response to this request the Tribunal delivered its Advisory Opinion in April 2015. One of the main conclusions reached by the Tribunal was that a "flag State is under the 'due diligence obligation' to take all necessary measures to ensure compliance and prevent IUU fishing by vessels flying its flag"[15] and that the flag State can be held liable if it fails "to comply with its 'due diligence' obligations concerning IUU fishing activities".[16] The Tribunal further emphasised that flag States are obliged to "take necessary measures, including those of enforcement"[17] and that, in flag States' domestic legislation, "[s]anctions applicable to involvement in IUU fishing activities must be sufficient to deter violations and deprive offenders of the benefits accruing from IUU fishing activities."[18]

Having established itself as a key player in the dispute settlement system under the Convention, the Tribunal has seen its case law diversify over the years and it has received a number of cases dealing with a wide range of matters under the Convention. Over the course of two decades, the Tribunal has consolidated its position as the pivotal forum for the peaceful settlement of disputes in the field of the law of the sea.

While the fundamental purpose of the Tribunal is to bring about the settlement of disputes in accordance with the Convention, the Tribunal, acting as "guardian" of legality, also plays a non-negligible role in the prevention of conflicts. The availability of judicial redress through the Tribunal encourages States to observe compliance with the international legal order for the seas and oceans established in the Convention. In playing this role, the Tribunal contributes to enhancing the international rule of law.

While the main function of international courts or tribunals is to apply the law, nevertheless, as noted by Sir Hersch Lauterpacht, "[t]his does not mean

14 *Ibid.*, at p. 43, para. 117.

15 *Request for an Advisory Opinion submitted by the Sub-Regional Fisheries Commission (SRFC), Advisory Opinion, 2 April 2015, ITLOS Reports 2015*, p. 4, at p. 40, para. 129.

16 *Ibid.*, at p. 44, para. 146.

17 *Ibid.*, at p. 42, para. 134.

18 *Ibid.*, para. 138.

that they do not in fact shape or even alter the law".[19] Indeed, an international judicial body has a role to play in the progressive development of international law, and this is particularly true of the Tribunal as regards the law of the sea.

It is in this spirit that we have brought together, in today's symposium, judges and former judges of the Tribunal, legal advisors, counsel who appear before the Tribunal, practitioners and scholars to reflect on the contribution made by the Tribunal to the rule of law and the progressive development of international law. This symposium also provides an opportunity to look to the future and find ways of improving our working methods.

---

19 H. Lauterpacht, *The Development of International Law by the International Court*, (Cambridge University Press, 1996), p. 75.

PART 1 / PARTIE 1

The Tribunal's Jurisprudence and Its Contribution to the Rule of Law

La jurisprudence du Tribunal et sa contribution à l'état de droit

The Tribunal's Jurisprudence and Its Contribution to the Rule of Law

David Anderson

The paper identifies some core elements in the international rule of law, before reviewing the jurisprudence of the Tribunal in relation to these elements.[1] As well as the Tribunal itself, decisions of its Special Chambers and the Seabed Disputes Chamber will also be covered, concentrating on what appear to be the leading cases in the context of the rule of law.[2] In this regard, the Tribunal's "Digest of Jurisprudence 1996–2016" is most helpful.[3]

The UN Charter laid down the current framework for international relations, but without mentioning the rule of law. However, one of the fundamental Charter principles is the peaceful settlement of disputes "in such a manner that international peace and security, and justice, are not endangered."[4] It is perhaps a sign of the progress that has been made since 1945 in the codification and progressive development of international law that increasing attention to the rule of law in international relations is now being paid by diplomats, statesmen and scholars.

I What are the Elements in the International Rule of Law?

The rule of law has been analysed by legal scholars primarily in the context of national legal systems. For example, in regard to the common law, Dicey produced a first analysis of the concept in the 19th century.[5] In German, the concept is that of *Rechtsstaat* or *Rechtsstaatlichkeit*. In French, the concept is that of *l'état de droit*.

1 The Tribunal's jurisprudence in relation to the development of the law of the sea is considered in other papers in this volume. The line between the rule of law and the development of international law is not always easy to discern. There may be some overlaps.

2 For a comprehensive survey, see P. Gautier, "The contribution of the International Tribunal for the Law of the Sea to the rule of law" in G. De Baere and J. Wouters (eds.), *The Contribution of International and Supranational Courts to the Rule of Law* (Elgar, 2015).

3 "Digest of Jurisprudence 1996–2016", (International Tribunal for the Law of the Sea, 2016).

4 Article 2(3) of the UN Charter.

5 A.V. Dicey, *Introduction to the Study of the Law of the Constitution* (Macmillan, 1885).

© 2018, BY INTERNATIONAL TRIBUNAL FOR THE LAW OF THE SEA | DOI 10.1163/9789004356832_005

Turning to the international arena, Wilfrid Jenks advanced the view that "[n]o legal system operates, or can operate, in a legal vacuum: no political system can provide good government, ensure justice, or preserve freedom, except on the basis of respect for law."[6]

In a similar vein, Nicholas Barber has argued that "[t]he rule of law can be presented as a set of qualities that ought to be present in all legal orders."[7] This includes, in the view of the present writer, the international legal order such as it exists at present.

The rule of law forms an essential precondition for order and justice, as well as the protection of human rights. As Michael Wood has written, "[r]ules of international law should uphold concepts such as fairness, security and justice for individuals, without limiting the proper authority of the State."[8]

However, it is apparent that the role played by the rule of law in inter-State relations is different in some ways from the role it plays in the domestic legal systems of democracies. Thus, a note of caution was struck by Rosalyn Higgins in her lecture at the London School of Economics: "[t]he difficulties of transposing the national rule of law model to the international context are … apparent. The concept of the 'international rule of law' is still a work in progress."[9]

Some of the differences are apparent. First, it is often pointed out that, in the present state of international society, there is no international legislature as such. Writing in 1928, Professor Brierly, after noting the defects in international law, argued that "the hope of advance must lie mainly in the development of the conventional element in the law."[10] The past 88 years have seen a remarkable development in the adoption of law-making conventions, especially since 1945. Many of these conventions were drafted by the ILC and adopted by global diplomatic conferences: today, they enjoy wide participation

6 C.W. Jenks, "The Rule of Law in World Affairs" in *The Prospects for International Adjudication* (Stevens and Sons, 1964), p. 757.

7 N. Barber, "The Rechtsstaat and the Rule of Law" 53 *University of Toronto Law Journal* (2003), p. 443, at p. 452.

8 M.C. Wood, "Public International Law and the Idea of the Rule of Law", in M. Pogačnik and others (eds.), *The Challenges of Contemporary International Law and International Relations – Liber Amicorum in Honour of Ernest Petrič* (European Faculty of Law, 2011), p. 450.

9 R. Higgins, "The ICJ, the UN System and the Rule of Law", Speech given at London School of Economics, 13 November 2006 (available at http://www.lse.ac.uk/website-archive/publicEvents/pdf/20061113_Higgins.pdf).

10 J.L. Brierly, *The Law of Nations*, 1st ed. (Oxford University Press, 1928).

and reflect customary law.[11] Professor Brierly's hoped-for advance has materialized. The lack of a single legislative organ has not prevented the codification and progressive development of large areas in international law, including the law of the sea. This latter part of the law was the subject of codification and progressive development in mid-century (the "Geneva Conventions") and also far-reaching and negotiated reform, as well as further development, at the end of the century in the form of the Convention and its implementing agreements. In other words, the UN system has provided the equivalent of a legislature.

Secondly, it remains true that international courts and tribunals, unlike national courts, have no jurisdiction over disputes without the consent of both parties. Part XV of the Convention provides an advance for the rule of law: the general rule in article 286 is that consent to jurisdiction over disputes concerning the interpretation or application of the terms of the Convention is conferred by the act of ratification or accession, subject always to the qualifications and exceptions provided for in the Convention. Finally, it is argued that there exists no international executive agency for law enforcement. While correct, it should be noted that studies of compliance with the decisions of international courts and tribunals indicate that judgments are complied with in the great majority of cases, thanks to the forces of international public opinion, often expressed through the UN and other international organizations.[12] This is true of the judgments of the Tribunal.

Particularly in regard to the law of the sea, the differences between national concepts of the rule of law and the international aspects should not be overstressed. The law of the sea is one part of general international law in which progress towards the effective rule of law can be confidently stated to be more advanced.

In recent years, Arthur Watts,[13] Simon Chesterman,[14] and Lord Bingham,[15] among others, have made important contributions to clarifying the core elements in the international rule of law. Arthur Watts argued that the protection of all States' interests and the creation of international stability required that

---

11 Leading examples include the *Vienna Convention on the Law of Treaties*, 23 May 1969, 1155 *UNTS* 331, and the *Vienna Convention on Diplomatic Relations*, 18 April 1961, 500 *UNTS* 95.

12 T. Koh, "Is there a Role for Law in a World ruled by Power?" in H.P. Hestermeyer et al. (eds.), *Coexistence, Cooperation and Solidarity: Liber Amicorum Rüdiger Wolfrum*, Vol. II (Brill, 2012), p. 1235.

13 A.D. Watts, "The International Rule of Law" 36 *GYBIL* (1991), p. 15.

14 "An International Rule of Law?" in "Rule of Law" by S. Chesterman, in *MPEPIL Online*, last updated July 2007.

15 T. Bingham, *The Rule of Law* (Allen Lane, 2010). He described the rule of law as an ideal.

inter-State relations be based on the rule of law. Writing after his retirement from the bench, Lord Bingham concluded that, in order to overcome the challenges facing the world, "it must be through the medium of rules internationally agreed, internationally implemented, and if necessary, internationally enforced."[16] Very recently Professor Robert McCorquodale has followed this three-fold approach and concluded that the elements of the international rule of law are "to uphold legal order and stability, to provide equality of application of the law … and to settle disputes before an independent legal body."[17]

Finally in this survey, the rule of law was the subject of a report by the UN Secretary-General (Kofi Annan), who opened the Tribunal's building some 15 years ago. Paragraph 6 of this report contains a helpful, even fuller, definition of the concept:

> The 'rule of law' … refers to a principle of governance in which all persons, institutions and entities, public and private, including the State itself, are accountable to laws that are publicly promulgated, equally enforced and independently adjudicated and which are consistent with human rights … standards. It requires, as well, measures to ensure adherence to the principles of supremacy of law, equality before the law, accountability to the law, fairness in the application of the law, separation of powers, participation in decision-making, legal certainty, avoidance of arbitrariness and procedural and legal transparency.[18]

Summing up, from these learned studies, it is clear that, while there exists no single definition of the rule of law in international relations, certain core elements can be discerned. These core elements will be examined under three headings.

A *The Rule of Law Requires the Existence of Settled Law with Agreed Rules*

1 The Status of the Convention

The Convention is a virtually complete statement of the modern law of the sea: it has been implemented and complemented by other international agreements; it forms the basis for the work of the UN and other international

16 *Ibid.*, p. 129.

17 R. McCorquodale, "Defining the International Rule of Law: Defying Gravity?" 65 *ICLQ* (2016), p. 277. The author speaks of degrees of compliance.

18 "The rule of law and transitional justice in conflict and post-conflict societies", Report of the Secretary-General, UN Doc. S/2004/616, 23 August 2004.

organizations in the maritime sector; and much of it reflects customary law.[19] The Convention has attracted ratifications and accessions from as many as 168 States Parties and the day-to-day support of many non-parties. The Convention has been described by Ambassador Tommy Koh as "A Constitution for the Oceans."[20] The Convention clearly contains elements that can be described as constitutional in nature. These include quasi-universal participation; the establishment of global standards protecting "community interests"[21] in the uses and health of the oceans (such as the freedom of navigation, the conservation and optimum utilization of the living resources of the sea, the protection and preservation of the marine environment, marine scientific research, and the peaceful settlement of disputes); the "common heritage" regime; and some compulsory jurisdiction. In other words, it contains some significant constitutional elements, while not amounting to a constitution in the strict sense of the word.

Clearly, the Convention's terms mark advances for the rule of law, but without expressly mentioning the concept. It represents a negotiated statement of the law for the 21st century, part codification, part progressive development, part reform and, at the same time, partly a framework for future developments. Importantly and unusually compared with other similar conventions, the substantive rules are underpinned to a large extent by the arrangements in Part XV for the settlement of disputes concerning the interpretation and application of these rules.[22]

Accordingly, as far as maritime issues are concerned, it can truly be stated that there exists an established law which is reasonably complete and certain. As Professor Oxman put it:

> In its most general sense, the Convention promotes the rule of law at sea by allocating authority to govern and by imposing qualifications on that authority in different situations. It articulates the relevant rights and duties of states in precise written form, converts those written articulations

19 For a survey from 1996, see B.H. Oxman, "The Rule of Law and the UN Convention on the Law of the Sea", 7 *EJIL* (1996), p. 353.

20 "Statement of Ambassador T. Koh, President of the Conference, at its final session in Montego Bay, Jamaica, 11 December 1982", (reprinted in *The Law of the Sea; Official Text of the United Nations Convention on the Law of the Sea* (United Nations, 1983), p. xxxiii.

21 On community interests, see D.W. Bowett, *The Law of the Sea* (Oceana, 1967), p. 62.

22 For a survey of the operation of Part XV up to 2015, see D. Anderson "Peaceful Settlement of Disputes under UNCLOS" in J. Barrett and R. Barnes (eds.), *Law of the Sea: UNCLOS as a Living Instrument* (BIICL, 2016).

> into binding treaty obligations expressly accepted by governments pursuant to their constitutional processes, and subjects most of those articulations to binding arbitration or adjudication.[23]

However, as with all other legal instruments, the terms of the Convention have to be interpreted and applied in relation to particular sets of facts; international courts and tribunals play an important role in settling disputes about the correct meaning.

Looking at its jurisprudence, the Tribunal can be said to have upheld order and stability in several important decisions. In particular, the Tribunal has had to rule on the meaning of wording about coastal State powers in the EEZ – wording which was controversial at the Conference. The decision of the Tribunal in the *M/V "SAIGA" (No. 2) Case (Saint Vincent and the Grenadines* v. *Guinea)* can be said to have upheld the "package deal."[24] It will be recalled that the respondent had first applied to a ship flying the flag of the applicant its pre-existing customs laws in a customs radius of 250 kilometres and then invoked a proposal made at the Conference in contending that its action was not contrary to article 56 of the Convention. The Tribunal rejected these arguments, finding that the Convention did not empower a coastal State to apply generally its customs laws to the EEZ.[25] As regards the unsuccessful proposal, Judge Nelson put the matter well in his Separate Opinion where he pointed out that the respondent's arguments contained within them the seeds of destruction of the Convention. "It would have the startling result that proposals which have not been accepted by the Conference would somehow still remain like shades waiting to be summoned, as it were, back to life if and when required."[26]

2 The Supremacy of the Law

The rule of law requires not only that there be a settled body of law but also that this body of law supersedes or over-rides inconsistent national claims and laws, as well as earlier international agreements. It is clear that the rules of the Convention apply as treaty rules to the States Parties; and that the Convention prevails over the Geneva Conventions and pre-existing customary law *inter*

---

23 B.H. Oxman, "Human Rights and the UN Convention on the Law of the Sea", 36 *Columbia Journal of Transnational Law* (1997), p. 399, at p. 402.

24 H. Caminos and M.R. Molitor, "Progressive Development of International Law and the Package Deal", 79 *AJIL* (1985), p. 871.

25 *M/V "SAIGA" (No. 2) (Saint Vincent and the Grenadines* v. *Guinea), Judgment, ITLOS Reports 1999*, p. 10, at p. 54, para 127.

26 *Ibid.*, at p. 124.

partes. Upon establishing their consent to be bound by the Convention, States are obliged to abandon claims that are inconsistent with the terms of the Convention, even if a particular claim has legislative or even constitutional status in the State concerned.[27] This requires the amendment of inconsistent legislation. Examples include the "roll-back" of claims to 200–mile territorial seas and the abandonment of claims to historic fishing rights in the EEZ, as well as claims to measure EEZs from rocks such as Rockall in compliance with article 121, paragraph 3. An instance before the Tribunal of an attempt to retain legislative claims pre-dating the Convention was the customs radius invoked by Guinea in the *M/V "SAIGA" (No. 2) Case*. A somewhat similar stance by China concerning its claims to the waters within the so-called "9-dash line" was rejected by the Tribunal constituted under Annex VII of the Convention in the case brought by the Philippines.[28] Ratification of the Convention requires inconsistent claims to be abandoned or withdrawn by States Parties.

B *The Rule of Law Requires the Settled Law to be Applied Consistently, Fairly and without Arbitrariness by All Concerned*

1 Equality before the Law

Equality before the law means that all States Parties to the Convention are subject in principle to the same rules. However, the Convention itself differentiates among States Parties: some are coastal States, others land-locked States, very many are flag States, etc. So far, all the contentious cases have concerned coastal States and flag States.

The European Union ("EU"), an organization, is a State Party according to the arrangements contained in Part IX and declarations made upon establishing consent to be bound. The EU became a party to a case before the Tribunal, namely, the *Case concerning the Conservation and Sustainable Exploitation of Swordfish Stocks in the South-Eastern Pacific Ocean* brought by Chile concerning fishing by vessels registered in an EU Member State in the South-Eastern Pacific Ocean.[29] The Tribunal further clarified the position of the EU in its Advisory Opinion given to the SRFC about IUU fishing, as follows:

27 This follows from article 26 of the Vienna Convention on the Law of Treaties: *Pacta sunt servanda*.

28 *The South China Sea Arbitration* (*The Republic of Philippines* v. *The People's Republic of China*), PCA Case No. 2013–19, 12 July 2016.

29 *Conservation and Sustainable Exploitation of Swordfish Stocks* (*Chile/European Community*), *ITLOS Reports 2000*, p. 148. The case was discontinued by agreement.

> 172. The Tribunal holds that in cases where an international organization, in the exercise of its exclusive competence in fisheries matters, concludes a fisheries access agreement with an SRFC Member State, which provides for access by vessels flying the flag of its member States to fish in the exclusive economic zone of that State, the obligations of the flag State become the obligations of the international organization. The international organization, as the only contracting party to the fisheries access agreement with the SRFC Member State, must therefore ensure that vessels flying the flag of a member State comply with the fisheries laws and regulations of the SRFC Member State and do not conduct IUU fishing activities within the exclusive economic zone of that State.
>
> 173. Accordingly, only the international organization may be held liable for any breach of its obligations arising from the fisheries access agreement, and not its member States. Therefore, if the international organization does not meet its "due diligence" obligations, the SRFC Member States may hold the international organization liable for the violation of their fisheries laws and regulations by a vessel flying the flag of a member State of that organization and fishing in the exclusive economic zones of the SRFC Member States within the framework of a fisheries access agreement between that organization and such Member States.
>
> 174. The SRFC Member States may, pursuant to article 6, paragraph 2, of Annex IX to the Convention, request an international organization or its member States which are parties to the Convention for information as to who has responsibility in respect of any specific matter. The organization and the member States concerned must provide this information. Failure to do so within a reasonable time or the provision of contradictory information results in joint and several liability of the international organization and the member States concerned.[30]

These findings clarify the status of the EU as a State Party in regard to fisheries in the EEZs of third States.

2 Accountability to the Law

All States Parties are accountable for their actions and incur responsibility for failures to respect the law. Issues of State responsibility were the subject of an

30 *Request for Advisory Opinion submitted by the Sub-Regional Fisheries Commission, Advisory Opinion, 2 April 2015, ITLOS Reports 2015*, p. 4, at p. 51.

Advisory Opinion by the Seabed Disputes Chamber, given at the request of the Authority. The opinion clarified the nature and scope of the obligations of sponsoring States, both obligations of "due diligence" towards contractors and direct obligations.[31] The Opinion has assisted the Authority in its important work. In contentious proceedings, issues of State responsibility and reparation for the violation of the applicant's rights as flag State, causing injuries to persons connected with or on board a vessel arrested at sea, arose in the *M/V "SAIGA" (No. 2) Case*. The Judgment sets out a carefully calibrated schedule of compensation.[32]

3 Upholding the Integrity of the Judicial Process

By prescribing provisional measures of protection in several pending cases, the Tribunal has upheld the integrity of the judicial process, an important aspect of the rule of law. The provisions in article 290 of the Convention reflect the general principle that, while a question remains pending before a court or tribunal, the *status quo ante* should not be changed by unilateral action.[33] Examples include the Tribunal's Order in the *Southern Bluefin Tuna Cases* (*New Zealand* v. *Japan; Australia* v. *Japan*)[34] and the *Case concerning Land Reclamation in and around the Straits of Johor* (*Malaysia* v. *Singapore*).[35]

The Statute provides that "[a]bsence of a party ... shall not constitute a bar to proceedings."[36] In other words, a non-appearing respondent cannot block further proceedings. The Tribunal has had occasion to apply this provision in the Statute in one case.[37] The Tribunal stated that:

> the absence of a party or failure of a party to defend its case does not constitute a bar to the proceedings and does not preclude the Tribunal from

---

31 *Responsibilities and obligations of States with respect to activities in the Area, Advisory Opinion, 1 February 2011, ITLOS Reports 2011*, p. 10.

32 *M/V "SAIGA" (No. 2) (Saint Vincent and the Grenadines* v. *Guinea), Judgment, ITLOS Reports 1999*, p. 10, at pp. 66–67, para. 175.

33 B. Cheng, *General Principles of Law* (Cambridge University Press, 1987), p. 140.

34 *Southern Bluefin Tuna (New Zealand* v. *Japan; Australia* v. *Japan), Provisional Measures, Order of 27 August 1999, ITLOS Reports 1999*, p. 280.

35 *Land Reclamation in and around the Straits of Johor (Malaysia* v. *Singapore), Provisional Measures, Order of 8 October 2003, ITLOS Reports 2003*, p. 10.

36 Article 28 of Annex VI to the Convention, second sentence.

37 *"Arctic Sunrise" (Kingdom of the Netherlands* v. *Russian Federation), Provisional Measures, Order of 22 November 2013, ITLOS Reports 2013*, p. 230.

> prescribing provisional measures, provided that the parties have been given an opportunity of presenting their observations on the subject.[38]

The Tribunal went on to find that the non-appearing State is nevertheless a party to the proceedings with the ensuing rights and obligations; and that:

> ... the prescription of provisional measures must also take into account the procedural rights of both parties and ensure full implementation of the principle of equality of the parties in a situation where the absence of a party may hinder the regular conduct of the proceedings and affect the good administration of justice.[39]

In my Separate Opinion as Judge *ad hoc* in this case, I pointed out that "[n]on-appearance does not serve the efficient application of Part XV of the Convention or, more widely, the rule of law in international relations."[40]

Judges Wolfrum and Kelly went further in a Joint Separate Opinion, stating that:

> there is a more fundamental consideration to be mentioned. In the case of States having consented to a dispute settlement system in general – such as the Netherlands and the Russian Federation by ratifying the Convention on the Law of the Sea – non-appearance is contrary to the object and purpose of the dispute settlement system under Part XV of the Convention.[41]

That view is perhaps difficult to reconcile with the terms of article 28 of the Statute which expressly contemplates the situation "when one of the parties does not appear before the Tribunal." Be that as it may, non-appearance is not unique to the Tribunal. Experience shows that the non-appearing respondent probably experiences a worse outcome by not appearing as compared with appearing, presenting the facts as known to it and arguing its legal position to the judges, even if the decision goes against the respondent.

---

38 *Ibid.*, at p. 242, para. 48.

39 *Ibid.*, paras. 51 and 53.

40 *Ibid.*, at p. 254.

41 *Ibid.*, at p. 258, para. 6.

4 Respect for Human Rights

The rule of law calls for respect for human rights at both the national and inter-State levels. In several cases, the Tribunal has taken considerations of human rights into account. Thus in *"Enrica Lexie" Incident* (*Italy* v. *India*), *Provisional Measures,* the Order of the Tribunal cited the *M/V "SAIGA"* (*No. 2*) *Case* and included the following recital: "Considering that the Tribunal reaffirms its view that considerations of humanity must apply in the law of the sea as they do in other areas of international law".[42]

In the prompt release cases submitted under article 292 of the Convention, the Tribunal has had regard for the human rights of the members of crews of detained vessels. The Tribunal has ordered the release of ships' officers who had been ordered to surrender their passports but were free to move around the port, treating them as detainees. An early example was the *"Camouco" Case* (*Panama* v. *France*), *Prompt Release,* where the Tribunal stated:

> That the *Camouco* has been in detention is not disputed. However, the parties are in disagreement whether the Master of the *Camouco* is also in detention. It is admitted that the Master is presently under court supervision, that his passport has also been taken away from him by the French authorities, and that, consequently, he is not in a position to leave Réunion. The Tribunal considers that, in the circumstances of this case, it is appropriate to order the release of the Master in accordance with article 292, paragraph 1, of the Convention.[43]

5 Separation of Powers

Separation of powers is a concept in domestic legal systems, but it is also relevant in the workings of a complex treaty regime which accords important roles to different international organizations and similar bodies. The Tribunal has shown great awareness of its role in regard to the separation of powers among the various bodies created by the Convention. In the *Dispute concerning delimitation of the maritime boundary between Bangladesh and Myanmar in the Bay of Bengal* (*Bangladesh/Myanmar*), the Tribunal considered its role in delimiting the continental shelf beyond 200 nautical miles, in relation to that of the Commission on the Limits of the Continental Shelf in considering

42 *"Enrica Lexie" Incident* (*Italy* v. *India*), *Provisional Measures, Order of 24 July 2015, ITLOS Reports 2015*, p. 182, at p. 204, para. 133.

43 *"Camouco"* (*Panama* v. *France*), *Prompt Release, Judgment, ITLOS Reports 2000*, p. 10, at pp. 32–33, para. 71.

submissions by the coastal States concerned.[44] The Tribunal concluded that "[a] decision ... not to exercise jurisdiction ... would not only fail to resolve a long-standing dispute, but also would not be conducive to the efficient operation of the Convention."[45]

In its Advisory Opinion on the *Responsibilities and obligations of States sponsoring persons and entities with respect to activities in the Area,* the Seabed Disputes Chamber considered its role in regard to the work of the organs of the Authority, noting that " ... the Chamber is part of the system in which the Authority's organs operate, but its task within the system is to act as an independent and impartial body."[46]

In these cases, the Tribunal has shown concern for the efficient operation of the Convention as a whole and its role within the system of the Convention as a complex treaty.

C Independent and Impartial Legal Bodies Exist for Settling Disputes

1 The Legal Bodies and Their Inter-relationships

The rule of law requires that there exist some courts and tribunals with appropriate jurisdiction to apply the law and to settle disputes on that basis. The limits of the jurisdiction must be respected. As is well-known, in the scheme of the Convention, there exist several bodies for settling disputes, as well as conciliation commissions acting under article 284.[47] Although the Convention is unusual in establishing and providing for some compulsory jurisdiction, the Convention also contains and allows for exceptions. Accordingly, each dispute settlement body has to decide, in a particular case, whether jurisdiction is established or whether an exception applies. Thus, in the *"Arctic Sunrise"Case (Netherlands* v. *Russian Federation), Provisional Measures,* the Tribunal found that an exception did not apply and that *prima facie* there was jurisdiction.[48]

Article 287 provides for the making of choices as regards the forum. The possible fora include the Tribunal, the ICJ and arbitration. Fears were expressed when the Tribunal was formed in 1996 about the risks of inconsistent decisions

44 *Delimitation of the maritime boundary in the Bay of Bengal (Bangladesh/Myanmar), Judgment, ITLOS Reports 2012*, p. 4, at p. 98, at paras. 373 ff.

45 *Ibid.*, at p. 102, para. 391.

46 *Responsibilities and obligations of States with respect to activities in the Area, Advisory Opinion, 1 February 2011, ITLOS Reports 2011*, p. 10, at p. 23, para. 26.

47 See, for example, the *Conciliation between The Democratic Republic of Timor-Leste and The Commonwealth of Australia*, PCA Case No. 2016–10.

48 *"Arctic Sunrise" (Kingdom of the Netherlands* v. *Russian Federation), Order of 25 October 2013, ITLOS Reports 2013*, p. 230, at p. 241.

being made and the fragmentation of the law of the sea. In its jurisprudence, the Tribunal has cited and followed relevant decisions of the Permanent Court of International Justice and the Court, as well as arbitral decisions. Recent judgments of the Court and some arbitral awards under Annex VII have cited the Tribunal. The fears expressed in 1996 have proved to have been exaggerated. There is developing a broadly consistent body of case-law concerning the interpretation of the Convention, whether the decision has been taken by this Tribunal, by the Court or by a tribunal constituted under Annex VII. I would note that many members of such tribunals have been serving or retired judges of this Tribunal or the Court, thereby helping to maintain consistency in decisions.

2 Independence and Impartiality

The rule of law calls for judges who are totally independent and impartial. The Tribunal is a collegiate judicial body composed of 21 members, elected by the regular meetings of the States Parties. Each judge is normally elected for a nine-year term. Both these factors accord a measure of independence, as do the grant of international diplomatic status and the requirement to give up inconsistent appointments and activities upon making the judicial solemn undertaking of impartiality. Fairness is ensured by the rules on the appointment of judges *ad hoc* in cases where one side is represented on the bench and the other is not.[49]

At the outset, the Tribunal adopted through its Rules a legal policy of handling cases without unnecessary delays by maintaining control of the proceedings, which are conducted to the greatest extent possible in public.[50] The Tribunal's Resolution on Internal Judicial Practice calls for the full participation in deliberations of all members of the bench. Judgments and orders are fully reasoned.[51] Each judge has the obligation to vote yes or no on every operative paragraph in a judgment or order. Further, each judge has the right to append a declaration or separate opinion, indicating any differences from the reasoning underpinning the majority decision or to append a dissenting opinion. Votes become public when the judgment or order is published. In this, the Tribunal follows the practice of the Court, not that of the European Court of Justice. Accordingly, procedural and legal transparency are guaranteed. Justice

49 As pointed out by T. Franck in *Fairness in International Law and Institutions* (Clarendon, 1995) at p. 324.

50 For a survey, see T. Treves, "The Rules of the ITLOS" in P. Chandrasekhara Rao and R. Khan (eds.), *The ITLOS: Law and Practice* (Kluwer, 2001), p. 111.

51 For a survey, see D. Anderson, "The Internal Judicial Practice of the ITLOS", in *ibid.*, p. 197.

is administered in public, subject to protecting the integrity of the judicial process and the confidentiality of commercial information concerning deep seabed mining. The Tribunal's Resolution ensures impartiality and provides reassurance to litigants that their arguments will all be considered and weighed against the terms of the Convention.

3 The Principle of Reasonableness and the Settlement of Disputes

The principle of reasonableness applies to the Convention as a whole and its terms should be interpreted in a reasonable manner.[52] Certain articles contain a specific rule of reasonableness. One example is provided by the "due regard" test in article 87, paragraph 2. Another is article 73, paragraph 2, which provides for the prompt release of fishing vessels arrested in the EEZ against the posting of a reasonable bond or other security. This bare obligation to release against a bond is developed to a certain extent in article 292 of the Convention, which has given the Tribunal, as the default jurisdiction, an important function in dealing with the question of release. However, the Convention is unspecific about the precise conditions and criteria to be applied. In a series of cases, the Tribunal has developed its jurisprudence concerning reasonable bonds. Thus in the *"Camouco" Case* (*Panama* v. *France*), *Prompt Release*, it was stated that:

> The Tribunal considers that a number of factors are relevant in an assessment of the reasonableness of bonds or other financial security. They include the gravity of the alleged offences, the penalties imposed or imposable under the laws of the detaining State, the value of the detained vessel and of the cargo seized, the amount of the bond imposed by the detaining State and its form.[53]

Later, in the *"Juno Trader" Case* (*Saint Vincent and the Grenadines* v. *Guinea-Bissau*), the Tribunal added:

> It is by reference to the penalties imposed or imposable under the law of the detaining State that the Tribunal may evaluate the gravity of the alleged offences, taking into account the circumstances of the case and the

52 See D. Anderson, "The Principle of Reasonableness" in H.P. Hestermeyer et al. (eds.), *Coexistence, Cooperation and Solidarity: Liber Amicorum Rüdiger Wolfrum*, Vol. I (Brill, 2012), p. 657. The principle was applied in the *Duzgit Integrity Arbitration* (*Malta* v. *São Tomé and Príncipe*), PCA Case No. 2014–07, 5 September 2016, para. 209.

53 *"Camouco"* (*Panama* v. *France*), *Prompt Release, Judgment, ITLOS Reports 2000*, p. 10, at p. 31, para. 67.

> need to avoid disproportion between the gravity of the alleged offences and the amount of the bond.[54]

The principle of reasonableness has arisen in a further context, namely the operation of "grey areas". Thus, in settling the maritime boundary dispute between Bangladesh and Myanmar and, in particular, delimiting the continental shelf beyond 200 nautical miles in such a way as to create a "grey area", the Tribunal applied the principle of reasonableness in stating:

> Under the Convention, as a result of maritime delimitation, there may also be concurrent exclusive economic zone rights of another coastal State. In such a situation, pursuant to the principle reflected in the provisions of articles 56, 58, 78 and 79 and in other provisions of the Convention, each coastal State must exercise its rights and perform its duties with due regard to the rights and duties of the other.[55]

In these and other cases, the Tribunal's jurisprudence has applied the principle of reasonableness and thereby contributed to the rule of law.

II Concluding Remarks

Litigation concerning the law of the sea is running at an all-time high.[56] Maritime cases have been submitted not only to the Tribunal but also to the Court and to *ad hoc* arbitration under Annex VII. For its part, this survey has shown that the Tribunal is making a significant contribution to the rule of law in the maritime sector of international relations. Several cases have concerned incidents affecting ships. Others have concerned maritime disputes between close neighbours. At present, a very interesting case about the delimitation of the EEZ and continental shelf is pending before a Special Chamber.[57] However, like all courts, the Tribunal is dependent on the willingness of States Parties to the Convention to submit their disputes to the Tribunal for adjudication.

---

54 *"Juno Trader" (Saint Vincent and the Grenadines* v. *Guinea-Bissau), Prompt Release, Judgment, ITLOS Reports 2004*, p. 17, at p. 41, para. 89.

55 *Delimitation of the maritime boundary in the Bay of Bengal (Bangladesh/Myanmar), Judgment, ITLOS Reports 2012*, p. 4, at p. 121, para. 475.

56 R. Churchill, "Dispute Settlement in the Law of the Sea: Annual Survey 2014, 30 *IJMCL* (2014), p. 585.

57 *Delimitation of the maritime boundary in the Atlantic Ocean (Ghana/Côte d'Ivoire).*

How can the Tribunal best contribute to the advancement of the rule of law? Judge Higgins answered this question for the ICJ as follows:

> In my view, the International Court need not do anything different from that which we always do, namely, meticulously apply international law in an impartial manner to the disputes before us. This is the best way for the International Court to protect and promote the rule of law.[58]

The same is true *mutatis mutandis* of the Tribunal. Let us conclude with the hope that the Tribunal continues to receive interesting cases. In this way, the Tribunal will surely enrich its jurisprudence and uphold the rule of law in the coming decades.

58 R. Higgins, *The ICJ and the Rule of Law*, Lecture to the United Nations University, 11 April 2007 (available at http://archive.unu.edu/events/files/2007/20070411_Higgins_speech.pdf).

The Tribunal's Jurisprudence and Its Contribution to the Rule of Law

José Luís Jesus

The celebration of the Tribunal's 20th anniversary provides me with an opportunity to take stock of its jurisprudence and its accomplishments since it received its first case in 1997.[1] Despite being a somewhat novel institution, the Tribunal has reached adulthood, by age, by accumulated judicial experience and by a meaningful jurisprudence it has developed over the last two decades, thus contributing to the better understanding and clarification of the rule of law, especially the international law of the sea.

There is much to be said about the Tribunal's accomplishments. I will, however, limit my remarks to a few observations of what appears to me to be the most salient points of the Tribunal's jurisprudence.

I Jurisprudence of the Tribunal

Since it started its functions in 1996, the Tribunal has received 25 cases, of which 16 were urgent proceedings (nine cases concerning prompt release of vessels and crews[2] under article 292 of the Convention and seven cases concerning provisional measures,[3] under article 290, paragraph 5, of the Convention,

1 *The M/V "SAIGA" Case* (*Saint Vincent and the Grenadines* v. *Guinea*), *Prompt Release.*

2 These cases are: Case No. 1, *The M/V "SAIGA" Case* (*Saint Vincent and the Grenadines* v. *Guinea*), *Prompt Release*; Case No. 5, *The "Camouco" Case* (*Panama* v. *France*), *Prompt Release*; Case No. 6, *The "Monte Confurco" Case* (*Seychelles* v. *France*), *Prompt Release*; *Case No. 8, The "Grand Prince" Case* (*Belize v. France*), *Prompt Release*; Case No. 9, *The "Chaisiri Reefer 2" Case* (*Panama* v. *Yemen*), *Prompt Release*; Case No. 11, *The "Volga" Case* (*Russian Federation* v. *Australia*), *Prompt Release*; Case No. 13, *The "Juno Trader" Case* (*Saint Vincent and the Grenadines* v. *Guinea-Bissau*), *Prompt Release*; Case No. 14, *The "Hoshinmaru" Case* (*Japan* v. *Russian Federation*), *Prompt Release*; and Case No. 15, *The "Tomimaru" Case* (*Japan* v. *Russian Federation*), *Prompt Release.*

3 See article 290, para. 5, of the Convention.

© 2018, BY INTERNATIONAL TRIBUNAL FOR THE LAW OF THE SEA | DOI 10.1163/9789004356832_006

pending the constitution of an Annex VII arbitral tribunal),[4] seven fully-fledged contentious cases[5] and two advisory opinions.[6]

These cases involved developed and developing countries from all regions of the world, as disputant States. The disputes submitted covered a wide range of issues pertaining to the law of the sea, such as the protection of the marine environment;[7] land reclamation;[8] conservation of marine living resources;[9] prompt release of vessels and crews; delimitation of maritime boundaries;[10] responsibilities and obligations of States sponsoring persons and entities with respect to activities in the Area;[11] obligations and liability of the flag State in

4 These cases are: Cases Nos 3 and 4, *Southern Bluefin Tuna Cases* (*New Zealand* v. *Japan*; *Australia* v. *Japan*), *Provisional Measures*; Case No. 10, *The MOX Plant Case* (*Ireland* v. *United Kingdom*), *Provisional Measures*; Case No. 12, *Case concerning Land Reclamation by Singapore in and around the Straits of Johor* (*Malaysia* v. *Singapore*), *Provisional Measures*; Case No. 20, *The "ARA Libertad" Case* (*Argentina* v. *Ghana*), *Provisional Measures*; Case No. 22, *The "Arctic Sunrise" Case* (*Netherlands* v. *Russian Federation*), *Provisional Measures*; Case No. 24, *The "Enrica Lexie" Incident* (*Italy* v. *India*), *Provisional Measures*.

5 These cases are: Case No. 2, *The M/V "SAIGA" (No. 2) Case* (*Saint Vincent and the Grenadines* v. *Guinea*); Case No. 7, *Case concerning the Conservation and Sustainable Exploitation of Swordfish Stocks in the South-Eastern Pacific Ocean* (*Chile/European Union*); Case No. 16, *Dispute concerning delimitation of the maritime boundary between Bangladesh and Myanmar in the Bay of Bengal* (*Bangladesh/Myanmar*); Case No. 18, *The M/V "Louisa" Case* (*Saint Vincent and the Grenadines* v. *Spain*); Case No. 19, *The M/V "Virginia G" Case* (*Panama/Guinea-Bissau*); Case No. 23, *Dispute concerning delimitation of the maritime boundary between Ghana and Côte d'Ivoire in the Atlantic Ocean* (*Ghana/Côte d'Ivoire*); Case No. 25, *The M/V "Norstar" Case* (*Panama v. Italy*).

6 Case No. 17, *Responsibilities and obligations of States sponsoring persons and entities with respect to activities in the Area* (*Request for Advisory Opinion submitted to the Seabed Disputes Chamber*); Case No. 21, *Request for an Advisory Opinion submitted by the Sub-Regional Fisheries Commission (SRFC)*(*Request for Advisory Opinion submitted to the Tribunal*).

7 See *The MOX Plant Case* (*Ireland* v. *United Kingdom*), *Provisional Measures*.

8 See *Case concerning Land Reclamation by Singapore in and around the Straits of Johor* (*Malaysia* v. *Singapore*), *Provisional Measures*.

9 See Cases No. 3 and 4, *Southern Bluefin Tuna Cases* (*New Zealand* v. *Japan*; *Australia* v. *Japan*), *Provisional Measures*.

10 See Case No. 16, *Dispute concerning delimitation of the maritime boundary between Bangladesh and Myanmar in the Bay of Bengal* (*Bangladesh/Myanmar*).

11 Case No. 17, *Responsibilities and obligations of States sponsoring persons and entities with respect to activities in the Area* (*Request for Advisory Opinion submitted to the Seabed Disputes Chamber*).

case of IUU fishing involving their vessels;[12] compensation for illegal seizure of vessels;[13] and sovereign immunity of warships,[14] just to name a few of the matters covered.

Though it has received 25 cases, the Tribunal actually entertained only 21 of them, as two cases were discontinued at the request of the parties[15] and two cases are still pending.[16] It is, therefore, in respect of the decisions taken by the Tribunal in these 21 cases that I will attempt to identify the main highlights of the jurisprudence it has developed over its lifetime.

As I see it, the jurisprudence of the Tribunal can be grouped in a nutshell in three categories, namely:

A. The positions it took on several issues of international law, by having recourse to and relying on the jurisprudence of other international courts and tribunals;
B. The specific jurisprudence it has developed, concerning cases of prompt release of vessels and crews, a procedure established in article 292 of the Convention; and
C. The new pathways it has established in pioneering some jurisprudential developments, particularly in the field of its specialization, the law of the sea.

I shall briefly outline the main aspects of these three categories.

A *Reliance on Other Courts' Jurisprudence*

I will first address the issue of the Tribunal's contribution to the strengthening of the jurisprudence that had already been set by other courts and tribunals, especially by the ICJ and the PCIJ.

In almost every case it has handled, the Tribunal has resorted to and relied on the jurisprudence of other courts and tribunals, mainly the ICJ and the PCIJ, as material sources of "other rules of international law", applicable pursuant

12 Case No. 21, *Request for an advisory opinion submitted by the Sub-Regional Fisheries Commission* (SRFC) (*Request for Advisory Opinion submitted to the Tribunal*).

13 Case No. 19, *The M/V "Virginia G" Case* (*Panama/Guinea-Bissau*).

14 Case No. 20, *The "ARA Libertad" Case* (*Argentina* v. *Ghana*), *Provisional Measures*.

15 Case No. 7, *Case concerning the Conservation and Sustainable Exploitation of Swordfish Stocks in the South-Eastern Pacific Ocean* (*Chile/European Union*) and Case No. 9, *The "Chaisiri Reefer 2" Case* (*Panama* v. *Yemen*).

16 These are: Case No. 23, *Dispute concerning delimitation of the maritime boundary between Ghana and Côte d'Ivoire in the Atlantic Ocean* (*Ghana/Côte d'Ivoire*); Case No. 25, *The M/V "Norstar" Case* (*Panama* v. *Italy*).

to article 293 of the Convention, in addressing particular issues raised in the context of the cases before it, whenever it did not find legal guidance in the provisions of the Convention.

Such issues include, *inter alia*, the definition or characterization of what is a "dispute", the exhaustion of local remedies, the nationality of claims, the modalities for the granting of nationalities to ships, the relationship between the national and the international law, the reparation for damages, the legal value of the minutes of negotiations, the clarification of the concepts of "public interests" and "state of necessity", the limits of the use of force in international relations and the non-appearance. I shall not detail here the Tribunal's reasoning in this regard.

The Tribunal's decisions in reliance on other courts' jurisprudence, while strengthening that jurisprudence, shows consistency with it, thus allaying the fears of some concerning a supposed danger of fragmentation of the jurisprudence of international courts and tribunals.

B *Prompt Release Jurisprudence*

Another set of cases that have been entertained by the Tribunal and which has given rise to some specific jurisprudential developments are cases of prompt release of vessels and crews pursuant to the procedure established in article 292 of the Convention. This procedure applies:

> [w]here the authorities of a State Party have detained a vessel flying the flag of another State Party and it is alleged that the detaining State has not complied with the provisions of this Convention for the prompt release of the vessel or its crew upon the posting of a reasonable bond or other financial security.[17]

This is a new procedure in international adjudication that is provided for in the Convention and may be resorted to by the flag State, by applying to the Tribunal for its vessel's prompt release, but not before ten days following the vessel's detention.

The prompt release procedure applies to vessels and/or their crews that have been arrested or detained for alleged violations of the fisheries laws and regulations of the coastal State in its EEZ.[18] It also applies to the vessel's prompt release from detention for violation of laws and regulations or international rules and standards for the protection and preservation of the marine

17 See article 292, para. 1, of the Convention.

18 See article 73, para. 2.

environment.[19] These are the only two situations to which the prompt release procedure set up in article 292 of the Convention applies. It may be noted that all of the nine cases of prompt release submitted to the Tribunal were based on alleged violation of the fisheries laws and regulations of the coastal State's EEZ.

The purpose of this procedure is to allow the flag State to obtain release of its vessels and crews by posting a "reasonable" bond with the detaining State, pending the final decision of the domestic court or other competent authorities of the detaining State on the merits of the case. The role of the Tribunal is to fix a bond it considers "reasonable" under the circumstances of the case and order the immediate release of the vessel and crew once the bond has been posted with the detaining State.[20] The Tribunal "shall deal only with the question of release, without prejudice to the merits of any case before the appropriate domestic forum against the vessel, its owner or its crew."[21]

Though the procedure of prompt release is an urgent proceeding, which usually is disposed of in a period of three to four weeks, the Tribunal has been able to develop a meaningful jurisprudence in this regard. I will refer to four salient points that seem to emerge from the prompt release jurisprudence. These points are: the setting up of the procedural framework itself for cases of prompt release, making it a procedure with a predictable outcome; the indication of factors that should be taken into account in the determination of the "reasonable bond" that should be posted for the release of the detained vessel and/or crew; the indication of several circumstances in which a bond is considered as not having been posted before the domestic authorities of the detaining State for the purposes of enabling the procedure of prompt release to take its course before the Tribunal; and finally the crafting of the ship-as-a-unit doctrine, allowing the flag State to extend its protection to foreign crew members and other foreign persons with an interest in the operations of a ship, as "the ship, everything on it and every person involved or interested in its operations are treated as an entity linked to the flag State."[22]

---

19 See article 226, para. 1–b.

20 See article 292, para. 4.

21 See article 292, para. 3.

22 This concept was first developed in the *M/V "SAIGA" (No. 2) Case*. In this case, the Tribunal stated that "The provisions [of articles 94, 106, 110, paragraph 3, 111, paragraph 8, and 217 of the Convention] referred to in the preceding paragraph indicate that the Convention considers a ship as a unit, as regards the obligations of the flag State with respect to the ship and the right of a flag State to seek reparation for loss or damage caused to the ship by acts of other States and to institute proceedings under article 292 of the Convention. Thus the ship, every thing on it, and every person involved or interested in its operations are treated as an entity linked to the flag State. The nationalities of these persons are not

As the prompt release procedure is new in international judicial practice and has so far been activated only before the Tribunal, the jurisprudence thereon has in fact been developed from scratch. In dealing with prompt releases cases, the Tribunal has drawn what could be called a "procedural itinerary" for such cases and, as a result, this procedure is now well known to the prospective parties to a dispute and the outcome of the prompt release case may be anticipated. Indeed, once a reasonable bond, as fixed by the Tribunal, is posted by the flag State or on its behalf in the form prescribed, the release of the vessel and crew is necessarily the expected outcome.

The Tribunal has also clearly identified different factors that should be taken into account in the composition of what is a "reasonable bond". As catalogued in the *"Camouco" Case* (*Panama* v. *France*), these factors are the gravity of the alleged offences, the penalties imposed or imposable, the value of the arrested vessel, the amount imposed as a bond by the detaining State and the form of the bond.[23] The Tribunal made it clear in the *"Monte Confurco" Case* (*Seychelles* v. *France*), that it did not "intend to lay down rigid rules as to the exact weight to be attached to each of [the criteria]".[24]

As the demonstration of the failure of the detaining State in complying with the requirement of article 73, paragraph 2, of the Convention on the release of the vessel and crew upon the posting of a reasonable bond or other security imposed by the detaining State is necessary for the prompt release procedure under article 292 of the Convention to be admissible, the Tribunal has also developed a jurisprudence on the issue of absence of a bond imposed by the detaining State. In accordance with this jurisprudence, failure of the detaining State to comply with article 73, paragraph 2, of the Convention includes situations in which the posting of a bond by the detaining State has not been possible; has been rejected by it; is not provided for in the coastal State's legislation; or it is alleged that the required bond is unreasonable.

The last prompt release case submitted to the Tribunal dates from 2007 when the *"Tomimaru" Case* (*Japan* v. *Russian Federation*), was filed.[25] It may well be that the clear jurisprudence developed by the Tribunal in prompt

relevant." *M/V "SAIGA" (No. 2)* (*Saint Vincent and the Grenadines* v. *Guinea*), *Judgment, ITLOS Reports 1999*, p. 10, at p. 48, para. 106.

23 *"Camouco"* (*Panama* v. *France*), *Prompt Release, Judgment, ITLOS Reports 2000*, p. 10, at p. 31, para. 67.

24 *"Monte Confurco"* (*Seychelles v. France*), *Prompt Release, Judgment, ITLOS Reports 2000*, p. 86, at p. 109, para. 76.

25 *The "Tomimaru" Case* (*Japan* v. *Russian Federation*), *Prompt Release*.

release cases is guiding States to solve their differences before resorting to the Tribunal. This may explain in part the reasons why no prompt release case has been filed before the Tribunal in the last eight years.

C *The Tribunal's Main Jurisprudential Contributions*

The Tribunal's main contribution to the development of international jurisprudence relates however to the setting of new jurisprudential pathways, especially in the field of its specialization, the law of the sea. I will underline in this regard only five areas where it has made noticeable contributions to the international jurisprudence. They relate to (1) maritime delimitation; (2) the nationality of vessels and the issue of the genuine link; (3) the rights of States in the exclusive economic zones of coastal States, pursuant to article 58 of the Convention; (4) the obligations and liability of the sponsoring State for activities in the Area; and (5) the obligations and liability of the flag State and international obligations regarding IUU fishing. I shall make the following few observations relating to these five points.

1 On Maritime Delimitation

Concerning the delimitation of maritime boundaries, the Tribunal has received two cases. They are Case 16 – the *Dispute concerning the delimitation of the maritime boundary between Bangladesh and Myanmar in the Bay of Bengal (Bangladesh/Myanmar)*, and Case 23 – the *Dispute concerning delimitation of the maritime boundary between Ghana and Côte d'Ivoire in the Atlantic Ocean (Ghana/Côte d'Ivoire)*. As this last case is still pending, I will only refer to the jurisprudential developments that emerged from Case 16.

In Case 16, the Tribunal proceeded to make a three-fold delimitation: delimitation of the territorial sea, delimitation of the EEZ and delimitation of the continental shelf beyond 200 nautical miles. This case, seen as a landmark in the Tribunal's case law, provided an opportunity for the Tribunal to make important contributions to international jurisprudence related to the delimitation of maritime borders. Reference will only be made here to some of these contributions relating to the delimitation of the territorial sea and the delimitation of the continental shelf beyond 200 nautical miles, for their novelty.

Regarding the delimitation of the territorial sea between the two countries, three salient points are to be highlighted: (a) the legal value of the minutes of negotiations in the delimitation of maritime boundaries; (b) the effect given to islands in maritime delimitation in general; and (c) the effect given to the Bangladeshi St. Martin's Island in delimitation of the territorial sea between Bangladesh and Myanmar, in contrast to the effect given to this island in the delimitation of the EEZ between the two countries.

The issue of the legal value of the minutes of negotiations came up in the context of the territorial sea delimitation. While Bangladesh claimed that the territorial sea delimitation between the two countries had been made through bilateral negotiations and exhibited the records of the negotiation which included a line claimed to be the negotiated delimitation line of the territorial sea between the two countries, Myanmar contested this claim, denying that such delimitation had been agreed upon through the negotiations.

The Tribunal concluded that the evidence presented by Bangladesh fell short of proving the existence of a tacit or *de facto* boundary agreement concerning the territorial sea[26] and, joining the ICJ's jurisprudence,[27] it pronounced that "evidence of a tacit legal agreement must be compelling."[28] It therefore did not accept Bangladesh's claim that the delimitation of the territorial sea had taken place through negotiations with Myanmar and proceeded, as requested, to decide the delimitation of the territorial sea itself.

On the issue of the effect to be given to St. Martin's Island in the delimitation of the territorial sea between the two countries, the issue was whether to give that island, a somewhat small feature, full effect in the delimitation of the territorial sea or partial or no effect at all, as argued by Myanmar.

Myanmar contended that the island could not be given full effect in the delimitation of the territorial sea because it was an important special circumstance which necessitated a departure from the median line, as the island lay immediately off the coast of Myanmar,[29] the island was a feature standing alone in the geography of Bangladesh, and that it was situated opposite the mainland of Myanmar, not Bangladesh. In Myanmar's view, granting St. Martin's Island full effect throughout the territorial sea delimitation would lead to a considerable distortion with respect to the general configuration of the coastline, created by a relatively small feature.[30] It argued that the island lay on Myanmar's side of any delimitation line constructed between mainland coasts. In Myanmar's view, St. Martin's Island was therefore "on the wrong side" of such delimitation line.[31] Relying on State practice, it observed that "small

26 *Delimitation of the maritime boundary in the Bay of Bengal (Bangladesh/Myanmar), Judgment, ITLOS Reports 2012*, p. 4, at p. 41, para. 118.

27 *Ibid.*, para. 117 citing to *Territorial and Maritime Dispute between Nicaragua and Honduras in the Caribbean Sea (Nicaragua v. Honduras), Judgment, I.C.J. Reports 2007*, p. 659, at p. 735, para. 253.

28 *Delimitation of the maritime boundary in the Bay of Bengal (Bangladesh/Myanmar), Judgment, ITLOS Reports 2012*, p. 4, at p. 40, para. 117.

29 *Ibid.*, at p. 43, para. 131.

30 *Ibid.*, para. 132.

31 *Ibid.*, para. 134.

or middle-size islands are usually totally ignored" and that the "predominant tendency is to give no or little effect to such maritime formations."[32]

Bangladesh, arguing for the full effect to be given to the island in the territorial sea delimitation, contended that Myanmar had "attempted to manufacture a 'special circumstance' where none exist[ed]" and stated that Myanmar had "ignored reality in order to provide itself with the desired result".[33] Responding to Myanmar's contention that St. Martin's Island was on the "wrong" side of the equidistance line between the coasts of Myanmar and Bangladesh and that this was an important special circumstance which necessitated a departure from the median line, Bangladesh stated that this contention marked a sharp departure from Myanmar's long-standing acceptance that St. Martin's Island was entitled to a 12 nm territorial sea.[34] Bangladesh further pointed out that the right of States to claim a territorial sea around islands was also a well established principle of customary international law and was recognized by Myanmar.[35] It stated that St. Martin's Island "is located 6.5 [nm] southwest of the land boundary terminus and an equivalent distance from the Bangladesh coast."[36]

The Tribunal first dealt with the effects of islands on maritime delimitation, as a general proposition, and then dealt with the issue of the specific effect of St. Martin's Island on the territorial sea delimitation. As for the effects of islands on delimitation in general, the Tribunal noted that neither the case law, nor State practice indicates that there is a general rule concerning the effect to be given to islands in maritime delimitation, adding that such effect depends on the particular circumstances of each case.[37] It observed that the effect to be given to islands in delimitation may differ, depending on whether the delimitation concerns the territorial sea or other maritime areas beyond it. Both the nature of the rights of the coastal State and their seaward extent may be relevant in this regard.[38]

The Tribunal observed that, while it is not unprecedented in case law for islands to be given less than full effect in the delimitation of the territorial sea, the islands subject to such treatment are usually "insignificant maritime

32 *Ibid.*, at p. 44, para. 137.
33 *Ibid.*, para. 138.
34 *Ibid.*, at p. 45, para. 139.
35 *Ibid.*, para. 142.
36 *Ibid.*, at p. 46, para. 143.
37 *Ibid.*, para. 147.
38 *Ibid.*, para. 148.

features".[39] Referring to the effect to be given to St. Martin's Island in the delimitation of the territorial sea, the Tribunal noted that St. Martin's Island is a significant maritime feature by virtue of its size and population and the extent of economic and other activities.[40] It concluded that, in the circumstances of this case, there were no compelling reasons that would justify treating St. Martin's Island as a special circumstance for the purposes of article 15 of the Convention or that would prevent the Tribunal from giving the island full effect in drawing the delimitation line of the territorial sea between the Parties.[41]

It is interesting to note that, while full effect was given to St Martin's Island in the delimitation of the territorial sea, in contrast no effect was given to it in the delimitation of the EEZ, contrary to Bangladesh's position. The Tribunal saw no reason under the circumstances of this case to give any effect to St. Martin's Island in the delimitation of the EEZ between the countries, based on two considerations: firstly because giving effect to the island in this respect would interfere with the natural projection of Myanmar's coast and secondly, because the equitable result to be achieved in the EEZ delimitation pursuant to article 74 of the Convention had been attained by the adjustment made to the provisional equidistance line prompted by the special circumstance of the concavity of the coast, thus making it unnecessary to consider any other special circumstances.

Another contribution that emerged from Case 16 relates to the Tribunal's pioneering role in the delimitation of the continental shelves of the two Parties beyond 200 nm. As it was the first case of delimitation of the continental shelf beyond 200 nm ever to be handled by a court or tribunal, and aware of its pioneering role in this field, the Tribunal made sure that its decision to proceed to this delimitation was based on the following assumptions and pronouncements: that the continental shelf, whether within or beyond 200 nm, is a single continental shelf;[42] that the delimitation of the continental shelf beyond 200 nm did not constitute an encroachment on the functions of the CLCS as the delimitation is without prejudice to the establishment of the outer limit of the continental shelf;[43] that there is a clear distinction between the delimitation of the continental shelf (article 83) and the delineation of the outer limits of the continental shelf beyond 200 nm (article 76);[44] that the establishment of the outer continental shelf limits did not need to be established prior to the

39 *Ibid.*, at p. 47, para. 151.

40 *Ibid.*, para. 151.

41 *Ibid.*, para. 152.

42 *Ibid.*, at p. 96, para. 361.

43 *Ibid.*, at p. 97, para. 367.

44 *Ibid.*, at p. 98, para. 370.

delimitation;[45] and that the rights over the continental shelf are inherent and therefore the entitlement to areas of extended continental shelf can exist independently of the establishment of the outer continental shelf limits.[46]

The Tribunal also clarified the concept of natural prolongation referred to in article 76 of the Convention. It stated that, while natural prolongation was introduced as a fundamental notion in continental shelf delimitation provisions, it was never defined and that the concept of natural prolongation and that of continental margin are closely inter-related and refer to the same area.[47] It therefore concluded that entitlement to a continental shelf beyond 200 nm should thus be determined by reference to the outer edge of the continental margin to be ascertained in accordance with article 76, paragraph 4, of the Convention.[48]

On the issue of the allocation of the so-called "grey area", the Tribunal once again played a pioneering role. As is well known, the issue of the grey area arises whenever adjustment is made to the equidistance line. In Case 16, adjustment was made to the equidistance line to obtain a line considered equitable pursuant to article 74 of the Convention. As a result a grey area of 1,000 km² was created. Bangladesh requested the Tribunal to decide on the grey area allocation and the Tribunal took up the challenge. No other court or tribunal had before taken a decision on this issue. As there was no delimitation to be made in this grey area, for there was no overlapping of the EEZs of the two countries involved, the Tribunal felt that it should solve the problem by granting continental shelf rights to Bangladesh as the grey area coincided with the extended continental shelf of Bangladesh while the rights and jurisdictions of the water column were granted to Myanmar.

By pioneering the delimitation of the continental shelf beyond 200 nm and the allocation of the grey area, the Tribunal set a precedent that may inspire other courts and tribunals to so proceed in future cases.

2 On the Nationality of Ships and the Issue of the Genuine Link

As for the nationality of ships, the Tribunal on two occasions had the opportunity to develop its jurisprudence on this issue.[49] The Tribunal's contribution in this respect becomes very important as it clarifies the interpretation of a

---

45 *Ibid.*, at p. 100, para. 379.

46 *Ibid.*, at p. 107, para. 409.

47 *Ibid.*, at p. 113, para. 432.

48 *Ibid.*, para. 434.

49 *M/V "SAIGA" (No. 2) (Saint Vincent and the Grenadines* v. *Guinea), Judgment, ITLOS Reports 1999*, p. 10, and *M/V "Virginia G" (Panama/Guinea-Bissau), Judgment, ITLOS Reports 2014*, p. 4.

ground rule of general international law embodied in article 91, paragraph 1, of the Convention regarding the nationality of ships. This clarification becomes even more important in the light of certain confusion amongst scholars as to the meaning and role to be given to the concept of "genuine link" in the granting of nationality to ships.

The Tribunal's jurisprudence in this regard is very clear. The first time it was confronted with this issue was in the *M/V "SAIGA" (No. 2) Case (Saint Vincent and the Grenadines* v. *Guinea)* where it held that

> the purpose of the provisions of the Convention on the need for a genuine link between a ship and its flag State is to secure more effective implementation of the duties of the flag State, and not to establish criteria by reference to which the validity of the registration of ships in a flag State may be challenged by other States.[50]

In the *M/V "Virginia G" Case (Panama/Guinea-Bissau)*, the Tribunal reaffirmed its previous jurisprudence and concluded that:

> [O]nce a ship is registered, the flag State is required, under article 94 of the Convention, to exercise effective jurisdiction and control over that ship in order to ensure that it operates in accordance with generally accepted international regulations, procedures and practices. This is the meaning of "genuine link".[51]

The jurisprudence set by the Tribunal on the issue of genuine link is a major stride in the judicial interpretation of article 91, paragraph 1, of the Convention and may provide guidance to the actions of governments and especially to counsels and lawyers appearing before courts and tribunals when arguing their case involving the issue of genuine link.[52]

---

50 *M/V "SAIGA" (No. 2) (Saint Vincent and the Grenadines* v. *Guinea), Judgment, ITLOS Reports 1999*, p. 10, at p. 42, para. 83.

51 *M/V "Virginia G" (Panama/Guinea-Bissau), Judgment, ITLOS Reports 2014*, p. 4, at p. 45, para. 113.

52 The main tenets of the Tribunal's jurisprudence in this regard may be summarised as follows: Article 91, para. 1, third sentence, of the Convention, requiring a genuine link between the flag State and the ship, should not be read as establishing prerequisites or conditions to be satisfied for the exercise of the right of the flag State to grant its nationality to ships; the purpose of the provisions of the Convention on the need for a genuine link between a ship and its flag State is to secure more effective implementation of the duties of the flag State, and not to establish criteria by reference to which the validity of the

3 On the Issue of other States Parties' Rights in the EEZ of Coastal States

The Tribunal has, on several occasions, clarified different aspects of the scope of article 58 of the Convention, concerning the identification of some of the rights of States whether coastal or land-locked, in the exclusive economic zones of the coastal States. One such clarification, which I believe is worth noting here, relates to the right of third States to undertake bunkering activities in that zone.

The Tribunal had to deal with the issue of bunkering of vessels in the EEZ of coastal States in two cases: the *M/V "SAIGA" (No. 2) Case (Saint Vincent and the Grenadines* v. *Guinea)* and the *M/V "Virginia G" Case (Panama/Guinea-Bissau)*. Though in the *M/V "SAIGA" (No. 2) Case* the Tribunal addressed the issue of bunkering in the exclusive economic zone of Guinea, it avowedly avoided taking position on the "broader question of the rights of the coastal States and other States with regard to bunkering in the exclusive economic zone."[53]

In the *M/V "Virginia G" Case*, the Tribunal further elaborated on its jurisprudence on bunkering activities in the EEZ of the coastal States by vessels flying a foreign flag. Here it made a distinction between bunkering activities regarding fishing vessels and other bunkering activities.

In this case, the Tribunal held the view that:

> the regulation by a coastal State of bunkering of foreign vessels fishing in its exclusive economic zone is among those measures which the coastal State may take in its exclusive economic zone to conserve and manage

---

registration of ships in a flag State may be challenged by other States; once a ship is registered, the flag State is required under article 94 of the Convention, to exercise effective jurisdiction and control over that ship in order to ensure that it operates in accordance with generally accepted international regulations, procedures and practices; article 94 of the Convention requires the flag State to effectively exercise its jurisdiction and control in administrative, technical and social matters over ships flying its flag; article 94, para. 6, of the Convention outlines the procedure to be followed where another State "has clear grounds to believe that proper jurisdiction and control with respect to a ship have not been exercised"; and there is nothing in article 94 to permit a State which discovers evidence indicating the absence of proper jurisdiction and control by a flag State over a ship to refuse to recognize the right of the ship to fly the flag of the flag State.

53 *M/V "SAIGA" (No. 2) (Saint Vincent and the Grenadines* v. *Guinea), Judgment, ITLOS Reports 1999*, p. 10, at p. 54, para. 138.

> its living resources under article 56 of the Convention read together with article 62, paragraph 4, of the Convention.[54]

However, it also made it clear that the coastal State does not have such competence with regard to other bunkering activities, unless otherwise determined in accordance with the Convention.[55] As the issue of bunkering is not expressly referred to in the Convention, the jurisprudence set by the Tribunal is a very important one and may serve as a guiding rule for those involved in bunkering operations in the EEZ of a coastal State.

4 On the Obligations and Liability of the Sponsoring State of Entities with Respect to Activities in the Area

Lastly, I will refer to the two advisory opinions given by the Tribunal. In these two advisory opinions, the Tribunal made significant contributions to international jurisprudence. In its Advisory Opinion in Case 17,[56] handled by its Seabed Disputes Chamber, it drew a kind of charter of the obligations and liability of the sponsoring State of entities carrying out activities in the Area. It identified the different obligations involved and detailed the several circumstances in which the sponsoring State may or may not incur liability. It made a clear distinction between the sponsoring State's due diligence obligations and its direct obligations and indicated what it meant by due diligence obligations.

On the issue of liability of the sponsoring State that Chamber of the Tribunal was very clear and to the point. After identifying the sponsoring State's failure to carry out its responsibilities under the Convention and the occurrence of damage as the conditions for this liability to arise, it indicated that the sponsoring State's liability results "from its failure to fulfil its obligations under the Convention and related instruments."[57] This case has cleared the way for sponsoring States, as it detailed their obligations and responsibilities.

54 *M/V "Virginia G" (Panama/Guinea-Bissau), Judgment, ITLOS Reports 2014*, p. 4, at p. 69, para. 217.

55 *Ibid.*, at p. 70, para. 223.

56 *Responsibilities and obligations of States with respect to activities in the Area, Advisory Opinion, 1 February 2011, ITLOS Reports 2011*, p. 10.

57 *Responsibilities and obligations of States with respect to activities in the Area, Advisory Opinion, 1 February 2011, ITLOS Reports 2011*, p. 10.

5 On Obligations and Liability of the flag State or the International Organization Relating to IUU Fishing

Another highlight in the jurisprudence of the Tribunal relates to the timely issue of IUU fishing. In Case 21, concerning an Advisory Opinion given at the request of the West African SFRC upon decision taken by its seven West-African Member States,[58] the Tribunal, in responding to the four questions raised in the request, clarified the issue of the flag State's obligations and liability in cases of IUU fishing activities carried out by its vessels in the EEZs of the SRFC Member States. It also addressed the liability of an international organization in situations where a fishing vessel violates the laws and regulations of the SRFC Member State while fishing under an authorization issued to it within the framework of an international agreement. Furthermore, it addressed the issue of rights and obligations of the SRFC Member States in ensuring the sustainable management of shared stocks and stocks of common interest, especially the small pelagic species and tuna.

As in Case 17, the Tribunal identified the direct obligations and the due diligence obligations of the flag State or, as the case may be, of the international organization involved. The liability of the flag State or, as the case may be, of the international organization, does not arise from the violation by the fishing vessel of the laws and regulations of coastal State but from the non-compliance by those entities with their obligations. If the flag State or the international organization comply with their obligations, they are not liable even when their vessels are found to have violated the coastal State laws and regulations.

Additionally, the Tribunal dealt with the issue of its own jurisdiction to deliver advisory opinions, as this issue was raised during the proceedings by some States participants. Here, the Tribunal drew attention to the fact that its jurisdiction as a *plenum* to entertain advisory cases is based on an international agreement related to the purposes of the Convention which specifically provides for that jurisdiction, pursuant to article 21 of its Statute.[59] Though the Convention did not directly refer to the advisory power of the Tribunal, acting as a *plenum*, it nonetheless opened the way for the Tribunal's advisory jurisdiction, whenever such was specifically provided for in international agreements, as referred to above. The SRFC Member States agreement, on the basis of which the request for the advisory opinion was made, fell totally under this category of agreement referred to in article 21 of the Statute.[60] This Advisory

58 The members are: Cabo Verde, Gambia, Guinea, Guinea-Bissau, Mauritania, Senegal, Sierra Leone.

59 See Annex VI to the Convention.

60 See Annex VI to the Convention.

Opinion may well have established a clearer legal landscape for those involved in or affected by IUU fishing activities.

II Concluding Remarks

As outlined above, the Tribunal's jurisprudence has touched upon several issues of the law of the sea, providing States with important clarifications of the provisions of the Convention and much needed legal guidance thereon. As the Convention is a complex legal instrument, the interpretation and application of which may demand expert judicial assistance, the Tribunal is well positioned to continue to give its contribution to that end. I am sure that if given the opportunity by States Parties, the Tribunal will continue to build on its jurisprudence on matters of the law of the sea, thus contributing to a better understanding of the provisions of the Convention and to the rule of law in international relations. The Tribunal's contribution to international jurisprudence in the last two decades augurs well for the future developments of its jurisprudence.

The Precautionary Approach in the Advisory Opinion Concerning the Responsibilities and Obligations of States Sponsoring Persons and Entities with Respect to Activities in the Area

Elsa Kelly

I Introduction and Preliminary Considerations

The International Tribunal for the Law of the Sea is commemorating the 20th anniversary of its creation this year. This is, therefore, the proper time to refer to the jurisprudence of the Tribunal and single out its contribution to the development of international law.

The Advisory Opinion of the Seabed Disputes Chamber, in response to the Request by the Council of the International Seabed Authority, set forth in the Council's decision ISBA/16/C/13 of 6 May 2010, is one of several decisions of the Tribunal dealing with environmental obligations of States Parties to the United Nations Convention on the Law of the Sea.[1]

Given the specific jurisdiction of the Seabed Disputes Chamber and the content of the questions in the request, the decision, in accordance with article 191 of the Convention, focuses primarily on Part XI, the Annexes relating thereto, the 1994 Agreement on Part XI, and the Regulations of the Authority.[2]

The precautionary approach is one of the legal issues dealt with in the Advisory Opinion which the Chamber addressed in the context of questions 1 and 3 of the request. Before turning to the consideration of the precautionary approach in the Advisory Opinion, it is convenient to refer briefly to its legal history and evolution.

The origin of the precautionary approach or principle can be traced back to the 1970's, when the concept was introduced for the first time in German legislation. In the following decades, the concept evolved with its inclusion in

1 *Responsibilities and obligations of States with respect to activities in the Area, Advisory Opinion, 1 February 2011, ITLOS Reports 2011*, p. 10.

2 The Regulations of the Authority are the Regulations on Prospecting and Exploration for Polymetallic Nodules in the Area of 2000 ("the Nodules Regulations"), and the Regulations on Prospecting and Exploration for Polymetallic Sulphides in the Area of 2010 ("the Sulphides Regulations").

© 2018, BY INTERNATIONAL TRIBUNAL FOR THE LAW OF THE SEA | DOI 10.1163/9789004356832_007

several regional and international instruments, such as the 1992 Convention on Biological Diversity which refers to the principle in its Preamble (without naming it);[3] the 1992 Rio Declaration on Sustainable Development (Principle 15);[4] the 1992 Framework Convention on Climate Change,[5] the 2000 Cartagena Protocol on Biosafety;[6] and the Treaty on the Functioning of the European Union ("TFEU"), articles 191 and 192.[7]

As can be ascertained from the examination of various regional and international instruments, different formulations of the principle exist, which clearly show that there is no uniform understanding of the precautionary approach concerning its content and application except for the basic notion that in cases of a threat of serious or irreversible damage to the environment, lack of scientific certainty should not be used as a reason for preventing action.

Nevertheless, this formulation, included in Principle 15 of the Rio Declaration, seems to have found a very wide acceptance at the international level and has been recognized by authors as the "core" content of the precautionary approach.

A more exhaustive formulation of the precautionary approach (or principle) may be found in the domestic legislation of European countries as, for example, in Germany, where the rule in article 20(a) of the German Constitution mandating that the State "shall protect the natural foundation of life and animals" is complemented by the inclusion of the precautionary approach (or principle) in different sectors regulated by German environmental legislation such as the Federal Emissions Control Act, the Atomic Energy Law, and the Genetic Engineering Act, and has been further developed in the jurisprudence of the German domestic courts.

The evolution of the precautionary approach in German legislation and jurisprudence seems to have developed differently in each sector in respect of its application and content and who is or may be affected with respect to the burden of proof. It also should be noted that the specific legislation concerning the subject matter dealt with here – the Seabed Mining Act – does not include an explicit reference to the precautionary approach. However, the legal obligation

3 *Convention on Biological Diversity*, 5 June 1992, 1760 *UNTS* 79.

4 *Rio Declaration on Environment and Development*, 13 June 1992, UN Doc. A/CONF.151/26 (vol. I).

5 *United Nations Framework Convention on Climate Change*, 9 May 1992, 1771 *UNTS* 107.

6 *Cartagena Protocol on Biosafety to the Convention on Biological Diversity*, 29 January 2000, 2226 *UNTS* 208.

7 *Consolidated version of the Treaty on the Functioning of the European Union*, 13 December 2007, OJ C 115/47 of 9 May 2008.

to apply this approach with respect to seabed mining activities in the Area may be inferred from its provisions.[8] In 2010, the German Government issued a statement in response to the Tribunal's invitation to States Parties to present written statements (regarding the Advisory Opinion requested by the Council concerning the responsibilities and obligations of States sponsoring persons and entities operating in the Area), in which it explained at length its position and the extent of the provisions contained in the Seabed Mining Act. This specific legislation was expressly mentioned by the Chamber in paragraph 237 of its Advisory Opinion stating that it "takes note of the Deep Seabed Mining Law adopted by Germany".[9]

Another important contribution is the Communication from the Commission of the European Union (the "Commission") on the precautionary principle (the "Communication").[10] In an explanatory note, the Commission declared that the objective of the Communication was to inform all interested parties as to how the European Union intended to apply the precautionary principle in cases:

> where scientific evidence is insufficient, inconclusive or uncertain and preliminary scientific evaluation indicates that there are reasonable grounds for concern that the potentially dangerous effects on the environment, human, animal, or plant health may be inconsistent with the high level protection chosen by the EU.[11]

It added that it also aimed to provide input to the ongoing debate both at the European Community and international levels.[12] The Commission gave further precisions with respect to its aims in adopting the Communication which were to: outline the Commission's approach to using the precautionary principle; establish the Commission's guidelines for applying it; build a common understanding of how to assess, appraise, manage, and communicate risks

8 Section 4, paragraph (6), of the German Seabed Mining Act provides that "[A]n applicant shall be approved if 1. The application and the plan of work meet the preconditions of the Convention, of the Implementing Agreement, and of the rules and regulations issued by the Authority for the conclusion of a contract and in particular the obligations pursuant to Article 4 (6) letters (a) to (c) of annex III to the Convention".

9 *Responsibilities and obligations of States with respect to activities in the Area, Advisory Opinion, 1 February 2011, ITLOS Reports 2011*, p. 10, at p. 73.

10 *Communication from the Commission on the precautionary principle*, COM(2000) 1 final, 2 February 2000, Commission of the European Communities.

11 *Ibid.*, p. 7.

12 *Ibid.*, p. 8.

that science is not able to evaluate fully; and avoid unwarranted recourse to the precautionary principle, as a disguised form of protectionism.[13]

The most important elements of the Communication concern the following aspects that define the functions of the precautionary principles and the different ways in which it may be applied:

1. The scope of the precautionary principle in practice goes beyond the declared objective in the TFEU "to protect the environment" and applies specifically "where preliminary objective science evaluation [...] indicates that there are reasonable grounds for concern that the potentially dangerous effects on the environment, human, animal or plant health may be inconsistent with the high level of protection chosen for the Community."[14]
2. The principle should be considered (applied) within:

   a structured decision making process with detailed scientific and other objective information. This structure is provided by the three elements of risk analysis: the assessment of risk, the choice of risk management strategy and the communication of the risk. The precautionary principle is particularly relevant to the element of risk management.[15]

3. The application of the precautionary principle "presupposes that potentially dangerous effects deriving from a phenomenon, product or process have been identified, and that scientific evaluation does not allow the risk to be determined with sufficient certainty."[16]
4. Implementation of "an approach based on the precautionary principle should start with a scientific evaluation as complete as possible, and where possible, identifying at each stage the degree of scientific uncertainty."[17]

The Commission also pointed out that, in considering the level of the risk and the degree of uncertainty, the response might be a decision to act or not to act (or not to establish a "binding legal measure"); and if action is the correct

13 *Ibid.*, p. 2, para. 2.
14 *Ibid.*, p. 2, para. 3.
15 *Ibid.*, p. 7.
16 *Ibid.*, p. 3.
17 *Ibid.*, p. 3.

answer, "a wide range of initiatives is available ... going from a legally binding measure to a research project or a recommendation."[18]

The Commission also stated that if action is recommended, measures based on the precautionary principle should be proportional to the chosen level of protection; non-discriminatory in their application; consistent with similar measures already taken; based, where feasible and appropriate, on a cost-benefit analysis concerning action or lack of action; subject to review in the light of new scientific information; and assign responsibility for producing scientific evidence (defining who should carry the burden of proof).[19]

The Communication provides very useful tools for determining the meaning, function and the different ways in which the principle may be applied and is extremely valuable for understanding a concept whose implementation, nevertheless, continues to raise difficulties and which remains ambiguous in many respects.

II Consideration of the Precautionary Approach in the Advisory Opinion

The Chamber's findings concerning the precautionary approach should be examined in the context of its advice in response to the questions in the request. The relevant questions are numbers 1 and 3. Question 1 concerns the legal responsibilities and obligations of sponsoring States with respect to sponsorship of activities in the Area in accordance with the Convention, in particular Part XI, and related instruments. Question 3 seeks clarification as to what constitutes the "necessary and appropriate measures" that a sponsoring State must take to fulfil its responsibility under the Convention, in particular article 139, Annex III and the 1994 Agreement on Part XI of the Convention. Some preliminary observations may be useful before considering the issues dealt with by the Chamber with respect to the precautionary approach:

(i) The term "precautionary approach" follows the English text of the Authority's Regulations, but the Chamber also observed that the French text calls it "*principe de précaution*" – "precautionary principle" – (as does the European Union in the TFEU and in the Communication), which implies that the expressions may be used synonymously.

18 *Ibid.*, p. 3, para. 5.

19 *Ibid.*, p. 3, para. 6.

(ii) The precautionary approach is not mentioned in the Convention as such. Both regulation 31, paragraph 2, of the Regulations on Prospecting and Exploration for Polymetallic Nodules in the Area of 2000 ("the Nodules Regulations"), and regulation 33 of the Regulations on Prospecting and Exploration for Polymetallic Sulphides in the Area of 2010 ("the Sulphides Regulations") provide that the Authority as well as sponsoring States shall apply a precautionary approach as defined in Principle 15 of the 1992 Rio Declaration on Environment and Development, which states that:

> [i]n order to protect the environment, the precautionary approach shall be widely applied by States according to their capabilities. Where there are threats of serious irreversible damage, lack of full scientific certainty shall not be used as a reason for postponing cost-effective measures to prevent environmental degradation.

Principle 15 by itself does not establish a legally binding obligation for States and it has been generally considered as a rule of "soft law". But, as contained in a regulation of the Authority, the principle becomes obligatory for the States Parties to the Convention. As noted by the Chamber, within the legal system set up in the Convention and related instruments, the Authority's Regulations have transformed non-binding Principle 15 of the Rio Declaration concerning the precautionary approach into a binding international obligation, applicable to both the Authority and the sponsoring States.[20]

(iii) The "Regulations" referred to above are the Nodules Regulations and the Sulphides Regulations, which were in force at the time of the decision.

(iv) The Nodules Regulations were subsequently amended, and later a third set of "Regulations on Prospecting and Exploration for Cobalt-rich Ferromanganese Crusts in the Area", were established in 2012 by the Council. Referring to future regulations by the Authority, the Chamber noted that, in the two sets of Regulations considered by it, the precautionary approach "applies specifically to the activities envisaged therein, namely prospecting and exploration for polymetallic nodules and polymetallic sulphides."[21] The Chamber further added that nevertheless, "it is to be expected that the Authority will either repeat or further develop this approach when it regulates exploitation activities and activities

20 *Responsibilities and obligations of States with respect to activities in the Area, Advisory Opinion, 1 February 2011, ITLOS Reports 2011*, p. 10, at p. 45, para. 127.

21 *Ibid.*, at p. 46, para. 130.

concerning other types of minerals";[22] and the Council certainly did so in the Cobalt-rich Regulations. It is also expected that the Authority will also apply and further develop the precautionary approach in its regulations concerning the exploitation of minerals in the Area.

A *The Precautionary Approach as a Direct Obligation of the Sponsoring State and as a Due Diligence Obligation "To Ensure"*

In its Advisory Opinion, the Chamber first ascertained that the Convention and related instruments (the Authority's Nodules and Sulphides Regulations) include provisions that establish direct obligations for sponsoring States that must be implemented by them independently of their due diligence obligation to ensure compliance by the contractor of a specific behaviour.[23]

The Chamber mentions a number of such direct obligations which it considers most important, and singles out the precautionary approach among them. However, the Chamber immediately states that these direct obligations (which include the precautionary approach) "can also be seen as a relevant factor in meeting the due diligence 'obligation to ensure' and that the said obligations are couched [formulated] as obligations to ensure compliance with a specific rule" of the Convention and related instruments.[24]

In the view of the Chamber this link between an obligation of due diligence and the precautionary approach may be traced back to the *Southern Bluefin Tuna Cases* (*New Zealand* v. *Japan; Australia* v. *Japan*) as emerges from the declaration by the Tribunal that the Parties "should in the circumstances act with prudence and caution to ensure that the conservation measures are taken…".[25] The Chamber also underlined that this statement is strengthened by further statements of the Tribunal concerning the existence of scientific uncertainty regarding the conservation measures to be taken, in the face of which it declared that "although the Tribunal cannot conclusively assess the scientific evidence presented by the parties, it finds that measures should be taken as a matter of urgency".[26]

---

22 *Ibid.*, para. 130.

23 *Ibid.*, at p. 44, para. 121.

24 *Ibid.*, para. 123.

25 *Ibid.*, at p. 46, para. 132.

26 *Ibid.*, at p. 46, para. 132 citing *Southern Bluefin Tuna* (*New Zealand* v. *Japan; Australia* v. *Japan*), *Provisional Measures, Order of 27 August 1999, ITLOS Reports 1999*, p. 280, at p. 296, para. 80.

Having asserted that compliance with "direct obligations" of sponsoring States is also a relevant factor"[27] for meeting the due diligence obligation to ensure compliance by the sponsored contractor of the provisions in Part XI of the Convention and related instruments (which include the Regulations established by the Authority), the Chamber went a step further from this general finding when it stressed that the precautionary approach "is applicable even outside the scope of the Regulations."[28] This statement by the Chamber is an important and significant interpretation of the applicable rules, because its effect is to refer back the question of the applicability of the precautionary principle to the provisions of the Convention, establishing that it should be considered as a due diligence obligation of sponsoring States independently of their obligations set forth in the Regulations.

The Chamber reinforced its findings with reference to the precautionary approach stating that, since the due diligence obligations of sponsoring States established in the Convention require them to take "all appropriate measures to prevent damage that might result from the activities of the contractors that they sponsor" (see articles 139, paragraph 1, 154, paragraph 4, annex III, article 4, paragraph 4, read together with article 145), this obligation applies "in situations where scientific evidence concerning the scope and potential negative impact of the activity in question is insufficient but where there are plausible indications of potential risks."[29]

Therefore, the sponsoring State, in the view of the Chamber, would not be fulfilling its due diligence obligation if it did not apply the precautionary approach in relation to those risks.

The Advisory Opinion referred also to Annex 4, section 5.1, of the Sulphides Regulations, that lays out a "standard clause" for exploration contracts which obliges the contractor to take necessary measures "to prevent, reduce and control pollution and other hazards to the marine environment arising from its activities in the Area as far as reasonably possible applying a precautionary approach and best environmental practices."[30]

The text of this "standard clause" establishes a contractual obligation of the sponsored contractor that, undoubtedly, widens the scope of the sponsoring State's obligation to apply "due diligence to ensure", as referred to above.

The interpretation provided by the Chamber implies that the implementation of the precautionary approach entails obligations for the Authority, the

27 *Ibid.*, at p. 44, para. 123.

28 *Ibid.*, at p. 46, para. 131.

29 *Ibid.*, para. 131.

30 *Ibid.*, at p. 47, para. 133.

sponsored contractor and the sponsoring States in the light of the provisions included in article 153 of the Convention concerning the system of exploration and exploitation of the Area, in particular paragraph 4, which reads:

> The Authority shall exercise such control over activities in the Area as is necessary for the purpose of securing compliance with the relevant provisions of this Part and the Annexes relating thereto, and the rules, regulations and procedures of the Authority, and the plans of work approved in accordance with paragraph 3. States Parties shall assist the Authority by taking all measures necessary to ensure such compliance in accordance with article 139.

It should be noted that, in the view of the Chamber, the Authority is responsible for establishing the rules, regulations and procedures, including those concerning the precautionary approach, taking into account all scientific information relevant to the protection of the marine environment and its resources which are the common heritage of mankind. It has the obligation to ensure that activities in the Area are carried out in accordance with Part XI of the Convention and related instruments, with the assistance of sponsoring States. In the event of a violation the Authority, pursuant to Annex III, article 18, is entitled to take enforcement action. The contractor has the obligation to fully implement the Authority's rules, regulations and procedures as well as the provisions established in the contract entered into with the Authority, including the standard clause concerning the application of the precautionary principle. As pointed out by the Chamber, the requirement to apply a precautionary approach is also a "contractual obligation" of the contractor.[31] Beyond this, the precautionary approach cannot be invoked as an excuse to create new obligations for a contractor.

The sponsoring State, for its part, is obliged to assist the Authority to implement the deep sea mining regime, including the precautionary approach, by taking all measures necessary to ensure its compliance by the contractor within its national legal system, in accordance with article 139.

The Chamber also maintained that the responsibility and obligations of the sponsoring State shall continue while the contract with the Authority is in force, and so should the laws, regulations and administrative measures adopted by it to ensure that the contractor complies with its obligations.

---

31 *Ibid.*, para. 133.

B Content and Scope of the Precautionary Approach

The reference to Principle 15 of the 1992 Rio Declaration in the Nodules and Sulphides Regulations (which, as indicated above, were the legal instruments considered by the Chamber at the time the decision was taken), is not very explicit in determining what the precautionary approach actually means.

It certainly indicates the situation in which the precautionary approach should be applied, that is "where there are threats of serious or irreversible damage" in which case "the lack of full scientific certainty shall not be used as a reason for postponing cost-effective measures to prevent environmental degradation". Principle 15 does not require that action must be taken, but allows action to be taken in cases of scientific uncertainty.

Most authors agree that the description of the content of the precautionary approach in Principle 15 of the Rio Declaration is insufficient and does not amount to a proper definition in a legal sense, since it uses a terminology that is imprecise, such as threats of "serious" damage, in a context of scientific uncertainty.

Furthermore, the principle indicates that States shall apply the approach "according to their capabilities"; this suggests that differences may affect the manner in which the precautionary approach may be applied if the capabilities of States do not meet the same standards. This makes the concept even more vague in relation to its concrete application by States.

Another source of uncertainty is the reference to "cost-effective" measures, which seems to refer to some kind of political decision concerning the cases or situations in which the application of the precautionary approach may or may not be considered acceptable.

In searching for a clearer meaning of the precautionary approach, with the aim of determining its content more accurately, some authors have suggested seeking clarification in legal texts that are more comprehensive than the 1992 Rio Declaration. In this respect, Judge Wolfrum refers to article 6 of the Straddling Fish Stocks Agreement as an example of "a more comprehensive circumscription of the precautionary approach".[32]

The Communication of the Council of the European Union on the precautionary principle is also an important source for grasping the meaning, content and applicability of the precautionary approach.

---

32 R. Wolfrum, "The Regulations of the Seabed Authority" in M. Lodge and M. Nordquist (eds.) *Peaceful Order in the World's Oceans – Essays in honour of Satya N. Nandan* (Brill, 2014), pp. 244 and 245.

C *The Chamber's Contribution Regarding the Content of the Precautionary Principle*

As observed above, the Advisory Opinion, in setting forth its interpretation of the Regulations of the Authority, read together with Part XI of the Convention and related instruments, gave further content to the precautionary approach when it affirmed that it must be considered as "an integral part of the general obligation of due diligence of sponsoring States which is applicable even outside the scope of the [Authority's] Regulations"[33] and that this general obligation under the Convention exists, independently of the Authority's Regulations, according to which "the sponsoring State has to take measures within the framework of its own legal system in order to oblige sponsored entities to adopt such an approach."[34]

Another aspect of the precautionary approach considered by the Chamber is the phrase in the first sentence of Principle 15 of the above-mentioned Rio Declaration that "the precautionary approach shall be ... applied by States according to their capabilities". The Chamber examines this question in relation to the preferential treatment awarded by the Convention to developing States as compared with that granted to developped States and refers to article 148, the general purpose of which is to promote the participation of developing States in activities in the Area.

In this respect, the Chamber considered that the statement in Principle 15 of the Rio Declaration concerning the different capabilities of States in the application of the precautionary approach implies that "the requirements for complying with the obligation to apply the precautionary approach may be stricter for the developed than for the developing sponsoring States."[35] The Chamber also considered that the reference to "capabilities" in the Rio Declaration is only "a broad and imprecise manner" of referring to the differences in developed and developing States, but pointed out that ultimately "what counts in a specific situation is the level of scientific knowledge and technical capability available to a given State in the relevant scientific and technical fields."[36]

The Chamber also cautioned in relation to the reference regarding "different capabilities", that this qualifier does not apply to the requirement, in regulation 33, paragraph 2, of the Sulphides Regulation, to follow "best environmental

---

33 *Responsibilities and obligations of States with respect to activities in the Area, Advisory Opinion, 1 February 2011, ITLOS Reports 2011*, p. 10, at p. 46, para. 131.

34 *Ibid.*, at p. 47, para. 134.

35 *Ibid.*, at p. 54, para. 161.

36 *Ibid.*, para. 162.

practices" (which the Chamber considered supplements the sponsoring State's obligation to apply the precautionary approach).[37]

It also should be noted, for clarification purposes, that this differentiation does not affect the ruling by the Chamber with respect to the issue as to whether, in the Convention, a preferential treatment exists for developing States concerning the obligations of sponsoring States, with respect to which the Chamber firmly established that none of the general provisions of the Convention grants such preferential rights. It therefore concluded "that the general provisions concerning the responsibility and liability of the sponsoring State apply equally to all sponsoring States, whether developing or developed."[38] In this context, the indication in Principle 15 of the Rio Declaration that the precautionary approach shall be applied by States "according to their capabilities" is an exception to the general rule mentioned above.

In the context of the third question, which refers, among other aspects, to the content of the measures that a sponsoring State must take in order to implement its obligations under the Convention and related instruments, the Chamber mentions the precautionary approach as one of those topics to be found in the provisions that establish direct obligations of the sponsoring States.[39] Nevertheless – and given the fact that the sponsoring State is obliged "to ensure" that the contractor complies with its contract, including the contractual clause provided in the Authority's Regulations concerning the implementation of the precautionary approach – the sponsoring State is under its due diligence obligation to include this approach in its laws and regulations. These cannot be less stringent than the regulations established by the Authority, but the sponsoring State may apply stricter requirements concerning environmental practices and precautions.

D *The Precautionary Approach and Its Consideration at the International Level*

The question concerning the legal status of the precautionary approach (or principle) at the international level is still under scrutiny from the academic and political perspectives, especially when considered in relation to certain specific areas such as the use of genetically modified organisms in industry or the installation of nuclear reactors.

Notwithstanding this ongoing debate, there is a fair amount of agreement in considering Principle 15 of the Rio Declaration as having achieved the status

---

37 *Ibid.*, para. 161.

38 *Ibid.*, at p. 53, para. 158.

39 *Ibid.*, at p. 44, para. 122.

of a rule of customary international law, even though there is no uniformity in its interpretation and application, since it is applied differently with respect to each sector.

In this respect, the Chamber observed that "the precautionary approach has been incorporated into a growing number of international treaties and other instruments many of which reflect the formulation of Principle 15 of the Rio Declaration" which in its view "has initiated a trend towards making this approach part of customary international law."[40]

The Advisory Opinion also finds that this trend is reinforced by the Authority's Regulations, in the above-mentioned "standard clause" contained in Annex IV, section 5.1 of the Sulphides Regulations, and by the Judgment of the ICJ in the *Case concerning the Pulp Mills on the River Uruguay*, which considered the precautionary approach to be a relevant factor for the interpretation of the environmental bilateral treaty between the Parties to that dispute (Argentina and Uruguay).[41]

This Advisory Opinion of the Chamber has had a considerable strengthening effect concerning the legal status of the precautionary approach, with respect to the "*opinio iuris*" given by many authors and international institutions, and by the practice of a considerable number of States, as reflecting customary international law. In fact, the Advisory Opinion has received wide international recognition as a guiding instrument concerning the interpretation of the Convention.

---

40 *Ibid.*, at p. 47, para. 135.

41 *Ibid.*, para. 135.

The Tribunal's Jurisprudence and Its Contribution to the Rule of Law

Jin-Hyun Paik

The 20th anniversary of the founding of the International Tribunal for the Law of the Sea is an appropriate time to reflect on and assess its work as a judicial institution. The Tribunal makes a contribution to the rule of law in two ways; first, by settling disputes peacefully, and second, by clarifying and developing international law. The two functions are closely interrelated. I will comment on each of these functions of the Tribunal.

I Role of the Tribunal in Dispute Settlement

First, let me address the role of the Tribunal as a means of dispute settlement under the United Nations Convention on the Law of the Sea. While the Tribunal was established by the Convention as a new, standing court twenty years ago,[1] it does not have the privilege of being the only and exclusive court to deal with disputes concerning the interpretation or application of the Convention. State Parties to such a dispute may choose any peaceful means to settle it, including any court or tribunal.[2] Even for compulsory procedures entailing binding decisions, the Tribunal is just one of the four means available under article 287, paragraph 1, of the Convention and is not even the residual means or default forum,[3] except for the two urgent proceedings, namely prompt release proceedings under article 292 and provisional measures proceedings under article 290, paragraph 5, of the Convention.

On the other hand, the jurisdiction of the Tribunal goes beyond the settlement of disputes submitted to it in accordance with the Convention. Article 21 of the Statute provides that its jurisdiction comprises "all matters specifically provided for in any other agreement which confers jurisdiction on the Tribunal".

1 Article 1, paragraph 1, of Annex VI to the Convention provides that "[t]he International Tribunal for the Law of the Sea is constituted and shall function in accordance with the provisions of this Convention and this Statute.

2 Article 280 of the Convention.

3 In accordance with article 287, paras. 3 and 4, of the Convention, an Annex VII arbitral tribunal is a residual forum.

© 2018, BY INTERNATIONAL TRIBUNAL FOR THE LAW OF THE SEA | DOI 10.1163/9789004356832_008

Based on this provision, the Tribunal gave an advisory opinion on the request submitted to it in accordance with the 2012 Convention on the Determination of the Minimal Condition for Access ("MCA Convention"), an international agreement concluded among seven Member States of the SRFC in West Africa. This was the first time that the Tribunal exercised its jurisdiction over matters specifically provided for in "any other agreement" which confers jurisdiction on it. It should also be noted that unlike the Tribunal, its Seabed Disputes Chamber has exclusive jurisdiction over certain categories of disputes arising from activities in the seabed and subsoil beyond national jurisdiction.[4]

Over the past 20 years, 25 cases have been submitted to the Tribunal.[5] Out of those 25 cases, 16 cases are concerned with either the prompt release of vessels or crews under article 292 or the prescription of provisional measures under article 290, paragraph 5, of the Convention. There have been two requests for an advisory opinion. The remaining seven are the cases on the merits. On the other hand, thirteen cases on the merits have been submitted to Annex VII arbitration.[6] These statistics suggest that the design of Part XV (especially section 2) of the Convention has worked as the drafters of the Convention intended in both a positive and negative sense.

In a positive sense, the high percentage of urgent cases the Tribunal has had to deal with vindicates its value as a standing court under the Convention that can respond to an urgent situation in a timely manner. In prompt release proceedings or provisional measures proceedings, the Tribunal usually gives its decision or order one month after an application or a request is filed with it. Such a prompt response cannot be expected from an *ad hoc* tribunal.

4 Article 187 of the Convention. Article 287, para. 2, of the Convention provides that "[a] declaration made under paragraph 1 shall not affect or be affected by the obligation of a State Party to accept the jurisdiction of the Seabed Disputes Chamber of the International Tribunal for the Law of the Sea to the extent and in the manner provided for in Part XV, section 5".

5 For the complete list of the cases, see https://www.itlos.org/en/cases/list-of-cases/

6 *Southern Bluefin Tuna Cases* (*New Zealand* v. *Japan, Australia* v. *Japan*) instituted in 1998; *The MOX Plant Case* (*Ireland* v. *United Kingdom*) instituted in 2001; *Malaysia* v. *Singapore*, instituted in 2003; *Guyana v. Suriname*, instituted in 2004; *Barbados* v. *Trinidad and Tobago*, instituted in 2004; *The Bay of Bengal Maritime Boundary Arbitration* (*Bangladesh* v. *India*) instituted in 2009; *The Chagos Marine Protected Area Arbitration* (*Mauritius* v. *United Kingdom*) instituted in 2010; *The ARA Libertad Arbitration* (*Argentina* v. *Ghana*) instituted in 2012; *The Republic of Philippines* v. *The Peoples' Republic of China*, instituted in 2013; *The Arctic Sunrise Arbitration* (*The Netherlands* v. *the Russian Federation*) instituted in 2013; *The Duzgit Integrity Arbitration* (*Malta* v. *Sao Tome and Principe*) instituted in 2013; *The Atlanto-Scandian Herring Arbitration* (*Denmark in respect of the Faroe Islands* v. *the European Union*) instituted in 2014; *The "Enrica Lexie" Incident* (*Italy* v. *India*) instituted in 2015.

The ability of the Tribunal to take urgent action needs to be appreciated because it is exactly why many States, especially maritime States, were in favour of establishing a new standing court at the Third United Nations Conference on the Law of the Sea ("UNCLOS III"). They considered that urgent actions by a standing court were essential to protecting their maritime interests in the new legal order of the oceans created by the Convention.

On the other hand, the limited number of disputes on the merits that have been submitted to the Tribunal is largely due to the fact that the Tribunal is not the residual forum under article 287 on the choice of procedures. While the largest number of States Parties chose the Tribunal as a preferred means under article 287, the number stands at 33, this represents less than one fifth of the total number of States Parties (as of 10 April 2013)[7]. Thus the statistical probability for a dispute subject to the compulsory procedures to be submitted to the Tribunal is rather low. By contrast, the number of States Parties which chose Annex VII arbitration is only nine.[8] However, the number of the cases on the merits that have been submitted to the Annex VII arbitration is almost twice as many as those submitted to the Tribunal.[9] This is so not because parties to the disputes chose Annex VII arbitration but rather because they chose different procedures or did not choose any procedure at all. Among the four procedures available under article 287 of the Convention, Annex VII arbitration has received the largest number of cases on the merits because it is the residual procedure. The Tribunal suffered from the relative paucity of merits cases because it is not such a procedure. In light of this structural disadvantage, it seems reasonable to expect that there will be no radical change in the number or nature of disputes to be submitted to the Tribunal at least in the near future. I hope that I prove to be wrong.

However, I can be optimistic about the long-term future of the Tribunal as a means of dispute settlement for the following reasons.

First, the Tribunal has been doing much better in receiving cases on the merits and requests for advisory opinions over the past several years.[10] This

---

7 United Nations, Oceans and Law of the Sea, http://www.un.org/Depts/los/index.htm.

8 *Ibid.*

9 Strictly speaking, only two cases (*The M/V "Louisa" Case* (*Saint Vincent and the Grenadines* v. *Kingdom of Spain*) and *The M/V "Norstar" Case* (*Panama* v. *Italy*)) have been submitted to the Tribunal pursuant to article 287 of the Convention. No case has ever been submitted to the ICJ in that way.

10 For example, since 2009 five contentious cases and two requests for advisory opinions have been submitted to the Tribunal. Before then, there had been only two contentious cases submitted to the Tribunal.

trend may have to do with the fact that the Tribunal has over time built up reputation and credibility as a judicial body. In this regard, it is interesting to note that parties to a dispute often agree to transfer to the Tribunal disputes that have been submitted to Annex VII arbitration in accordance with article 287 of the Convention. This was the case with the *M/V "SAIGA" (No. 2) Case*, the *Dispute concerning delimitation of the maritime boundary between Bangladesh and Myanmar in the Bay of Bengal* and the *Dispute concerning delimitation of the maritime boundary between Ghana and Côte d'Ivoire in the Atlantic Ocean*. It is also interesting to note that a party to a dispute often makes a declaration to choose the Tribunal in accordance with article 287, paragraph 1, of the Convention immediately prior to the institution of the proceedings so that the dispute is submitted to the Tribunal rather than to Annex VII arbitration. This was the case with the *M/V "Louisa" Case* and with the *M/V "Norstar" Case* currently pending before the Tribunal.

Another development worth noting is the utilization of a special chamber. Article 15, paragraph 2, of Annex VI to the Convention provides that the Tribunal shall form a chamber for dealing with a particular dispute submitted to it, if the parties so request. The composition of such a chamber shall be determined by the Tribunal with the approval of the parties. A special chamber was first composed to deal with the *Case concerning the Conservation and Sustainable Exploitation of Swordfish Stocks in the South-Eastern Pacific Ocean* between Chile and European Union. Another was formed again lately in the *Dispute concerning delimitation of the maritime boundary between Ghana and Côte d'Ivoire in the Atlantic Ocean*. The latter chamber was composed of three judges selected from the members of the Tribunal and two *ad hoc* judges from outside the Tribunal. Considering that an Annex VII arbitral tribunal usually includes at least two or three judges from the Tribunal, in practice there is little difference between a special chamber and an Annex VII arbitral tribunal in terms of the parties' flexibility in selecting judges. On the other hand, a special chamber has an advantage in terms of facilities, cost and time. I therefore think that a special chamber of the Tribunal can be an alternative to Annex VII arbitration.

Second, as more activities take place in the area beyond national jurisdiction, as it appears to be in light of the fact that the Authority is currently preparing for the regulation for the exploitation of the area, diverse types of disputes will be sure to arise and be submitted to the Seabed Disputes Chamber which has exclusive jurisdiction over them under article 187.

Finally, although this potential has yet to be tested, it should be recalled that access to the Tribunal is not limited to States Parties. Article 20, paragraph 2, of the Statute stipulates that the Tribunal shall be open to "entities other than States Parties in any case expressly provided for in Part XI or in any case submitted pursuant to any other agreement conferring jurisdiction on the Tribunal which is accepted by all the parties to that case". Thus it appears that the Tribunal is open to a wider range of parties, including non-State entities. Exactly who has such access to the Tribunal remains to be seen but the wider access can have important implications for the future of the Tribunal as a means of dispute settlement.[11] Furthermore, article 37 of the Statute provides that the Seabed Disputes Chamber shall be open to the State Parties, the Authority and "the other entities referred to in Part XI, section 5". Such entities encompass the Enterprise, state enterprises, natural or judicial persons. Thus the Chamber has the potential to serve as the primary means to settle disputes arising from activities in the area as seabed mining becomes a reality.

In summing up, the Tribunal is structurally disadvantaged by the design of the choice of procedures set out in article 287 of the Convention. This is reflected in the number and nature of the cases that have been submitted to the Tribunal in the past two decades. However, there have been some encouraging developments such as transfer of cases from Annex VII arbitral tribunals to the Tribunal and the utilization of a special chamber. The exclusive jurisdiction of the Seabed Disputes Chamber as well as potentially wider access to the Tribunal is another factor with positive implications for the Tribunal as a means of dispute settlement. For these reasons, I am cautiously optimistic about the future role of the Tribunal.

II Tribunal's Jurisprudence on the Legal Issues Related to Ships

Now let me turn to the jurisprudence of the Tribunal and its contribution to the rule of law. Here I will focus on one area to which the Tribunal has made a unique contribution rather than canvass the overall jurisprudence of the Tribunal and assess its contribution. That area concerns the legal notion of a ship and related issues. It is no accident that the Tribunal, as a specialized court created to settle maritime disputes, has made a special contribution to the rule of law by clarifying the notion of a ship and addressing several intricate legal issues related to ships.

---

11 Alan Boyle suggests that access is probably the most significant difference between the Tribunal and the International Court of Justice. According to him, broader access to the Tribunal has an advantage to allow non-State entities to participate in the international legal system. See A. Boyle, "Dispute Settlement and the Law of the Sea Convention: Problems of Fragmentation and Jurisdiction", 46 *ICLQ* (1997), p. 51.

A ship is the principal, if not exclusive, means to use the ocean. A ship is used for various purposes encompassing, among others, navigation, fishing, exploration and exploitation of offshore oil and gas, marine scientific research, seabed mining, law enforcement at sea and naval warfare. Indeed it is impossible to think of the ocean without ships.

Thus the Convention refers to a ship in numerous provisions. Many disputes that have been submitted to the Tribunal have been concerned with ships, such as prompt release of vessels and crews, compensation for damage arising from the illegal arrest and detention of a ship and the immunity of a warship. In fact, the very first case submitted to the Tribunal, the *M/V "SAIGA" Case* (*Saint Vincent and the Grenadines* v. *Guinea*), was concerned with a dispute over the compensation for damage arising from the illegal arrest and detention of the M/V *Saiga*.

Despite the omnipresence of ships in the law of the sea, the notion of a ship is by no means clear. In fact, the meaning, nationality, nature and status of a ship are riddled with uncertainty and ambiguity. For example, when article 110, paragraph 1, of the Convention provides that on the high seas a warship is not justified in boarding a foreign "ship", what does the term foreign "ship" refer to? When the same provision provides that boarding is justified when there is reasonable ground for suspecting that the "ship" is engaged in piracy, the slave trade, or unauthorized broadcasting, what does the term "ship" refer to in this situation? Further, when paragraph 3 of the same article stipulates that if the suspicion proves to be unfounded, the "ship" shall be compensated for any loss or damage, what does "ship" in this context refer to? On the other hand, when articles 17, 38, 53, of the Convention provide that "ships" enjoy the rights of innocent passage, transit passage, and of archipelagic sea lane passage, what does the term "ships" in those provisions refer to?

More questions can be raised as to the nationality as well as the nature and status of a ship. For example, when article 91 of the Convention on the nationality of ships provides that there must exist a genuine link between the State and the ship, what does the requirement of genuine link mean? Is the registration of a ship in the absence of genuine link invalid and thus can the nationality of such a ship be refuted? Today a ship often has a multinational crew and carries cargo belonging to many different nationalities. In a dispute involving compensation for loss and damage caused to such a ship, can the flag State make claims with respect to persons who are not its nationals or cargos which do not belong to its nationals? Again, in a dispute involving international wrongful act committed against a ship, local remedies must be exhausted before the flag State makes claims against the State responsible for such wrongful act. What is the nature of injury caused to a ship? Is it injury to the rights of the flag State or to the rights of the owner or operator of the ship?

The answers to these questions have far reaching implications, both procedural and substantive, for the settlement of disputes involving a ship. In fact, several States in the proceedings before the Tribunal raised the above issues to challenge the jurisdiction of the Tribunal and the admissibility of claims, as well as to present a claim for damages.[12] For example, an objection to jurisdiction and admissibility on the basis of the nationality of a ship has been made in a few proceedings. In other proceedings involving disputes over injury to a ship resulting from an internationally wrongful act, objections have been made based on the nationality of claims or the exhaustion of local remedies. Those objections, if accepted, terminate the proceedings before examining the merits of the case. Thus the clarification of the notion of a ship, a principal means for the use and protection of the ocean, is a prerequisite to the effective disposal of disputes involving a ship.

The term "ship" has multiple meanings, referring to movable property, the owner or operator of a ship, or the ship's flag State, depending on the context and situation in which the term is employed.[13] Returning to the question raised above, when article 110, paragraph 1, of the Convention stipulates that a warship is not justified in boarding a foreign "ship", the term "ship" in that context may refer to movable property. On the other hand, the term "ship" in paragraph 3 of the same article[14] may indicate the owner of the ship or the operator who charted the ship. Yet all "ships" enjoying the rights of innocent passage, transit passage and archipelagic passage in articles 17, 38 and 53, of the Convention may be understood to mean the ship's flag State rather than the owner or operator of the ship. In any case, different meanings of the term "ship" in different contexts and situations have given rise to confusion and could be a serious obstacle to the effective resolution of ship-related disputes.

I believe that the Tribunal has made a significant contribution to overcoming the confusion and difficulty related to the notion of "ship" by clarifying the relevant provisions of the Convention and developing the international law

---

12 In the *M/V "Virginia G" Case* (*Panama/Guinea-Bissau*), Guinea-Bissau presented a counter-claim that the case involved damages caused to it as a result of Panama's violation of article 91 of the Convention by granting its nationality to a ship which had no genuine link with it.

13 D.P. O'Connell, *The International Law of the Sea, Vol. II* (Oxford University Press, 1984), pp. 747–8; see also H. Meyers, *The Nationality of Ships* (Martinus Nijhoff, 1967), pp. 8–13.

14 "If the suspicions prove to be unfounded, and provided that the ship boarded has not committed any act justifying them, it shall be compensated for any loss or damage that may have been sustained."

of the sea pertaining to this matter. Let me highlight some key findings of the Tribunal in this regard.

First, the Tribunal clarified the concept of the nationality of a ship. In the *M/V "SAIGA" (No. 2) Case (Saint Vincent and the Grenadines* v. *Guinea)*, the Tribunal observed that "[a]rticle 91 [of the Convention] leaves to each State exclusive jurisdiction over the granting of its nationality to ships."[15] It further observed that "the nationality of a ship is a question of fact to be determined … on the basis of evidence adduced by the parties."[16] Therefore, in case of dispute over the nationality of a ship, parties have the burden of proof to establish that the ship is registered in and has the nationality of either of them.

With respect to the requirement of a genuine link, the Tribunal stated in the *M/V "SAIGA" (No. 2) Case* that

> the purpose of the provisions of the Convention on the need for a genuine link between a ship and its flag State is to secure more effective implementation of the duties of the flag State, and not to establish criteria by reference to which the validity of the registration of ships in a flag State may be challenged by other States.[17]

In the *M/V "Virginia G" Case (Panama/Guinea-Bissau)*, the Tribunal reaffirmed its previous jurisprudence by stating that "article 91, paragraph 1, third sentence, of the Convention requiring a genuine link between the flag State and the ship should not be read as establishing prerequisites or conditions to be satisfied for the exercise of the right of the flag State to grant its nationality to ships."[18] The Tribunal pointed out that "once a ship is registered, the flag State is required, under article 94 of the Convention, to exercise effective jurisdiction and control over that ship in order to ensure that it operates in accordance with generally accepted international regulations, procedures and practices", and that "[t]his is the meaning of 'genuine link'."[19]

Second, the Tribunal clarified the unique nature of a ship as a unit. This finding has particular relevance to the right of the flag State to seek redress for the ship's crew who are not its nationals. In the *M/V "SAIGA" (No. 2) Case*,

15 *M/V "SAIGA" (No. 2) (Saint Vincent and the Grenadines* v. *Guinea), Judgment, ITLOS Reports 1999*, p. 10, at p. 36, para. 63.

16 *Ibid.*, at p. 37, para. 66.

17 *Ibid.*, at p. 42, para. 83.

18 *M/V "Virginia G" (Panama/Guinea-Bissau), Judgment, ITLOS Reports 2014*, p. 4, at p. 44, para. 110.

19 *Ibid.*, at p. 45, para. 113.

responding to the argument that the flag State has no right to seek redress for non-national crew members, the Tribunal stated that:

> the Convention considers a ship as a unit, as regards the obligations of the flag State with respect to the ship and the right of a flag State to seek reparation for loss or damage caused to the ship by acts of other States and to institute proceedings under article 292 of the Convention. Thus the ship, every thing on it, and every person involved or interested in its operations are treated as an entity linked to the flag State. The nationalities of these persons are not relevant.[20]

The Tribunal supported this finding with practical considerations based on the realities of modern maritime transport that any large ships could have a crew comprising persons of several nationalities and "[i]f each person sustaining damage were obliged to look for protection from the State of which such person is a national, undue hardship would ensue."[21] This finding has subsequently influenced the work of the ILC in preparing the Draft Articles on Diplomatic Protection and was instrumental in the adoption of article 18 on the protection of ships' crews.[22]

In the *M/V "Virginia G" Case*, the Tribunal reaffirmed its jurisprudence by finding that "the *M/V Virginia G*, its crew and cargo on board as well as its owner and every person involved or interested in its operations are to be treated as an entity linked to the flag State."[23] Likewise the Tribunal in the latest *M/V "Norstar" Case* took the same view.[24]

Third, the Tribunal addressed the question as to what is the nature of an injury to a ship resulting from an internationally wrongful act; namely, whether it is injury to persons with interest in the ship or to the ship's flag State. The

20 *M/V SAIGA (No. 2) (Saint Vincent and the Grenadines* v. *Guinea), Judgment, ITLOS Reports 1999*, p. 10, at p. 48, para. 106.

21 *Ibid.*, para. 107.

22 Article 18 reads: "The right of the State of nationality of the members of the crew of a ship to exercise diplomatic protection is not affected by the right of the State of nationality of a ship to seek redress on behalf of such crew members, irrespective of their nationality, when they have been injured in connection with an injury to the vessel resulting from an internationally wrongful act." See *Draft Articles on Diplomatic Protection with commentaries, 2006, Yearbook of the International Law Commission*, 2006, vol. II, Part Two.

23 *M/V "Virginia G" (Panama/Guinea-Bissau), Judgment, ITLOS Reports 2014*, p. 4, at p. 48, para. 127.

24 *M/V "Norstar" (Panama* v. *Italy), Preliminary Objections, Judgment, ITLOS Reports 2016*, p. 44, at p. 95, para. 231.

answer to this question has an implication for the applicability of the rule of the exhaustion of local remedies stipulated in article 95 of the Convention.

In the *M/V "SAIGA" (No. 2) Case*, the Tribunal noted that "in this case the rights which Saint Vincent and the Grenadines claims have been violated by Guinea are all rights that belong to Saint Vincent and the Grenadines under the Convention (articles 33, 56, 58, 111 and 292) or under international law"[25] and that "[n]one of the violations of rights claimed by Saint Vincent and the Grenadines ... can be described as breaches of obligations concerning the treatment to be accorded to aliens."[26] The Tribunal concluded that "[a]ccordingly, the claims in respect of such damage are not subject to the rule that local remedies must be exhausted."[27]

In the *M/V "Virginia G" Case*, the Tribunal also examined the nature of the rights which Panama claimed had been violated by Guinea-Bissau. The Tribunal noted that "most provisions of the Convention referred to in the final submissions of Panama confer rights mainly on States" and that "in some of the provisions referred to by Panama, however, rights appear to be conferred on a ship or persons involved."[28] The Tribunal observed in this regard that "[w]hen the claim contains elements of both injury to a State and injury to an individual, for the purpose of deciding the applicability of the exhaustion of local remedies rule, the Tribunal has to determine which element is preponderant."[29] The Tribunal then took the view that the principal rights that Panama alleges have been violated by Guinea-Bissau are rights that belong to Panama under the Convention, and "the alleged violations of them thus amount to direct injury to Panama."[30] The Tribunal accordingly concluded that "the claims in respect of such damage are not subject to the rule of exhaustion of local remedies."[31]

In the latest *M/V "Norstar" Case*, the Tribunal followed the same approach as in the *M/V "SAIGA" (No. 2) Case* and the *M/V "Virginia G" Case*.[32] Having examined Panama's rights that it claims have been violated by Italy, the Tribunal found that "the right of Panama to enjoy freedom of navigation on the high

---

25 *M/V SAIGA (No. 2) (Saint Vincent and the Grenadines* v. *Guinea), Judgment, ITLOS Reports 1999*, p. 10, at p. 45, para. 97.

26 *Ibid.*, para. 98.

27 *Ibid.*, para. 98.

28 *M/V "Virginia G" (Panama/Guinea-Bissau), Judgment, ITLOS Reports 2014*, p. 4, at p. 54, para. 156.

29 *Ibid.*, para. 157.

30 *Ibid.*

31 *Ibid.*, at p. 55, para. 158.

32 *M/V "Norstar" (Panama* v. *Italy), Preliminary Objections, Judgment, ITLOS Reports 2016*, p. 44, at p. 103, para. 268.

seas is a right that belongs to Panama under article 87 of the Convention, and that a violation of that right would amount to direct injury to Panama".[33] Accordingly, the Tribunal came to the conclusion that "the claims in respect of such damage are not subject to the rule of exhaustion of local remedies."[34]

With those findings, the Tribunal has considerably clarified the legal notion of a ship and issues related thereto. To be sure, this crucial notion needs to be further clarified and elaborated and there are many other legal issues still to be addressed. However, I believe that the Tribunal has developed solid jurisprudence on the meaning, nationality, and nature and status of a ship and thus made a valuable contribution to the peaceful settlement of disputes involving ships.

III Conclusion

Before concluding, it is worth reflecting briefly on what is required to strengthen the rule of law in international relations. I can think of three elements: first, a well-developed body of laws; second, a well-developed body of institutions to apply and implement such laws in a fair and equal manner; and third, a positive attitude of the members of the international community towards the rule of law. These three elements are inherently inter-related. They are also mutually reinforcing.

Understood this way, I think that the Tribunal as a standing, specialized court established to deal with maritime disputes is one of the most important institutions in strengthening the rule of law at sea. The Tribunal peacefully settles maritime disputes by interpreting and applying the Convention and other international law. In so doing, the Tribunal clarifies and develops the international law of the sea. As a consequence, it can foster the positive attitude of States toward the rule of law. In the past two decades, the Tribunal has made a valuable contribution to the rule of law at sea by effectively performing those tasks. Admittedly its full potential has yet to be realized. I hope that we will be able to celebrate the thirtieth anniversary in ten years' time with a lot more confidence and pride.

33 *Ibid.*, para. 270.

34 *Ibid.*, para. 271.

The International Tribunal for the Law of the Sea and the Rule of Law

Tullio Treves

Before examining the contribution made by the Tribunal to the rule of law, it seems necessary to examine briefly the contribution made to the rule of law by the Convention. The reason is the connection between the Tribunal and the Convention. Indeed, the Tribunal has been established by the States Parties to the Convention in compliance with obligations set out in it. Moreover, the task of the Tribunal is to settle disputes concerning the interpretation or application of the Convention.

I The Contribution of the Convention

The contribution of the Convention to the rule of law may be seen from a substantial and from a procedural point of view. From both points of view, the Convention marks significant progress in the expansion of the rule of law on the oceans. There are, however, limits to such expansion on which I will direct some observations.

Substantially, the Convention tries to deal comprehensively with all aspects of the law of the sea. Its provisions are also drafted so as to encompass, in most cases, new problems not envisaged at the time of the Third United Nations Conference on the Law of the Sea. Bunkering is a clear example of one of these problems. The Judgment of the Tribunal in the *M/V "Virginia G" Case* shows that the rules set out in the Convention may be interpreted so as to encompass an activity not considered by the drafters of the Convention.[1]

Admittedly, there are limits to the comprehensiveness of the Convention. Practice since 1982 shows that some issues envisaged in the Convention require further conventional developments. This was the case of straddling stocks and highly migratory species for which an "implementing agreement" was concluded in 1995

Recent practice also shows that there are activities whose regulation within the framework of the Convention is difficult to achieve and which require new

1 *M/V "Virginia G" (Panama v. Guinea Bissau), Judgment, ITLOS Reports 2014*, p. 4, at pp. 66–68, paras. 209–215.

© 2018, BY INTERNATIONAL TRIBUNAL FOR THE LAW OF THE SEA | DOI 10.1163/9789004356832_009

negotiations and the development of new rules. This is the case of activities concerning the exploitation of biodiversity and genetic resources beyond the limits of national jurisdiction, on which negotiations with a view to concluding a binding instrument are in progress.

Procedurally, the main contribution of the Convention to the rule of law consists in its provisions on the settlement of disputes and, especially, in the fact that, under these provisions, disputes concerning the interpretation or application of the Convention may be submitted to arbitral or judicial settlement at the request of one party, without needing the specific agreement of the other party. This is what is commonly called compulsory settlement of disputes, well described by article 282 of the Convention when it mentions a dispute which "shall, at request of one party to the dispute, be submitted to a procedure that entails a binding decision".

As is well known, compulsory settlement under the Convention is not without exceptions. According to a view put forward in the *Southern Bluefin Tuna* arbitral award of 2000, the limitations concerning disputes involving the exercise of sovereign rights or jurisdiction of the coastal State set out in article 297 and the possibility of excluding from compulsory settlement certain categories of disputes, such as those dealing with delimitation of maritime areas set out in article 298, would justify the conclusion that compulsory settlement is not the rule but the exception under UNCLOS.[2]

I personally do not agree with this view. The number of issues concerning the high seas, the formulation of article 297 allowing exceptions to the exception, and the fact that a majority of States Parties have not made the declarations provided for in article 298, seem to me to justify the conclusion that what is indicated by the Convention as a "limitation" or "exception" is indeed a limitation or an exception. Admittedly, however, articles 297 and 298 carve out of compulsory settlement a substantial number of the possible disputes concerning the interpretation or application of the Convention.[3]

Perhaps the most important limitation to the dispute-settlement mechanism set out in the Convention is that it deals with disputes concerning "the interpretation or application" of the Convention. This description of the scope

---

2 *Southern Bluefin Tuna Case* (*Australia* v. *Japan and New Zealand* v. *Japan*), 4 August 2000, *RIAA* Vol. XXIII, pp. 1–57, at p. 46, para. 63.

3 See T. Treves, "The Exclusive Economic Zone and the Settement of Disputes", in E. Franckx and P. Gautier (eds), *La zone économique exclusive et la Convention des Nations Unies sur le droit de la mer, 1982–2000: un premier bilan de la pratique des Etats /The Exclusive Economic Zone and the United Nations Convention on the Law of the Sea, 1982–2000: a preliminary assessment of State practice* (Bruylant, 2003), at pp. 94–96.

ratione materiae of the disputes which may be submitted to adjudication under the Convention, which one finds in almost all articles of Part XV of the Convention, and consequently also of the scope *ratione materiae* of the jurisdiction of the judges and arbitrators to whom such disputes may be submitted, seems obvious in a Convention dealing with a particular, although vast, sector of international law. This limitation has, nonetheless, proved to be very important and marks a difference between law of the sea – and, in particular, delimitation – disputes submitted to the ICJ or to arbitral tribunals on the basis of instruments other than the Convention, and disputes submitted to adjudication under the dispute-settlement provisions of the Convention.

Before the ICJ it is normal that questions concerning sovereignty over land features and delimitation of maritime areas be submitted together as parts of the same dispute. *Cameroon* v. *Nigeria* and *Nicaragua* v. *Colombia* are clear examples among others, and so is *Eritrea v. Yemen* as regards arbitration proceedings. In these cases the Court, and the arbitral tribunal, decided on sovereignty over certain land features and, on the basis of such decision, on the delimitation of the parties' maritime zones. The jurisdiction conferred to them by the relevant instruments (Article 36, paragraph 2, of the ICJ Statute, Pact of Bogotá, special agreement) permitted the adjudicating bodies to deal with questions concerning sovereignty as well as with those concerning maritime delimitation issues.

This possibility is, nevertheless, excluded as regards cases in which the jurisdiction of the adjudicating body is based on the Convention because the Convention does not contain provisions concerning sovereignty over land. A dispute concerning sovereignty over land as a premise for delimitation of maritime areas would not be a dispute concerning the interpretation or application of the Convention. This has been the premise upon which the Philippines framed the case they brought to arbitration under the Convention against China. Even though the two States notoriously disagreed as regards sovereignty over a number of land features, the Philippines avoided making any request concerning sovereignty in order to overcome the objection that disputes concerning sovereignty were not among those covered by compulsory settlement under the Convention. As is well known, the arbitral tribunal accepted the position taken by the Philippines, even though China, in a "Position Paper" submitted to the arbitrators, put forward the view that the "real" dispute was about sovereignty over land features and consequently not included, under the Convention, within the scope of the arbitral tribunal's jurisdiction.[4]

---

4 *The South China Sea Arbitration* (*The Republic of Philippines* v. *The People's Republic of China*), PCA Case No. 2013–19, 29 October 2015, para. 152.

In the *Chagos Marine Protected Area Arbitration*, Mauritius shaped one of the submissions in its application as concerning a question of interpretation of the term "coastal State" under the Convention, in order to support the conclusion that the United Kingdom, not being a "coastal State" of the Chagos archipelago, was not entitled to proclaim a "marine protected area" in the Archipelago. The United Kingdom objected that this was an indirect way to have the arbitral tribunal make a statement as to sovereignty over the archipelago, which would be beyond its jurisdiction, as it would not concern the interpretation or application of the Convention. The arbitral tribunal accepted this objection. In light of the record of the discussions between the parties, it stated that the "real" dispute concerned sovereignty over the Chagos archipelago.[5] Consequently, the arbitral tribunal lacked jurisdiction. While the "real issue in the case" did not relate to the interpretation or application of the Convention, the arbitral tribunal specified that "an incidental connection between the dispute and some matter regulated by the Convention [was] insufficient to bring the dispute, as a whole, within the ambit of article 288(1)."[6] It did not, however, "categorically exclude that in some instances a minor issue of territorial sovereignty could indeed be ancillary to a dispute concerning the interpretation or application of the Convention."[7]

The limitations and exceptions to the compulsory jurisdiction of adjudicating bodies competent under the Convention have probably had the effect that certain disputes existing between States Parties have not been submitted to adjudication under the Convention.

The question of whether the Tribunal would be competent to decide on a mixed land sovereignty and law of the sea question on the basis of a special agreement between the parties remains open.

II The Contribution of the Tribunal

Coming now to the contribution of the Tribunal to the rule of law, it may be wondered what is the reason to dwell on the contribution of the Tribunal in a celebration of the 20th anniversary of its establishment. The Tribunal is but one of the adjudicating bodies to which compulsory jurisdiction is granted under article 287, and not even the default one. Still, the contribution

5 *Chagos Marine Protected Area Arbitration* (*Mauritius* v. *United Kingdom*), PCA Case No. 2011–03, 18 March 2015, paras. 211–2012.

6 *Ibid.*, para 220.

7 *Ibid.*, para 221.

made by the Tribunal to the expansion of the substantive rules set out in the Convention and to the procedural mechanisms aimed at eliminating doubts as to the meaning and scope, as well as to the application in concrete situations of the Convention's provisions, is quite relevant.

Before looking at this contribution, it seems useful to observe that the Tribunal's role goes much beyond that of one of the adjudicating bodies which may, if the conditions are met, exercise compulsory jurisdiction under the Convention. Its being a permanent body makes it possible for it to develop a jurisprudence of its own and to participate in the development of the jurisprudence of other adjudicating bodies called to settle law of the sea disputes. Moreover, because of the fact that it is a pre-constituted body, the Convention has granted it a practically exclusive role in dealing, under article 290, paragraph 5, with requests for provisional measures pending the establishment of a competent arbitral tribunal and, under article 292, with requests for the prompt release of vessels and crews.

As it emerges especially from its frequent reference to the jurisprudence of the ICJ and of other international courts and tribunals, and from its Judgment in the *Delimitation of the maritime boundary in the Bay of Bengal* (*Bangladesh/Myanmar*),[8] the Tribunal has proven that the concerns about its becoming a factor of fragmentation of international law were unfounded. May I be permitted to recall the views I expressed on this subject in the declaration I made as a Judge in that case. I stated that:

> all courts and tribunals called to decide on the interpretation and application of the Convention, including its provisions on delimitation, should … consider themselves as parts of a collective interpretative endeavour, in which, while keeping in mind the need to ensure consistency and coherence, each contributes its grain of wisdom and its particular outlook.[9]

In light of its jurisprudence spanning two decades, it seems possible to state that the Tribunal has played its part in this collective endeavour.

Being the only permanent adjudicating body specialized in the law of the sea and having been established on the basis of the Convention, commonly referred to as the "constitution for the oceans", the Tribunal has sometimes felt encouraged to adopt extensive interpretations of certain substantive rules

8 *Delimitation of the maritime boundary in the Bay of Bengal* (*Bangladesh/Myanmar*), *Judgment, ITLOS Reports 2012*, p. 4.

9 *Declaration of Judge Treves, ITLOS Reports 2012*, at p. 141, para. 2.

or of its jurisdiction. Some of these have been criticized, but most others have been met with favour and are often referred to in judgments and awards.

Starting with the Tribunal's contribution to the rule of law through the interpretation and application of the substantive rules of the Convention, we may first of all refer to the already mentioned jurisprudence on bunkering. After having reviewed the possible answers to the question of the legal regime of bunkering in the first *M/V "SAIGA" Case*,[10] and after having stated, in the *M/V "SAIGA" (No. 2) Case*, that it was not necessary to take a position,[11] almost two decades later, in the *M/V "Virginia G"* Judgment, the Tribunal took a position assimilating the regime applicable to bunkering of fishing vessels in the EEZ to that of the vessels receiving bunker.[12] It left open the question concerning the regime of bunkering of vessels exercising an activity different from fishing.[13]

Important statements are set out in the Judgment on the first contentious case decided by the Tribunal, the *M/V "SAIGA" (No. 2) Case (Saint Vincent and the Grenadines v. Guinea)*. The statement in the Judgment of 1999 that:

> the Convention considers a ship as a unit, as regards the obligations of the flag State with respect to the ship and the right of a flag State to seek reparation for loss or damage caused to the ship by acts of other States and to institute proceedings under article 292 of the Convention. Thus the ship, every thing on it, and every person involved or interested in its operations are treated as an entity linked to the flag State. The nationalities of these persons are not relevant[14]

seems to have become part of existing customary international law or at least the accepted interpretation of the Convention. The same may be said of another statement set out in the same Judgment:

> Although the Convention does not contain express provisions on the use of force in the arrest of ships, international law, which is applicable by

10 *M/V "SAIGA", (Saint Vincent and the Grenadines v. Guinea), Prompt Release, Judgment, ITLOS Reports 1997*, p. 16, at pp. 29–30, paras. 57–58.

11 *M/V "SAIGA" No. 2 (Saint Vincent and the Grenadines v. Guinea), Judgment, ITLOS Reports 1999*, p. 10, at pp. 56–57, paras. 137–138.

12 *M/V "Virginia G" (Panama/Guinea-Bissau), Judgment, ITLOS Reports 2014*, p. 4, at pp. 67–69, paras. 211–217.

13 *Ibid.*, at p. 70, para. 223.

14 *M/V "SAIGA" (No. 2) (Saint Vincent and the Grenadines v. Guinea), Judgment, ITLOS Reports 1999*, p. 10, at p. 48, para 106.

> virtue of article 293 of the Convention, requires that the use of force must be avoided as far as possible and, where force is unavoidable, it must not go beyond what is reasonable and necessary in the circumstances. Considerations of humanity must apply in the law of the sea, as they do in other areas of international law.[15]

Yet another statement in the *M/V "SAIGA" (No. 2)* Judgment that has raised a lot of attention, although not all commentators were favourable, is that according to which:

> the purpose of the provisions of the Convention on the need for a genuine link between a ship and its flag State is to secure more effective implementation of the duties of the flag State, and not to establish criteria by reference to which the validity of the registration of ships in a flag State may be challenged by other States.[16]

It would be too long to list the other important contributions of the Tribunal to the rule of law by its interpretations and applications of the Convention. Suffice it to recall the numerous developments found in its decisions on matters of international environmental law. They range from the distinction between procedural and substantial obligations, the precautionary principle, and the obligation to conduct environmental impact assessments.[17] The analysis of the obligation "to ensure" and of its relevance in determining the responsibilities, including for environmentally harmful activities, of States sponsoring persons conducting deep seabed mining operations and of flag States of fishing vessels has been clarified in the Advisory Opinion of 2011 of the Tribunal's Seabed Disputes Chamber[18] and in that of 2014 of the Tribunal in plenary formation.[19]

The Tribunal has interpreted its jurisdictional powers extensively. It has done so, notably, as regards provisional measures and advisory opinions. As regards provisional measures, taking as a basis the obligation to cooperate regarding the prevention of pollution, the Tribunal used its provisional measures orders

---

15 *Ibid.*, at p. 61, para. 155.

16 *Ibid.*, at p. 42, para. 83.

17 These Judgments are reviewed in T. Treves, "Disputes concerning the protection of the environment; the practice of ITLOS", in B. Cortese (ed.), *Studi in onore di Laura Picchio Forlati* (Giappichelli, 2014), pp.135–143.

18 *Responsibilities and obligations of States with respect to activities in the Area, Advisory Opinion, 1 February 2011, ITLOS Reports 2011*, p. 10.

19 *Request for an Advisory Opinion submitted by the Sub-Regional Fisheries Commission, Advisory Opinion, 2 April 2015, ITLOS Reports 2015*, p. 4.

to bring the parties to conduct jointly activities permitting them to settle the dispute. In particular, in the Order in the *Case concerning Land Reclamation by Singapore in and around the Straits of Johor*, the Tribunal prescribed, as a provisional measure, that the parties establish a group of independent experts with the mandate to propose measures to cope with the possible harmful consequences of the land reclamation work started by Singapore.[20] The parties complied: they established the expert group, took note of the report it submitted, concluded an agreement in conformity with the measures proposed in it and declared that the agreement contained the final settlement of the dispute.[21] While it is far from certain that other international courts and tribunals would have read their mandate in provisional measures proceedings in the same way, it is beyond doubt that with this decision the Tribunal contributed constructively to the elimination of the dispute.

As regards advisory opinions, while fully aware that the Convention only provides for advisory opinions of the Seabed Disputes Chamber and not of the Tribunal in its plenary composition, the Tribunal has tried to overcome this limitation for the future. It introduced in the Rules article 138 which declares the readiness of the Tribunal as a whole to deal with requests for advisory opinions provided that they are submitted by "a body" under an international agreement concerning the law of the sea specifically providing for such submission. This provision has encouraged a West-African fishery organization to submit a request for an advisory opinion to the Tribunal. Notwithstanding strong opposition voiced as regards the alleged lack of jurisdictional basis for dealing with the request, and arguments that article 138 was adopted *ultra vires*, the Tribunal, in its Advisory Opinion of 2014, affirmed its jurisdiction on the basis of article 21 of the Statute. Although controversial, this decision may be seen as an effort to expand the rule of law on the oceans.

In conclusion, the Tribunal is an efficient instrument for the expansion of the rule of law on the oceans. It may be said that it has exercised wisely its powers to this end. A word of caution seems, nonetheless, necessary: the Tribunal must be careful in not going beyond what can be done without raising reactions which may, in the long run, prove to be counterproductive.

---

20 *Land Reclamation in and around the Straits of Johor* (*Malaysia* v. *Singapore*), *Provsional Measures, Order of 8 October 2003, ITLOS Reports 2003*, p. 10, at p. 27, para 106.

21 See Press Release, *Case Concerning Land Reclamation by Singapore In and Around the Straits of Johor* (*Malaysia* v. *Singapore*), 14 January 2005, Permanent Court of Arbitration, available at https://www.pcacases.com/web/sendAttach/1127.

PART 2 / PARTIE 2

The Contribution of the Tribunal to the Progressive Development of International Law

La contribution du Tribunal au développement progressif du droit international

The Contribution of the Tribunal to the Progressive Development of International Law

Shunji Yanai

Opening Remarks

I would like to make some short opening remarks by touching upon some of the salient points of the jurisprudence of the Tribunal which, in my view, have contributed to the progressive development of international law, in particular in the field of the law of the sea. Then I will ask the distinguished panellists to express their respective views of the topic under consideration. This will be followed by an exchange of views among the panellists and a question and answer session with the audience.

The Tribunal is celebrating its 20th anniversary today, but it is still a young judicial institution as compared with the ICJ which recently celebrated its 70th anniversary. International arbitration has an even longer history in the field of the settlement of international disputes entailing binding decisions. Since 1996, 25 cases have been brought to the Tribunal. Out of the 13 cases filed in the first decade, seven concerned the prompt release of foreign fishing vessels arrested in the EEZs of coastal States, followed by four provisional measures cases, and two cases on the merits. In the second decade a greater variety of cases started coming to the Tribunal, including two maritime boundary delimitation cases and two requests for an advisory opinion.

It is a well-known fact that the Convention contains many ambiguous provisions as a result of compromises reached among States in order to reconcile their conflicting interests and differing views. Many provisions were thus left for future development through the interpretation or application of the Convention. One typical example of such provisions is the method by which the delimitations of the EEZ and the continental shelf are to be effected. The Convention provides that such delimitations "shall be effected by agreement on the basis of international law [...] in order to achieve an equitable solution." The Convention only sets a goal, without indicating the method to be applied to achieve it.

When a cargo ship is arrested by a coastal State, an issue arises as to whether or not the rule of diplomatic protection applies to the claims brought by its flag State in respect of loss or damage sustained by the ship, its crew and other persons concerned. Another example of provisions which need clarification

© 2018, BY INTERNATIONAL TRIBUNAL FOR THE LAW OF THE SEA | DOI 10.1163/9789004356832_010

is those concerning exploration and exploitation of deep seabed mineral resources. On the other hand, the progress of human activities on the seas and oceans has brought a series of entirely new problems. For instance, bunkering, or fuelling at sea, of fishing vessels within the EEZ of other States is a practice which was developed after the adoption of the Convention. The Convention does not give clear guidance as to whether such activities belong to the freedom of navigation or fall under the coastal State's jurisdiction in its EEZ. In 2013 the Sub-Regional Fisheries Commission, consisting of Seven West African countries, transmitted to the Tribunal a request for an advisory opinion on several questions concerning IUU fishing activities in their EEZs. While the advisory jurisdiction of the Seabed Disputes Chamber is expressly provided for in the Convention (article 191), there is no express provision concerning such jurisdiction of the full Tribunal. Views were divided among the States Parties which participated in the written and oral proceedings regarding this request for an advisory opinion. Therefore, the Tribunal had to decide first on the question of the advisory jurisdiction of the full Tribunal.

These are some of the areas where provisions of the Convention are expected to be clarified by international courts and tribunals. I would now like to cite some cases in which the Tribunal has, in my view, contributed to the progressive development of international law, in particular, in the law of the sea.

The ICJ devised a two-stage method of delimitation which has come to be known as the "equidistance/relevant circumstances method" according to which a median line is drawn at the first stage as the provisional delimitation line. Then at the second stage, if an adjustment proves necessary in light of special circumstances, the provisional delimitation line is modified in order to achieve an equitable solution. This method later evolved into the three-stage method by the addition of the third stage to verify that the adjusted delimitation line does not lead to an inequitable result. The Tribunal applied this three-stage method of delimitation in the *Dispute concerning delimitation of the maritime boundary between Bangladesh and Myanmar in the Bay of Bengal*. This was the first delimitation case brought to the Tribunal which involved the delimitation of the territorial sea, the EEZ, and the continental shelf within and beyond 200 nm. The Tribunal concluded that the same equidistance/relevant circumstances method should be applied both to the continental shelf within 200 nm and beyond 200 nm in the Bay of Bengal. The Judgment in this case is the first one in international adjudication where the continental shelf beyond 200 nm has been delimited. This delimitation line employed for the continental shelf beyond 200 nm gives rise to an area of limited size located beyond 200 nm from the coast of Bangladesh but within 200 nm from that of

Myanmar, which is commonly referred to as a "grey zone". The Tribunal adds in its Judgment that "there are many ways in which the Parties may ensure the discharge of their obligations in this respect, including the conclusion of specific agreements or the establishment of appropriate cooperative arrangements."

In its Judgment in the *M/V "SAIGA" (No. 2) Case* (1999), the Tribunal provided remarkable guidance regarding the issue as to whether or not the rule of diplomatic protection applies to the claims brought by a flag State in respect of loss or damage sustained by the cargo ship navigating under its flag, the crew and other persons concerned when the ship is arrested by a coastal State. The Tribunal clarifies in this Judgment that the Convention considers a ship as a unit as regards the obligations of the flag State with respect to the ship and its right to seek reparation for loss or damage caused to the ship by the act of another State. The Judgment further explains that "the ship, everything on it, and every person involved or interested in its operations are treated as an entity linked to the flag State," and that "the nationalities of these persons are not relevant." Thus, the Tribunal rejected the application of the rule of diplomatic protection to this case. Recently in the *M/V "Virginia G" Case* (2014), the Tribunal applied this "a ship as a unit" principle.

With respect to the provisions of the Convention concerning exploration of deep seabed mineral resources, the Seabed Disputes Chamber of the Tribunal rendered an Advisory Opinion in 2011 in response to the request made by the International Seabed Authority on several questions regarding the responsibilities and obligations of States sponsoring persons and entities with respect to activities in the international seabed Area. The Chamber pointed out, in particular, that sponsoring States have two kinds of obligations under the Convention and related instruments: the obligation to ensure compliance by sponsored contractors with the terms of the contract and the obligations under the Convention and related instruments (an obligation of "due diligence"), yet others being the "direct obligations" which sponsoring States must comply with, independently of their obligation to ensure a certain conduct on the part of the sponsored contractors.

Regarding "bunkering" of foreign vessels fishing in the EEZ of a coastal State which is a practice developed after the adoption of the Convention, the Tribunal made the following ruling in the *M/V "Virginia G" Case* (*Panama* v. *Guinea-Bissau*) (2014): the regulation by a coastal State of bunkering of foreign vessels fishing in its EEZ is among those measures which the coastal State may take in its EEZ to conserve and manage its living resources under the Convention. While finding that by boarding, inspecting and arresting the *M/V Virginia G*, Guinea-Bissau had not violated the relevant provisions of the

Convention, the Tribunal did find that Guinea-Bissau had violated these provisions by confiscating the vessel and the gas oil on board, and therefore decided to award Panama, the flag State, compensation for the gas oil.

With respect to the advisory jurisdiction of the full Tribunal, the Tribunal carefully considered Article 21 of the Tribunal's Statute, which is an integral part of the Convention. This article provides that "the jurisdiction of the Tribunal comprises all disputes and all applications submitted to it in accordance with this Convention and all matters specifically provided for in any other agreement which confers jurisdiction on the Tribunal." The Tribunal noted that, in the present case, the MCA Convention is an international agreement concluded by the seven Member States of the SRFC. The Tribunal further noted that under the MCA Convention, the Conference of Ministers of the SRFC authorized its Permanent Secretary to bring a given legal matter before the Tribunal for an advisory opinion. This MCA Convention is the "agreement which confers jurisdiction on the Tribunal" by virtue of Article 21 of its Statute. On the basis of the foregoing, the Tribunal unanimously decided that it has jurisdiction to give an advisory opinion requested by the SRFC. The Tribunal then replied to the four questions asked by the SRFC including those concerning the obligation of the flag State of vessels fishing in the EEZ of the SRFC member States, the liability of the flag State in case of violation of the laws and regulations of the SRFC member States, the obligations of the European Union in respect of fishing vessels flying the flag of its member States, and the rights and obligations of the coastal States in ensuring the sustainable development of shared stocks and stocks of common interest. It is gratifying to note that this Advisory Opinion helped the SRFC and its member States promote cooperation among themselves and with the European Union.

I would now like to invite the distinguished panellists to express their respective views on the contribution of the Tribunal to the progressive development of international law.

The Elaboration of Due Diligence Obligations as a Mechanism to Ensure Compliance with International Legal Obligations by Private Actors

Doris König

First of all, I want to congratulate President Golitsyn, all the present and former judges and the staff members of the Tribunal on the 20th anniversary of International Tribunal for the Law of the Sea. It's an honour and a pleasure for me to celebrate with you, and to give a short presentation on the Tribunal's contribution to the progressive development of international law.

In my opinion, one important contribution to the development of international law can be found in the Tribunal's two Advisory Opinions. In these Advisory Opinions, the Tribunal elaborated on the due diligence obligations of States sponsoring business entities with respect to deep seabed mining on the one hand, and those of flag States in cases where IUU fishing activities are conducted by vessels under their flag within the EEZs of third States on the other.

I General Considerations

In 2012, the International Law Association ("ILA") established a "Study Group on Due Diligence in International Law" that delivered two reports, in 2014 and 2016. The First Report (2014) provided information on the history of due diligence in international law, the development of due diligence in the context of State responsibility, and the role of due diligence in several specific areas of international law, such as international investment law, international humanitarian and human rights law, transnational criminal law, international environmental law, and – last but not least – international law of the sea.[1] The Second Report (2016) focused on broader, more analytical questions concerning what functions the concept of due diligence serves, and why it is employed as a standard of conduct in many and varied areas of international law.[2]

---

1 T. Stephens (Rapporteur) and D. French (Chair), ILA Study Group on Due Diligence in International Law, First Report, March 2014, available at: http://www.ila-hq.org/en/committees/study_groups.cfm/cid/1045.

2 See T. Stephens (Rapporteur) and D. French (Chair), ILA Study Group on Due Diligence in International Law, Second Report, July 2016, p. 1, available at: http://www.ila-hq.org/en/study-groups/index.cfm/cid/1045.

© 2018, BY INTERNATIONAL TRIBUNAL FOR THE LAW OF THE SEA | DOI 10.1163/9789004356832_011

The Study Group found out that the resort to due diligence as a standard of conduct has to be seen against the backdrop of general approaches to accountability in international law and that it can be characterised as a "standard of reasonableness, or reasonable care, that seeks to take account of the consequences of wrongful conduct and the extent to which such consequences could feasibly have been avoided by the State or international organisation that either commissioned the relevant act or which omitted to prevent its occurrence".[3] Thus the over-arching standard is reasonableness. As the ILA Study Group put it in its Second Report, "one might describe a due diligence obligation as an obligation for a State to take all measures it could reasonably be expected to take".[4] Since the term "reasonable" is very broad, it is difficult to define *in abstracto*, and leaves States much discretion in the choice of means. It is, in particular, not clear whether the assessment of reasonableness of the measures taken by a State depends, *inter alia*, on the level of development of that State.[5]

In international environmental law, the concept of due diligence has become a key component of the obligation to prevent harm. Since environmental harm to other States' territories or to areas beyond national jurisdiction is often caused by private actors, it is generally accepted that not each and every failure to prevent harm by private actors can be attributed to the State under the jurisdiction or control of which the activities are planned or carried out (State of origin). Therefore, the so-called "principle of no-harm" is breached only when the State of origin has not acted diligently with regard to its own activities, over state-owned enterprises, or private activities.[6] The ILA Study Group found out that some principles with regard to the due diligence standard in international environmental law appear to be broadly accepted. In respect of the material content of due diligence, the State of origin is expected to prevent foreseeable significant damage, or at least minimize the risk of such harm.[7] It was debated, however, whether the precautionary principle or

3 *Ibid.*, p. 2.

4 *Ibid.*, p. 8, with reference to J.W. Salacuse, *The Law of Investment Treaties* (Oxford University Press, 2010), p. 217 (see note 23).

5 *Ibid.*, p. 9.

6 ILA Study Group on Due Diligence in International Law, First Report, March 2014 (*op. cit.* at note 1), p. 25 *et seq.*

7 *Ibid.*, p. 26, with reference to the ILC Draft Articles on Prevention of Transboundary Harm from Hazardous Activities, with commentaries, *Yearbook of the International Law Commission*, 2001, vol. II, Part Two, at p. 154, commentary to article 3, according to which due diligence is "manifested in reasonable efforts by a State to inform itself of factual and legal components that relate foreseeably to a contemplated procedure and to take appropriate

approach is part of the concept of due diligence. With regard to the procedural content, States have to establish certain procedures, such as environmental impact assessment and permit procedures, notification and consultation with potentially affected States, and procedures to monitor the implementation of the activity.[8]

Against this backdrop, the Seabed Disputes Chamber and the Tribunal as a whole had to find the appropriate criteria of the due diligence standard for the cases at hand, answer open questions with regard to contentious issues, such as the applicability of the principle of common but differentiated responsibilities, and by doing so, develop the due diligence concept in international law in general.

II Advisory Opinion on Responsibilities and Obligations of States Sponsoring Persons and Entities with Respect to Activities in the Area

In its first Advisory Opinion concerning deep seabed mining[9], the Seabed Disputes Chamber had to interpret the expression "responsibility to ensure" in article 139, paragraph 1, of the Convention, establish a standard of performance for sponsoring States, and determine the degree of liability if a State did not carry out its responsibilities. The Chamber pointed out that the "responsibility to ensure" confers upon the sponsoring State an obligation under international law. By stipulating such an obligation for the sponsoring State, the Convention establishes a legal mechanism through which the rules of the Convention, although being treaty law and as such binding only on States Parties, become effective for sponsored contractors which are established under and regulated in domestic law. The Seabed Disputes Chamber stated:

---

measures in a timely fashion to address them. Thus States are under an obligation to take unilateral measures to prevent significant transboundary harm, or at any event to minimize the risk thereof".

8 ILA Study Group on Due Diligence in International Law, First Report, March 2014 (*op. cit.* at note 1), p. 28 *et seq.*

9 *Responsibilities and obligations of States with respect to activities in the Area, Advisory Opinion, 1 February 2011, ITLOS Reports 2011*, p. 10. For an analysis in German see *H. Jessen*, "Staatenverantwortlichkeit und seevölkerrechtliche Haftungsgrundsätze für Umweltschäden durch Tiefseebodenbergbau", *Zeitschrift für Umweltrecht* (2012), pp. 71–81.

> "Responsibility to ensure" points to an obligation of the sponsoring State under international law. It establishes a mechanism through which the rules of the Convention concerning activities in the Area, although being treaty law and thus binding only on the subjects of international law that have accepted them, become effective for sponsored contractors which find their legal basis in domestic law. *This mechanism consists in the creation of obligations which States Parties must fulfil by exercising their power over entities of their nationality and under their control.*[10]

In a way, the State acts as a "transformer" who transposes its international obligation to protect the marine environment into national laws and regulations which are then binding on private entities. Since the State is not expected to prevent each and every violation by private actors, the Chamber characterised this obligation "to ensure" as an obligation of conduct rather than an obligation of result.[11]

Referring to the Judgment of the ICJ in the *Pulp Mills* case,[12] the Chamber revealed an intrinsic connection between obligations of conduct and obligations of due diligence.[13] Obligations of conduct must be carried out with due diligence which means that a State is obliged "to deploy adequate means, to exercise best possible efforts, to do the utmost" to obtain the requested result – in the case at hand the result that the sponsored contractor complies with its obligation not to do harm to the Area.[14] According to the Chamber, due diligence obligations are often found in international legal instruments

10 *Responsibilities and obligations of States with respect to activities in the Area, Advisory Opinion, 1 February 2011, ITLOS Reports 2011*, p. 10, at p. 40, para. 108 (emphasis added). For the responsibility of States for activities of private persons or entities see A. Seibert-Fohr, "Die völkerrechtliche Verantwortung des Staats für das Handeln von Privaten: Bedarf nach Neuorientierung? 73 *Zeitschrift für öffentliches Recht und Völkerrecht* (2013), pp. 55 *et seq.*

11 *Responsibilities and obligations of States with respect to activities in the Area, Advisory Opinion, 1 February 2011, ITLOS Reports 2011*, p. 10, at p. 41, para. 110.

12 *Pulp Mills on the River Uruguay (Argentina* v. *Uruguay), Judgment, I.C.J Reports 2010*, p. 14. For an analysis in German see A. Proelß, "Das Urteil des Internationalen Gerichtshofs im Pulp Mills-Fall und seine Bedeutung für die Entwicklung des Umweltvölkerrechts", in M. Ruffert (ed.), *Dynamik und Nachhaltigkeit des Öffentlichen Rechts, Festschrift für Professor Dr. Meinhard Schröder zum 70. Geburtstag* (Duncker & Humblot, 2012) p. 611 *et seq.*

13 *Responsibilities and obligations of States with respect to activities in the Area, Advisory Opinion, 1 February 2011, ITLOS Reports 2011*, p. 10, at p. 41, para. 111.

14 *Ibid.*, p. 41, para. 110.

> to refer to obligations in respect of which, while it is not considered reasonable to make a State liable for each and every violation committed by persons under its jurisdiction, it is equally not considered satisfactory to rely on mere application of the principle that the conduct of private persons or entities is not attributable to the State under international law.[15]

In this respect, due diligence obligations are a necessary and reasonable compromise between too far-reaching obligations of result on the one hand, and a non-acceptable release from any obligation on the other.

As to the standard of performance, the Chamber pointed out that due diligence is a variable concept that may change overtime, for example in light of new scientific or technological knowledge. As a general rule, due diligence obligations have to be adapted in relation to the risks involved. Thus, the standard of due diligence has to be stricter for riskier activities.[16] This thought is also reflected in Article 3 of the ILC's Draft Articles on the Prevention of Transboundary Harm.[17] In the issue at hand, the Chamber determined that to fulfil its due diligence obligation, the sponsoring State is required to take measures within its legal system which must be "reasonably appropriate".[18] Referring to article 139, paragraph 2, in connection with article 153, paragraph 4, and Annex III, article 4, paragraph 4, of the Convention, the Chamber concluded that the sponsoring State has to adopt laws and regulations and to take administrative measures in order to fulfil the due diligence standard.[19] These national measures should be kept under review so as to ensure that they are adapted to new developments and current international standards.[20] In addition, the Chamber stated for good reason that it is inherent in the due diligence obligation to ensure that the obligations of a sponsored contractor are made enforceable.[21] It is thus not sufficient to adopt new laws and regulations

15 *Ibid.*, para. 112.

16 *Ibid.*, p. 43, para. 117.

17 ILA Study Group on Due Diligence in International Law, Second Report, July 2016 (*op. cit.* at note 2), p. 12, with reference to ILC Draft Articles on Prevention of Transboundary Harm from Hazardous Activities, with commentaries, *Yearbook of the International Law Commission*, 2001, vol. II, Part Two, at p. 154, para. 11, commentary to article 3, where it is stated that due diligence standard should be "appropriate and proportional to the degree of risk of the transboundary harm".

18 *Responsibilities and obligations of States with respect to activities in the Area, Advisory Opinion, 1 February 2011, ITLOS Reports 2011*, p. 10, at p. 44, para. 120.

19 *Ibid.*, para. 218.

20 *Ibid.*, para. 222.

21 *Ibid.*, para. 239.

on paper; compliance has to be supervised, and in cases of non-compliance enforcement measures have to be taken.

Most noteworthy, the Chamber established a link between the obligation of due diligence and the precautionary approach as stipulated in the Authority's Nodules and Sulphides Regulations. As a consequence, it characterized the precautionary approach as an integral part of the general obligation of due diligence of sponsoring States which is applicable even outside the scope of the Authority's Regulations. Therefore, sponsoring States are required to take appropriate preventive measures in situations where scientific evidence concerning the scope and potential harm of the activity in question is insufficient but where there are plausible indications of potential risks. In this respect, the Chamber made it clear that disregarding such potential risks would be a failure to fulfil the due diligence obligation and a failure to comply with the precautionary approach which would entail the sponsoring State's liability. The Seabed Disputes Chamber stated:

> it is appropriate to point out that *the precautionary approach is also an integral part of the general obligation of due diligence* of sponsoring States, which is applicable even outside the scope of the Regulations. The due diligence obligation of the sponsoring States requires them to take all appropriate measures to prevent damage that might result from the activities of contractors that they sponsor. This obligation applies in situations where scientific evidence concerning the scope and potential negative impact of the activity in question is insufficient but where there are plausible indications of potential risks. *A sponsoring State would not meet its obligation of due diligence if it disregarded those risks.* Such disregard would amount to a failure to comply with the precautionary approach.[22]

Moreover, the precautionary approach is supplemented by the obligation to apply "best environmental practices" which also forms part of the sponsoring State's obligation of due diligence.[23] This legal construction is a novelty which might play an important role in international environmental law in general. The link between due diligence obligations and the precautionary approach, coupled with best environmental practices which are by now incorporated in a number of international treaties, has a strong potential to prevent harm to the environment and the global commons by activities of private entities.

---

22 *Ibid.*, para. 131 (emphasis added).

23 *Ibid.*, para. 136.

Furthermore, the Chamber adopted an objective (rather than a subjective) standard of due diligence, i.e. developed and developing States have to meet the same standard, irrespective of their individual capabilities and financial means.[24] This issue was highly contentious in the statements before the Chamber. A number of developing States including the applicant State Nauru and international institutions such as the UN Environment Programme ("UNEP")[25] argued that developing States' duties should be limited to the use of best practicable means at their disposal and in accordance with their capabilities. Less strict standards for developing countries could be based on the preamble and various provisions in Part XI, especially article 148 which promotes the "effective participation of developing States in activities in the Area ... as specifically provided for in this Part [Part XI], having due regard to their special interests and needs ...". The Chamber interpreted this provision in a strict way, finding that no provision in Part XI specifically provides for preferential treatment to developing States. It pointed out:

> However, none of the general provisions of the Convention concerning the responsibilities (or the liability) of the sponsoring State "specifically provides" for according preferential treatment to sponsoring States that are developing States. As observed above, there is no provision requiring the consideration of such interests and needs beyond what is specifically stated in Part XI. It may therefore be concluded that the *general provisions concerning responsibilities and liability of the sponsoring State apply equally to all sponsoring States*, whether developing or developed.[26]

The reasoning behind this conclusion is twofold: First, the Chamber was concerned about a potential spread of sponsoring States "of convenience", because it is easy for business enterprises in developed States to set up companies in developing States in the expectation of less burdensome standards and controls. Secondly – and more importantly – the Chamber aimed at guaranteeing the uniform application of the highest standards of protection of the marine environment and of the common heritage of mankind. In this respect it stated:

---

24 *Ibid.*, para. 158.

25 Written Statement by UNEP, available at: https://www.itlos.org/fileadmin/itlos/documents/cases/case_no_17/UNEP.pdf, Annex, p.1; see also H. Zhang, "The Sponsoring State's 'Obligation to Ensure' in the Development of the International Seabed Area", 28 *IJMCL* (2013), pp. 681, 689, 693 *et seq.*

26 *Responsibilities and obligations of States with respect to activities in the Area, Advisory Opinion, 1 February 2011, ITLOS Reports 2011*, p. 10, at pp. 53–54, para. 158 (emphasis added).

> Equality of treatment between developing and developed sponsoring States is consistent with the need to prevent commercial enterprises based in developed States from setting up companies in developing States, acquiring their nationality and obtaining their sponsorship in the hope of being subjected to less burdensome regulations and controls. The *spread of sponsoring States "of convenience" would jeopardize uniform application of the highest standards of protection of the marine environment*, the safe development of activities in the Area and protection of the common heritage of mankind.[27]

It defined the role of the sponsoring State as one of contributing to the common interest of all States in the proper implementation of the principle of the common heritage of all mankind.[28] On balance, this fundamental common interest of the international community outweighs the interest of developing States to be treated according to their capabilities – or, in other words, according to the principle of common but differentiated responsibilities which is well established in international environmental law. The Chamber made an exception with regard to the precautionary approach. Since Principle 15 of the 1992 Rio Declaration on Environment and Development provides that the precautionary approach shall be applied by States "according to their capabilities", the requirements for complying with that obligation may be stricter for developed than for developing States. This exception, however, does not encompass the supplemental obligation to follow "best environmental practices".[29]

Finally, the Chamber clarified the relationship between the obligation of due diligence and State liability.[30] It held that the liability of a sponsoring State arises only from its failure to carry out its own due diligence obligation and is triggered by the damage caused by a sponsored contractor.[31] The sponsoring State, therefore, is only liable for damages caused by one of its sponsored entities if it fails to discharge its own obligation of due diligence. Otherwise, it is exempted from liability. This view rules out the application of strict liability,[32]

---

27 *Ibid.*, para. 159 (emphasis added).

28 *Ibid.*, para. 226.

29 *Ibid.*, para. 161.

30 For a detailed analysis of the connection between State responsibility, liability and the concept of due diligence see J. Kulesza, *Due Diligence in International Law* (Brill, 2016), p. 136 *et seq.*

31 *Responsibilities and obligations of States with respect to activities in the Area, Advisory Opinion, 1 February 2011, ITLOS Reports 2011*, p. 10, at p. 60, para. 184.

32 *Ibid.*, para. 189.

a standard of liability which was demanded in several statements during the proceedings.

III Advisory Opinion Requested by the Sub-Regional Fisheries Commission (SRFC)

The second Advisory Opinion concerning IUU fishing[33] was given by the full Tribunal in accordance with article 21 of the Statute and article 138 of the Rules. In my opinion, the Tribunal's arguments with regard to its jurisdiction to give the Advisory Opinion are convincing,[34] and its advisory jurisdiction is a means to clarify legal issues and to make use of the Tribunal's expertise *before* a dispute arises.[35]

With regard to the issue of due diligence, the Tribunal confirmed the Seabed Disputes Chamber's reasoning. It held that, in case of IUU fishing in the EEZs of the States which are members of the SRFC, the obligation of a flag State to ensure that vessels flying its flag are not involved in IUU fishing is also an obligation of conduct and, as such, a due diligence obligation. The Tribunal stated:

> It follows from article 58, paragraph 3, and article 62, paragraph 4, as well as from article 192, of the Convention that flag States are obliged to take the necessary measures to ensure that their nationals and vessels flying their flag are not engaged in IUU fishing activities.... In other words, while under the Convention the primary responsibility for the conservation and management of living resources in the exclusive economic zone, including the adoption of such measures as may be necessary to ensure compliance with the laws and regulations enacted by the coastal State in this regard, rests with the coastal State, *flag States also have the responsibility*

33 *Request for an Advisory Opinion submitted by the Sub-Regional Fisheries Commission, Advisory Opinion, 2 April 2015, ITLOS Reports 2015*, p. 4. For an analysis see V.J. Schatz, "Combating Illegal Fishing in the Exclusive Economic Zone – Flag State Obligations in the Context of the Primary Responsibility of the Coastal State", 7 *Goettingen Journal of International Law* (2015), p. 1 *et seq.*

34 *Request for an Advisory Opinion submitted by the Sub-Regional Fisheries Commission, Advisory Opinion, 2 April 2015, ITLOS Reports 2015*, p. 4, paras. 37 *et seq.*, esp. 52–60.

35 Critical, however, T. Ruys and A. Soete, "'Creeping' Advisory Jurisdiction of International Courts and Tribunals? The Case of the International Tribunal for the Law of the Sea", 29 *Leiden Journal of International Law* (2016), p. 155 *et seq.*

> *to ensure that vessels flying their flag do not conduct IUU fishing activities* within the exclusive economic zones of the SRFC Member States.[36]

Although, for procedural reasons, the scope of the Advisory Opinion is limited to the EEZs of the SRFC Member States, the Tribunal's findings can be transferred to the EEZs of other coastal States.

For the Tribunal is was important to point out that, under the Convention, the primary responsibility for the conservation and management of living resources in the EEZ rests with the coastal State. To meet its responsibilities, the coastal State must adopt the necessary laws and regulations, including enforcement procedures.[37] In this context, the Tribunal emphasised that the primary responsibility of coastal States in cases of IUU fishing in their EEZs does not release other States from their obligations in this respect. Consequently, flag States also have general and specific obligations with regard to the conservation and management of marine living resources.[38] They have, in particular, the "responsibility to ensure" that vessels flying their flag do not conduct IUU activities within the EEZs of third States.[39]

The expression "responsibility to ensure" was interpreted in the same way as the Seabed Disputes Chamber did in the context of deep seabed mining.[40] Consequently, flag States are under the due diligence obligation to take all necessary measures including enforcement mechanisms to ensure compliance by fishing vessels flying their flag with the requirement not to engage in IUU fishing. It was stated:

> In the case of IUU fishing in the exclusive economic zones of the SRFC Member States, the obligation of a flag State not party to the MCA Convention [Convention on the Determination of the Minimal Conditions for Access and Exploitation of Marine Resources within the Maritime Areas under Jurisdiction of the Member States of the Sub-Regional Fisheries Commission] to ensure that vessels flying its flag are not involved in IUU fishing is also an obligation "of conduct". In other words, as stated in the Advisory Opinion of the Seabed Disputes Chamber, *this is an obligation "to deploy adequate means, to exercise best*

36 *Request for an Advisory Opinion submitted by the Sub-Regional Fisheries Commission, Advisory Opinion, 2 April 2015, ITLOS Reports 2015*, p. 4, at p. 38, para. 124 (emphasis added).

37 *Ibid.*, paras. 104–106.

38 *Ibid.*, para. 110.

39 *Ibid.*, para. 124.

40 *Ibid.*, para. 125 *et seq.*

> *possible efforts, to do the utmost" to prevent* IUU *fishing by ships flying its flag*. However, as an obligation "of conduct" this is a "due diligence obligation", not an obligation "of result". This means that this is *not an obligation of the flag State to achieve compliance by fishing vessels flying its flag in each case* with the requirement not to engage in IUU fishing in the exclusive economic zones of the SRFC Member States. The flag State is *under the "due diligence obligation" to take all necessary measures to ensure compliance and to prevent* IUU *fishing* by fishing vessels flying its flag.[41]

The same should be true, by the way, for those parts of the high seas which are covered by regional fisheries management organization conservation and management measures. The Tribunal expressly stated that if, nevertheless, violations occur and are reported by other States, the flag State is obliged to investigate and, if appropriate, take any action to remedy the situation as well as inform the reporting State of that action.[42] In this regard, the Tribunal underlined that the duty to cooperate is a fundamental principle in the prevention of pollution of the marine environment and in general international law and that this obligation extends to cases of alleged IUU fishing activities.[43]

In addition, the Tribunal held that the flag State has the obligation to set up enforcement mechanisms to monitor and secure compliance with its laws and regulations. In cases of IUU fishing, sanctions must be adequate and sufficient to deter future violations:

> While the nature of the laws, regulations and measures that are to be adopted by the flag State is left to be determined by each flag State in accordance with its legal system, the flag State nevertheless has the obligation to include in them *enforcement mechanisms to monitor and secure compliance* with these laws and regulations. Sanctions applicable to involvement in IUU fishing activities must be *sufficient to deter violations and to deprive offenders of the benefits* accruing from their IUU fishing activities.[44]

Even though the Tribunal did not mention it, it became clear that all flag States have to meet the same standards. This should allow measures against "flags of convenience" in the fisheries sector.

41 *Ibid.*, para. 129 (emphasis added).
42 *Ibid.*, para. 119, 139.
43 *Ibid.*, para. 140.
44 *Ibid.*, para. 138 (emphasis added).

As in the case of sponsoring States, the violation of laws and regulations by private entities are not *per se* attributable to the flag State. The liability of the flag State arises from its own failure to comply with its due diligence obligations. The Tribunal stated:

> In the present case, the liability of the flag State does not arise from a failure of vessels flying its flag to comply with the laws and regulations of the SRFC Member States concerning IUU fishing activities in their exclusive economic zones, as the violation of such laws and regulations by vessels is not *per se* attributable to the flag State. *The liability of the flag State arises from its failure to comply with its "due diligence" obligations* concerning IUU fishing activities conducted by vessels flying its flag in the exclusive economic zones of the SRFC Member States.[45]

This, in turn, means that the flag State is exempted from liability if it has taken all necessary and appropriate measures to meet its due diligence obligations.[46] Since the flag State's liability only depends on the nature of the measures taken and their proper enforcement, the frequency of IUU fishing activities by its vessels are irrelevant to the issue as to whether there is a breach of its due diligence obligation. In this respect, the Tribunal clarified:

> The Tribunal also wishes to address the issue as to whether isolated IUU fishing activities or only a repeated pattern of such activities would entail a breach of "due diligence" obligations of the flag State. As explained in paragraphs 146 and 148, the Tribunal finds that a breach of "due diligence" obligations of a flag State arises if it has not taken all necessary and appropriate measures to meet its obligations to ensure that vessels flying its flag do not conduct IUU fishing activities in the exclusive economic zones of the SRFC Member States. Therefore, the frequency of IUU fishing activities by vessels in the exclusive economic zones of the SRFC Member States is not relevant to the issue as to whether there is a breach of "due diligence" obligations by the flag State.[47]

Frequent violations might, however, be an indicator for deficient regulations or enforcement mechanisms. This might also be a deterrent to States offering

45 *Ibid.*, para. 146 (emphasis added).
46 *Ibid.*, para. 148.
47 *Ibid.*, para. 150.

"flags of convenience" to fishing vessels the owners of which are located in States which are able to conduct stricter controls.

IV Concluding Remarks

In conclusion, it is the Tribunal that deserves the credit for elaborating upon the details of due diligence obligations and their connection with the concept of State liability. The Seabed Disputes Chamber confirmed that the due diligence concept is a flexible and dynamic legal concept that develops over time and might change in view of new scientific or technological knowledge. It pointed out that due diligence obligations establish a mechanism through which the rules of the Convention, although being treaty law and as such binding only on States Parties, become effective for private entities.[48] This legal mechanism puts the State into the role of a "transformer" and makes use of the State's regulating and enforcement capacities which are usually lacking at the international level. For States, this means that rights like the right to sponsor contractors in deep seabed mining or the right to fish always come with the corresponding due diligence obligation to regulate and effectively control the behaviour of the private actors involved in such activities.

The connection between the fulfilment of these due diligence obligations and State liability enables other States to ask for compensation and remedial action before international courts or arbitral tribunals. Since in both advisory cases dealt with by the Tribunal, the ultimate goal is the protection of the common heritage of mankind *viz.* common goods, this mechanism also serves the purpose to preserve such goods in the interest of the international community as a whole. Drawing on the jurisprudence of the ICJ and the work of the ILC, the Tribunal developed the due diligence concept in a progressive manner. This was also acknowledged by the ILA Study Group on Due Diligence in International Law which examined the question of whether there is emerging a common standard of due diligence across the range of different areas of international law.[49] The Tribunal has paved the way for a better understanding and a more effective application of this concept in international law.

48 *Responsibilities and obligations of States with respect to activities in the Area, Advisory Opinion, 1 February 2011, ITLOS Reports 2011*, p. 10, at pp. 40–41, para. 108.

49 ILA Study Group on Due Diligence in International Law, Second Report, July 2016 (*op. cit.* at note 2), p. 47.

The Contribution of the Tribunal to the Progressive Development of International Law

Francisco Orrego Vicuña

I The Tribunal's Contribution to the Development of International Law in Context

It is a well-known fact that the development of international law is to a large extent the outcome of a steady jurisprudential evolution. It is here where the role of judicial decisions as an auxiliary source of international law manifests itself with full strength either by clarifying the meaning of treaties, identifying the rules emanating from customary international law or even applying general principles of law and equity. While this is true generally it is still more evident in the case of specialized jurisdictions such as that of the Tribunal and its contribution to the progressive development of the law of the sea. This is not to ignore the fact that jurisprudence has not always succeeded in providing for systematic development of the law in view of the limited issues brought to adjudication, but even those failures have helped to reorient the meaning of the law by way of the major codification conferences on the law of the sea and their own contribution to its progressive development.

The Tribunal's contribution can thus only be appreciated in its full dimension by taking into account the manner how it is inserted into the mainstream of international jurisprudence as established by both the PCIJ and the ICJ, a host of international arbitration tribunals and the conferences which step by step have provided for the systematic codification and development of this major aspect of international law. The emblematic cases of the *Bering Sea Fur Seals Arbitration* in 1893,[1] the *North Atlantic Coast Fisheries Case* in 1910,[2] or the *El Salvador* v. *Nicaragua* case concerning the legal status of the Gulf of Fonseca in 1917[3] are not only interesting from the point of view of their historical setting, but above all show how a number of the concepts and solutions devised by

1 *Award between the United States and the United Kingdom relating to the rights of jurisdiction of United States in the Bering's sea and the preservation of fur seals*, 15 August 1893, RIAA Vol. XXVIII, pp. 263–276.

2 *The North Atlantic Coast Fisheries Case* (*Great Britain, United States*), 7 September 1910, RIAA Vol. XI, pp. 167–226.

3 *El Salvador* v. *Nicaragua*, Central American Court of Justice, 9 March 1917, 11 AJIL 674 (1917).

© 2018, BY INTERNATIONAL TRIBUNAL FOR THE LAW OF THE SEA | DOI 10.1163/9789004356832_012

those decisions were later reflected in the jurisprudence of international tribunals, whether in terms of the conservation and sustainable exploitation of the living resources of the sea, the use of closing lines in the case of bays or the specific issues concerning a particular geographical area, developments which in turn would be translated into the corresponding articles of the Geneva Conventions and the Law of the Sea Convention.

Ever since the *Grisbadarna* arbitration in 1909[4] the question of maritime delimitation has figured prominently in international jurisprudence, having approached for the first time the question of inter-temporal law, the role of "*effectivités*" or the use of straight baselines and geographical orientations for the attribution of maritime areas. Not every decision, however, provided a positive start-up in the development of the law of the sea, a case in point being of course that of the *S. S. "Lotus"* in connection with the jurisdiction on the high seas,[5] but even then it helped to form a consensus about a different view as reflected in a host of treaties, including the major conventions on the law of the sea. In a different matter, the case of the *S.S. Wimbledon* evidenced the concern for the rights of navigation in international waterways, again a recurrent subject in international jurisprudence and legislation.[6] Since the early years the subject matter with which jurisprudence has been concerned has constantly expanded.

II Facilitating Rights of Navigation in Maritime Areas

A first major line of jurisprudential development and the role of the Tribunal therein concerns the navigation of major waterways necessary for maritime communications, particularly in the light of the jurisdiction of coastal States in those areas, as became evident in the connection with the *Corfu Channel* case in 1949[7] and its later reflection in the codification conventions and the precision of the conditions for the exercise of both navigational rights and coastal State sovereignty in such areas. A prior development of particular interest was that of the *I'm Alone*, which, in 1935, dealt with the right of hot pursuit in the high seas and its limits.[8] Since its early decisions in the *M/V "SAIGA" Case* (*Saint Vincent and the Grenadines* v. *Guinea*), *Prompt Release* and the *M/V*

4 *Grisbadarna Arbitration* (*Norway/Sweden*), 23 October 1909, *RIAA* Vol. XI, pp. 147–166.

5 *"Lotus", Judgment No. 9, 1927, P.C.I.J. Series A, No 10.*

6 *S.S. "Wimbledon", Judgments, 1923, P.C.I.J., Series A, No 1.*

7 *Corfu Channel, Merits, Judgment, I.C.J. Reports 1949*, p. 4.

8 *S.S. "I'm Alone"* (*Canada, United States*), 30 June 1933 and 5 January 1935, *RIAA* Vol. III, pp. 1609–1618.

"SAIGA" (No. 2) Case,[9] the Tribunal sought to clarify the issue of hot pursuit in the continuous zone and the exclusive economic zone as key maritime areas where hot pursuit needed to be updated as required by the development of the Law of the Sea within the framework of the Convention. Questions concerning the prompt release of vessels, the role of judicial procedures in the courts of the costal State and compensation, together with the precision of the regime of the exclusive economic zone, nationality of claims and proportionality in the use of force became paramount elements of the new jurisprudence emanating from the Tribunal.

It is of interest to note that while questions concerning financial matters have seldom been taken to permanent international courts, the Tribunal has been faced with claims in this matter concerning the amount of the bond required, their proportionality in connection with the gravity of the offence and the criteria for deciding on such measures.[10] A balanced approach to the safeguarding of the interest of coastal States' sovereignty and the interest of the State of nationality in prompt release was also well attained in the *"Camouco" Case (Panama* v. *France), Prompt Release* and the *"Monte Confurco" Case (Seychelles* v. *France), Prompt Release* in 2000.[11] These decisions were the first concerning non-authorized fishing in Sub-Antarctic waters under French jurisdiction. An important line of cases were decided subsequently on questions of prompt release,[12] adoption of provisional measures[13] and the exercise of jurisdiction by the courts of the coastal State, as shown prominently in the

9 *M/V "SAIGA" (Saint Vincent and the Grenadines* v. *Guinea), Prompt Release, Judgment, ITLOS Reports 1997*, p. 16; *M/V "SAIGA" (No. 2) (Saint Vincent and the Grenadines* v. *Guinea), Judgment, ITLOS Reports 1999*, p. 10.

10 *"Volga" (Russian Federation* v. *Australia), Prompt Release, Judgment, ITLOS Reports 2002*, p. 10.

11 *"Camouco" (Panama* v. *France), Prompt Release, Judgment, ITLOS Reports 2000*, p. 10, *"Monte Confurco" (Seychelles* v. *France), Prompt Release, Judgment, ITLOS Reports 2000*, p. 86.

12 See for example, *"Grand Prince" (Belize* v. *France), Prompt Release, Judgment, ITLOS Reports 2001*, p. 17, *"Chaisiri Reefer 2" (Panama* v. *Yemen), Order of 13 July 2001, ITLOS Reports 2001*, p. 82, *"Juno Trader" (Saint Vincent and the Grenadines* v. *Guinea-Bissau), Prompt Release, Judgment, ITLOS Reports 2004*, p. 17, *"Hoshinmaru" (Japan* v. *Russian Federation), Prompt Release, Judgment, ITLOS Reports 2005–2007*, p. 18, *"Tomimaru" (Japan* v. *Russian Federation), Prompt Release, Judgment, ITLOS Reports 2005–2007*, p. 74.

13 *M/V "Louisa" (Saint Vincent and the Grenadines* v. *Kingdom of Spain), Provisional Measures, Order of 23 December 2010, ITLOS Reports 2008–2010*, p. 58, *"Arctic Sunrise" (Kingdom of the Netherlands* v. *Russian Federation), Provisional Measures, Order of 22 November 2013, ITLOS Reports 2013*, p. 230.

"ARA Libertad" Case (*Argentina* v. *Ghana*)[14] and the *"Enrica Lexie" Incident* (*Italy* v. *India*).[15] On occasion, while provisional measures have not been granted, a declaration by the coastal State has been noted by the Tribunal in lieu thereof, as was the case in the *M/V "Louisa" Case* (*Saint Vincent and the Grenadines* v. *Kingdom of Spain*), where a declaration was made by Spain on the protection of the marine environment.

III The Tribunal's Role in Providing Certainty to the Law on Maritime Delimitation

A second major jurisprudential line in which the contribution of the Tribunal to the development of international law can be assessed is that concerning maritime delimitation. This contribution can only be evaluated if the broader context of the law on maritime delimitation is examined, including most prominently therein the case law of the ICJ. It is well known that the ICJ chose at the start the wrong approach to this matter as evidenced in the *North Sea Continental Shelf* cases[16] and the *Tunisia/Libya Continental Shelf* dispute a few years later.[17] The essential difficulty was here the understanding of the Court that judges could operate in an entirely discretionary manner where the meaning of equity within the system of international law could be done away with because what mattered was only to achieve an equitable result. The same approach was followed in the *Gulf of Maine* case[18] resulting in what Prosper Weil appropriately described as plunging jurisprudence into total subjectivity.

The criticism of this approach by distinguished authors, Prosper Weil and Sir Elihu Lauterpacht in particular, as well as the views of influential judges, including Jennings, Gros, Oda and Schwebel, gradually came to change the original misunderstanding as the *Libya/Malta Continental Shelf* case began to show as from 1985.[19] Equity increasingly became associated to international law with a view to introduce a corrective function capable of ensuring security,

14 *"ARA Libertad" (Argentina* v. *Ghana), Provisional Measures, Order of 15 December 2012, ITLOS Reports 2012*, p. 332.

15 *"Enrica Lexie" Incident (Italy* v. *India), Provisional Measures, Order of 24 August 2015, ITLOS Reports 2015*, p. 182.

16 *North Sea Continental Shelf (Federal Republic of Germany/Denmark; Federal Republic of Germany/Netherlands), Judgment, I.C.J. Reports 1969*, p. 3.

17 *Continental Shelf (Tunisia/Libyan Arab Jamahiriya), Judgment, I.C.J. Reports 1982*, p. 18.

18 *Delimitation of the Maritime Boundary in the Gulf of Maine Area (Canada/United States of America), Judgment, I.C.J. Reports 1984*, p. 246.

19 *Continental Shelf (Libyan Arab Jamahiriya/Malta), Judgment, I.C.J. Reports 1985*, p. 13.

foreseeability and the general application of a normative system of law. At the same time an enhanced role of special circumstances in the implementation of equitable principles became an important tool for facilitating the necessary flexibility so as to attend to the different characteristics of each case. The cases of *Qatar* v. *Bahrain*,[20] *Cameroon* v. *Nigeria*,[21] *Jan Mayen* (*Denmark* v. *Norway*)[22] and others gradually led to the identification of a common methodology for delimitation, with particular reference to the pertinent coasts, base points, provisional equidistance subject to verification in the light of special circumstances and a final verification of proportionality.

The ICJ came to fully accept these changing conceptual and methodological approaches in the Black Sea delimitation case between Romania and Ukraine in 2009,[23] as the arbitrations between Barbados and Trinidad & Tobago and Guyana and Suriname had also accepted in the preceding years.[24] This is not to say that progress has always been a process of steady development as there have also been recent cases where the ICJ appears to have returned to early approaches where equity does not appear to have faithfully followed its attachment to the law, the cases of *Nicaragua* v. *Colombia* in 2012[25] and *Peru* v. *Chile* in 2014[26] bearing witness to such departures as to the role of equity in the delimitation process.

As a consequence of the uncertainties surrounding the role of equity and the law in maritime delimitation generally the cases on this matter have not been many before the Tribunal. But here lies precisely the Tribunal's contribution to the development of the law governing this kind of adjudication. In point of fact the case concerning the *Delimitation of the maritime boundary in*

20 *Maritime Delimitation and Territorial Questions between Qatar and Bahrain* (*Qatar* v. *Bahrain*), *Merits, Judgment, I.C.J. Reports 2001*, p. 40.

21 *Land and Maritime Boundary between Cameroon and Nigeria* (*Cameroon* v. *Nigeria: Equatorial Guinea intervening*), *Judgment, I.C.J. Reports 2002*, p. 303.

22 *Maritime Delimitation in the Area between Greenland and Jan Mayen* (*Denmark* v. *Norway*), *Judgment, I.C.J. Reports 1993*, p. 38.

23 *Maritime Delimitation in the Black Sea* (*Romania* v. *Ukraine*), *Judgment, I.C.J. Reports 2009*, p. 61.

24 *Arbitration between Barbados and the Republic of Trinidad and Tobago, relating to the delimitation of the exclusive economic zone and the continental shelf between them*, 11 April 2006, *RIAA* Vol. XXVII pp. 147–251; *Award in the arbitration regarding the delimitation of the maritime boundary between Guyana and Suriname*, 17 September 2007, *RIAA* Vol. XXX pp. 1–144.

25 *Territorial and Maritime Dispute* (*Nicaragua* v. *Colombia*), *Judgment, I.C.J. Reports 2012*, p. 624.

26 *Maritime Dispute* (*Peru* v. *Chile*), *Judgment, I.C.J. Reports 2014*, p. 3.

the Bay of Bengal (*Bangladesh/Myanmar*) in 2012[27] relies on a uniform method of delimitation and its various successive stages of identification and verification. Thereby the cycle begun by the ICJ in 1969, the adaptation that followed in that very court and arbitration tribunals, became to a meaningful extent consolidated under the Tribunal, thus providing for a degree of certainty that made it fully compatible with the meaning of international law on this issue. It could reasonably be expected that in the future this contribution will open the gates of further submissions on maritime delimitation cases before ITLOS, a process already underway at the ICJ[28] and the PCA.[29]

An additional contribution of the Tribunal in respect of maritime delimitation must also be noted. In the *Bangladesh/Myanmar* case referred to above, the Tribunal for the first time undertook the delimitation of the continental shelf beyond the 200 mile distance, a possibility that the *Barbados/Trinidad and Tobago* arbitration had envisaged but not implemented in view of the circumstances of that case. Such a trend found its confirmation in the *Bangladesh* v. *India* maritime delimitation case before an Annex VII Tribunal under the Convention where a grey area of continental shelf beyond 200 miles was appropriately noted.[30] Cases concerning this extended continental shelf jurisdiction have also been brought before the ICJ as evidenced by those between Nicaragua and Colombia[31] and Somalia and Kenya.[32] Natural prolongation has reacquired in consequence a role but in a different context to that which characterized the *North Sea Continental Shelf* cases as it is no longer substituting for a 200 mile distance but rather supplementing this uniform limit.[33]

---

27 *Delimitation of the maritime boundary in the Bay of Bengal* (*Bangladesh/Myanmar*), *Judgment, ITLOS Reports 2012*, p. 4.

28 *Maritime Delimitation in the Caribbean Sea and the Pacific Ocean* (*Costa Rica* v. *Nicaragua*), Application of 26 February 2014.

29 *Arbitration between the Republic of Croatia and the Republic of Slovenia*, PCA Case No. 2012–04.

30 *Bay of Bengal Maritime Boundary Arbitration between Bangladesh and India*, PCA Case No. 2010–16, 7 July 2014.

31 *Question of the Delimitation of the Continental Shelf between Nicaragua and Colombia beyond 200 nautical miles from the Nicaraguan coast*, (*Nicaragua* v. *Colombia*), Application of 16 September 2013.

32 *Maritime Delimitation in the Indian Ocean* (*Somalia* v. *Kenya*), Application of 28 August 2014.

33 The *Arbitration under the Timor Sea Treaty* (*Timor-Leste* v. *Australia*), PCA Case No. 2013–6, pending before the PCA, concerns yet a different situation where treaties in force have been called into question because of applying historical understandings about the continental shelf delimitation. The case is currently under conciliation proceedings (PCA Case No. 2016–10).

Certainty and foreseeability have substituted for the guess work with which the process of maritime delimitation started before international courts and tribunals, resulting in a greater clarity and uniformity in the prevailing approaches, particularly insofar the role of equity in harmony with the rules of international law had been generally accepted. The Tribunal's contribution to this development represents an important stage in the evolution undertaken. In the end, the criticism occasionally made of articles 74, paragraph 1, and 83, paragraph 1, of the Convention as being too vague and general so as to provide for guidance in delimitation has proven wrong as an equitable solution was therein always conceived in strict association with international law.

IV Clarifying the Regime for Management and Exploitation of Living Resources

The cases concerning disputes on the management and exploitation of living resources of the sea have been less frequent in international jurisprudence generally and also in the role of the Tribunal in this context. In fact, the contribution made by the *Bering Sea Fur Seals Arbitration* has been hardly surpassed by international jurisprudence. The ICJ judgment on *Fisheries Jurisdiction* in 1974[34] followed the wrong approach to this question by deciding that the vessels of third parties could not be excluded from the 50 mile jurisdictional zone proclaimed by Iceland at the time, disregarding what was already an emerging trend in the early law of the sea negotiations insofar the 200 mile jurisdictional area was concerned. Questions of preferential access, conservation of resources and the interests of third parties were to a useful extent clarified.

As with other aspects of the law of the sea later decisions also evidence an evolution concerning issues of conservation of resources in a contemporary perspective, as shown by the ICJ in the case regarding *Whaling in the Antarctic*.[35] Management measures under the Convention on the Conservation and Management of High Seas Fishery Resources in the South Pacific Ocean have also been brought to the PCA.[36] A number of disputes of interest in this matter failed to proceed to the merits on jurisdictional grounds.

34 *Fisheries Jurisdiction (United Kingdom* v. *Iceland), Merits, Judgment, I.C.J. Reports 1974*, p. 3.

35 *Whaling in the Antarctic (Australia* v. *Japan: New Zealand intervening), Judgment, I.C.J. Reports 2014*, p. 226.

36 *Review Panel established under the Convention on the Conservation and Management of High Seas Fishery Resources in the South Pacific Ocean*, PCA Case No. 2013–14, 5 July

Only one case concerning specifically the living resources of the sea has been submitted to the Tribunal. This was the dispute between Chile and the European Union ("EU") on the exploitation and conservation of swordfish in the South East Pacific, which was simultaneously taken to the World Trade Organization ("WTO") by the EU.[37] The case was settled and could not thus reach the merits stage. It must be noted, however, that tribunals tend to be cautious when the request for provisional measures envisages the suspension of an ongoing activity, as was the case of the provisional measures decided by a Special Chamber of the Tribunal in respect of the delimitation of the maritime boundary between Ghana and Côte d'Ivoire in the Atlantic Ocean, a case at first submitted to Annex VII arbitration by Ghana, followed next by the submission to a special chamber of ITLOS, upon agreement of the parties.[38]

The interaction between the Tribunal and arbitration procedures under Annex VII of the Convention must also be kept in mind. In the *Southern Blue Fin Tuna Cases* ((*New Zealand v. Japan; Australia v. Japan*), a jurisdictional decision of an Annex VII tribunal interacted with an Order for provisional measures issued by the Tribunal.[39] This interaction, however, would not survive the jurisdictional decision reached in that arbitration. Although much criticized, the jurisdictional decision cannot be considered wrong as the rules governing the dispute prevented the arbitral tribunal from affirming jurisdiction in the light of the choices made by the parties. The Tribunal's Order was, however, of lasting interest insofar it dealt with the conditions of the Convention for the issuance of provisional measures and the limits to be applied by the parties in their activities concerning the fishing of these species.

V Environmental Protection as a New Area of Concern of the Tribunal

Environmental protection has provided yet another line of jurisprudential developments in the law of the sea. While not yet abundant this line evidences

2013. See also *Request for an Advisory Opinion submitted by the Sub-Regional Fisheries Commission, Advisory Opinion, 2 April 2015, ITLOS Reports 2015*, p. 4.

37 *Case concerning the Conservation and Sustainable Exploitation of Swordfish Stocks in the South-Eastern Pacific Ocean (Chile/European Union)*.

38 *Delimitation of the maritime boundary in the Atlantic Ocean (Ghana/Côte d'Ivoire), Provisional Measures, Order of 25 April 2015, ITLOS Reports 2015*, p. 146.

39 *Southern Bluefin Tuna (New Zealand* v. *Japan; Australia* v. *Japan), Provisional Measures, Order of 27 August 1999, ITLOS Reports 1999*, p. 280.

both at the ICJ and the Tribunal a growing sensibility in connection with this subject. The disputes concerning the living resources of the sea provide a first point of contact with environmental issues. This was noticeable in the historic cases discussed above but also more recently. The Denmark-EU dispute on the fishing of Atlantic herring,[40] just like that noted between Chile and the EU on swordfish, while both settled by agreement of the parties, are indicative of this connection between the environment and the exploitation of living resources. International arbitrations have also been important in this matter, cases in point being those of the *Gulf of St. Lawrence between Canada and France*[41] and the *Chagos Marine Protected Area Arbitration* (*Mauritius* v. *United Kingdom*).[42]

The Tribunal's contribution on this aspect is best known in the light of the *MOX Plant Case* (*Ireland* v. *United Kingdom*) and the issuance of the Order on provisional measures in 2001,[43] with particular reference to the obligations of the parties to assess the risks to maritime areas associated to this nuclear plant and the related obligation on prevention of pollution in the marine environment, all of which came to be ratified by the 2003 Annex VII arbitration on this matter. These expressions of concern would last beyond the fact that the case was in the end withdrawn by Ireland. It should not pass unnoticed, however, that in so doing the Tribunal has also been tempted by developments hardly compatible with the current state of international law, as the suggestion of the Seabed Disputes Chamber dispute that the precautionary principle embodied in the Rio Declaration and its incorporation in a number of treaties and instruments "has initiated a trend towards making this approach part of customary international law".[44] While this view has not been endorsed by the full Tribunal, it is indicative of the need to light a yellow warning sign in respect of some well-meant interpretations that stand in contrast with the more cautious attitude of the ICJ.

40 *The Atlanto-Scandian Herring Arbitration* (*The Kingdom of Denmark in respect of the Faroe Islands v. The European Union*), PCA Case No 2013–20, discontinued in 2014, having also been submitted in parallel to the WTO, where it was also discontinued.

41 *Filleting within the Gulf of St. Lawrence between Canada and France*, 17 July 1986, *RIAA* Vol. XIX, pp. 225–296.

42 *Chagos Marine Protected Area Arbitration* (*Mauritius* v. *United Kingdom*), PCA Case No. 2011–03, 18 March 2015.

43 *MOX Plant* (*Ireland* v. *United Kingdom*), *Provisional Measures, Order of 3 December 2001, ITLOS Reports 2001*, p. 95.

44 *Responsibilities and obligations of States with respect to activities in the Area, Advisory Opinion, 1 February 2011, ITLOS Reports 2011*, p. 10, at p. 47, para. 135.

VI Emerging Developments Concerning Maritime Areas in Association with Claims to Sovereignty

There is still a more recent line of developments in international jurisprudence of particular significance as it concerns the question of maritime entitlements of areas recognized or claimed to be under the territorial sovereignty of disputing States. Historically this matter was directly or indirectly involved in the many cases that have addressed questions of baselines of maritime areas, including bays and other geographical features. In contemporary terms, however, the issue is less technical and relates to matters of great complexity associated to State sovereignty. The question arose in the *Chagos Marine Protected Area Arbitration* (*Mauritius* v. *United Kingdom*) noted above, where in spite of the fact that jurisdiction was not accepted in connection with the status of the United Kingdom as a coastal State in that archipelago, fishing rights were recognized in favor of Mauritius. To a more limited extent the question also came to the Tribunal in the case concerning *Land Reclamation in and around the Straits of Johor* (*Malaysia* v. *Singapore*), *Provisional Measures*, where the safeguard of the latter's navigational rights in the area was sought in association with the land works undertaken therein by Singapore, a case also settled by agreement of the parties.[45]

VII In Search of a New Balance

The latest case where maritime jurisdiction in association with territorial sovereignty came to be the core of the dispute is the 2016 Annex VII arbitration between the Philippines and the People's Republic of China concerning the South China Sea and the issue of islands and other features above or below water at high tide.[46] While the case was decided in the framework of the PCA and not that of the Tribunal, the interrelationship between these two major specialized jurisdictional institutions is unavoidable as it became evident in prior cases concerning proceedings under Annex VII of the Convention.

Disputes touching upon such sensitive questions have in reality two dimensions. The first is the legal reasoning of the award, which correctly interpreted the meaning of the Convention in this matter. The second dimension is

---

45 *Land Reclamation in and around the Straits of Johor* (*Malaysia* v. *Singapore*), *Provisional Measures, Order of 8 October 2003, ITLOS Reports 2003*, p. 10.

46 *The South China Sea Arbitration* (*The Republic of Philippines* v. *The People's Republic of China*), PCA Case No. 2013–19, 12 July 2016.

different and concerns the perception of one of the parties that its fundamental interests were not duly taken into account. This is where the appropriate balance is on occasions altered to the point of making the implementation of the award very difficult to achieve and eventually alienating the aggrieved party from international dispute settlement proceedings.

However different the legal and geographical aspects of the *Beagle Channel Arbitration* were,[47] there is nonetheless a striking similarity with the case now under consideration. Queen Elizabeth's award with the advice of a distinguished arbitration commission, composed of five judges of the ICJ, was legally of high quality and fully consistent with the interpretation of treaties in force and the consideration of geographical circumstances in the area. The fact is, however, that one of the parties perceived that its fundamental interests had not been duly taken into account, refused to recognize and implement the award and proceeded to its unilateral annulment, prompting extremely strained relations between the parties.

Negotiations followed and good offices and mediation by the late Pope John Paul II intervened to find a solution to the problem. After eight years of hard work the process succeeded and a Treaty of Peace and Friendship was signed and implemented, bringing the dispute to an end. One of the key contributions made by that mediation was the identification of the precise interests of each party. While for Chile such interest was the sovereignty over the disputed islands and the respect of the delimitation line of the award in the Beagle Channel, for Argentina the major interest was to avoid that Chile's maritime jurisdiction might be extended to the South Atlantic Ocean.

The Treaty fully respected these two essential interests. Even if the award is not mentioned by name in the Treaty, the Beagle Channel arbitration line of delimitation and the consequential sovereignty over the islands is kept intact, while at the same time Argentina's concern was addressed by a line of delimitation drawn in the open seas beyond the territorial sea.

As has already been repeatedly proposed by the People's Republic of China the answer to the dispute is to be found in the context of negotiations between the parties concerned, having also considered that the award is null and void. To the extent that such negotiations are undertaken and come to the precise identification of the fundamental interests of the parties, if necessary accompanied by some form of mediation, the very role of the award might be safeguarded while in some way taking care of the aggrieved interest. Evidently this is a long term effort, evidencing that the award is not the end of the dispute

47 *Dispute between Argentina and Chile concerning the Beagle Channel*, 18 February 1977, *RIAA* Vol. XXI pp. 53–264.

settlement process but only its beginning. While conceived in a different context the conciliation provided for under article 298 of the Convention and Annex V pursues a similar objective of securing a friendly settlement between the parties.[48]

The significant contribution of the Tribunal to the development of international law that has been outlined would be certainly enhanced if awards and judgments dealing specifically with the law of the sea come to bear fruit, a proposition none too evident in the light of the recent case law of the ICJ and some of the awards noted. The participation of major actors of the international legal system in dispute settlement proceedings would be certainly strengthened as a result.

---

48 *Conciliation between The Democratic Republic of Timor-Leste and The Commonwealth of Australia*, PCA Case No. 2016–10.

The Principle of Due Regard

Bernard H. Oxman

In the course of the past twenty years, the Tribunal has made significant contributions to the progressive development of international law. I would propose to focus on one object of those contributions, namely the principle of due regard, which has emerged from the opinions of the Tribunal as one of the great organizing principles of the law of the sea.

One of law's most important functions is to advance common interests. This includes the shared interest in accommodation of competing interests. Law advances this shared interest in many different ways. One way is through rules of self-restraint. The importance of such rules is particularly apparent in two contexts that intersect in the law of the sea.

One context is regimes that confer freedom of action. The enjoyment of such freedom demands self-restraint. It requires that others respect our freedom. And so it requires us to respect theirs.

The other context is regimes that allocate jurisdiction. The exercise of jurisdiction also demands self-restraint. It requires that others respect our jurisdiction. And so it requires us to respect theirs.

The high seas regime, which has long been a central part of the law of the sea, has two characteristics that illustrate this intersection. One is the freedom of all States to use the high seas. The other is the authority of every State to confer its nationality on ships (and later aircraft) and grant them the privilege of making use of the freedom of the seas.

As lawyers, we know that rules of self-restraint are what distinguishes the regime for a common area from anarchy. This is true of any commons, be it the high seas or a public park. And thus we probably should not be surprised that, in its 1956 Report to the UN General Assembly, the ILC referred to the basic principle of self-restraint not in the text of its draft article 27 on freedom of the high seas, but rather in its commentary on that article. The Commission said: "States are bound to refrain from any acts which might adversely affect the use of the high seas by nationals of other States."[1]

1 ILC, Report on the Work of Its Eighth Session, UN Doc. A/3159, at p. 278, Art. 27, commentary, para. 1 (1956).

© 2018, BY INTERNATIONAL TRIBUNAL FOR THE LAW OF THE SEA | DOI 10.1163/9789004356832_013

The text that emerged as article 2 of the 1958 Convention on the High Seas explicitly articulates the basic principle of self-restraint: it says the freedoms of the high seas "shall be exercised by all States with reasonable regard to the interests of other States in their exercise of the freedom of the high seas".[2] This rule is repeated in article 87 of the Convention, but with the term "reasonable regard" changed to "due regard". This textual change was not substantive. I first pointed this out in 1982 with respect to the French text,[3] and repeated the point in 1984 with respect to the English text in the following terms:

> The change from "reasonable regard" in the English text of article 2 of the 1958 Convention on the High Seas to "due regard" in the English text of the 1982 Convention is the result of a retranslation of the Spanish term "debida consideración" (which is the Spanish equivalent of "reasonable regard" in the Convention on the High Seas) as "due regard" or "due consideration" in proposed Second Committee texts originally drafted by Spanish speaking delegates. There was no suggestion that the change was substantive. On the other hand, paragraphs 1 and 3 of article 147, a First Committee text, were drawn directly from proposals by the United States, and thus retained the "reasonable regard" terminology. In this connection, it should be noted that articles 87, paragraph 2, and 147, paragraph 3, in part address the same duty, but use "due regard" and "reasonable regard" respectively to express that duty.[4]

2 Convention on the High Seas, 29 April 1958, 450 *UNTS*, 11.

3 B.H. Oxman, "Le Régime des navires de guerre dans le cadre de la Convention des Nations Unis sur le Droit de la Mer", 28 *Annuaire français de droit international* (1982) p. 823, n. 22. ("Le changement de l'expression 'en tenant raisonnablement compte', employée dans le texte de la Convention sur la haute mer, en 'en tenant dûment compte', formule qui figure dans le texte de la nouvelle convention, vient de ce que la formule espagnole 'debida consideraciôn' (qui, dans la Convention de 1958, est l'équivalent espagnol de 'en tenant raisonnablement compte') a été retraduite en 'en tant dûment compte' dans les propositions initialement rédigées par des délégations hispanophones.").

4 B.H. Oxman, "The Regime of Warships under the United Nations Convention on the Law of the Sea", 24 *Virginia Journal of International Law* (1984), p. 827, n. 52. The rendering in four of the authentic texts of the basic provisions of the Convention setting forth the duty and of article 2 of the 1958 Convention on the High Seas is as follows:

I was subsequently pleased to discover that Judge Nelson, citing the foregoing passage in a 1989 essay on the high seas regime,[5] and Judge Anderson, citing Judge Nelson in a 2005 paper, agreed that the change was not substantive.[6]

Use of the term "due regard" to articulate the underlying duty of self-restraint has a respectable pedigree. The term is used in that context in the

---

Article	English	French	Russian	Spanish
56(2)	shall have due regard	tient dûment compte	должным образом учитывает	tendrá debidamente en cuenta
58(3)	shall have due regard	tiennent dûment compte	должным образом учитывают	tendrán debidamente en cuenta
87(2)	with due regard	en tenant dûment compte	должным образом учитывая	teniendo debidamente en cuenta
147(1) 147(3)	with reasonable regard	en tenant raisonnablement compte	с разумным учетом	teniendo razonablemente en cuenta
1958 *HS Art.* 2	with reasonable regard	en tenant raisonnablement compte	разумно учитывая	con la debida consideración

5 L.D.M. Nelson, "Certain Aspects of the Legal Regime of the High Seas", in Y. Dinstein (ed.), *International Law at a Time of Perplexity, Essays in Honour of Shabtai Rosenne* (Springer, 1989), p. 527, n. 31.

6 D. Anderson, "Freedoms of the High Seas in the Modern Law of the Sea", in D. Freestone, R. Barnes, and D. Ong (eds.), *The Law of the Sea: Progress and Prospects* (Oxford University Press, 2006), p. 327, 332 ("So far as I am aware, there was no intention at the Conference to change the content of the 'reasonable regard' test. The change from the well-known term 'reasonable' to the rather less familiar word 'due' is no more than semantic. The due regard test is an element in the principle of good faith: rights must be exercised reasonably. The interests of others in their exercise of the same or similar freedoms must be taken into account and not simply ignored. The selfish disregard of the interests of others could well amount to an abuse of rights, contrary to article 300.") *But see* the Separate Opinion of Judge Laing in *M/V "SAIGA" (No. 2)* (*Saint Vincent and the Grenadines* v. *Guinea*), *Judgment, ITLOS Reports 1999*, p. 10 at p. 175, para. 32 (the "standard of 'due regard' is less ambulatory and open-textured than is the standard of 'reasonable regard' in the counterpart article 2 of the High Seas Convention").

1944 Convention on International Civil Aviation,[7] in the 1967 Outer Space Treaty,[8] and in the 1974 judgment of the International Court of Justice in the *Fisheries Jurisdiction* case.[9]

In the sense of a rule of self-restraint requiring respect for the rights and freedoms of other actors, I count some 10 specific provisions in which a "due regard" obligation is set forth in the Convention.[10] To this I would add the two paragraphs of article 147 that use "reasonable regard" to make the same point.

---

7 Convention on International Civil Aviation, 7 December 1944, 15 *UNTS* 295, Art. 3(d) (state aircraft "will have due regard for the safety of navigation of civil aircraft").

8 Treaty on Principles Governing the Activities of States in the Exploration and Use of Outer Space, including the Moon and Other Celestial Bodies, 27 January 1967, 610 *UNTS* 205, Art. 9 ("States Parties to the Treaty ... shall conduct all their activities in outer space, including the Moon and other celestial bodies, with due regard to the corresponding interests of all other States Parties to the Treaty").

9 *Fisheries Jurisdiction (United Kingdom* v. *Iceland), Merits, Judgment, I.C.J. Reports 1974*, p. 3, para. 72, and *Fisheries Jurisdiction (Federal Republic of Germany* v. *Iceland), Merits, Judgment, I.C.J. Reports 1974*, p. 175, para. 64, ("the former laissez-faire treatment of the living resources of the sea in the high seas has been replaced by a recognition of a duty to have due regard to the rights of other States and the needs of conservation for the benefit of all").

10 United Nations Convention on the Law of the Sea, 10 December, 1982, 1833 *UNTS* 3 (hereafter "UNCLOS"):

- Art. 27, para. 4 ("In considering whether or in what manner an arrest should be made, the local authorities shall have due regard to the interests of navigation");
- Art. 39, para. 3(a) (State aircraft "will have due regard for the safety of navigation of civil aircraft"); see *supra* at note 7;
- Art. 56, para. 2 ("[i]n exercising its rights and performing its duties under this Convention in the exclusive economic zone, the coastal State shall have due regard to the rights and duties of other States");
- Art. 58, para. 3 ("[i]n exercising their rights and performing their duties under this Convention in the exclusive economic zone, States shall have due regard to the rights and duties of the coastal State");
- Art. 60, para. 3 ("Such removal [of installations and structures] shall also have due regard to fishing, the protection of the marine environment and the rights and duties of other States");
- Art. 66, para. 3(a) ("States concerned shall maintain consultations with a view to achieving agreement on terms and conditions of [fishing for anadromous stocks beyond the outer limits of the EEZ] giving due regard to the conservation requirements and the needs of the State of origin in respect of these stocks");
- Art. 79, para. 5 ("When laying submarine cables or pipelines, States shall have due regard to cables or pipelines already in position") (incorporated by reference in article 112);

Article 22, paragraph 1, uses only the term "regard" without any adjective. Other terms are also used in the Convention to convey the same underlying idea. Following the lead of the 1958 Convention on the Continental Shelf,[11] four provisions of the Convention articulate the point in the negative, requiring States to avoid "unjustifiable interference" with the rights and interests of others.[12] In a similar vein, two provisions dealing with the seabed proscribe infringement.[13] Following the lead of the 1958 Convention on the Territorial Sea and the

---

- Art. 87, para. 2 ("These freedoms shall be exercised by all States with due regard for the interests of other States in their exercise of the freedom of the high seas, and also with due regard for the rights under this Convention with respect to activities in the Area");
- Art. 142, para. 1 ("Activities in the Area, with respect to resource deposits in the Area which lie across limits of national jurisdiction, shall be conducted with due regard to the rights and legitimate interests of any coastal State across whose jurisdiction such deposits lie");
- Art. 234 (coastal State laws and regulations for the prevention, reduction and control of marine pollution from vessels in ice-covered areas within the limits of the EEZ "shall have due regard to navigation and the protection and preservation of the marine environment based on the best available scientific evidence").

11 *Convention on the Continental Shelf*, Art. 5, para. 1, 29 April 1958, 499 *UNTS* 311 ("exploration of the continental shelf and the exploitation of its natural resources must not result in any unjustifiable interference with navigation, fishing or the conservation of the living resources of the sea").

12 The provisions are:
- UNCLOS, art. 78, para. 2 ("The exercise of the rights of the coastal State over the continental shelf must not infringe or result in any unjustifiable interference with navigation and other rights and freedoms of other States as provided for in this Convention");
- UNCLOS, art. 194, para. 4 ("In taking measures to prevent, reduce or control pollution of the marine environment, States shall refrain from unjustifiable interference with activities carried out by other States in the exercise of their rights and in pursuance of their duties in conformity with this Convention");
- UNCLOS, art. 240(c) ("marine scientific research shall not unjustifiably interfere with other legitimate uses of the sea compatible with this Convention and shall be duly respected in the course of such uses");
- UNCLOS, art. 246, para. 8 ("Marine scientific research activities referred to in this article [in the EEZ and continental shelf] shall not unjustifiably interfere with activities undertaken by coastal States in the exercise of their sovereign rights and jurisdiction provided for in this Convention").

13 The provisions are:
- UNCLOS, art. 78, para. 2 ("The exercise of the rights of the coastal State over the continental shelf must not infringe or result in any unjustifiable interference with navigation and other rights and freedoms of other States as provided for in this Convention");
- UNCLOS, art. 142, para. 2 ("Consultations, including a system of prior notification, shall be maintained with the State concerned, with a view to avoiding infringement of such rights and interests").

Contiguous Zone,[14] four provisions of the Convention prohibit hampering of navigation rights of other States in areas subject to the sovereignty of the coastal State.[15]

Taken together, the provisions of the Convention that set forth the underlying rule substantially broaden the circumstances in which the rule of self-restraint is expressly applicable. But that said, it is evident that most remain rooted in the classic high seas regime in the sense that the duty applies either to protect, or to limit, the exercise of freedoms of the sea. This of course does not exhaust the possibilities. And it is in addressing newer issues that the Tribunal has made two things clear: first, that the specific provisions in the Convention are manifestations of a more general organizing principle of due regard in the law of the sea; and second, that the underlying duty is not only a negative one, but requires due diligence by a state, including regulatory and enforcement action, to secure compliance by its nationals and vessels with the duty of due regard.

As to the first point: in the *Bay of Bengal* (*Bangladesh/Myanmar*) case,[16] the Tribunal was faced with an issue that had intrigued law of the sea aficionados for many years, especially after the emergence in the Convention of the 200 mile limit of the EEZ. As the ICJ observed in the *North Sea Continental Shelf* cases, in certain circumstances the use of an equidistance line to delimit overlapping entitlements may not bear an appropriate relation to the respective coasts of the parties, and the magnitude of a cut-off effect may increase with distance from the coast.[17] Citing that observation, the Tribunal in the *Bay of Bengal* case adjusted the provisional equidistance line it had drawn so that the

---

14 *Convention on the Territorial Sea and the Contiguous Zone,* Art. 15, para. 1, 29 April, 1958, 516 *UNTS* 205 ("The coastal State must not hamper innocent passage through the territorial sea").

15 The provisions are:
- UNCLOS, *supra*, at note 12, Art. 24 ("The coastal State shall not hamper the innocent passage of foreign ship through the territorial sea");
- UNCLOS, art. 42, para. 2 (straits State "laws and regulations shall not ... in their application have the practical effect of denying, hampering or impairing the right of transit passage as defined in this section");
- UNCLOS, art. 44 ("States bordering straits shall not hamper transit passage"); – UNCLOS, art. 211, para. 4 (coastal State laws and regulations for the prevention, reduction and control of marine pollution from foreign vessels in the territorial sea "shall ... not hamper innocent passage of foreign vessels").

16 *Delimitation of the maritime boundary in the Bay of Bengal* (*Bangladesh/Myanmar*), *Judgment, ITLOS Reports 2012*, p. 4 (hereafter "*Bay of Bengal* case").

17 *North Sea Continental Shelf* (*Federal Republic of Germany/Denmark; Federal Republic of Germany/Netherlands*), *Judgment, I.C.J. Reports 1969*, p. 3.

seaward segment of the maritime boundary would bear a more appropriate relation to the respective coasts of the parties.

The difficulty is that if a line of delimitation reaches the 200 mile limit of one of the States at a point that is not equidistant from the respective coasts of the parties, continuation of that line in the same direction beyond 200 nm may result in what has been called a "grey area" that is seaward of the 200 nm zone of one State and beyond the line of delimitation that limits the jurisdiction of the other.[18]

One possible response by a tribunal is to defer the problem by stopping the maritime boundary where it reaches the nearest 200 mile limit; that is what a chamber of the ICJ did in the *Gulf of Maine* case.[19] Another is to avoid the problem by changing the direction of the line and continuing it along the nearest 200 mile limit until it reaches a point that is equidistant (namely 200 nm) from both coasts; that is what the ICJ did in the *Peru* v. *Chile* case.[20]

In the *Bay of Bengal* case the Tribunal was faced with a continental shelf that unquestionably extended beyond 200 nm, as the Law of the Sea Conference itself expressly recognized. Moreover, the Tribunal concluded that the reasons for adjusting the provisional equidistance line within 200 nm remained relevant to delimitation of the continental shelf beyond 200 nm as well. But because only the continental shelf entitlements of the parties overlapped beyond the nearest 200 mile limit, the delimitation would produce a triangular area between the respective 200 mile limits that was subject to the rights of one coastal State with respect to the seabed and subsoil but did not otherwise limit the other coastal State's rights pursuant to the regime of the EEZ, notably with respect to the superjacent waters.[21]

The text of the Convention makes no express provision for this situation. The Tribunal held that the underlying principle of due regard reflected in many provisions of the Convention applies in this situation as well. The Tribunal recalled:

> the legal regime of the continental shelf has always coexisted with another legal regime in the same area. Initially that other regime was that of the high seas and the other States concerned were those exercising high seas freedoms. Under the Convention, as a result of maritime delimita-

18 See *Bay of Bengal* case, *supra* at note 16, at p. 119, para. 464.

19 *Delimitation of the Maritime Boundary in the Gulf of Maine Area (Canada/United States of America), Judgment, I.C.J. Reports 1984*, p. 246, para. 228.

20 *Maritime Dispute (Peru* v. *Chile), Judgment, I.C.J. Reports 2014*, p. 3, para. 198(4).

21 *Bay of Bengal* case, *supra* at note 16, at p. 121, para. 474.

> tion, there may also be concurrent exclusive economic zone rights of another coastal State. In such a situation, pursuant to the principle reflected in the provisions of articles 56, 58, 78 and 79 and in other provisions of the Convention, each coastal State must exercise its rights and perform its duties with due regard to the rights and duties of the other.[22]

Similarly, while the due regard provisions of articles 56 and 58 of the Convention are focused on the reciprocal obligations of coastal States and flag States in the EEZ, in its Advisory Opinion on fisheries in 2015, the Tribunal reached essentially the same conclusion regarding the mutual obligations of coastal States in their respective EEZs. It observed that while States have sovereign rights to explore, exploit, conserve and manage the living resources in their EEZs, "in exercising their rights and performing their duties under the Convention in their respective exclusive economic zones, they must have due regard to the rights and duties of one another."[23] The Tribunal explained that this "flows from articles 56, paragraph 2, and 58, paragraph 3, of the Convention and from the States Parties' obligation to protect and preserve the marine environment, a fundamental principle underlined in articles 192 and 193 of the Convention."[24]

As to the second point, the Convention does of course contain specific provisions requiring a State to take affirmative steps to ensure respect for international regulations that implement the duty of due regard. The best known relate to the duties of a State under article 94 to assume jurisdiction over each ship flying its flag and it master, officers and crew, to take such measures for those ships as are necessary to ensure safety at sea with regard to the use of signals, the maintenance of communication and the prevention of collisions, and in doing so to conform to generally accepted international regulations, procedures and practices and to take any steps which may be necessary to secure their observance. In rejecting challenges to the status of a State as the flag State on grounds of the genuine link requirement, the Tribunal has twice underscored the importance of ensuring that there is a flag State to carry out the foregoing duties. In 1999, in the *M/V "SAIGA" (No. 2) Case (Saint Vincent and the Grenadines* v. *Guinea)*, the Tribunal concluded that "the purpose of the provisions of the Convention on the need for a genuine link between a ship and its flag State is to secure more effective implementation of the duties of the flag State, and not to establish criteria by reference to which the validity of

22 *Ibid.*, para. 475.

23 *Request for an Advisory Opinion submitted by the Sub-Regional Fisheries Commission, Advisory Opinion, 2 April 2015, ITLOS Reports 2015*, p. 4, at p. 61, para. 216.

24 *Ibid.*

the registration of ships in a flag State may be challenged by other States."[25] In 2014, in the *M/V "Virginia G" Case* (*Panama/Guinea-Bissau*), the Tribunal reaffirmed this statement, adding that "once a ship is registered, the flag State is required, under article 94 of the Convention, to exercise effective jurisdiction and control over that ship in order to ensure that it operates in accordance with generally accepted international regulations, procedures and practices. This is the meaning of 'genuine link'."[26]

The Convention and the regulations of the Authority also set forth specific duties of a State that sponsors mining activities in the international seabed "Area" as well as the obligations of the sponsored contractor. In its 2011 Advisory Opinion, the Tribunal's Seabed Disputes Chamber's comprehensive analysis of the duties of the sponsoring State included the following observation: "It is inherent in the 'due diligence' obligation of the sponsoring State to ensure that the obligations of a sponsored contractor are made enforceable."[27]

In its 1974 Judgment in the *Fisheries Jurisdiction* case, the ICJ observed: "It is one of the advances in maritime international law, resulting from the intensification of fishing, that the former laissez-faire treatment of the living resources of the sea in the high seas has been replaced by a recognition of a duty to have due regard to the rights of other States and the needs of conservation for the benefit of all."[28] This duty is reflected in the Convention's provisions on conservation and management of living resources and in the Convention's 1995 Implementation Agreement on fisheries. The Tribunal signaled its willingness to enforce this duty in its 1999 provisional measures Order in the *Southern Bluefin Tuna Cases* (*New Zealand* v. *Japan; Australia* v. *Japan*).[29] This stands in marked contrast to the subsequent decision of the first arbitral tribunal constituted under the Convention to decline jurisdiction in that case;[30] it did so on

25 *M/V "SAIGA" (No. 2)*, *supra* at note 6, at p. 42, para. 83.

26 *M/V "Virginia G" (Panama* v. *Guinea Bissau), Judgment, ITLOS Reports 2014*, p. 4, at p. 14, para. 113.

27 *Responsibilities and obligations of States with respect to activities in the Area, Advisory Opinion, 1 February 2011, ITLOS Reports 2011*, p. 10, at p. 73, para. 239.

28 *Fisheries Jurisdiction (United Kingdom* v. *Iceland), Merits, Judgment, I.C.J. Reports 1974*, p. 3, para. 72, and *Fisheries Jurisdiction (Federal Republic of Germany* v. *Iceland), Merits, Judgment, I.C.J. Reports 1974*, p. 175, para. 64.

29 *Southern Bluefin Tuna (New Zealand* v. *Japan; Australia* v. *Japan), Provisional Measures, Order of 27 August 1999, ITLOS Reports 1999*, p. 280.

30 *Southern Bluefin Tuna (Australia* v. *Japan; New Zealand* v. *Japan)*, 4 August 2000, *RIAA* Vol. XXIII, p. 48, para. 72.

controversial grounds that were recently rejected by another arbitral tribunal constituted under the Convention.[31]

The elaboration of the regime of the EEZ, including the sovereign rights of the coastal State to conserve and manage the living resources of the zone, is a major element of the Convention's response to the problems to which the ICJ adverted in its 1974 judgment. But this did not displace the due regard duty. The Tribunal elaborated on this point in the *Request for an Advisory Opinion submitted by the Sub-Regional Fisheries Commission* of April 2015. Citing the flag State's duty under article 58, paragraph 3, to have due regard to the rights and duties of the coastal State in the EEZ, the obligation of all States under article 192 to protect and preserve the marine environment, and the requirement under article 62, paragraph 4, that nationals of other States fishing in the EEZ comply with coastal State regulations, the Tribunal concluded that "while under the Convention the primary responsibility for the conservation and management of living resources in the exclusive economic zone ... rests with the coastal State, flag States also have the responsibility to ensure that vessels flying their flag do not conduct [illegal, unreported and unregulated] fishing activities within the exclusive economic zones" of other States.[32] Referring to this analysis, an arbitral tribunal constituted under the Convention recently observed that "anything less than due diligence by a State in preventing its nationals from unlawfully fishing in the exclusive economic zone of another would fall short of the regard due pursuant to Article 58(3) of the Convention."[33]

Lawyers around the world are well aware that new tribunals may be created for the purpose of explicating a new constitutional order, thereby facilitating its effective implementation. So it is with the law of the sea. As the decisions of the Tribunal to which I have adverted make clear, those of us who were, as they say, present at the creation of the Tribunal can take particular satisfaction in the way in which it has fulfilled this function during the past two decades. The Tribunal has discerned in the underlying structure of the law of the sea under the Convention a duty of due regard that has emerged as a basic organizing principle, and it has provided wise guidance to states on how that principle may be applied to confront challenges old and new, foreseen and unforeseen.

---

31 *The South China Sea Arbitration* (*The Republic of Philippines* v. *The People's Republic of China*), PCA Case No. 2013–19, 29 October 2015, para. 223.

32 *Request for Advisory Opinion submitted by the Sub-Regional Fisheries Commission, Advisory Opinion, 2 April 2015, ITLOS Reports 2015*, p. 4, at p. 38, para. 124.

33 *The South China Sea Arbitration, supra* at note 31, 12 July 2016, para. 744.

The Contribution of the Tribunal to the Progressive Development of International Law

Tullio Scovazzi

I The Role of Courts in the Progressive Development of International Law

In addressing cases submitted to them, courts can contribute to the progressive development of international law in two different ways, depending on whether treaty or customary rules are involved. First, courts can be called to make a choice among divergent interpretations of the applicable treaty provisions; second, they can have the opportunity to take part in the process of formation and evolution of customary rules. Some considerations may be useful as regards the latter instance.

The assumption that courts apply customary international rules and cannot create them finds support in Article 38, paragraph 1(d), of the Statute of the ICJ, according to which judicial decisions are only subsidiary means for the determination of rules of law. The idea is that, as an international customary rule already exists in the form of a general practice accepted as law, a judicial decision can only ascertain the content of it. The court makes the determination that in fact a settled practice is taking place (*repetita iuvant*) and the corresponding behaviour is believed by States or other international law subjects to be legally obligatory (*opinio iuris sive necessitatis*).[1]

However, the assumption that courts can only apply legal rules is not completely true. For a number of reasons, creative aspects can be found in several

1 As stated by the ICJ in the Judgment of 20 February 1969 in the *North Sea Continental Shelf* cases, "not only must the acts concerned amount to a settled practice, but they must also be such, or be carried out in such a way, as to be evidence of a belief that this practice is rendered obligatory by the existence of a rule of law requiring it. The need for such a belief, i.e., the existence of a subjective element, is implicit in the very notion of the *opinio juris sive necessitatis*. The States concerned must therefore feel that they are conforming to what amounts to a legal obligation. The frequency or even habitual character of the acts is not in itself enough. There are many international acts, e.g., in the field of ceremonial and protocol, which are performed almost invariably, but which are motivated only by considerations of courtesy, convenience or tradition, and not by any sense of legal duty", *North Sea Continental Shelf (Federal Republic of Germany/Denmark; Federal Republic of Germany/Netherlands), Judgment, I.C.J. Reports 1969*, p. 3, para. 77.

© 2018, BY INTERNATIONAL TRIBUNAL FOR THE LAW OF THE SEA | DOI 10.1163/9789004356832_014

court decisions, at least in the sense that courts orientated the evolution of customary international law.

First, although they do not have the authority of binding precedents, courts' decisions, when they confirm existing rules, also strengthen such rules. As it has been remarked with regard to the ICJ – but the same can be repeated today also for the Tribunal – a court's reasoning in law "enters into the general storehouse of public international law"[2].

Second, as customary international law is not published in written form in any official journal, in certain cases it is not easy to determine if and when a new rule has come into effect. Instances where two different normative propositions are put forward, and where it is difficult to balance the weight of each of them, are an inevitable occurrence in a system where non-written rules have an important role to play. The former rule is put into question and is progressively eroded by an innovating trend until the moment, if any, when a reversal of positions takes place and the trend becomes the new rule. In the foggy weather when the distinction between the old and the new law remains blurred, courts can make a choice on what actually is the applicable regime.

Third, in certain cases a customary rule presents a quite general character and courts are called to give a more precise content to it.[3] Here courts disclose what may be considered as implicit in the rule, but in fact is the result of their understanding of the object and purpose of the rule in the light of the specific case.[4]

---

2 "The Court's reasoning in law – its statement of what it regards as the correct legal position *and why* – enters into the general storehouse of public international law. That is why the decisions of the International Court become one of the most important reservoirs today for the rules of international law, and indeed one of the law's most powerful instruments for adaptation to the constantly changing conditions", S. Rosenne, *The World Court*, 5th ed. (Martinus Nijhoff, 1995), p. 148.

3 "In fact, the role performed by the ICJ often goes beyond the mere stating of existing customary law. By stating what is implied in existing rules and extracting general principles from such rules, the ICJ has developed important chapters of international law, such as the law of delimitation of maritime areas and the law of effective nationality, and added density to many areas of the law. In doing so the Court deploys a relevant amount of creativity, adopting in many cases an inductive approach that contrasts with the deductive process it describes as appropriate for determining the contents of international customary law", T. Treves, "International Law: Achievements and Challenges" in *Cursos Euromediterráneos Bancaja de Derecho International* (2006), p. 85.

4 "Here (…) the customary norm has no existence until the judge determines its content. It is this determination which gives it life and identity. Custom is here defined without reference to any State conduct. It is disembodied custom. The content of customary law no longer derives from a combination of State practice and *opinio juris* but directly from the law-making

Fourth, it may also happen that, in cases where the actual legal regime is felt to be inadequate, courts determine that a completely new rule has emerged and becomes applicable to the specific instance. Here the creative role of courts assumes its most evident dimension, as they exercise a quasi-legislative function.[5]

While opportunities to orientate the progressive development of international law do not often arise, they should be given serious consideration by courts when they occur. This would be consistent with the assumption that the main purpose of law is not conservation, but development and change.

II The Evolutionary Aspects of Judgments Relating to Law of the Sea

Evidence of the creative role of courts are found in a number of international decisions, starting from the case-law of the ICJ itself. Since some notable instances relate to law of the sea, they can be usefully recalled also in the context of an analysis intended to mainly focus on the Tribunal.

A *Where the ICJ Created a Rule (Straight Baselines)*

A meaningful decision, from the point of view of the creation of a customary international rule, is the ICJ Judgment of 18 December 1951 in the *Fisheries* case (*United Kingdom* v. *Norway*).[6]

As an exception to the rule that coastal zones are measured from the low water mark, Norway was the first State to establish a straight baseline system from which the breadth of its territorial sea was measured (by a Royal Decree of 12 July 1935).[7] The segments of the baselines were drawn in the sea and joined appropriate points located on headlands or on the numerous islands and islets in the vicinity of the coastline. The preamble of the 1935 decree made reference to "the geographic conditions prevailing on the Norwegian coast" and the

power of the international courts. In short, customary law is none other than judge-made law", P. Weil, *The Law of Maritime Delimitation – Reflections*, (Cambridge University Press, 1989), p. 155.

5 A well-known instance is the award of 11 March 1941 in the *Trail smelter case* (*United States, Canada*) (*RIAA* Vol. III, p. 1965), where the arbitral tribunal established by Canada and the United States enunciated the rule on the prohibition of transboundary pollution.

6 *Fisheries* (*United Kingdom* v. *Norway*), *Judgment, I.C.J. Reports 1951*, p. 116. The decisions on the two questions submitted to the ICJ were taken by ten votes to two and by eight votes to four, respectively.

7 The 1935 decree applied to the Norwegian coasts located beyond the Polar Circle.

need to "safeguard the vital interest of the inhabitants of the northernmost parts of the country". In fact, no general practice existed in this regard and no precedent for such a measure could be found in the legislation of other States. The closing by a line of the entrance to a single bay – a measure that some States had previously taken – was not comparable to a straight baseline system composed of 47 segments along a coast which was over 1,500 kilometres in length.

The legality of the method of straight baselines was questioned by the United Kingdom before the ICJ. By finding in its 1951 Judgment that the Norwegian baselines were not contrary to international law, the ICJ provided a significant contribution to the evolution of (or, better, determined a radical change in) international law of the sea. To reach its conclusion, the ICJ relied on three different and concurring kinds of factors of geographic, economic and historical character. First, the ICJ took into full consideration the almost unique geographic features of the Norwegian coastline, in particular the typical deep indentations (fjords) and the numerous islands and islets fringing it (the *skjærgård*, composed of almost 120,000 insular formations of different size).[8] According to the ICJ, geographic realities dictated that, in the specific case, the baseline could depart from the natural limit of the low water mark and be drawn according to a method based on a geometric construction.[9] Second, the ICJ took into consideration the weight of the economic factors existing in the region, in particular the traditional fishing activities which by far represented the main source of earnings for the local population.[10] Third, historic factors also influenced the decision, since previous measures adopted by Norway, although not as extensive as the 1935 decree, had not given rise to opposition by other States.[11]

Such a thorough explanation about the reasonableness of the new rule applied by the ICJ was probably intended to replace the absence of any general practice that could support it. The creative character of the 1951 judgment is impressive. Can a number of factors that would qualify a national measure as *per se* reasonable overcome a total lack of precedents and justify a radical departure from a consolidated customary rule? In 1951 the ICJ gave a positive

8 *Fisheries (United Kingdom* v. *Norway), Judgment, I.C.J. Reports 1951*, p. 116, at p. 127.

9 *Ibid.*, at p. 129. Rather than prescribing precise limits of length for the single segments of the baseline, as was suggested by the United Kingdom, the ICJ preferred to enunciate the flexible condition that straight baselines must not depart to any appreciable extent from the general direction of the coast (ibid., p. 133).

10 *Ibid.*, at p. 127 and 133. Oil had not yet been discovered in the Norwegian continental shelf.

11 *Ibid.*, at p. 138.

answer to the question, probably because it felt that the change corresponded to an improvement in international law and that it could be confined to the rare situations of Norwegian-type coastlines.

The position taken by the ICJ influenced the drafters of subsequent codification treaties to such an extent that some key passages of the 1951 Judgment were literally reproduced in the wording of the relevant provisions of the 1958 Convention on the Territorial Sea and the Contiguous Zone and, thereafter, the Convention: "where the coastline is deeply indented and cut into" (article 7, paragraph 1, of the Convention) reflects "where a coast is deeply indented and cut into" (1951 Judgment);[12] "the drawing of straight baselines must not depart to any appreciable extent from the general direction of the coast" (article 7, paragraph 3, of the Convention) reflects "the drawing of baselines must not depart to any appreciable extent from the general direction of the coast" (1951 Judgment);[13] "the sea areas lying within the lines must be sufficiently closely linked to the land domain to be subject to the regime of internal waters" (article 7, paragraph 3, of the Convention) reflects "areas lying within these lines are sufficiently closely linked to the land domain to be subject to the regime of internal waters" (1951 Judgment);[14] "economic interests peculiar to the region concerned, the reality and the importance of which are clearly evidenced by long usage" (article 7, paragraph 5, of the Convention) reflects "certain economic interests peculiar to a region, the reality and importance of which are clearly evidenced by a long usage" (1951 Judgment).[15] The ICJ Judgment could also have influenced the choice of not indicating in the 1958 Geneva Convention and the Convention any maximum length for segments of a straight baseline.

However, the effects of the choice made by the ICJ did not remain confined to the specific case of Norwegian-type coastlines. The 1951 Judgment determined a widespread practice among coastal States, including several whose coastline is geographically very different from the Norwegian one. As the majority of coastal States have today established straight baselines, present international practice follows a much more liberal trend than the literal reading of the 1951 Judgment and the provisions of the Convention would allow. This gave rise to some concerns within the ICJ itself, which, in deciding on 16 March 2001 the case on the *Maritime Delimitation and Territorial Questions between Qatar and Bahrain*, pointed out that "the method of straight baselines, which is

12 *Ibid.*, at p. 128.

13 *Ibid.*, at p. 133.

14 *Ibid.*

15 *Ibid.*

an exception to the normal rules for the determination of baselines, may only be applied if a number of conditions are met. This method must be applied restrictively."[16]

B Where the ICJ Did Not Contribute to the Creation of a Rule (Exclusive Economic Zone)

In the *Fisheries Jurisdiction* cases (*United Kingdom* v. *Iceland; Federal Republic of Germany* v. *Iceland*), both decided by the ICJ on 25 July 1974, the question at stake was the limit of coastal States' fisheries jurisdiction: whether it was restricted to a 12 mile coastal belt, as put forward by many developed States, or whether it could extend far beyond such a distance, reaching 50 nautical miles, as established by the Icelandic legislation, or even further up to 200 nautical miles, as already claimed by several Latin American and African States.[17]

Here, in a frequently quoted sentence, the ICJ pointed out that a court of law cannot anticipate the legislator, that is, the results of the conference of codification of law of the sea that was then taking place (incidentally, this is the contrary of what happened with the 1951 Judgment,[18] where the ICJ anticipated the future legislator):

> In recent years the question of extending the coastal State's fisheries jurisdiction has come increasingly to the forefront. The Court is aware that a number of states have asserted an extension of fishery limits. The Court is also aware of present endeavours, pursued under the auspices of the United Nations, to achieve in a third Conference on the Law of the Sea the further codification and progressive development of this branch of the law, as it is of various proposals and preparatory documents produced in this framework, which must be regarded as manifestations of the views and opinions of individual States and as vehicles of their aspirations, rather than as expressing principles of existing law. The very fact of convening the third Conference on the Law of the Sea evidences a manifest desire on the part of all States to proceed to the codification of that law on a universal basis, including the question of fisheries and conservation of the living resources of the sea. Such a general desire is

---

16 *Maritime Delimitation and Territorial Questions between Qatar and Bahrain (Qatar v. Bahrain), Merits, Judgment, I.C.J. Reports 2001*, p. 40, para. 212.

17 *Fisheries Jurisdiction (United Kingdom* v. *Iceland), Merits, Judgment, I.C.J. Reports 1974*, p. 3. *Fisheries Jurisdiction (Federal Republic of Germany* v. *Iceland), Merits, Judgment, I.C.J. Reports 1974*, p. 175.

18 *Supra*, section II.A.

> understandable since the rules of international maritime law have been the product of mutual accommodation, reasonableness and co-operation. So it was in the past, and so it is necessarily today. In the circumstances, the Court, as a court of law, cannot render judgment *sub specie legis ferendae*, or anticipate the law before the legislator has laid it down.[19]

The ICJ found that the extension of the exclusive fishing rights of Iceland to 50 nautical miles was not opposable to the United Kingdom and the Federal Republic of Germany.[20] This does not seem fully convincing. The crucial question was not whether a court can anticipate the legislator. As stated by the same ICJ in the Judgment of 20 February 1969 in the *North Sea Continental Shelf* cases, what becomes relevant for a customary rule is an extensive and virtually uniform State practice, including that of States whose interests are specifically affected.[21] If such a practice does not exist, because of a clash in the positions put forward by different groups of States, a court is called upon to weigh the opposing positions and make a choice on the content of the rule that it deems applicable. This may be quite a difficult choice. But there are no definite reasons why the choice should necessarily be oriented towards the past and disregard the future, that is, the evolutionary trends. Unlike what it did in 1951, in 1974 the ICJ did not take into consideration the geographic, economic and historical factors that could justify an extension of coastal States' jurisdiction as regards fisheries,[22] nor did it weigh these factors against the opposite position put forward by the major maritime powers.

---

19 *Fisheries Jurisdiction (United Kingdom* v. *Iceland), Merits, Judgment, I.C.J. Reports 1974*, p. 3, para. 53, and *Fisheries Jurisdiction (Federal Republic of Germany* v. *Iceland), Merits, Judgment, I.C.J. Reports 1974*, p. 175, para. 45.

20 The decision was taken by ten votes to four. The ICJ also found that the parties were under a mutual obligation to undertake negotiations in good faith for the equitable solution of their differences concerning fishing rights.

21 "Although the passage of only a short period of time is not necessarily, or of itself, a bar to the formation of a new rule of customary international law on the basis of what was originally a purely conventional rule, an indispensable requirement would be that within the period in question, short though it might be, State practice, including that of States whose interests are specifically affected, should have been both extensive and virtually uniform in the sense of the provision invoked; and should moreover have occurred in such a way to show a general recognition that a rule of law or legal obligation is involved" *North Sea Continental Shelf (Federal Republic of Germany/Denmark; Federal Republic of Germany/Netherlands), Judgment, I.C.J. Reports 1969*, p. 3, para. 74.

22 These reasons were already explained in the declaration on the maritime zone (*zona marítima*), jointly adopted by Chile, Ecuador and Peru on 18 August 1952. For example:

Within a short time, the 1974 Judgments were overtaken by State practice, also as a consequence of the general acceptance already in 1975 of the 200 nautical mile EEZ by the States participating in the negotiations for the future Convention. Impressive is also the fact that Iceland took the liberty to execute the 1974 Judgments in a reverse fashion: not only did it not abrogate its 50 mile fishing zone, but it also proceeded in the same year to extend it to 200 nautical miles.

C *Where Courts Give Content to a Rule* (*Maritime Delimitation*)

In the field of maritime delimitations, courts – be they the ICJ, arbitral tribunals or, more recently, the Tribunal[23] – are currently providing a decisive contribution to the clarification of the content of the applicable rule. Strangely enough, in this regard the content of the customary rule, as it results from international jurisprudence, is much more detailed than the relevant treaty provision, that is article 74, paragraph 1, of the Convention:

> The delimitation of the exclusive economic zone between States with opposite or adjacent coasts shall be effected by agreement on the basis of international law, as referred to in Article 38 of the Statute of the International Court of Justice, in order to achieve an equitable solution.[24]

The provision confirms the general obligation of the States concerned to behave in good faith in order to reach an agreement on a maritime delimitation.[25] However, article 74, paragraph 1, does not say what the content of the

---

"Los factores geológicos y biológicos que condicionan la existencia, conservación y desarrollo de la fauna y flora marítimas en las aguas que bañan las costas de los países declarantes, hacen que la antigua extensión del mar territorial y de la zona contigua sean insuficientes para la conservación, desarrollo y aprovechamiento de esas riquezas a que tienen derecho los países costeros."

23 See *infra*, section IX.

24 Article 83, para. 1, of the Convention (Delimitation of the continental shelf between States with opposite or adjacent coasts) corresponds to article 74, the only change being the words "continental shelf" instead of "exclusive economic zone".

25 The content of this obligation was specified by the ICJ in the already mentioned 1969 Judgment on the *North Sea Continental Shelf* cases: "The parties are under an obligation to enter into negotiations with a view to arriving at an agreement, and not merely to go through a formal process of negotiation as a sort of a prior condition for the automatic application of a certain method of delimitation in the absence of agreement; they are under an obligation so to conduct themselves that the negotiations are meaningful, which will not be the case when either of them insists upon its own position without contemplat-

substantive rules that become applicable if the States concerned do not reach an agreement is. The reference to Article 38 of the Statute of the ICJ, which specifies the categories of rules that the ICJ must apply, does not give any guidance on how to address the substance of the problem, that is, how to draw a line on a map. The indication of the objective of achieving an equitable solution seems pleonastic, as any agreement which has been freely negotiated by the parties embodies by definition an equitable solution.[26]

The elusive content of article 74, paragraph 1, was due to practical reasons. During the negotiations, States involved in thorny issues of maritime delimitation strongly opposed specific solutions which would have played in favour of their opposite or adjacent neighbouring countries. Also States facing manifold issues of delimitations, depending on the characteristics of their coastlines and those of the different neighbouring States concerned, preferred a vague provision which would grant them enough flexibility to play different games in different fields. It was unwise to force the situation by trying to set forth a clear-cut solution in the text of the Convention. This explains the choice of the drafters of the Convention to leave the very controversial issue of delimitation unresolved and thus avoid opening a Pandora's box that could have precluded the adoption of the Convention itself or its general acceptance.[27]

Today, starting from the already mentioned 1969 ICJ Judgment on the *North Sea Continental Shelf* cases, we can rely on a notable body of international decisions on maritime delimitations.[28] They demonstrate the use of a number of "methods" (such as equidistance, proportionality, reduced effect of certain

---

ing any modification of it" *North Sea Continental Shelf, Judgment, I.C.J. Reports 1969*, p. 3, para. 85.

26 It may be added that para. 4 of article 74 ("Where there is an agreement in force between the States concerned, questions relating to the delimitation of the exclusive zone shall be defined in accordance with the provisions of that agreement") recalls the story of Monsieur de la Palice.

27 The stalemate in the Convention is so evident that in the award rendered on 17 December 1999 in the *Eritrea – Yemen Arbitration* (*Second Stage: Maritime Delimitation*) the arbitral tribunal made the following remark: "In any event there has to be room for differences of opinion about the interpretation of articles [articles 74 and 83 of the Convention] which, in a last minute endeavour at the Third United Nations Conference on the Law of the Sea to get agreement on a very controversial matter, were consciously designed to decide as little as possible. It is clear, however, that both articles envisage an equitable result". *Second stage of the proceedings between Eritrea and Yemen* (*Maritime Delimitation*), 17 December 1999, *RIAA* Vol. XXII pp. 335–410, para. 116.

28 An interesting point, on which no elaboration can be made hereunder, is that there are sometimes inconsistencies, between one decision and another.

islands, shifting of the equidistance line, drawing of a corridor, etc.) that, in the light of the circumstances which are relevant in each specific case, are found by courts to be appropriate for delimiting maritime zones in order to achieve an equitable solution. In this regard, a logical process has been developed by courts and followed in most decisions (so-called "equitable principles/relevant circumstances method"): to draw the equidistance line, as a first criterion for reference, and then evaluate whether or not such delimitation does lead to an equitable solution; if not, an adjustment or a shifting of the line is made. As recalled in the arbitral award of 11 April 2006 on the maritime delimitation between Barbados and Trinidad and Tobago:

> the determination of the line of delimitation thus normally follows a two-step approach. First, a provisional line of equidistance is posited as a hypothesis and a practical starting point. While a convenient starting point, equidistance alone will in many circumstances not ensure an equitable result in the light of the peculiarities of each specific case. The second step accordingly requires the examination of this provisional line in the light of relevant circumstances, which are case specific, so as to determine whether it is necessary to adjust the provisional equidistance line in order to achieve an equitable result.[29]

As far as maritime delimitations are concerned, courts have provided a decisive contribution in giving a more precise content to article 74 of the Convention. In fact, they have circumvented such an elusive provision in order to revert to the previous article 6 of the 1958 Geneva Convention on the Continental Shelf, where something very close to the equitable principles/relevant circumstances method was already envisaged.[30]

29 *Arbitration between Barbados and the Republic of Trinidad and Tobago, relating to the delimitation of the exclusive economic zone and the continental shelf between them*, 11 April 2006, *RIAA* Vol. XXVII pp. 147–251, para. 242.

30 "Where the same continental shelf is adjacent to the territories of two or more States whose coasts are opposite each other, the boundary of the continental shelf appertaining to such States shall be determined by agreement between them. In the absence of agreement, and unless another boundary line is justified by special circumstances, the boundary is the median line, every point of which is equidistant from the nearest points of the baselines from which the breadth of the territorial sea of each State is measured" (para. 1; para. 2 provides in the same way for the delimitation between adjacent States).

III The Tribunal's Jurisprudence in General

As provided for in article 293 of the Convention, the Tribunal is called upon to apply the Convention and other rules of international law not incompatible with it.[31] It could thus have opportunities to orientate the progressive evolution of international law in regard to both the interpretation of treaty law (mainly the Convention) and the determination of the content of customary rules.

Although for chronological reasons limited to 12 judgments (eight of which relate to the special procedure of prompt release of vessels and crews under article 292 of the Convention), two advisory opinions and several orders,[32] the Tribunal's case law (contentious cases and advisory proceedings) has provided an important contribution to the interpretation of a number of the provisions of the Convention, as well as to the progressive development of customary international law of the sea, in fields such as fisheries,[33] maritime delimitation,[34] and use of force at sea.[35] Moreover, the Tribunal's Advisory Opinions are relevant also for other areas of customary international law, including international responsibility,[36] due diligence obligations[37] and protection of the environment in general.[38] Some doubts can be cast about the decision on the first case submitted to the Tribunal, insofar as the thorny question of the nationality of ships was addressed.[39]

The instances that seem most notable are considered hereunder.[40]

---

31 Article 293 of the Convention is recalled by article 23 of Annex VI to the Convention (Statute of the Tribunal), according to which the Tribunal "shall decide all disputes and applications in accordance with article 293".

32 The case-law of the Tribunal is periodically reviewed, together with other decisions on the law of the sea, in the *IJCML*. See most recently R. Churchill, "Dispute Settlement in the Law of the Sea: Survey for 2015 – Part I" *IJCML* (2016), p. 555.

33 See *infra*, section VII.

34 See *infra*, section IX.

35 See *infra*, section X.

36 See *infra*, section IV.

37 See *infra*, section IV.A.

38 See *infra*, section VI.

39 See *infra*, section XIII.

40 This paper will not consider the procedural questions or the questions related to the special procedures falling under the Tribunal's jurisdiction, such as provisional measures (article 290 of the Convention) or prompt release of vessels and crews (article 292).

IV International Responsibility

A *Responsibility for Breaches of Due Diligence Obligations*

In the Advisory Opinion of 1 February 2011 on the *Responsibilities and obligations of States sponsoring persons and entities with respect to activities in the Area*,[41] the Tribunal's Seabed Disputes Chamber clarified the content of the provisions of the Convention relating to the responsibility or liability of States for mining activities carried out by entities sponsored by them.[42]

Article 153, paragraph 2(b), of the Convention allows activities in the Area to be carried out by "natural or juridical persons which possess the nationality of States Parties or are effectively controlled by them or their nationals, when sponsored by such States". In this regard, Article 139, paragraph 2, and Annex III of the Convention set forth a special liability regime by providing that a sponsoring State is not "liable for damage caused by any failure of a contractor sponsored by it to comply with its obligations if that State Party has adopted laws and regulations and taken administrative measures which are, within the framework of its legal system, reasonably appropriate for securing compliance by persons under its jurisdiction" (article 4, paragraph 4, of Annex III). The questions asked by the Council to the Seabed Disputes Chamber related, *inter alia*, to the precise content of responsibilities and obligations of sponsoring States and the extent of their liability for the conduct of sponsored contractors.[43]

---

41 *Responsibilities and obligations of States with respect to activities in the Area, Advisory Opinion, 1 February 2011, ITLOS Reports 2011*, p. 10. The opinion was adopted unanimously.

42 Important for the clarification of legal concepts are the remarks made by the Seabed Disputes Chamber on the meaning of the English words "responsibility" and "liability": "the term 'responsibility' refers to the primary obligation whereas the term 'liability' refers to the secondary obligation, namely, the consequences of a breach of the primary obligation" (para. 66 of the 2011 Advisory Opinion). This distinction does not exist in the other five official texts of the Convention that use the same term (for example, "responsabilité" in French and "responsabilidad" in Spanish).

43 The questions asked by the Council were the following: "1. What are the legal responsibilities and obligations of States Parties to the Convention with respect to the sponsorship of activities in the Area in accordance with the Convention, in particular Part XI, and the 1994 Agreement relating to the Implementation of Part XI of the United Nations Convention on the Law of the Sea of 10 December 1982? 2. What is the extent of liability of a State Party for any failure to comply with the provisions of the Convention, in particular Part XI, and the 1994 Agreement, by an entity whom it has sponsored under Article 153, paragraph 2 (b), of the Convention? 3. What are the necessary and appropriate measures that a sponsoring State must take in order to fulfil its responsibility under the Convention, in particular Article 139 and Annex III, and the 1994 Agreement?"

According to the Seabed Disputes Chamber, the responsibility of States for activities carried out by sponsored contractors arises from a failure to comply with an obligation of due diligence. The expression "responsibility to ensure", which is often used in international instruments, indicates an obligation of conduct and of due diligence, and not an obligation of result:

> The sponsoring State's obligation "to ensure" is not an obligation to achieve, in each and every case, the result that the sponsored contractor complies with the aforementioned obligations. Rather, it is an obligation to deploy adequate means, to exercise best possible efforts, to do the utmost, to obtain this result. To utilize the terminology current in international law, this obligation may be characterized as an obligation "of conduct" and not "of result", and as an obligation of "due diligence".[44]

In a passage that can be considered as an important contribution to the law of State responsibility, the Seabed Disputes Chamber clarified in what cases the breach of an obligation of due diligence may entail the responsibility of a State. In this regard, the Seabed Disputes Chamber emphasized the relative character of the content of an obligation of due diligence, adding some remarks on the standards relevant in the case of deep seabed mining activities:

> The expression "to ensure" is often used in international legal instruments to refer to obligations in respect of which, while it is not considered reasonable to make a State liable for each and every violation committed by persons under its jurisdiction, it is equally not considered satisfactory to rely on mere application of the principle that the conduct of private persons or entities is not attributable to the State under international law (…).[45]

The Seabed Disputes Chamber continued:

> The content of "due diligence" obligations may not easily be described in precise terms. Among the factors that make such a description difficult is the fact that "due diligence" is a variable concept. It may change over time as measures considered sufficiently diligent at a certain moment

---

44 *Responsibilities and obligations of States with respect to activities in the Area, Advisory Opinion, 1 February 2011, ITLOS Reports 2011*, p. 10, at p. 41, para. 110.

45 *Ibid.*, para. 112. This kind of responsibility does not seem to be covered in the Draft Articles on State Responsibility, adopted in 2001 by the ILC (see, in particular, Article 8).

> may become not diligent enough in light, for instance, of new scientific or technological knowledge. It may also change in relation to the risks involved in the activity. As regards activities in the Area, it seems reasonable to state that prospecting is, generally speaking, less risky than exploration activities which, in turn, entail less risk than exploitation. Moreover, activities in the Area concerning different kinds of minerals, for example, polymetallic nodules on the one hand and polymetallic sulphides or cobalt rich ferromanganese crusts on the other, may require different standards of diligence. The standard of due diligence has to be more severe for the riskier activities.[46].

The Seabed Disputes Chamber also gave a more precise content to the Convention obligation of the sponsoring State to adopt laws and regulations and to take administrative measures which are, within the framework of its legal system, reasonably appropriate for securing compliance by persons under its jurisdiction.[47] The content of such legislation and measures can be determined by the sponsoring State within the framework of its legal system.[48] However, the sponsoring State does not have an absolute discretion in this regard. It must act in good faith, taking into account "objectively, the relevant options in a manner that is reasonable, relevant and conducive to the benefit of mankind as a whole."[49] In particular, the Seabed Disputes Chamber held that:

> the sponsoring State may find it necessary, depending upon its legal system, to include in its domestic law provisions that are necessary for implementing its obligations under the Convention. These provisions may concern, inter alia, financial viability and technical capacity of sponsored contractors, conditions for issuing a certificate of sponsorship and penalties for non-compliance by such contractors.[50]
>
> [...]
>
> Other indications may be found in the provisions that establish direct obligations of the sponsoring States [...]. These include: the obligations to assist the Authority in the exercise of control over activities in the Area; the obligation to apply a precautionary approach; the obligation to apply best environmental practices; the obligation to take measures to ensure

46 *Ibid.*, at p. 43, para. 117.

47 Also this obligation can be seen as a manifestation of the obligation of due diligence.

48 *Ibid.*, at p. 70, para. 229.

49 *Ibid.*, at p. 71, para. 230.

50 *Ibid.*, at p. 72, para. 234.

> the provision of guarantees in the event of an emergency order by the Authority for protection of the marine environment; the obligation to ensure the availability of recourse for compensation in respect of damage caused by pollution; and the obligation to conduct environmental impact assessments. It is important to stress that these obligations are mentioned only as examples.[51]

Subsequently, in the Advisory Opinion of 2 April 2015 on the *Request for an Advisory Opinion submitted by the Sub-Regional Fisheries Commission* (SRFC), the Tribunal found that due diligence obligations exist also in the field of fisheries. In particular, the Tribunal remarked that the liability of a State does not arise from any failure of vessels flying its flag to comply with the laws and regulations of coastal States concerning IUU fishing activities in their EEZ, "as the violation of such laws and regulations by vessels is not *per se* attributable to the flag State." The liability of the flag State arises instead from its failure to comply with its due diligence obligations concerning IUU fishing,[52] in particular the obligation to take the necessary measures to ensure that its nationals and vessels flying its flag are not engaged in IUU fishing activities.[53]

B *Rejection of a Double Standard of Responsibility*

Insofar as responsibility or liability of sponsoring States is concerned, in the 2011 Advisory Opinion the Seabed Disputes Chamber rejected the assumption that developing States enjoy preferential treatment as compared to developed States.[54] Such an assumption cannot find any basis either in customary international law or in the Convention. Moreover, it would run against the need to prevent the birth of so-called sponsoring States of convenience and to ensure the highest standards of protection of the marine environment and safety in deep seabed mining activities:

> Equality of treatment between developing and developed sponsoring States is consistent with the need to prevent commercial enterprises based in developed States from setting up companies in developing States, acquiring their nationality and obtaining their sponsorship in the

51 *Ibid.*, at p. 73, para. 236.

52 *Request for Advisory Opinion submitted by the Sub-Regional Fisheries Commission, Advisory Opinion, 2 April 2015, ITLOS Reports 2015*, p. 4 at p. 44, para. 146.

53 *Ibid.*, at p. 38, para. 124.

54 *Responsibilities and obligations of States with respect to activities in the Area, Advisory Opinion, 1 February 2011, ITLOS Reports 2011*, p. 10, at p. 53, para. 158.

hope of being subjected to less burdensome regulations and controls. The spread of sponsoring States "of convenience" would jeopardize uniform application of the highest standards of protection of the marine environment, the safe development of activities in the Area and protection of the common heritage of mankind.[55]

C Entitlement to Invoke Responsibility

Important considerations were made by the Seabed Disputes Chamber that rendered the 2011 Advisory Opinion also with regard to the right to invoke responsibility and claim compensation for damage to the marine environment beyond national jurisdiction. The Chamber found that, in the presence of an *erga omnes partes* obligation, such a right belongs to each State party to the Convention, as well as to the Authority, which is entitled to act on behalf of mankind as a whole (article 137, paragraph 2, of the Convention).[56] This shows an important vision of the Authority's competences.

Moreover, in cases where the sponsored entity was not able to meet its liability in full and the sponsoring State was not liable, the Chamber, relying on article 235, paragraph 3, of the Convention,[57] went as far as suggesting to the Authority that it should consider the establishment of a trust fund to compensate for all the damage not covered.[58]

D Responsibility of International Organizations

One of the questions answered by the Tribunal in the 2015 Advisory Opinion was the subject of the responsibility of an international organization for

---

55 *Ibid.*, at p. 54, para. 159

56 *Ibid.*, at p. 59, para. 180. According to the already mentioned 2001 Draft Articles on State Responsibility, "any State other than the injured State is entitled to invoke the responsibility of another State (...) if: (*a*) the obligation breached is owed to a group of States including that State, and is established for the protection of a collective interest of that group; or (*b*) the obligation breached is owed to the international community as a whole" (Article 48, para. 1).

57 "With the objective of assuring prompt and adequate compensation in respect of all damage caused by pollution of the marine environment, States shall cooperate in the implementation of existing international law and the further development of international law relating to responsibility and liability for the assessment of and compensation for damage and the settlement of related disputes, as well as, where appropriate, development of criteria and procedures for payment of adequate compensation, such as compulsory insurance or compensation funds".

58 *Responsibilities and obligations of States with respect to activities in the Area, Advisory Opinion, 1 February 2011, ITLOS Reports 2011*, p. 10, at p. 65, at paras. 205 and 209.

wrongful acts committed by its member States,[59] with specific reference to violations of the fishing licenses granted by a coastal State within the framework of an agreement with the international organization. It is easy to identify the European Union as implicitly involved, since this organization has been granted by its member States the exclusive competence to enter into international agreements with third States in the field of fisheries and has in fact concluded several fishing agreements, including with the West African States members of the SRFC.

Relying also on article 6, paragraph 1, of Annex IX (Participation by international organizations) of the Convention,[60] the Tribunal linked liability to competence as follows:

> The liability of an international organization for an internationally wrongful act is linked to its competence. [...] It follows that an international organization which in a matter of its competence undertakes an obligation, in respect of which compliance depends on the conduct of its member States, may be held liable if a member State fails to comply with such obligation and the organization did not meet its obligation of "due diligence."[61]

The Tribunal found that the international organization is under an obligation to ensure that vessels flying the flag of its member States comply with the obligations arising from the agreements it has concluded and is consequently liable for a failure to do so:

> The Tribunal holds that in cases where an international organization, in the exercise of its exclusive competence in fisheries matters, concludes a fisheries access agreement with an SRFC Member State, which provides for access by vessels flying the flag of its member States to fish in the exclusive economic zone of that State, the obligations of the flag State become the obligations of the international organization. The interna-

59 The question, asked by the SRFC, was the following: "Where a fishing license issued to a vessel within the framework of an international agreement with the flag State or with an international agency, shall the State or international agency be held liable for the violation of the fisheries legislation of the coastal State by the vessel in question?".

60 "Parties which have competence under article 5 of this Annex shall have responsibility for failure to comply with obligations or for any other violation of this Convention".

61 *Request for Advisory Opinion submitted by the Sub-Regional Fisheries Commission, Advisory Opinion, 2 April 2015, ITLOS Reports 2015*, p. 4, at p. 49, para. 168.

> tional organization, as the only contracting party to the fisheries access agreement with the SRFC Member State, must therefore ensure that vessels flying the flag of a member State comply with the fisheries laws and regulations of the SRFC Member State and do not conduct IUU fishing activities within the exclusive economic zone of that State.
>
> Accordingly, only the international organization may be held liable for any breach of its obligations arising from the fisheries access agreement, and not its member States. Therefore, if the international organization does not meet its "due diligence" obligations, the SRFC Member States may hold the international organization liable for the violation of their fisheries laws and regulations by a vessel flying the flag of a member State of that organization and fishing in the exclusive economic zones of the SRFC Member States within the framework of a fisheries access agreement between that organization and such Member States.[62]

Here the exclusive competence of the organization to conclude fisheries agreements entails the consequence of channeling the liability on the organization itself.[63] However, since also the member States should be under an obligation to ensure that vessels flying their flag do not engage in IUU fishing, it is not clear why the 2015 Advisory Opinion seems to exclude the concurrent responsibility of such States. The uncertain and sometimes mysterious aspects of the allocation of competences between an international organization (in practice, only the European Union so far) and its member States[64] should not play to the prejudice of non-member States.

---

62 *Ibid.*, at p. 51, paras. 172 and 173.

63 If so, this kind of responsibility could fall under the situation envisaged in Article 64 (*Lex specialis*) of the Draft Articles on Responsibility of International Organizations, adopted in 2011 by the ILC: "These articles do not apply where and to the extent that the conditions for the existence of an internationally wrongful act or the content or implementation of the international responsibility of an international organization, or a State in connection with the conduct of an international organization, are governed by special rules of international law. Such special rules of international law may be contained in the rules of the organization applicable to the relations between an international organization and its members".

64 From the declaration made on 1 April 1998 by the European Community (now European Union) on depositing its formal confirmation of the Convention it can be inferred that the commonly called "exclusive" competence of the Union in the field of fisheries is not fully exclusive: "The Community points out that its Member States have transferred competence to it with regard to the conservation and management of sea fishing resources. Hence in this field it is for the Community to adopt the relevant rules and regulations

An interesting remark is that that, in the explanatory memorandum for a new draft European Union Regulation on the sustainable management of external fishing fleets, the European Commission pointed out that "ITLOS stresses the liability of the Union, and not its Member States, for any breach of the fisheries access agreements it has with coastal States."[65]

V Abuse of Rights

In the Judgment of 28 May 2013 in the *M/V "Louisa" Case* (*Saint Vincent and the Grenadines* v. *Spain*), the Tribunal remarked that article 300 of the Convention ("Abuse of rights") cannot be invoked on its own and becomes relevant only when the rights, jurisdiction and freedoms recognized in the Convention are exercised in an abusive manner.[66] This finding is questionable, at least by those who consider abuse of right as belonging to the category of general principles of law.[67]

(which are enforced by the Member States) and, within its competence, to enter into external undertakings with third States or competent international organizations. This competence applies to waters under national fisheries jurisdiction and to the high seas. Nevertheless, in respect of measures relating to the exercise of jurisdiction over vessels, flagging and registration of vessels and the enforcement of penal and administrative sanctions, competence rests with the Member States whilst respecting Community law. Community law also provides for administrative sanctions."

65 European Union document COM(2015) 636 final of 10 December 2015, p. 3.

66 *M/V "Louisa" (Saint Vincent and the Grenadines* v. *Kingdom of Spain), Judgment, ITLOS Reports 2013*, p. 4, at p. 43, para. 137.

67 As pointed out in the Dissenting Opinion of Judge Jesus, "indeed, as postulated by the abuse-of-right principle, no right, whether concerning the sea or the land, should be exercised in an arbitrary or malicious manner in such a way as to cause unnecessary harm or injury to others. Article 300 merely states, in a direct way, for the law of the sea a general principle of law that applies equally to other fields of law, internal and international. The principle of abuse of right is a natural offspring of the good faith principle and, as such, its general applicability is to be expected even in situations in which it is not incorporated into a particular provision of a treaty or any other legal text. Its observance is of the essence if justice and peace are to prevail in inter-State relations", *M/V "Louisa" (Saint Vincent and the Grenadines* v. *Kingdom of Spain), Dissenting Opinion of Judge Jesus, ITLOS Reports 2013*, p. 149, paras. 44 and 45.

VI Protection of the Environment

Two findings of the Tribunal on the protection of the marine environment do not seem confined to law of the sea, but have a broader relevance for customary international law in general.

A *Precautionary Approach*

In the 2011 Advisory Opinion, the Seabed Disputes Chamber pointed out that the obligations of sponsoring States are not limited to the due diligence "obligation to ensure",[68] but include also a number of direct obligations. One of them, also resulting from the relevant Authority regulations, is to apply a precautionary approach, as reflected in Principle 15 of the 1992 Rio Declaration on Environment and Development.[69] According to the prudent words of the Seabed Disputes Chamber:

> the precautionary approach has been incorporated into a growing number of international treaties and other instruments, many of which reflect the formulation of Principle 15 of the Rio Declaration. In the view of the Chamber, this has initiated a trend towards making this approach part of customary international law.[70]

In fact, the precautionary approach has been so frequently incorporated in international practice, especially in multilateral treaties on the protection of the

68 *Supra*, section IV.A.

69 "In order to protect the environment, the precautionary approach shall be widely applied by States according to their capabilities. Where there are threats of serious or irreversible damage, lack of full scientific certainty shall not be used as a reason for postponing cost-effective measures to prevent environmental degradation."

70 *Responsibilities and obligations of States with respect to activities in the Area, Advisory Opinion, 1 February 2011, ITLOS Reports 2011*, p. 10, at p. 47, para. 135. The precautionary approach was only hinted at in the Tribunal's Order of 27 August 1999 in the *Southern Bluefin Tuna Cases, Provisional Measures*, as remarked upon in the Separate Opinion of Judge Treves: "This approach, which may be called precautionary, is hinted at in the Order, in particular in paragraph 77. However, that paragraph refers it to the future conduct of the parties. While, of course, a precautionary approach by the parties in their future conduct is necessary, such precautionary approach, in my opinion, is necessary also in the assessment by the Tribunal of the urgency of the measures it might take. In the present case, it would seem to me that the requirement of urgency is satisfied only in the light of such precautionary approach. I regret that this is not stated explicitly in the Order", *Separate Opinion of Judge Treves, ITLOS Reports 1999*, at p. 317, para. 8.

environment, that the trend noted by the Seabed Disputes Chamber as being only at its initial stage can today be considered as successfully concluded.

B *Environmental Impact Assessment*

The Seabed Disputes Chamber also found that the obligation to conduct an environmental impact assessment is another direct obligation of sponsoring States under both the Convention and customary international law, stating "[I]t should be stressed that the obligation to conduct an environmental impact assessment is a direct obligation under the Convention and a general obligation under customary international law."[71]

Here the Seabed Disputes Chamber quoted a passage in the ICJ Judgment of 20 April 2010 in the *Pulp Mills on the River Uruguay* case, according to which the carrying out of an environmental impact assessment may now be considered a requirement under general international law in cases where there is a risk that a proposed industrial activity may have a significant adverse impact in a transboundary context, in particular on a shared resource.[72] The Seabed Disputes Chamber broadened the ICJ's reasoning to include within its scope mining activities in the Area.[73]

VII Fisheries

A *Flag States' Obligations*

In its 2015 Advisory Opinion, the Tribunal confirmed that the primary responsibility for taking the necessary measures to prevent, deter and eliminate IUU

71 *Responsibilities and obligations of States with respect to activities in the Area, Advisory Opinion, 1 February 2011, ITLOS Reports 2011*, p. 10, at p. 50, para. 145.

72 *Pulp Mills on the River Uruguay (Argentina* v. *Uruguay), Judgment, I.C.J. Reports 2010*, p. 14, at p. 83, para. 204.

73 See *Advisory Opinion, 1 February 2011, ITLOS Reports 2011*, p. 10, at p. 51, para. 148: "Although aimed at the specific situation under discussion by the Court, the language used seems broad enough to cover activities in the Area even beyond the scope of the Regulations. The Court's reasoning in a transboundary context may also apply to activities with an impact on the environment in an area beyond the limits of national jurisdiction; and the Court's references to 'shared resources' may also apply to resources that are the common heritage of mankind. Thus, in light of the customary rule mentioned by the ICJ, it may be considered that environmental impact assessments should be included in the system of consultations and prior notifications set out in article 142 of the Convention with respect to 'resource deposits in the Area which lie across limits of national jurisdiction'".

fishing in the EEZ rests with the coastal State.[74] However, this does not release other States from their obligations. In particular, giving a broad interpretation to article 94, paragraph 2(b), of the Convention,[75] the Tribunal held that the flag State:

> in fulfilment of its responsibility to exercise effective jurisdiction and control in administrative matters, must adopt the necessary administrative measures to ensure that fishing vessels flying its flag are not involved in activities which will undermine the flag State's responsibilities under the Convention in respect of the conservation and management of marine living resources. If such violations nevertheless occur and are reported by other States, the flag State is obliged to investigate and, if appropriate, take any action necessary to remedy the situation.[76]

This is a clear indication of the existence of obligations that are not directly addressed in the Convention, but are consistent with the Convention's general objective of conservation of marine living resources and the content of many fishing agreements.

B *Bunkering of Fishing Vessels*

In the Judgment of 14 April 2014 in the *M/V "Virginia G" Case* (*Panama/Guinea-Bissau*), the Tribunal addressed the question whether the sale of gas oil to fishing vessels (so-called offshore bunkering) within the exclusive economic zone falls under the sovereign rights granted to the coastal State or under the freedom of navigation and other internationally lawful uses of the sea granted to other States. There is no specific provision in this regard in the Convention. To answer the question, the Tribunal analyzed a number of provisions in the Convention on the EEZ and took into consideration State practice in the field of bunkering.

As regards the Convention provisions, the Tribunal preferred a broad interpretation of the list of matters falling under the coastal State's jurisdiction given by article 62, paragraph 4, reaching the conclusion that the coastal State

74 *Advisory Opinion, 2 April 2015, ITLOS Reports 2015*, p. 4, at p. 33, para. 106.

75 Article 94, para. 2(b), of the Convention provides: "In particular every State shall: (…) (b) assume jurisdiction under its internal law over each ship flying its flag and its master, officers and crew in respect of administrative, technical and social matters concerning the ship". On this provision see also *infra*, para. XIII. A.

76 *Request for Advisory Opinion submitted by the Sub-Regional Fisheries Commission, Advisory Opinion, 2 April 2015, ITLOS Reports 2015*, p. 4, at p. 36, para. 119.

is granted the right to regulate all activities having a direct connection to fishing. Such activities include bunkering, as it allows fishing vessels to fish without interruption:

> The Tribunal [...] is of the view that it is apparent from the list in article 62, paragraph 4, of the Convention that for all activities that may be regulated by a coastal State there must be a direct connection to fishing. The Tribunal observes that such connection to fishing exists for the bunkering of foreign vessels fishing in the exclusive economic zone since this enables them to continue their activities without interruption at sea.[77]
>
> [...]
>
> The Tribunal is of the view that the regulation by a coastal State of bunkering of foreign vessels fishing in its exclusive economic zone is among those measures which the coastal State may take in its exclusive economic zone to conserve and manage its living resources under article 56 of the Convention read together with article 62, paragraph 4, of the Convention.[78]

This conclusion is supported by the definitions of "fishing" and "fishing-related activities" given by a number of international agreements[79] and by the national legislation of several States.[80] However, coastal States' rights are strictly related to the bunkering of fishing vessels and cannot be extended to the bunkering of vessels engaged in other activities.[81]

The position taken by the Tribunal in regard to the bunkering of fishing vessels in the EEZ is well grounded and persuasively explained. It contributes in a decisive way to the clarification of a question left open by the Convention.

---

77 *M/V "Virginia G" (Panama/Guinea-Bissau), Judgment, ITLOS Reports 2014*, p. 4, at p. 68, para. 215.

78 *Ibid.*, at p. 69, para. 217.

79 *Ibid.*, at p. 68, para. 216.

80 *Ibid.*, at p. 69, para. 218.

81 *Ibid.*, at p. 70, para. 223. In the specific case, the Tribunal found that the charging of fees for bunkering by Guinea-Bissau was not guided by fiscal interests, but was established for services rendered in connection with the authorization of bunkering (para. 234) and that the procedure for obtaining such authorization was not unduly burdensome for an applicant (para. 235).

VIII Rights of Coastal States in the EEZ or on the Continental Shelf

Besides the case of bunkering,[82] the Tribunal had two other opportunities to clarify the content of the coastal State's rights in maritime zones beyond the territorial sea.

In the Judgment of 1 July 1999 in the *M/V "SAIGA" (No. 2) Case (Saint Vincent and the Grenadines* v. *Guinea*), the Tribunal held that by applying its customs legislation to a customs radius which included parts of the EEZ, Guinea acted in a manner contrary to the Convention.[83] The customs legislation of the coastal State cannot extend beyond the territorial sea,[84] and no reasons of public interest could justify exceptions to this rule:

> In the view of the Tribunal, recourse to the principle of "public interest", as invoked by Guinea, would entitle a coastal State to prohibit any activities in the exclusive economic zone which it decides to characterize as activities which affect its economic "public interest" or entail "fiscal losses" for it. This would curtail the rights of other States in the exclusive economic zone. The Tribunal is satisfied that this would be incompatible with the provisions of articles 56 and 58 of the Convention regarding the rights of the coastal State in the exclusive economic zone.[85]

It was evident that Article 34 of the Guinean Customs code, providing for the establishment of a "customs radius" (*rayon des douanes*) of 250 kilometres from the coast, went far beyond the rights granted by the Convention to the coastal State. Accordingly, the Tribunal held that the arrest and detention of a ship flying a foreign flag, the prosecution and conviction of its master, the confiscation of the cargo and the seizure of the ship were all actions contrary to the Convention.

In the Order of 25 April 2015 on the *Dispute concerning delimitation of the maritime boundary between Ghana and Côte d'Ivoire in the Atlantic Ocean,*

---

82 *Supra*, section VII.B.

83 *M/V "SAIGA" (No. 2) (Saint Vincent and the Grenadines* v. *Guinea), Judgment, ITLOS Reports 1999*, p. 10, at p. 56, para. 136.

84 Yet article 33 of the Convention (Contiguous zone) does not say that the customs legislation applies within the 24-mile contiguous zone. It provides that in the contiguous zone the coastal State can prevent and punish infringements of its customs legislation in its territory or territorial sea.

85 *M/V "SAIGA" (No. 2) (Saint Vincent and the Grenadines* v. *Guinea), Judgment, ITLOS Reports 1999*, p. 10, at p. 55, para. 131.

a Special Chamber of the Tribunal clarified the extent of the coastal State's rights as regards access to information on the resources of the continental shelf:

> the Special Chamber considers that the rights of the coastal State over its continental shelf include all rights necessary for and connected with the exploration and exploitation of the natural resources of the continental shelf and that the exclusive right to access to information about the resources of the continental shelf is plausibly among those rights.[86]

IX Maritime Delimitation

In deciding its first maritime boundary case – the *Dispute concerning delimitation of the maritime boundary between Bangladesh and Myanmar in the Bay of Bengal*[87] – the Tribunal followed the already consolidated jurisprudence of the ICJ and arbitral tribunals on this kind of dispute. The Tribunal remarked in this regard that courts and tribunals have developed a body of case law on maritime delimitations which has reduced the elements of subjectivity and uncertainty in the determination of maritime boundaries and in the choice of methods employed to that end.[88] As to the specific case, the Tribunal:

- applied the so-called three-stage approach (construction of a provisional equidistance line, based on the geography of the parties' coasts and mathematical calculations; determination of whether there are relevant circumstances requiring adjustment of this line; checking whether the line results in any significant disproportion between the ratio of the respective coastal lengths and the ratio of the relevant maritime areas allocated to each party);[89]

---

86 *Delimitation of the maritime boundary in the Atlantic Ocean (Ghana/Côte d'Ivoire), Provisional Measures, Order of 25 April 2015, ITLOS Reports 2015*, p. 146, at p. 164, para. 94.

87 A second case, relating to the delimitation of the maritime boundary between Ghana and Côte d'Ivoire, is pending.

88 *Delimitation of the maritime boundary in the Bay of Bengal (Bangladesh/Myanmar), Judgment, ITLOS Reports 2012*, p. 4, at p. 64, para. 226.

89 *Ibid.*, at p. 76, para. 240.

- gave full effect to an island of Bangladesh for the purpose of the delimitation of the territorial sea (article 15 of the Convention);[90]
- gave no effect to the same island in drawing the delimitation line for the EEZ and the continental shelf,[91] as "the effect to be given to islands in delimitation may differ, depending on whether the delimitation concerns the territorial sea or other maritime areas beyond it";[92]
- determined what were the relevant coasts of the parties, noting that "for a coast to be considered as relevant in maritime delimitation it must generate projections which overlap with those of the coast of another party";[93]
- took into account the concavity of the coast of Bangladesh and adjusted the equidistance line accordingly in order to avoid a cut-off effect;[94]
- did not consider the Bengal depositional system as relevant to the delimitation of the EEZ and the continental shelf, remarking that "the location and direction of the single maritime boundary applicable both to the seabed and subsoil and to the superjacent waters within the 200 n.m. limit are to be determined on the basis of geography of the coasts of the Parties in relation to each other and not on the geology or geomorphology of the seabed of the delimitation area."[95]

In the 2012 Judgment the Tribunal, for the first time in the international jurisprudence on maritime boundaries, also delimited the continental shelf beyond the 200 nautical mile limit (the so-called "extended continental shelf")

---

90 *Ibid.*, at p. 47, para. 151: "While it is not unprecedented in case law for islands to be given less than full effect in the delimitation of the territorial sea, the islands subject to such treatment are usually 'insignificant maritime features' (…) In the view of the Tribunal, St. Martin's Island is a significant maritime feature by virtue of its size and population and the extent of economic and other activities."

91 *Ibid.*, at p. 86, paras. 318–319: "St. Martin's Island is an important feature which could be considered a relevant circumstance in the present case. However, because of its location, giving effect to St. Martin's Island in the delimitation of the exclusive economic zone and the continental shelf would result in a line blocking the seaward projection from Myanmar's coast in a manner that would cause an unwarranted distortion of the delimitation line. The distorting effect of an island on an equidistance line may increase substantially as the line moves beyond 12 nm from the coast. For the foregoing reasons, the Tribunal concludes that St. Martin's Island is not a relevant circumstance and, accordingly, decides not to give any effect to it in drawing the delimitation line of the exclusive economic zone and the continental shelf."

92 *Ibid.*, at p. 46, para. 148.

93 *Ibid.*, at p. 58, para. 198.

94 *Ibid.*, at p. 81, para. 293.

95 *Ibid.*, at p. 87, para. 322.

to which, for geological reasons, both Bangladesh and Myanmar were entitled. The Tribunal disregarded the concept of "natural prolongation", referred to in article 76, paragraph 1, of the Convention,[96] as it does not constitute "a separate and independent criterion a coastal State must satisfy in order to be entitled to a continental shelf beyond 200 nm",[97] and concluded that natural prolongation was to be understood in light of the subsequent paragraphs of article 76 defining the continental shelf and the continental margin.[98] In other words:

> Entitlement to a continental shelf beyond 200 nm should thus be determined by reference to the outer edge of the continental margin, to be ascertained in accordance with article 76, paragraph 4.[99]

While the Bay of Bengal presents the unique situation of a thick layer of sediments which covers practically the entire floor of the bay,[100] the Tribunal found that article 76 of the Convention

> does not support the view that the geographic origin of the sedimentary rocks of the continental margin is of relevance to the question of entitlement to the continental shelf or constitutes a controlling criterion for determining whether a State is entitled to a continental shelf.[101]

Noting that article 83 of the Convention (Delimitation of the continental shelf between States with opposite or adjacent coasts) "applies equally to the delimitation of the continental shelf both within and beyond 200 n.m.",[102] the Tribunal decided that the adjusted equidistance line delimiting both the EEZ

96 Article 76, para. 1, of the Convention provides: "The continental shelf of a coastal State comprises the seabed and subsoil of the submarine areas that extend beyond its territorial sea throughout the natural prolongation of its land territory to the outer edge of the continental margin, or to a distance of 200 nautical miles from the baselines from which the breadth of the territorial sea is measured where the outer edge of the continental margin does not extend up to that distance".

97 *Delimitation of the maritime boundary in the Bay of Bengal (Bangladesh/Myanmar), Judgment, ITLOS Reports 2012*, p. 4, at p. 113, para. 435.

98 *Ibid.*

99 *Ibid.*, at p. 114, para. 437.

100 *Ibid.*, at p. 115, para. 444: "the sea floor of the Bay of Bengal is covered by a thick layer of sediments some 14 to 22 kilometres deep originating in the Himalayas and the Tibetan Plateau, having accumulated in the Bay of Bengal over several thousands of years."

101 *Ibid.*, para. 447.

102 *Ibid.*, at p. 117, para. 454.

and the continental shelf within 200 nautical miles between the parties continued in the same direction beyond the 200 nautical mile limit of Bangladesh until it reached the area where the rights of third States may be affected.[103]

X Use of Force Against Individuals at Sea

In its Judgment in the *M/V "Saiga" (No. 2) Case (Saint Vincent and the Grenadines* v. *Guinea)*, the Tribunal dealt with the question of the use of force in arresting ships, a matter that is not expressly regulated by the Convention and falls under general international law.

In the specific case, the officers of a fast-moving Guinean patrol boat fired with live ammunition at a foreign tanker almost fully laden and low in the water that could be boarded without much difficulty. They used force without issuing any of the signals and warnings required by international law and practice.[104] Their behaviour was even worse when on board:

> The Guinean officers also used excessive force on board the *Saiga*. Having boarded the ship without resistance, and although there is no evidence of the use or threat of force from the crew, they fired indiscriminately while on the deck and used gunfire to stop the engine of the ship. In using firearms in this way, the Guinean officers appeared to have attached little or no importance to the safety of the ship and the persons on board. In the process, considerable damage was done to the ship and to vital equipment in the engine and radio rooms. And, more seriously, the indiscriminate use of gunfire caused severe injuries to two of the persons on board.[105]

The Tribunal held that, in arresting ships, the use of force must be avoided as far as possible and must never go beyond what is reasonable and necessary in the circumstances:

> In considering the force used by Guinea in the arrest of the *Saiga*, the Tribunal must take into account the circumstances of the arrest in the context of the applicable rules of international law. Although the

103 *Ibid.*, at p. 118, para. 462.

104 *M/V "SAIGA" (No. 2) (Saint Vincent and the Grenadines* v. *Guinea), Judgment, ITLOS Reports 1999*, p. 10, at p. 62, para. 157.

105 *Ibid.*, at p. 63, para 158.

> Convention does not contain express provisions on the use of force in the arrest of ships, international law, which is applicable by virtue of article 293 of the Convention, requires that the use of force must be avoided as far as possible and, where force is unavoidable, it must not go beyond what is reasonable and necessary in the circumstances. Considerations of humanity must apply in the law of the sea, as they do in other areas of international law.[106]

The Tribunal specified that the normal practice in arresting ships as follows:

> These principles have been followed over the years in law enforcement operations at sea. The normal practice used to stop a ship at sea is first to give an auditory or visual signal to stop, using internationally recognized signals. Where this does not succeed, a variety of actions may be taken, including the firing of shots across the bows of the ship. It is only after the appropriate actions fail that the pursuing vessel may, as a last resort, use force. Even then, appropriate warning must be issued to the ship and all efforts should be made to ensure that life is not endangered [...].[107]

The Tribunal's conclusion was that Guinea used excessive force and endangered human life before and after boarding the *Saiga* and thereby violated the rights of the flag State (Saint Vincent and the Grenadines) under international law.[108]

Perhaps, considering that it is entitled to apply any rule of international law not incompatible with the Convention (in accordance with article 293, paragraph 1, of the Convention), the Tribunal could have taken a step further than merely stating that "considerations of humanity must apply in the law of the

---

106 *Ibid.*, at p. 61, para 155.

107 *Ibid.*, at p. 62, para. 156. The Tribunal quoted Article 22, para. 1, *f*, of the *Agreement for the Implementation of the Provisions of the United Nations Convention on the Law of the Sea of 10 December 1982 relating to the Conservation and Management of Straddling Fish Stocks and Highly Migratory Fish Stocks* (4 August 1995, 2167 *UNTS* 3): "1. The inspecting State shall ensure that its duly authorized inspectors: (...) (f) avoid the use of force except when and to the degree necessary to ensure the safety of the inspectors and where the inspectors are obstructed in the execution of their duties. The degree of force used shall not exceed that reasonably required in the circumstances."

108 *Ibid.*, at p. 63, para 159. The same standards were applied by the Tribunal also in the 2014 Judgment in the *M/V "Virginia G" Case* (*Panama/Guinea-Bissau*). Here the Tribunal concluded that the State involved (Guinea-Bissau) did not use excessive force in boarding a foreign ship engaged in bunkering.

sea." In customary international law there are rules on human rights, in particular the right to life, that set forth strict limits on the lethal use of force by States against individuals. These rules are embodied in a number of treaties and are applied by the competent courts, such as the European and the Inter-American Court on Human Rights. The Tribunal could have made a direct reference to the applicable human rights rules.

XI The Right of Ships to Leave Foreign Ports

In the 2013 Judgment in the *M/V "Louisa" Case* (*Saint Vincent and the Grenadines* v. *Kingdom of Spain*), the Tribunal was called to decide whether the right of freedom of navigation on the high seas implied also the right for a foreign ship to leave a port, notwithstanding its detention because of legal proceedings against it.[109] As it could be expected given the oddity of the question, the answer was a negative one:

> The Tribunal notes that article 87 of the Convention deals with the freedom of the high seas, in particular the freedom of navigation, which applies to the high seas and, under article 58 of the Convention, to the exclusive economic zone. It is not disputed that the M/V "Louisa" was detained when it was docked in a Spanish port. Article 87 cannot be interpreted in such a way as to grant the M/V "Louisa" a right to leave the port and gain access to the high seas notwithstanding its detention in the context of legal proceedings against it.[110]

XII Warships

In the Order of 15 December 2012 in the *"ARA Libertad" Case* (*Argentina* v. *Ghana*), *Provisional Measures*, the Tribunal remarked that a warship is "an expression of the sovereignty of the State whose flag it flies"[111] and that, in

109 In the specific case, the ship was detained in the context of criminal proceedings relating to alleged violations of Spanish laws on the protection of the underwater cultural heritage in the Spanish maritime internal waters and territorial sea and the possession and handling of weapons of war in Spanish territory.

110 *M/V "Louisa" (Saint Vincent and the Grenadines* v. *Kingdom of Spain), Judgment, ITLOS Reports 2013*, p. 4, at p. 36, para. 109.

111 *Ibid.*, at p. 33, para. 94.

accordance with general international law, a warship enjoys immunity, including in internal waters.[112] This implies that article 32 of the Convention (Immunities of warships and other government ships operated for non-commercial purposes),[113] which is included in the section of the Convention relating to innocent passage in the territorial sea, has a broader scope of application and can be referred to all kinds of marine waters.

XIII Nationality of Ships

The Tribunal seems less convincing when, in deciding in 1999 the already mentioned *M/V "SAIGA" (No. 2) Case*, it addressed the questions of the genuine link and the attribution of nationality to ships.

A *Genuine Link between a State and a Ship Flying Its Flag*

Under article 91, paragraph 1, of the Convention, a genuine link must exist between a State and a ship flying its flag.[114]

The *M/V "SAIGA" (No. 2) Case* related to the arrest by Guinea of a tanker flying the flag of Saint Vincent and the Grenadines that was engaged in selling gas oil as bunker to vessels fishing off the coast of West Africa. The ship was owned by a Cypriot company, managed by a British company and chartered by a Swiss company. The master of the ship was of Ukrainian nationality and the crew was composed of nationals of Ukraine or Senegal. The owner of the cargo of gas oil was a Swiss company.

The Tribunal first addressed the question of whether the absence of a genuine link between a flag State and a ship entitles another State to refuse to recognize the nationality of the flag State. It gave to the question a negative answer.[115] In particular, the Tribunal recalled that the ILC, in its 1956 Draft Articles on the Law of the Sea, understood the genuine link as a criterion for the recognition

---

112 *Ibid.*, at p. 34, para. 95.

113 Article 32 of the Convention provides: "With such exceptions as are contained in subsection A and in articles 30 and 31, nothing in this Convention affects the immunities of warships and other government ships operated for non-commercial purposes."

114 Article 91, para. 1, of the Convention provides: "Every State shall fix the conditions for the grant of its nationality to ships, for the registration of ships in its territory, and for the right to fly its flag. Ships have the nationality of the State whose flag they are entitled to fly. There must exist a genuine link between the State and the ship."

115 *M/V "SAIGA" (No. 2) (Saint Vincent and the Grenadines* v. *Guinea), Judgment, ITLOS Reports 1999*, p. 10, at p. 41, para. 82.

by other States of the nationality granted by a State to ships.[116] However, in the final text of the 1958 Convention on the High Seas, the corresponding provision was substantively changed as follows: "[t]here must exist a genuine link between the State and the ship; in particular, the State must effectively exercise its jurisdiction and control in administrative, technical and social matters over ships flying its flag."[117]

From this change the Tribunal drew the conclusion that the existence of a genuine link is not a condition for the recognition of nationality of ships: "[t]hus, while the obligation regarding a genuine link was maintained in the 1958 Convention, the proposal that the existence of a genuine link should be a basis for the recognition of nationality was not adopted."[118]

The same conclusion could be repeated for article 91, paragraph 1, of the Convention, which is based on article 5 of the 1958 Geneva Convention.[119]

The Tribunal further pointed out that article 94, paragraph 6, of the Convention already provides for the consequences to be drawn from the lack of a genuine link, that is, the right of other States to report the matter to the flag State. According to the Tribunal, the need for a genuine link is established in the Convention for the mere purpose "to secure more effective implementation of the duties of the flag State":

> Paragraphs 2 to 5 of article 94 of the Convention outline the measures that a flag State is required to take to exercise effective jurisdiction as envisaged in paragraph 1. Paragraph 6 sets out the procedure to be followed where another State has "clear grounds to believe that proper jurisdiction and control with respect to a ship have not been exercised". That State

116 Article 29 of the 1956 Draft Articles on the Law of the Sea provides: "Ships have the nationality of the State whose flag they are entitled to fly. Nevertheless, for purposes of the recognition of the national character of the ship by other States, there must exist a genuine link between the State and the ship." The question of the genuine link was not addressed by the ICJ in *Constitution of the Maritime Safety Committee of the Inter-Governmental Maritime Consultative Organization, Advisory Opinion, I.C.J. Reports 1960*, p. 150, at p. 171.

117 Article 5, para. 1, of the *Convention on the High Seas*, 29 April 1958, 450 *UNTS* 11.

118 *M/V "SAIGA" (No. 2) (Saint Vincent and the Grenadines* v. *Guinea), Judgment, ITLOS Reports 1999*, p. 10, at p. 41, para. 80.

119 *Ibid.*, para. 81: "The Convention follows the approach of the 1958 Convention. Article 91 retains the part of the third sentence of article 5, paragraph 1, of the 1958 Convention which provides that there must be a genuine link between the State and the ship. The other part of that sentence, stating that the flag State shall effectively exercise its jurisdiction and control in administrative, technical and social matters over ships flying its flag, is reflected in article 94 of the Convention, dealing with the duties of the flag State."

> is entitled to report the facts to the flag State which is then obliged to "investigate the matter and, if appropriate, take any action necessary to remedy the situation". There is nothing in article 94 to permit a State which discovers evidence indicating the absence of proper jurisdiction and control by a flag State over a ship to refuse to recognize the right of the ship to fly the flag of the flag State.
>
> The conclusion of the Tribunal is that the purpose of the provisions of the Convention on the need for a genuine link between a ship and its flag State is to secure more effective implementation of the duties of the flag State, and not to establish criteria by reference to which the validity of the registration of ships in a flag State may be challenged by other States.[120]

In other words, according to the Tribunal in its 1999 Judgment, the Convention does not allow other States to call into question the criteria followed by the flag State to grant registration and nationality to ships, including in the cases where there is no genuine link between the flag State and the ship. This conclusion is far from being convincing.

Irrespective of what might have been the drafting history of article 5 of the 1958 Geneva Convention and article 91, paragraph 1, of the Convention, recourse to the preparatory works of a treaty can be made only as a supplementary means, where the interpretation according to the general rule leaves the meaning ambiguous or obscure or leads to a result which is manifestly absurd or unreasonable (see article 32 of the 1969 Vienna Convention on the Law of Treaties).[121] In article 91, paragraph 1, of the Convention the sentence "there must exist a genuine link between the State and the ship" is very simple and fully clear in itself. It is expressed in mandatory terms and, being connected to the previous sentence in the same provision, can easily be understood in the sense that the conditions established under the national legislation of a State for granting its nationality to ships must be based on the existence of a genuine

---

120 *Ibid.*, paras. 82 and 83. The Tribunal added (at para. 84) that "[T]his conclusion is not put into question by the United Nations Convention on Conditions for Registration of Ships of 7 February 1986 invoked by Guinea. This Convention (which is not in force) sets out as one of its principal objectives the strengthening of 'the genuine link between a State and ships flying its flag'." The 1986 Convention has not entered into force even today.

121 Under the general rule of interpretation, article 31, para. 1, of the Vienna Convention on the Law of Treaties provides "a treaty shall be interpreted in good faith in accordance with the ordinary meaning to be given to the terms of the treaty in their context and in the light of its object and purpose." Vienna Convention on the Law of Treaties 115 *UNTS* 331.

link between such State and the ship. In other words, any State can specify in its national legislation the conditions for the granting of its flag to ships, provided that, as required by article 91, paragraph 1, there is a genuine link between the State and the ship. The consequence to be drawn is that, if there is no genuine link, the right to grant the national flag cannot be exercised. If so, there cannot be any obligation for other States to recognize a flag that cannot be granted. This is the self-evident result of the reading of a clearly written provision.

Also questionable is the Tribunal's conclusion that the only remedy for the violation of the obligation to ensure a genuine link is to report the facts to the flag State, as provided for in article 94, paragraph 6, of the Convention as follows:

> A State which has clear grounds to believe that proper jurisdiction and control with respect to a ship have not been exercised may report the facts to the flag State. Upon receiving such a report, the flag State shall investigate the matter and, if appropriate, take any action necessary to remedy the situation.

Indeed, article 94, paragraph 6, is a very unfortunate provision that brings problems to solutions rather than solutions to problems. It gives to other States a so-called right to report the facts to a State that is allegedly responsible for an internationally wrongful act. However, in cases where the genuine link does not exist, the mere right to report to a State that already knows the wrong it is doing is not likely to lead to any tangible remedy for the reporting State.

Such a situation seems so unsatisfactory that the Tribunal itself, in the already mentioned 2015 Advisory Opinion, felt it appropriate to add something that does not result from the reading of article 94, paragraph 6, namely that the flag State:

> is obliged to investigate the matter upon receiving such a report and, if appropriate, take any action necessary to remedy the situation. The Tribunal is of the view that the flag State is under the obligation to inform the reporting State about the action taken.[122]

To clarify that the flag State is bound to do something more than what is literally required by article 94, paragraph 6, of the Convention is a useful addition to the picture. But it is not enough. It is true that, as the Tribunal remarks in

122 *Request for Advisory Opinion submitted by the Sub-Regional Fisheries Commission, Advisory Opinion, 2 April 2015, ITLOS Reports 2015*, p. 4, at p. 36, para. 118.

the 1999 Judgment, article 94 of the Convention does not point out that a State can refuse to recognize the right of a ship to fly the flag of a State that does not comply with the obligation of ensuring the genuine link. But article 94 does not say either that reporting the facts to the flag State is the only way in which the other States can invoke the responsibility of the flag State for the lack of a genuine link. Reporting under article 94, paragraph 6, can be understood as a first step which should lead to investigation and appropriate measures by the flag State. However, if this does not occur, the consequences remain those resulting from the application of the ordinary rules on State responsibility for internationally wrongful acts (namely, cessation and non-repetition of the act, re-establishment of the situation which existed before, compensation if damage has occurred, satisfaction, right of other States to adopt countermeasures under certain conditions).[123] For instance, the non-recognition of the right to grant the national flag could be a rightful countermeasure against a State that has persistently violated the obligation to ensure the existence of a genuine link. However, from the reading of the Tribunal's 1999 Judgment, article 94, paragraph 6, of the Convention seems to be a sort of *lex specialis*[124] which, on the question of the genuine link, would prevent the application of the ordinary rules of general international law on the consequences of an internationally wrongful act.

Where the approach taken by the Tribunal's 1999 Judgment appears even less convincing, speaking with all the due respect, is in the passage stating that "the purpose of the provisions of the Convention on the need for a genuine link between a ship and its flag State is to secure more effective implementation of the duties of the flag State."[125] According to the Tribunal, a rule in a treaty that provides for a quite precise obligation, as the rule on the genuine link does, would exist only for the benefit of the State that has allegedly violated the obligation in question. Such an unwarranted conclusion appears in full contradiction with the normal function of legal provisions, that is, to set forth obligations for one subject and corresponding rights for another

123 See the relevant provisions of the ILC Draft Articles on Responsibility of States for Internationally Wrongful Acts, *Official Records of the General Assembly, Fifty-sixth session, Supplement No. 10* (A/56/10), chp.IV.E.1), November 2001.

124 See Article 55 (*Lex specialis*) of the Draft articles on Responsibility of States for Internationally Wrongful Acts: "These articles do not apply where and to the extent that the conditions for the existence of an internationally wrongful act or the content or implementation of the international responsibility of a State are governed by special rules of international law."

125 *M/V "SAIGA" (No. 2) (Saint Vincent and the Grenadines v. Guinea), Judgment, ITLOS Reports 1999*, p. 10, at p. 42, para. 83.

subject.[126] This should happen also for the rule on the genuine link. Today the main purpose of this rule is to ensure the safety of navigation and to give to all other States in general the right to prevent a State from allowing ships to sail in unsafe conditions that create a danger to human life and to the protection of the marine environment. The present orientation towards the objective of safety of navigation is clearly shown in article 94, paragraphs 1 to 5, of the Convention, which specify in great detail in what matters and manners the flag State is bound to effectively exercise its jurisdiction and control over ships flying its flag.

In the Judgment in the *M/V "SAIGA" (No. 2) Case*, the Tribunal did not state that, according to the spirit of the Convention, the right to grant a flag is given only to those States that ensure that ships flying their flag navigate in safe conditions.[127] Nor did the Tribunal make use of the category of due diligence obligations, that would bind flag States to adopt laws and regulations and to take administrative measures which are reasonably appropriate for securing compliance by ships flying their flag with the rules on safety of navigation.[128] Here the Tribunal missed a unique opportunity to provide a major contribution to the progressive development of international law of the sea, despite the fact that in some provisions of the Convention, such as the already mentioned article 94, paragraphs 1 to 5, the legal basis could be found for choosing a progressive orientation. The fact that the Seabed Disputes Chamber later took a position against sponsoring States of convenience in deep seabed

126 For example, it is evident that a rule such as "there must be a helmet on the head of every worker employed in the construction of buildings" sets forth an obligation for the employer and a corresponding right for the worker and the State, acting for the general interest of the safety in working conditions. This rule has not been adopted only to secure more effective implementation of the duties of the employer. If it is violated, the legal remedies cannot only consist in reporting the facts to the employer.

127 It is sometimes pointed out that today the attraction exercised by flags of convenience is less related to the possibility to circumvent the rules on the safety of navigation, which most ship-owners are willing to comply with, than to the possibility to depart from stringent contractual and social requirements for seafarers, starting from their salaries. However, this would not change the substance of the matter, as sub-standard qualifications and salaries also affect safety of navigation, and would not be a good reason to condone flags of convenience.

128 As already remarked upon (*supra*, section IV.A), the Tribunal later made use of the category of due diligence obligations in its Advisory Opinions relating to deep seabed mining activities and fishing.

mining activities[129] does not wipe out the impression that the Tribunal's 1999 Judgment provided implicit support to States granting flags of convenience.

It may be added that, in the specific case, the Tribunal found that "the evidence adduced by Guinea was not sufficient to justify the contention that there was no genuine link between the ship *Saiga* and Saint Vincent and the Grenadines".[130] It thus appears that there was in fact no practical need for the Tribunal to elaborate in general on the content of the obligation to ensure a genuine link and to reach the conclusion that such an obligation only works in favour of the flag State.

The question of the genuine link was also discussed in the already mentioned 2014 Judgment in the *M/V "Virginia G" Case*, relating to an oil tanker flying the flag of Panama and engaged in supplying gas oil to fishing vessels. The tanker was owned by a Panamanian company and was chartered to an Irish company. Again the Tribunal, quoting the precedent of the *M/V "SAIGA" (No. 2)* decision, reached the conclusion that the existence of a genuine link is not a condition for the granting of nationality to ships.[131] However, here the Tribunal added that the obligation to ensure a genuine link applies only after registration of a ship:

> In the view of the Tribunal, once a ship is registered, the flag State is required, under article 94 of the Convention, to exercise effective

129 See *supra*, section IV.B.

130 *M/V "SAIGA" (No. 2) (Saint Vincent and the Grenadines* v. *Guinea), Judgment, ITLOS Reports 1999*, p. 10, at p. 42, para. 87. In summarizing the position of the flag State, the Tribunal remarked (at para. 78) that "Saint Vincent and the Grenadines calls attention to various facts which, according to it, provide evidence of this link. These include the fact that the owner of the *Saiga* is represented in Saint Vincent and the Grenadines by a company formed and established in that State and the fact that the *Saiga* is subject to the supervision of the Vincentian authorities to secure compliance with the International Convention for the Safety of Life at Sea (SOLAS), 1960 and 1974, the International Convention for the Prevention of Pollution from Ships, 1973, as modified by the Protocol of 1978 relating thereto (MARPOL 73/78), and other conventions of the International Maritime Organization to which Saint Vincent and the Grenadines is a party. In addition, Saint Vincent and the Grenadines maintains that arrangements have been made to secure regular supervision of the vessel's seaworthiness through surveys, on at least an annual basis, conducted by reputable classification societies authorized for that purpose by Saint Vincent and the Grenadines. Saint Vincent and the Grenadines also points out that, under its laws, preference is given to Vincentian nationals in the manning of ships flying its flag."

131 *M/V "Virginia G" (Panama/Guinea-Bissau), Judgment, ITLOS Reports 2014*, p. 4, at p. 44, para. 110.

> jurisdiction and control over that ship in order to ensure that it operates in accordance with generally accepted international regulations, procedures and practices. This is the meaning of "genuine link".[132]

Does the sentence above mean that, if the obligation to ensure a genuine is not complied with by a State during the time subsequent to the registration, the right of a ship to fly the flag of that State is lost? Although this would seem a logical consequence, the Tribunal did not draw such a conclusion. It was satisfied with the fact that, in the specific case, there was no reason to question that Panama exercised effective jurisdiction and control over the *M/V "Virginia G"* at the time of the incident.[133]

B *Nationality of Ships by Conduct*

Another question relating to the nationality of ships addressed by the Tribunal in the *M/V "SAIGA" (No. 2)* Judgment was whether the *Saiga* was a ship without nationality. It appears the she had a provisional certificate of registration issued by Saint Vincent and the Grenadines which had expired on 12 September 1997. On 28 November 1997, she was granted a permanent certificate of registration. This explains the objection raised by Guinea that Saint Vincent and the Grenadines had no legal standing to bring a claim before the Tribunal, as at the time of the facts (27 October 1997) the *Saiga* was a ship without nationality. Saint Vincent and the Grenadines controverted Guinea's objection referring, *inter alia*, to some aspects of the national legislation and to a declaration dated 1 March 1999 by the national Deputy Commissioner for Maritime Affairs which stated that the *Saiga* remained validly registered in the register of ships as at 27 October 1997.

The Tribunal remarked in general that, "in the case of merchant ships, the normal procedure used by States to grant nationality is registration in accordance with domestic legislation adopted for that purpose."[134] In the specific case, the Tribunal found that Saint Vincent and the Grenadines had produced sufficient evidence to support its assertion that the *Saiga* was a national ship at the time of the incident,[135] that such evidence has been reinforced by the

---

132 *Ibid.*, at p. 45, para. 113.

133 *Ibid.*, at pp. 45–46, paras. 114 to 117.

134 *M/V "SAIGA" (No. 2) (Saint Vincent and the Grenadines* v. *Guinea), Judgment, ITLOS Reports 1999*, p. 10, at p. 37, para. 64.

135 *Ibid.*, para. 67: "Saint Vincent and the Grenadines has produced evidence before the Tribunal to support its assertion that the *Saiga* was a ship entitled to fly its flag at the time of the incident giving rise to the dispute. In addition to making references to the relevant

conduct of the State in question[136] and that Guinea did not challenge or raise any doubts about the registration or nationality of the ship at any time until the submission of its counter-memorial in October 1998.[137] The Tribunal's conclusions were the following:

(a) it has not been established that the Vincentian registration or nationality of the *Saiga* was extinguished in the period between the date on which the Provisional Certificate of Registration was stated to expire and the date of issue of the Permanent Certificate of Registration;
(b) in the particular circumstances of this case, the consistent conduct of Saint Vincent and the Grenadines provides sufficient support for the conclusion that the *Saiga* retained the registration and nationality of Saint Vincent and the Grenadines at all times material to the dispute;
(c) in view of Guinea's failure to question the assertion of Saint Vincent and the Grenadines that it is the flag State of the *Saiga* when it had every reasonable opportunity to do so and its other conduct in the case, Guinea cannot successfully challenge the registration and nationality of the *Saiga* at this stage;
(d) in the particular circumstances of this case, it would not be consistent with justice if the Tribunal were to decline to deal with the merits of the dispute.[138]

These conclusions leave many doubts, especially as regards the assumption that nationality to ships can be granted by conduct. If registration is the normal procedure to grant nationality to ships, why should the expiration of a

provisions of the Merchant Shipping Act, Saint Vincent and the Grenadines has drawn attention to several indications of Vincentian nationality on the ship or carried on board. These include the inscription of 'Kingstown' as the port of registry on the stern of the vessel, the documents on board and the ship's seal which contained the words 'SAIGA Kingstown' and the then current charter-party which recorded the flag of the vessel as 'Saint Vincent and the Grenadines'."

136 *Ibid.*, para. 68: "The evidence adduced by Saint Vincent and the Grenadines has been reinforced by its conduct. Saint Vincent and the Grenadines has at all times material to the dispute operated on the basis that the *Saiga* was a ship of its nationality. It has acted as the flag State of the ship during all phases of the proceedings. It was in that capacity that it invoked the jurisdiction of the Tribunal in its Application for the prompt release of the *Saiga* and its crew under article 292 of the Convention and in its Request for the prescription of provisional measures under article 290 of the Convention."

137 *Ibid.*, at p. 38, para. 69.

138 *Ibid.*, para. 73.

certificate of registration not also automatically entail that the nationality has expired? What other factual evidence would be needed to reach this simple conclusion?[139] Why should Guinea be under the burden to prove what is already stated in a certificate issued by the other party to the dispute? Why should Saint Vincent and the Grenadines be allowed to prove something which is in full contradiction with the clear content of its own certification? On the one hand, the Tribunal held that the nationality of ships is based on a formality, such as a certificate, rather than on a matter of fact, such as a genuine link.[140] On the other hand, the Tribunal held that a formality, such as the expiration of a certificate, is not enough to prove the loss of nationality and may be overcome by a matter of fact, such as the conduct of the alleged flag State. The two assumptions are in contradiction, as consistency would require formalities to be given the same value. The sudden appearance in the Tribunal's Judgment of a sort of "nationality of ships by conduct" is not a promising addition to international law of the sea and seems in conflict with article 91, paragraph 2, of the Convention.[141]

The position taken in the *M/V "SAIGA" (No. 2) Case* Judgment was so questionable that, in a subsequent case, the Tribunal itself preferred a completely different solution in a similar situation. In deciding, on 20 April 2001, the

139 See the *Separate Opinions of President Mensah, ITLOS Reports 1999*, p. 86, para. 15, and *of Vice-President Wolfrum, ITLOS Reports 1999*, p. 99, para. 26, as well as the *Dissenting Opinion of Judge Warioba, ITLOS Reports 1999*, p. 212–213, paras. 46 and 47: "The second ground on which the Judgment is based is what is termed as the consistent behaviour of the Applicant. It is argued that the Applicant has operated at all times as the flag State in all the phases of the case. This is indeed a strange argument in the context of article 91 of the Convention. Under that article, as has already been stated, States have exclusive jurisdiction to set the conditions for the grant of nationality to ships. Saint Vincent and the Grenadines has set those conditions in the Merchant Shipping Act. Either a ship is registered under those conditions or it is not registered. The behaviour of Saint Vincent and the Grenadines will not change what is in its law, it will not change the words on the Certificate of Registration, and it will not change what is inscribed in the Book of Registry. The Tribunal is in a way trying to amend the Convention by introducing new conditions outside article 91. Under that article it is only the flag State which can fix conditions for registration of ships. If the Tribunal determines that the consistent behaviour of a State should lead other States to accept it as a condition of registration it will be a violation of the principle of exclusive jurisdiction enshrined in article 91 of the Convention."

140 See *supra*, section XIII.A.

141 Article 91, para. 2, of the Convention provides that "[e]very State shall issue to ships to which it has granted the right to fly its flag documents to that effect."

"Grand Prince" Case (*Belize* v. *France*), *Prompt Release*,[142] the Tribunal found that a provisional registration that had expired at the time of the application was not a sufficient basis for holding that Belize was the flag State of a ship.[143] This despite the fact that the Administration of the International Merchant Marine Register of Belize issued a certification in which it was stated that the ship was still considered as registered in Belize until final decision by it.[144]

C *Right of the Flag State to Bring Claims in Cases Involving Ships*

In deciding the *M/V "SAIGA" (No. 2) Case*, the Tribunal addressed Guinea's assumption that Saint Vincent and the Grenadines was not entitled to act in diplomatic protection of individuals, namely the ship-owners, the master, the members of the crew and the owners of the cargo, who were not its own nationals. According to Tribunal, a number of provisions of the Convention[145] show that the ship is one single entity necessarily linked to the flag State. This particular situation grants to the flag State a sort of exclusive right to bring claims relating to the operation of a ship:

> the Convention considers a ship as a unit, as regards the obligations of the flag State with respect to the ship and the right of a flag State to seek reparation for loss or damage caused to the ship by acts of other States and to institute proceedings under article 292 of the Convention. Thus the ship, every thing on it, and every person involved or interested in its operations are treated as an entity linked to the flag State. The nationalities of these persons are not relevant.[146]
>
> The Tribunal must also call attention to an aspect of the matter which is not without significance in this case. This relates to two basic characteristics of modern maritime transport: the transient and multinational composition of ships' crews and the multiplicity of interests that may be involved in the cargo on board a single ship. A container vessel carries a large number of containers, and the persons with interests in them may

142 The case related to the special procedure for prompt release of vessels and crews pursuant to article 292 of the Convention.

143 *"Grand Prince"* (*Belize* v. *France*), *Prompt Release, Judgment, ITLOS Reports 2001*, p. 17, at p. 42, para. 85.

144 *Ibid.*, at p. 38, para. 70.

145 In particular, articles 94, 106, 110, para. 3, 111, para. 8, 217, 292 of the Convention. See *M/V "SAIGA" (No. 2)* (*Saint Vincent and the Grenadines* v. *Guinea*), *Judgment, ITLOS Reports 1999*, p. 10, at p. 47, para. 105.

146 *Ibid.*, at p. 48, para. 106. In fact, the nationality of persons on board could become relevant for other purposes, such issues relating to human rights or criminal jurisdiction.

> be of many different nationalities. This may also be true in relation to cargo on board a break-bulk carrier. Any of these ships could have a crew comprising persons of several nationalities. If each person sustaining damage were obliged to look for protection from the State of which such person is a national, undue hardship would ensue.[147]

Also in the *M/V "Virginia G"* Judgment, the Tribunal found that the flag State is entitled to make claims relating to the ship, irrespective of the fact that the ship-owner and the crew are not its own nationals.[148]

The Tribunal's conclusion on this question seems fully in conformity with both the Convention and customary international law.[149]

XIV Concluding Remarks

The Tribunal's jurisprudence is always remarkable for textual and conceptual clarity,[150] as well as care in legal analysis.[151] It leaves a general impression of solidity and reliability, which is typically evidenced by the Judgment in the *Dispute concerning delimitation of the maritime boundary in the Bay of Bengal (Bangladesh/Myanmar)*.

In deciding the first case submitted to it, the Tribunal missed an opportunity of orientating the progressive development of international law of the sea.

---

147 *Ibid.*, para. 107.

148 *M/V "Virginia G" (Panama/Guinea-Bissau), Judgment, ITLOS Reports 2014*, p. 4, at p. 49, paras. 119–129.

149 See the decision on question two by the Arbitral Tribunal that on 7 September 1910 settled the dispute between the United Kingdom and the United States, *The North Atlantic Coast Fisheries Case (Great Britain, United States)*, 7 September 1910, RIAA Vol. XI, pp. 167–226.

150 See, for example, the clear explanation that, in the 2012 Judgment on the delimitation in the Bay of Bengal, the Tribunal gives about what is estoppel – a notion difficult to be seized by lawyers coming from non-common law countries: "in international law, a situation of estoppel exists when a State, by its conduct, has created the appearance of a particular situation and another State, relying on such conduct in good faith, has acted or abstained from an action to its detriment. The effect of the notion of estoppel is that a State is precluded, by its conduct, from asserting that it did not agree to, or recognize, a certain situation." *Delimitation of the maritime boundary in the Bay of Bengal (Bangladesh/Myanmar), Judgment, ITLOS Reports 2012*, p. 4, at p. 42, para. 124.

151 See, for example, the care devoted by the Seabed Disputes Chamber in interpreting the relevant provisions of the Convention in all six official texts, *Responsibilities and obligations of States with respect to activities in the Area, Advisory Opinion, 1 February 2011, ITLOS Reports 2011*, p. 10, at p. 30, paras. 64–71.

Called to make a choice that presented both legal and political aspects, the Tribunal neglected the general concerns for safety of navigation and protection of the environment that are implied in the Convention notion of "genuine link". But subsequent elements in the Tribunal's case-law, in particular the two Advisory Opinions, show that this court has taken a more progressive attitude towards the needs of the protection of the environment and the conservation of marine living resources. The use by the Tribunal of the notion of due diligence obligations as regards mining activities and fishing also constitutes a promising development in international law of the sea.

The Impacts of the Tribunal's Jurisprudence on the Development of International Law

Yoshifumi Tanaka

I Introduction

Whilst the primary task of international courts and tribunals is to settle international disputes, judicial organs also perform an important function in the development of international law through their jurisprudence and the same holds true of the Tribunal. In fact, the jurisprudence of the Tribunal can be said to make an important contribution to the development of international law in three ways.

First, by confirming *dicta* and/or precedents of other judicial organs with regard to the interpretation and application of rules of international law, the Tribunal contributes to further consolidating the normative status of these rules (the consolidation of rules).

Second, more often than not, the meaning of rules of international law, customary or conventional, becomes a subject of international disputes. Like other international courts and tribunals, the Tribunal clarifies the meaning and scope of relevant rules of international law in its jurisprudence (the clarification of rules).

Third, the procedural law of international courts and tribunals evolves through their jurisprudence over time and the same applies to the Tribunal. In fact, the Tribunal develops procedural rules concerning judicial proceedings through its jurisprudence (the development of procedural law). Evolution of procedural rules of international courts and tribunals can also be regarded as part of the development of international law.

Noting these three points, this article seeks to succinctly examine the impacts of the Tribunal's jurisprudence on the development of international law. Because of limitations of space, no comprehensive analysis of this subject can be made here. This article has only the modest aim of examining some remarkable examples in this matter. The following section addresses state of necessity and the basic principle concerning the use of force in law enforcement operations at sea as examples of the consolidation of rules of international law. The article then moves on to discuss the clarification of rules of international law with specific focus on bunkering in the EEZ and State responsibility. Next, the

© 2018, BY INTERNATIONAL TRIBUNAL FOR THE LAW OF THE SEA | DOI 10.1163/9789004356832_015

article examines the development of procedural rules through the Tribunal's jurisprudence, before offering conclusions.

II Consolidation of the Existing Rules of International Law

A *State of Necessity*

The first issue to be examined concerns the "state of necessity" as a legal basis for precluding wrongfulness. According to the commentary of the ILC to the Draft Articles on Responsibility of States for Internationally Wrongful Acts ("the ILC Draft Articles on State Responsibility"), "[t]he term 'necessity' ('état de necessité') is used to denote those exceptional cases where the only way a State can safeguard an essential interest threatened by a grave and imminent peril is, for the time being, not to perform some other international obligation of lesser weight or urgency."[1] In the view of the ILC, this is a highly exceptional plea.[2]

In the *Gabčíkovo-Nagymaros Project* case, "state of necessity" was invoked by Hungary as a legal ground to suspend and abandon works that it had been committed to perform under the 1977 Treaty on the Construction and Operation of the Gabčíkovo-Nagymaros Barrage System and related instruments. In this regard, the ICJ held that: "[T]he state of necessity is a ground recognized by customary international law for precluding the wrongfulness of an act not in conformity with an international obligation."[3]

Furthermore, the Court approved the customary law character of conditions which must be cumulatively satisfied to invoke "necessity" as a plea for precluding wrongfulness set forth in article 33 of the ILC Draft Articles on State Responsibility.[4] However, the Court offered scant explanation of the reasons why state of necessity and its conditions can be regarded as part of customary international law. After examining the question of whether the conditions on "state of necessity" were fulfilled, the Court, in the *Gabčíkovo-Nagymaros Project* Judgment, concluded that: "Hungary would not have been permitted to

1 J. Crawford, *The International Law Commission's Articles on State Responsibility: Introduction, Text and Commentaries* (Cambridge University Press, 2002), p. 178.

2 *Ibid.*

3 *Gabčíkovo-Nagymaros Project (Hungary/Slovakia), Judgment, I.C.J Reports 1997*, p. 40, para. 51.

4 *Ibid.*, p. 41, para. 52.

rely upon that state of necessity in order to justify its failure to comply with its treaty obligations, as it had helped, by act or omission to bring it about."[5]

Subsequently, by referring to cases and incidents on this subject, including the *Gabčíkovo-Nagymaros Project* Judgment, the ILC concluded that: "[o]n balance, State practice and judicial decisions support the view that necessity may constitute a circumstance precluding wrongfulness under certain very limited conditions, and this view is embodied in article 25."[6]

The *dictum* in the *Gabčíkovo-Nagymaros Project* Judgment was also confirmed by the ICJ in the *Wall* case, stating that:

> As the Court observed in the case concerning *Gabčíkovo-Nagymaros Project (Hungary/Slovakia)*, "the state of necessity is a ground recognized by customary international law" that "can only be accepted on an exceptional basis"; it "can only be invoked under certain strictly defined conditions which must be cumulatively satisfied; and the State concerned is not the sole judge of whether those conditions have been met."[7]

The Court then applied one of the conditions stated in article 25 of the ILC Draft Articles on State Responsibility.[8] Here one may find an "institutional circularity."[9]

The application of the defence of "state of necessity" was also at issue in the *M/V "SAIGA" (No. 2)* Case before the Tribunal. In this case, the Tribunal considered whether the otherwise wrongful application by Guinea of its customs laws to the EEZ could be justified under general international law by Guinea's appeal to "state of necessity". Here the Tribunal relied on the ICJ's view in the *Gabčíkovo-Nagymaros Project* Judgment, stating that:

> 133. In the *Case Concerning the Gabčíkovo-Nagymaros Project* (*Gabčíkovo-Nagymaros Project (Hungary/ Slovakia), Judgment, I.C.J. Reports 1997*, pp. 40 and 41, paragraphs 51 and 52), the International Court of Justice noted with approval two conditions for the defence based on "state of

5 *Ibid.*, p. 46, para. 57.

6 Crawford, *supra* at note 1, p. 183.

7 *Legal Consequences of the Construction of a Wall in the Occupied Palestinian Territory, Advisory Opinion, I.C.J Reports 2004*, p. 195, para. 140.

8 *Ibid.*

9 R.D. Sloane, "On the Use and Abuse of Necessity in the Law of State Responsibility", 106 *AJIL* 3 (2012), p. 453. See also T. Yamada, *Necessity in International Law* (in Japanese) (Yuhikaku, 2014), p. 75.

necessity" which in general international law justifies an otherwise wrongful act. These conditions, as set out in article 33, paragraph 1, of the International Law Commission's Draft Articles on State Responsibility, are:

(a) the act was the only means of safeguarding an essential interest of the State against a grave and imminent peril; and

(b) the act did not seriously impair an essential interest of the State towards which the obligation existed.

134. In endorsing these conditions, the Court stated that they "must be cumulatively satisfied" and that they "reflect customary international law."[10]

By applying the conditions set out in article 33(1) of the ILC Draft Articles on State Responsibility, the Tribunal ruled that application of Guinea's customs laws to a customs radius was contrary to the Convention; and that the arrest and detention of the *Saiga*, the prosecution and conviction of its Master, the confiscation of the cargo and the seizure of the ship were contrary to the Convention.[11] Overall, the Tribunal seemed to approve the rule of the state of necessity as formulated by the ILC Draft Articles on State Responsibility.[12]

The Tribunal did not clarify its view with regard to the customary law nature of the state of necessity, by examining State practice and *opinio juris*. Even so, by endorsing the views of the ILC and the ICJ in this matter, it can be argued that the Tribunal contributed to consolidating the normative status of "state of necessity" in customary international law.

B *The Basic Principle Concerning the Use of Force in Law Enforcement Operations at Sea*

The second issue to be addressed pertains to the basic principle concerning the use of force in law enforcement operations at sea. The Tribunal, in the *M/V "SAIGA" (No. 2) Case* between Saint Vincent and the Grenadines and Guinea, examined the legality of the force used by Guinea in the arrest of the *Saiga*. Referring to the *I'm Alone* and the *Red Crusader* cases, the Tribunal ruled that:

10 *M/V "SAIGA" (No. 2) (Saint Vincent and the Grenadines* v. *Guinea), Judgment, ITLOS Reports 1999*, p. 10, at p. 56, paras. 133–134.

11 *Ibid.*, para. 136.

12 S. Heathcote, « Est-ce que l'état de nécessité est un principe de droit international coutumier? » 1 *Revue belge de droit international* (2007), p. 59.

> Although the Convention does not contain express provisions on the use of force in the arrest of ships, international law, which is applicable by virtue of article 293 of the Convention, requires that the use of force must be avoided as far as possible and, where force is unavoidable, it must not go beyond what is reasonable and necessary in the circumstances. Considerations of humanity must apply in the law of the sea, as they do in other areas of international law.[13]

According to the Tribunal, these principles have been followed over the years in law enforcement operations at sea.[14] Furthermore, the Tribunal took the view that the basic principles concerning the use of force in the arrest of a ship at sea have been reaffirmed by article 22(1)(f) of the 1995 Fish Stocks Agreement.[15] Even though the meaning of "international law" was not explained in the *M/V "SAIGA" (No. 2)* Judgment, the term "international law" in this context can be thought to be customary international law. It would seem to follow that the Tribunal, in the *M/V "SAIGA" (No. 2) Case*, confirmed the customary law nature of the basic principles by confirming precedents in this matter.

Related to this, it is of particular interest to note that the Tribunal explicitly referred to considerations of humanity. A classical reference to considerations of humanity can be seen in the 1949 *Corfu Channel* Judgment. In this case, the ICJ ruled that the obligations incumbent upon the Albanian authorities consisted in notifying, for the benefit of shipping in general, the existence of a minefield in Albanian territorial waters and in warning the approaching British warships of the imminent danger to which the minefield exposed them. In the view of the Court, such obligations are based on "certain general and well-recognized principles, namely: elementary considerations of humanity, even more exacting in peace than in war; the principle of the freedom of maritime communication; and every State's obligation not to allow knowingly its territory to be used for acts contrary to the rights of other States."[16] An issue

---

13 *M/V "SAIGA" (No. 2)*, *supra* at note 10, at p. 61, para. 155.

14 *Ibid.*, at p. 62, para. 156.

15 *Ibid.*. Likewise, article 8 bis, paragraph 9, of the 2005 SUA Convention provides that: "[a]ny use of force pursuant to this article shall not exceed the minimum degree of force which is necessary and reasonable in the circumstance." *Protocol of 2005 to the Convention for the Suppression of Unlawful Acts Against the Safety of Maritime Navigation*, 14 October 2005.

16 *Corfu Channel (United Kingdom* v. *Albania), Merits, Judgment, I.C.J. Reports 1949*, p. 4, at p. 22.

that arises here is where "certain general and well-recognized principles" of elementary considerations of humanity derives from. The ICJ offered scant explanation about this issue. Fifty years later, however, the *dictum* of the ICJ was confirmed by the Tribunal, in the *M/V "SAIGA" (No. 2) Case*. Like the ICJ, the Tribunal did not clarify the legal basis of considerations of humanity. By confirming the *dictum* of the ICJ in the *Corfu Channel* Judgment, however, the Tribunal can be said to have contributed to consolidating the normative status of considerations of humanity.[17]

C *Commentary*

On the basis of the above cursory survey, two brief comments can be made.

First, the Tribunal's jurisprudence demonstrates that in some cases, the Tribunal identified rules of international law applicable to a specific case by relying on the jurisprudence of the ICJ and/or other precedents. The practice of the Tribunal contributes to consolidating the normative status of the rules concerned. At the same time, it prevents the fragmentation of international law by maintaining consistency with the ICJ jurisprudence and other precedents.

Second, simplification of the identification process of rules of customary international law in international jurisprudence leaves some room for discussion. For instance, before the *Gabčíkovo-Nagymaros Project* Judgment, it was less clear whether state of necessity enjoyed universal acceptance in international law.[18] In fact, the arbitral tribunal in the *Rainbow Warrior* arbitration considered the state of necessity as the "controversial doctrine" and concluded that there is no general principle allowing the defence of necessity.[19] However, the ICJ, in the *Gabčíkovo-Nagymaros Project* Judgment, admitted the customary law character of state of necessity, without examining State practice and *opinio juris*. The Court's view affected the work of the ILC when drafting a rule concerning state of necessity in its Draft Articles on State Responsibility. The *dictum* of the ICJ in the *Gabčíkovo-Nagymaros Project* Judgment and the ILC Draft Articles on State Responsibility were also applied by the Tribunal in the *M/V "SAIGA" (No. 2) Case*. Thus, it can be argued that the state of necessity

17 Considerations of humanity are embodied in treaties, for instance, in the *International Convention on Maritime Search and Rescue*, 27 April 1979, 1405 *UNTS* 119. It can also be observed that several provisions of the Convention, such as articles 18, para. 2, 24, para. 2, 44 and 98, reflect considerations of humanity.

18 D. Bodansky and J.R. Crook, "Symposium: The ILC's State Responsibility Articles", 96 *AJIL* 4 (2002), p. 788.

19 *Case concerning the difference between New Zealand and France concerning the interpretation or application of two agreements, concluded on 9 July 1986 between the two States and which related to the problems arising from the Rainbow Warrior Affair*, 30 April 1990, *RIAA* Vol. XX, pp. 215–284, at p. 254.

was consolidated as customary international law through the ICJ, ILC and the Tribunal. As Bodansky and Crook observed, it may be said that "legal development of state of necessity had a circular quality."[20] In this regard, there may be a need to consider the question whether the development of a rule of customary international law through institutional circularity may entail the risk of detaching the rule from actual State practice.[21]

III Clarification of Rules of International Law

A *Bunkering in the EEZ of a Third State*

Even though the Convention is intended to be a comprehensive treaty,[22] it does not provide rules applicable to each and every issue that may arise from human activities in the oceans. The legality of bunkering in an EEZ of a foreign State is a case in point.

This issue was raised, for the first time in the Tribunal's jurisprudence, in the 1999 *M/V "SAIGA" (No. 2) Case*. A central question in this case was whether or not Guinea was entitled to apply its customs laws in order to regulate bunkering in its EEZ. In this regard, the Tribunal held that whilst the coastal State has jurisdiction to apply customs laws and regulations in respect of artificial islands, installations and structures in the EEZ pursuant to article 60, paragraph 2, of the Convention, the Convention does not empower a coastal State to apply its customs laws in respect of any other parts of the EEZ not mentioned in that provision.[23]

Subsequently, a similar dispute arose between Panama and Guinea-Bissau. On 20 August 2009, the *M/V "Virginia G"*, an oil tanker flying the flag of Panama, supplied gas oil to fishing vessels flying the flag of Mauritania in the EEZ of Guinea-Bissau. On 21 August 2009, the *M/V "Virginia G"* was arrested by the authority of Guinea-Bissau and the tanker, along with its gear, equipment and products on board, was confiscated. Panama subsequently instituted arbitral proceedings against Guinea-Bissau pursuant to Annex VII of the Convention in a dispute concerning the *M/V "Virginia G"*. Later the dispute was transferred to the Tribunal.

20 Bodansky and Crook, *supra* at note 18, p. 788. Yet, they did not refer to the *M/V "SAIGA" (No. 2) Case.*

21 Heathcote called the state of necessity developed by the ICJ and ILC "plantes de serre, [ou] perles de culture". Heathcote *supra* at note 12, p. 63.

22 Article 156, para. 2, of the Convention.

23 *M/V "SAIGA" (No. 2)*, *supra* at note 10, p. 54, para. 127.

A pivotal issue to be addressed by the Tribunal was whether Guinea-Bissau, in the exercise of its sovereign rights in respect of the conservation and management of natural resources in its EEZ, had the competence to regulate bunkering of foreign vessels fishing in this zone. In this regard, the Tribunal took the view that the regulation by a coastal State of bunkering of foreign vessels fishing in its EEZ is among those measures which the coastal State may take in its EEZ to conserve and manage its living resources under articles 56 and 62, paragraph 4, of the Convention.[24] According to the Tribunal, the coastal State's jurisdiction over bunkering of foreign vessels fishing in its EEZ derives from the sovereign rights of that State to explore, exploit, conserve and manage natural resources. At the same time, the Tribunal added that the coastal State does not have such competence with regard to other bunkering activities, unless otherwise determined in accordance with the Convention.[25] All in all, the Tribunal in the *M/V "Virginia G" Case* can be thought to clarify rules concerning the regulation of bunkering in the EEZ by the coastal State through interpretation of relevant provisions of the Convention.

B *International Responsibility*

Attention must also be paid to the Tribunal's view with regard to international responsibility. The Seabed Disputes Chamber of the Tribunal, in its 2011 Advisory Opinion, specified the circle of subjects that can invoke State responsibility for damage arising from seabed activities in the Area. In this regard, the Chamber ruled that: "[s]ubjects entitled to claim compensation may include the Authority, entities engaged in deep seabed mining, other users of the sea, and coastal States."[26]

Moreover, by referring to Article 48 of the ILC Draft Articles on State Responsibility, the Chamber made an important statement: "[e]ach State Party may also be entitled to claim compensation in light of the *erga omnes* character of the obligations relating to preservation of the environment of the high seas and in the Area."[27]

In the above passage, the Seabed Disputes Chamber provides scant explanation about the meaning of the term "*erga omnes*". In light of the term "[e]ach State Party", however, there appears to be some scope to consider that the

---

24 *M/V "Virginia G" (Panama* v. *Guinea-Bissau), Judgment, ITLOS Reports 2014*, p. 4, at pp. 66–69, paras. 208–217.

25 *Ibid.*, at p. 70, paras. 222–223.

26 *Responsibilities and obligations of States with respect to activities in the Area, Advisory Opinion, 1 February 2011, ITLOS Reports 2011*, p. 10, at p. 59, para. 179.

27 *Ibid.*

obligation relating to preservation of the environment of the high seas can be considered as *erga omnes partes* under the Convention. If this is the case, the *dictum* of the Chamber will mean that States Parties to the Convention may invoke responsibility for the breach of obligations in this matter.[28]

This view seems to be echoed by the ICJ in the 2012 *Belgium* v. *Senegal* case. In this case, the Court considered that the States Parties to the Convention against Torture[29] have a common interest to ensure, in view of their shared values, that acts of torture are prevented and that, if they occur, their authors do not enjoy impunity.[30] According to the Court, "[t]he common interest in compliance with the relevant obligations under the Convention against Torture implies the entitlement of each State party to the Convention to make a claim concerning the cessation of an alleged breach by another State party."[31] It follows that any State Party to the 1984 UN Convention against Torture may invoke the responsibility of another State Party with a view to ascertaining the alleged failure to comply with its obligation *erga omnes partes*.[32] The Court thus held that Belgium, as a State Party to the Convention against Torture, had standing to invoke the responsibility of Senegal for the alleged breaches of its obligations under articles 6(2) and 7(1) of the 1984 Convention.[33]

Related to this, the 2014 *Whaling in the Antarctic* case merits particular mention. Australia suffered no material damage as a result of Japan's scientific whaling in the Antarctic. Nonetheless, Australia referred the dispute to the ICJ to uphold its "collective interest, an interest it shares with all other parties" to the International Convention for the Regulation of Whaling[34] and the ICJ accepted the *locus standi* of Australia in this case. Therefore, there may be some scope to consider that in the *Whaling in the Antarctic* case, the ICJ accepted *locus standi* on the basis of obligation *erga omnes parties*, even though the Court did not explicitly refer to the obligation. Although further accumulation

28 R.L. Johnstone, *Offshore Oil and Gas Development in the Arctic under International Law: Risk and Responsibility* (Nijhoff, 2015), p. 223.

29 *Convention against Torture and Other Cruel, Inhuman or Degrading Treatment or Punishment*, 10 December 1984, 1465 *UNTS* 85.

30 *Questions relating to the Obligation to Prosecute or Extradite* (*Belgium* v. *Senegal*), *Judgment, I.C.J. Reports 2012*, p. 422, at p. 449, para. 68.

31 *Ibid.*, at p. 450, para. 69.

32 *Ibid.*

33 *Ibid.*, para.70. See also *Separate Opinion of Judge Cançado Trindade, ibid.*, pp. 527–529, paras. 104–108.

34 *Whaling in the Antarctic* (*Australia* v. *Japan: New Zealand Intervening*), Presentation by H. Burmester, Verbatim Record, CR 2013/18, 9 July 2013, p. 28, para. 19. See also presentation by L. Boisson de Chazournes, *ibid.*, pp. 33–34, paras. 18–20.

of case-law is needed to draw more general conclusions, the Tribunal's 2011 Advisory Opinion and the jurisprudence of the ICJ appear to hint at the direction that not directly injured States can invoke responsibility of another State on the basis of the alleged breach of obligations *erga omnes partes*.

IV Development of Procedural Rules

As noted, evolution of procedural rules can be regarded as an important function of the Tribunal. In this regard, one may take provisional measures and advisory jurisdiction as examples.

A *Provisional Measures*

In the ICJ jurisprudence, the requirements for the Court to indicate provisional measures have evolved over the years through its jurisprudence.[35] Likewise the Tribunal has also developed the requirements to prescribe provisional measures through its jurisprudence. In this regard, two points can be made.

The first point concerns a parallel development of the requirements to prescribe provisional measures in the ICJ and the Tribunal's jurisprudence. The requirement of the plausible character of the alleged rights in the principal request is a case in point. Until recently, the Court had not explicitly examined the plausibility of the alleged rights in the principal request as a distinct condition for provisional measures.[36] However, the Court in its Order in the *Belgium*

---

35 R. Higgins, "Interim Measures for the Protection of Human Rights" 36 *Columbia Journal of Transnational Law*, (1997), p. 108.

36 T. Sugihara, *Kokusai Shiho Saiban Seido* (in Japanese, *Institution of the International Court of Justice*) (Yuhikaku, 1996) p. 282. See also J. Sztucki, *Interim Measures in the Hague Court* (Kluwer, 1983), p. 123 and 259. An exceptional case may be the *Lockerbie* case. After the proceedings had been instituted, the UN Security Council adopted a resolution under Chapter VII of the UN Charter calling upon Libya to surrender two Libyan nationals who had been charged with responsibility for the destruction of the PanAm flight. The Court held that under Article 103 of the UN Charter, the obligations of the parties under the Charter prevail over their obligations under any other international agreement, including the Montreal Convention. Thus, the ICJ declined Libya's request for the indication of provisional measures on the ground that the rights claimed by Libya under the Montreal Convention could not be regarded as appropriate for protection by the indication of provisional measures. *Questions of Interpretation and Application of the 1971 Montreal Convention arising from the Aerial Incident at Lockerbie (Libyan Arab Jamahiriya* v. *United Kingdom), Provisional Measures, Order of 14 April 1992, I.C.J. Reports 1992*, p. 3, at p. 15, paras. 39–40; *Questions of Interpretation and Application of the 1971 Montreal Convention arising*

v. *Senegal* case referred to the plausibility test, stating that: "[T]he power of the Court to indicate provisional measures should be exercised only if the Court is satisfied that the rights asserted by a party are at least plausible".[37] In the *Belgium* v. *Senegal* case, the plausibility test was discussed in connection with the link between the right to be protected and the measures requested. In the *Costa Rica* v. *Nicaragua* case of 2011, this element was explicitly considered as a distinct requirement for indicating provisional measures. In the words of the Court, "for the purposes of considering the request for the indication of provisional measures, the Court needs only to decide whether the rights claimed by the Applicant on the merits, and for which it is seeking protection, are plausible."[38]

Subsequently the plausibility test was, for the first time in the jurisprudence of the Tribunal, discussed in the *Ghana/Côte d'Ivoire* provisional measures proceedings 2015. According to the Special Chamber, while it need not concern itself with the competing claims of the Parties, it needed to satisfy itself that the rights which Côte d'Ivoire claims on the merits and seeks to protect were at least plausible.[39] In this regard, the Special Chamber, in the *Ghana/Côte d'Ivoire* case, ruled that Côte d'Ivoire had presented enough material to show that the rights it sought to protect in the disputed area were plausible.[40] Likewise, the Tribunal in the 2015 *"Enrica Lexie" Incident* case considered that both Parties had sufficiently demonstrated that the rights they seek to protect regarding the *"Enrica Lexie"* incident were plausible.[41] It seems that this is in line with the development of the ICJ jurisprudence in this matter.

---

from the Aerial Incident at Lockerbie (*Libyan Arab Jamahiriya* v. *United States of America*), *Provisional Measures, Order of 14 April 1992, I.C.J. Reports 1992*, p. 114, at pp. 126–127, paras. 42–43.

37 *Questions relating to the Obligation to Prosecute or Extradite* (*Belgium* v. *Senegal*), *Provisional Measures, Order of 28 May 2009, I.C.J. Reports 2009*, p. 139, at p. 151, para. 57.

38 *Certain Activities carried out by Nicaragua in the Border Area* (*Costa Rica* v. *Nicaragua*) (hereafter "the *Costa Rica/Nicaragua* case"), *Provisional Measures, Order of 8 March 2011, I.C.J. Reports 2011*, p. 6, at p. 19, para. 57.

39 *Delimitation of the maritime boundary in the Atlantic Ocean* (*Ghana/Côte d'Ivoire*), *Provisional Measures, Order of 25 April 2015, ITLOS Reports 2015*, p. 146, at p. 158, para. 58.

40 *Ibid.*, at p. 159, para. 62.

41 *"Enrica Lexie" Incident* (*Italy* v. *India*), *Provisional Measures, Order of 24 August 2015, ITLOS Reports 2015*, p. 182, at p. 197, para. 85. For a brief outline of this incident, see Y. Jie Wu, "The Enrica Lexie Incident: Jurisdiction in the Contiguous Zone?" *Cambridge International Law Journal Blog*, 19 April 2014, available at: http://cjicl.org.uk/2014/04/19/enrica-lexie-incident-jurisdiction-contiguous-zone/.

However, the Court, in its jurisprudence, did not clarify the standard for the plausibility test. Likewise the Tribunal and its Special Chamber provided no further precision with regard to the criterion for determining the plausibility of the claim of the disputing party. The vagueness of the test may entail the risk of undermining the predictability of orders of the Court and the Tribunal with regard to provisional measures.[42] Furthermore, as stressed by the PCIJ in the *Factory at Chorzów* case,[43] provisional measures must be distinct from interim judgments. Yet, the examination of the plausibility of the alleged rights at the stage of provisional measures may run the risk of dealing with matters which should be examined at the stage of the merits and, consequently, the order of provisional measures may come close to the interim judgment. If this is the case, there is a concern that the plausibility test may make the distinction between provisional measures and pre-judgment obscure.[44]

The second point relates to a difference of interpretation of the requirements for the granting of provisional measures in the jurisprudence of the ICJ and that of the Tribunal. The interpretation of the requirement of "urgency" is an example. Urgency is an essential requirement of the prescription of provisional measures.[45] In the ICJ jurisprudence, it appears that the requirement of urgency is connected to an imminent risk that irreparable prejudice may be caused to the rights in dispute before the Court.[46] For example, execution of an individual within a very short period of time in the *LaGrand* case can be considered as an imminent risk.[47] In this case, urgency means imminence. However, it appears that the time-frame of the concept of urgency in

42 Separate Opinion of Judge Koroma in the *Costa Rica/Nicaragua* case, *I.C.J. Reports 2011*, p. 31, paras. 7–8.

43 *Order of 21 November 1927, P.C.I.J., Series A, No. 12*, p. 10. See also Declaration of Judge Oda in *LaGrand (Germany* v. *United States of America), Provisional Measures, Order of 3 March 1999, I.C.J. Reports 1999*, at p. 19, para. 6.

44 T. Sugihara, *Kokusai Shiho, supra.* note 36, p. 285.

45 *Separate Opinion of Judge Treves, Southern Bluefin Tuna (New Zealand* v. *Japan; Australia* v. *Japan), Provisional Measures, Order of 27 August 1999, ITLOS Reports 1999*, p. 280, at p. 316, para. 2. See also article 290, para. 5, of the Convention and article 89, para. 4, of the Rules.

46 *Questions relating to the Obligation to Prosecute or Extradite (Belgium* v. *Senegal), Provisional Measures, I.C.J Reports 2009*, p. 152, para. 62; *Certain Activities Carried Out by Nicaragua in the Border Area (Costa Rica v. Nicaragua), Provisional Measures, Order of 8 March 2011, ICJ Reports 2011*, p. 21, para. 64. See also E. Roucounas, "L'urgence et le droit international", in Société française pour le droit international, *Le droit international et le temps: Colloque de Paris* (Pedone, 2011), pp. 201–203.

47 *LaGrand (Germany* v. *United States of America), Provisional Measures, Order of 3 March 1999, I.C.J. Reports 1999*, p. 14, para. 14, and p. 15, para. 26.

the Tribunal's jurisprudence needs different consideration. For instance, the decline of fish stocks may be caused by cumulative effects of various elements, including the over-exploitation. The phenomenon of the exhaustion of marine living resources is a continuous process. One cannot deny the possibility that pending the final decision, a certain conduct of a disputing party might accelerate the decline of the fish stock or cause novel deterioration of the stock.[48] Hence it can be considered that, as Judge Laing stated in the *Southern Bluefin Tuna Cases*, "urgency or imminence is of the activity causing the harm, not necessarily the harm itself."[49]

In light of cumulative effects on the fish stock and the need for precaution, there appears to be a need to consider the question as to whether or not there is the urgency of situation which requires provisional measures to prevent *a trend* of decline towards a collapse of the fish stock. In this regard, notably Judge Treves in the *Southern Bluefin Tuna Cases* stated that: "The urgency concerns the stopping of a trend towards such collapse."[50] In relation to this, it must also be noted that normally scientific uncertainty exists in conservation of marine living resources. Accordingly, as the Tribunal stated in the *Southern Bluefin Tuna Cases*,[51] "prudence and caution" may be required when assessing the existence of urgency. Hence the concept of urgency in the context of conservation of marine living resources is to be closely linked to the precautionary approach.[52] In this regard, Judge Treves took the view that "the requirement of urgency is satisfied only in the light of such precautionary approach."[53] The learned judge also highlighted the inter-linkage between provisional measures and the precautionary approach, stating: "[A] precautionary approach seems to me inherent in the very notion of provisional measures."[54] Thus three

48 P. Gautier, "Mesures conservatoires, préjudice irréparable et protection de l'environnement", in *Liber Amicorum, Jean-Pierre Cot, Le procès international* (Bruylant, 2009), p. 149.

49 *Separate Opinion of Judge Laing* in the *Southern Bluefin Tuna* cases, *supra* at note 45, *ITLOS Reports 1999*, p. 308, para. 8.

50 *Separate Opinion of Judge Treves, supra* at note 45, *ITLOS Reports 1999*, p. 318, para. 8 (emphasis added).

51 *Southern Bluefin Tuna (New Zealand* v. *Japan; Australia* v. *Japan), Provisional Measures, Order of 27 August 1999, ITLOS Reports 1999*, p. 280, at p. 296, para. 77.

52 The customary law nature of the precautionary approach or principle remains a matter for discussion. Even so, it is possible that a court of tribunal takes account of the precautionary approach as an element of interpretation of the law applicable to a specific case. *See* Y. Tanaka, "Rethinking *Lex Ferenda* in International Adjudication", 51 *German Yearbook of International Law* (2008), p. 492.

53 *Separate Opinion of Judge Treves, supra* at note 45, *ITLOS Reports 1999*, p. 318, para. 8.

54 *Ibid.*, para. 9.

elements, i.e. urgency, the precautionary approach and provisional measures, are intimately inter-linked in the context of conservation of marine living resources.

It is true that under article 290, paragraph 5, of the Convention, the Tribunal is required to determine whether or not the urgency of the situation exists pending the constitution of the Annex VII arbitral tribunal.[55] As the Tribunal itself pointed to, however, "there is nothing in article 290 of the Convention to suggest that the measures prescribed by the Tribunal must be confined to that period."[56] As the Annex VII arbitral tribunal in the *Southern Bluefin Tuna* case stated, revocation of the Tribunal's Order prescribing provisional measures did not "mean that the Parties may disregard the effects of that Order or their own decisions made in conformity with it."[57] Thus the concept of urgency in the context of conservation of marine living resources needs to be considered in a longer time-frame than an imminent risk, taking account of consideration of "prudence and caution." In this sense, the interpretation of the requirement of urgency in the jurisprudence the Tribunal may differ from that in the ICJ jurisprudence.

B *Advisory Jurisdiction*

Finally, some mention must be made of advisory jurisdiction of the Tribunal as a full Tribunal. Whereas the Seabed Disputes Chamber of the Tribunal is explicitly empowered to give advisory opinions under the Convention,[58] the Convention contains no explicit provision concerning the advisory jurisdiction of the Tribunal as a full court.[59] An issue thus arises as to whether an advisory jurisdiction is conferred to the full Tribunal under the Convention. This was one of the debatable issues in the Advisory Opinion concerning the questions submitted by the SRFC. Indeed, opinions of States are sharply divided on this matter.

---

55 Article 290, paras. 1 and 5, of the Convention.

56 *Land Reclamation in and around the Straits of Johor (Malaysia* v. *Singapore), Provisional Measures, Order of 8 October 2003, ITLOS Reports 2003*, p. 10, at p. 22, para. 67. See also paras. 68–69.

57 *Southern Bluefin Tuna (New Zealand-Japan, Australia-Japan)*, 4 August 2000, *RIAA* Vol. XXIII, p. 47, para. 67.

58 Article 191 of the Convention. See also article 159, para. 10, of the Convention. Annexes, including the Statute (Annex VI), form an integral part of the Convention (article 318).

59 *Request for Advisory Opinion submitted by the Sub-Regional Fisheries Commission, Advisory Opinion, 2 April 2015, ITLOS Reports 2015*, p. 4 (hereafter "the 2015 Advisory Opinion"), at p. 21, para. 53.

While some ten States, out of 22 States which submitted written statements to the Tribunal, took the position that Tribunal as a full court does not have an advisory jurisdiction under the Convention,[60] the Tribunal ruled that the full Tribunal has advisory jurisdiction. When examining this issue, the Tribunal, in its Advisory Opinion, gave much weight to article 21 of the Statue, which reads: "[t]he jurisdiction of the Tribunal comprises all disputes and all applications submitted to it in accordance with this Convention and all matters specifically provided for in any other agreement which confers jurisdiction on the Tribunal."

According to the Tribunal, article 21 contains three elements:

(i) All "disputes" submitted to the Tribunal in accordance with the Convention,
(ii) All "applications" submitted to the Tribunal in accordance with the Convention, and
(iii) All "matters" specifically provided for in any other agreement which confers jurisdiction on the Tribunal.[61]

As the Tribunal observed, it is apparent that the term "disputes" under article 21 relates to the contentious jurisdiction of the Tribunal. Similarly, the word "applications" refers to applications in contentious cases submitted to the Tribunal in accordance with the Convention. This is clear from article 23 of the Statute which lays down that: "[t]he Tribunal shall decide all disputes and applications in accordance with article 293", which is part of Part XV of the Convention dealing with "Settlement of Disputes."[62]

On the other hand, the words "all matters" need different consideration. According to the Tribunal, the words "all matters" should not be interpreted as covering only "disputes" because, if that were to be the case, article 21 would have used the word "disputes". The Tribunal thus considered that the words must mean something more than only "disputes" and that something "must include advisory opinions, if specifically provided for in 'any other agreement

60 Those States are: Argentina, Australia, the People's Republic of China, France, the Republic of Ireland, Portugal, Spain, Thailand, the United Kingdom as well as the United States. The tone of the argument differs though. Whereas the United States is not a party to the Convention, on 1 April 2014, the Tribunal decided that the statement presented by the United States should be considered as part of the case file. *Ibid.*, at p. 13, para. 24.

61 *Ibid.*, at p. 21, para. 54.

62 *Ibid.*, para. 55.

which confers jurisdiction on the Tribunal'."[63] In this regard, the Tribunal held that: "[T]he expression 'all matters specifically provided for in any other agreement which confers jurisdiction on the Tribunal' does not by itself establish the advisory jurisdiction of the Tribunal", but "it is the 'other agreement' which confers such jurisdiction on the Tribunal".[64] In summary, article 21 and the "other agreement" conferring jurisdiction on the Tribunal constitute the legal basis of the advisory jurisdiction of the full Tribunal.[65]

As already discussed elsewhere, there appears to be some scope to reconsider the question of whether article 21 of the Statute, along with the "other agreement" conferring jurisdiction on the Tribunal, can provide an adequate legal basis of the advisory opinion of the full Tribunal.[66] If the interpretation of the Tribunal is correct, theoretically at least, the Tribunal could have whatsoever jurisdiction in so far as the jurisdiction is conferred by "any other agreement" than the Convention.[67] Yet, it is hard to imagine that the drafters of the Convention intended to take such an unreasonable interpretation.

---

63 *Ibid.*, para. 56. This interpretation is supported by: written statement of New Zealand, 27 November 2013, p. 4, para. 10; written statement of the Federal Republic of Somalia, 27 November 2013, p. 4, para. 3; written statement of Japan, 29 November 2013, pp. 2–3, para. 5; written statement of the Caribbean Regional Fisheries Mechanism, 27 November 2013, p. 17, para. 48; written statement of the SRFC version 2, March 2014, pp. 11–12; Presentation by Mr Ney, Verbatim Record, ITLOS/PV.14/C21/2, 3 September 2014, p. 2. Written statements and verbatim record are available at: https://www.itlos.org/. See also P. Gautier, "The Settlement of Disputes", in D.J. Attard et al. (eds.), *The IMLI Manual on International Maritime Law*, Vol. I, (Oxford University Press, 2014), p. 565.

64 The 2015 Advisory Opinion, *supra,* at note 59, at p. 22, para. 58.

65 *Ibid.* See also Statement by Mr Rüdiger Wolfrum on Agenda Item 75(a), 9–10, para. 16 (28 November 2005); written statement by the Federal Republic of Germany, 6, para. 8 (18 November 2013).

66 For a critical assessment of advisory jurisdiction of the Tribunal as a full Tribunal, see Y. Tanaka, "Reflections on the Advisory Jurisdiction of ITLOS as a Full Court: The ITLOS Advisory Opinion of 2015", 14 *The Law and Practice of International Courts and Tribunals* (2015), pp. 318–339; M. Lando, "The Advisory Jurisdiction of the International tribunal for the Law of the Sea: Comments on the Request for an Advisory Opinion Submitted by the Sub-Regional Fisheries Commission", 29 *Leiden Journal of International Law* (2016) pp. 441–461.

67 Written statement by the United States of America, 27 November 2013, p. 7, para. 25. Related to this, Judge Armand Ugon stated that: "The Parties to a dispute cannot depart from the Statute of the Court unilaterally or by agreement between themselves". Dissenting Opinion of Judge Ugon, *Interhandel (Switzerland* v. *United States of America), Judgment, I.C.J. Reports 1959*, p. 93, para. 6. See also written statement of Australia, 28 November 2013, p. 7, para. 14.

Furthermore, it has been suggested that article 21 of the Statute reflects the approach of Article 36, paragraph 1, of the Statute of the ICJ.[68] Even though Article 36, paragraph 1, also refers to the words "all matters", this provision has not been interpreted as conferring the advisory jurisdiction to the ICJ.[69] The words "all matters" under Article 36, paragraph 1, of the ICJ Statute refer to "disputes" in future cases. If the phrase "all matters" in article 21 of the Statute has a meaning different from that in Article 36, paragraph 1, of the ICJ Statute, there is a need to prove it. It seems that the advisory jurisdiction of the full Tribunal declared in the 2015Advisory Opinion is a judicial innovation. In any case the voting record of the Advisory Opinion does seem to imply that the Tribunal is ready to perform a more positive role in the interpretation and application of the law of the sea through advisory proceedings.

V Concluding Remarks

The above consideration reveals that the Tribunal's jurisprudence affects the progressive development of international law in three ways.

First, by confirming or relying on the *dictum* of the ICJ or other precedents with regard to a rule of international law, the Tribunal contributes to consolidating the normative status of the rules concerned. Examples include confirmation of customary law character of "state of necessity" and the basic principle concerning the use of force in law enforcement operations at sea. This practice can also prevent the fragmentation of international law. At the same time, there may be a need to consider the question of whether it is relevant to determine the customary law nature of a rule of international law within the circle of the international jurisprudence only, without examining State practice and *opinio juris*.

Second, by applying relevant rules to a particular case, the Tribunal clarifies the scope and meaning of the rules. By way of example, it is argued that the Tribunal in the *M/V "Virginia G" Case* clarified rules concerning the regulation of bunkering in the EEZ by the coastal State through the interpretation of relevant provisions of the Convention. It is also important that the Seabed Disputes Chamber accepted the *erga omnes* character of the obligations relating to preservation of the environment of the high seas and in the Area. The Chamber's view provides an important insight into the entitlement of not

68 M. Nordquist et al. (eds.), *United Nations Convention on the Law of the Sea: A Commentary*, Vol. V, (Nijhoff, 1989), p. 378.

69 Written statement of the Portuguese Republic, 27 November 2013, p. 4, para. 10.

directly injured States to invoke the responsibility of another State which has breached the obligations concerning the preservation of the environment of the high seas and in the Area.

Third, the Tribunal develops procedural rules with regard to its judicial proceedings. In this regard, commonalities and differences between the jurisprudence of the Tribunal and that of the ICJ merit particular attention. On the one hand, one can witness a parallel development of the requirements to prescribe provisional measures in the ICJ and the Tribunal's jurisprudence. On the other hand, the interpretation of the requirements in the Tribunal's jurisprudence may differ from that in the ICJ jurisprudence. The requirement of urgency is a case in point. In the particular context of marine environmental protection and conservation of marine living resources, it is argued that the concept of urgency may need to be considered in a longer time-frame than an imminent risk.

The Contribution of the International Tribunal for the Law of the Sea to the Progressive Development of International Law

*Peter Tomka**

Introduction

Before the Tribunal started its work 20 years ago, certain scholars questioned whether it was wise for the drafters of the Convention to provide States with a choice of forum – the Tribunal, the ICJ or arbitral tribunals, the latter being the default option – to settle their disputes.[1] This short paper considers how the Tribunal has largely refuted concerns with respect to fragmentation by contributing to the harmonized application and development of the international law of the sea.[2] The Tribunal's decisions are discussed in four categories: maritime

* This is a revised version of a speech that was delivered on 5 October 2016 in Hamburg as part of the Symposium on "The Contribution of the Tribunal to the Rule of Law" celebrating the 20th anniversary of the International Tribunal for the Law of the Sea. The excellent research and editorial assistance of Jessica Howley and Daniel Kaasik is gratefully acknowledged.

1 See C. Greenwood, "Statement on behalf of the ICJ to the UN General Assembly on the occasion of the commemoration of the thirtieth anniversary of the opening for signature of UNCLOS", 10 December 2012, para. 7, available at http://www.icj-cij.org/presscom/files/9/17229.pdf (visited 15 November 2016) and P. Gautier, "The Contribution of the International Tribunal for the Law of the Sea to the Rule of Law" in G. De Baere and J. Wouters (eds.), *The Contribution of International and Supranational Courts to the Rule of Law* (Edward Elgar, 2015), pp. 211–2. For such views, see, most notably, S. Oda, "Dispute Settlement Prospects in the Law of the Sea" 44 *ICLQ* 4 (1995) p. 864 (considering that the creation of the Tribunal "will prove to have been a great mistake" in this respect as "[t]he law of the sea must be interpreted in the light of the uniform development of jurisprudence within the international community and must not be dealt with in a fragmentary manner"). *Cf.*, on the other hand, J.I. Charney, "The Implications of Expanding International Dispute Settlement Systems: The 1982 Convention on the Law of the Sea" 90 *AJIL* 1 (1996) p. 72; and S. Rosenne, "Establishing the International Tribunal for the Law of the Sea" 89 *AJIL* 4 (1995) p. 814. The choice of procedures is provided under article 287 of the Convention. See generally N. Klein, *Dispute Settlement in the UN Convention on the Law of the Sea* (Cambridge University Press, 2005), pp. 53–9.

2 See also C. Greenwood, *supra* note 1, para. 7; P. Gautier, *supra* at note 1, pp. 211–2; and S. Yanai, "Statement of the President of the Tribunal to the UN General Assembly on the occasion of the commemoration of the thirtieth anniversary of the opening for signature of UNCLOS", 10 December 2012, available at https://www.itlos.org/fileadmin/itlos/documents/

© 2018, BY INTERNATIONAL TRIBUNAL FOR THE LAW OF THE SEA | DOI 10.1163/9789004356832_016

delimitation, provisional measures proceedings, prompt release proceedings and advisory opinions. It is also noted how the Tribunal's jurisprudence includes a rather prominent environmental aspect, which may be seen as corresponding to a more general rise in international environmental litigation.[3]

I Maritime Delimitation

The Tribunal made various important contributions to international law in its first maritime delimitation case, the *Delimitation of the maritime boundary in the Bay of Bengal* case,[4] and two of these may be mentioned here.[5] The first relates to the methodology adopted by international courts and tribunals to delimit the continental shelf or EEZ, or to draw a single delimitation line. Over time, the ICJ has developed a three-step methodology for addressing such delimitation, which was clearly encapsulated in the Court's unanimous 2009 Judgment in the *Black Sea* case.[6] The methodology was also followed by the Court in the later 2012 *Territorial and Maritime Dispute* between Nicaragua and Colombia.[7] In the *Bay of Bengal* case, while the Tribunal acknowledged that there may be circumstances in which an alternative method would be called for,[8] it held that "in the present case the appropriate method to be applied [...] is the equidistance/relevant circumstances method"[9] and observed that "taking into account the jurisprudence of international courts and tribunals on

statements_of_president/yanai/GA_Statement_30th_anniversary_101212.E_FINALE.pdf (visited 15 November 2016). See *infra* at note 76.

3 See generally T. Stephens, "International Environmental Disputes: To Sue or Not to Sue?" in N. Klein, *Litigating International Law Disputes* (Cambridge University Press, 2014), pp. 291–302.

4 *Delimitation of the maritime boundary in the Bay of Bengal (Bangladesh/Myanmar), Judgment, ITLOS Reports 2012*, p. 4. There is one other maritime delimitation dispute currently pending before a Chamber of the Tribunal, namely the *Dispute concerning delimitation of the Maritime Boundary between Ghana and Côte d'Ivoire in the Atlantic Ocean*.

5 See also V. Golitsyn, "Judicial Practice of the International Tribunal for the Law of the Sea – An Overview" 47 *Revue belge de droit international* 1 (2014), pp. 228–30.

6 *Maritime Delimitation in the Black Sea (Romania v. Ukraine), Judgment, I.C.J. Reports 2009*, p. 61, paras. 115–22. For an overview of the "three-stage approach", see S. Fietta and R. Cleverly, *Practitioner's Guide to Maritime Boundary Delimitation* (Oxford University Press, 2016), pp. 52–95. For the development of the law generally, see *ibid.*, Part A.

7 *Territorial and Maritime Dispute (Nicaragua v. Colombia), Judgment, I.C.J. Reports 2012*, p. 624, paras. 190–247.

8 *Bay of Bengal*, *supra* at note 4, at pp. 66–67, paras. 234–235.

9 *Ibid.*, at p. 67, para. 239.

this matter, [it] will follow the three-stage approach, as developed in the most recent case law on the subject."[10] The Tribunal thus confirmed the methodology developed by the ICJ as applicable more broadly under international law.

Secondly, the Tribunal determined that it was able to delimit the continental shelf between the parties in the area beyond 200 nm from the respective States' coasts, notwithstanding the role of the CLCS in issuing recommendations to States regarding the outer limits of the continental shelf.[11] Although the Tribunal considered that "the determination of whether an international court or tribunal should exercise its jurisdiction depends on the procedural and substantive circumstances of each case",[12] it may be noted that recently the ICJ adopted a similar approach in the case concerning *Question of the Delimitation of the Continental Shelf between Nicaragua and Colombia beyond 200 nautical miles from the Nicaraguan Coast*.[13]

The first maritime delimitation dispute argued before the Tribunal thus demonstrates how the approaches of the Tribunal and the ICJ have been similar,[14] notwithstanding that they are different institutions with different histories, roles and jurisdiction.

II Provisional Measures

Such harmonization between the ICJ and the Tribunal can also be noted in provisional measures proceedings. In the dispute settlement mechanism established in Part XV of the Convention, so-called Annex VII arbitral tribunals are the default adjudicatory bodies for the settlement of disputes concerning the interpretation or application of the Convention.[15] However, the Tribunal has compulsory jurisdiction as the default adjudicatory body in cases concerning the prompt release of vessels and crews[16] – discussed in the following section – and provisional measures proceedings pending the establishment of

10 *Ibid.*, para. 240.

11 *Ibid.*, at p. 103, para. 394.

12 *Ibid.*, at p. 101, para. 384.

13 *Question of the Delimitation of the Continental Shelf between Nicaragua and Colombia beyond 200 nautical miles from the Nicaraguan Coast* (*Nicaragua* v. *Colombia*), *Preliminary Objections, Judgment of 17 March 2016*, paras. 106–14, available at http://www.icj-cij.org/docket/files/154/18956.pdf (visited 15 November 2016).

14 See also D.H. Anderson, "Delimitation of the Maritime Boundary in the Bay of Bengal (Bangladesh/Myanmar)" 106 *AJIL* 4 (2012), p. 823.

15 Article 287, para. 5, of the Convention.

16 Article 292 of the Convention.

an Annex VII arbitral tribunal.[17] As long as the requisite conditions are met, the Tribunal may prescribe provisional measures even in cases where it does not have compulsory jurisdiction over the merits of the dispute, namely in cases brought before an arbitral tribunal yet to be constituted.[18]

So far, the Tribunal has considered requests for provisional measures in ten cases,[19] in which it has clarified and developed the applicable conditions of law and fact pertaining to the exercise of this jurisdiction. Most of these conditions are similar to the conditions applied by the ICJ, which makes the practice of the Tribunal and the Court mutually relevant and complementary.[20] In the following, attention is drawn again to two developments in the jurisprudence of the Tribunal.[21]

---

17 Article 290 of the Convention.

18 Article 290, para. 5, of the Convention.

19 Three of the ten requests have been submitted under article 290, paragraph 1, of the Convention: *M/V "SAIGA" (No. 2) (Saint Vincent and the Grenadines* v. *Guinea), Provisional Measures, Order of 11 March 1998, ITLOS Reports 1998*, p. 24 (originally submitted under article 290, paragraph 5); *M/V "Louisa" (Saint Vincent and the Grenadines* v. *Kingdom of Spain), Provisional Measures, Order of 23 December 2010, ITLOS Reports 2008–2010*, p. 58; and *Delimitation of the maritime boundary in the Atlantic Ocean* (Ghana/Côte d'Ivoire), *Provisional Measures, Order of 25 April 2015, ITLOS Reports 2015*, p. 146 ("*Gulf of Guinea*"). Seven of the ten requests have been submitted under article 290, paragraph 5, pending the constitution of an arbitral tribunal: *Southern Bluefin Tuna (New Zealand* v. *Japan; Australia* v. *Japan), Provisional Measures, Order of 27 August 1999, ITLOS Reports 1999*, p. 280; *MOX Plant (Ireland* v. *United Kingdom), Provisional Measures, Order of 3 December 2001, ITLOS Reports 2001*, p. 95; *Land Reclamation in and around the Straits of Johor (Malaysia* v. *Singapore), Provisional Measures, Order of 8 October 2003, ITLOS Reports 2003*, p. 10; *"ARA Libertad" (Argentina* v. *Ghana), Provisional Measures, Order of 15 December 2012, ITLOS Reports 2012*, p. 332; *"Arctic Sunrise" (Kingdom of the Netherlands* v. *Russian Federation), Provisional Measures, Order of 22 November 2013, ITLOS Reports 2013*, p. 230; and *"Enrica Lexie" Incident (Italy* v. *India), Provisional Measures, Order of 24 August 2015, ITLOS Reports 2015*, p. 182.

20 See further C.A. Miles, "The Influence of the International Court of Justice on the Law of Provisional Measures" in M. Andenas and E. Bjorge (eds), *A Farewell to Fragmentation: Reassertion and Convergence in International Law* (Cambridge University Press, 2015), pp. 218–71 and P. Tomka and G.I. Hernández, "Provisional Measures in the Tribunal for the Law of the Sea" in H.P. Hestermeyer et al. (eds), *Coexistence, Cooperation and Solidarity: Liber Amicorum Rüdiger Wolfrum* (Martinus Nijhoff, 2012) pp. 1763–85.

21 It is noted that the Tribunal has also contributed to the development of the condition of "urgency", arising from article 290 of the Convention, which is a question of particular circumstances, with decisions only taken "on a case by case basis in light of all relevant factors": *Gulf of Guinea, supra* at note 19, p. 156, para. 43. The condition of "urgency" has been applied by the Tribunal or its Chamber to very different factual circumstances, which

First, the Tribunal has consistently affirmed that for the prescription of provisional measures, it is not necessary to definitively establish the existence of the rights claimed by the parties.[22] In the recent case of the *Dispute concerning delimitation of the maritime boundary between Ghana and Côte d'Ivoire in the Atlantic Ocean* (*Ghana/Côte d'Ivoire*) ("*Gulf of Guinea*"), the Special Chamber of the Tribunal specified or re-articulated this latter condition by suggesting that it is necessary for the Special Chamber to satisfy itself that the rights claimed by the parties are at least "plausible".[23] This approach taken in *Gulf of Guinea* was followed in the case of the *"Enrica Lexie" Incident* (*Italy* v. *India*), *Provisional Measures* in 2015,[24] meaning that the jurisprudence of the Tribunal is now aligned with the recent jurisprudence of the ICJ in provisional measures cases.[25] Indeed, the ICJ itself first explicitly introduced the criterion of "plausibility of rights" only in 2009 in a case between Belgium and Senegal,[26] although traces of the same principle can be found in earlier jurisprudence.[27] The criterion of "plausibility of rights" has been seen to reflect the consideration that "unless it is apparent that the applicant has at least some prospect of success on the merits, it is inappropriate for the Court to indicate provisional measures."[28] This principle, which is of special importance in the context of the principle of consensual jurisdiction, can also be referred to as the principle

---

naturally leads to a more nuanced understanding thereof. See also C. Miles, *supra* at note 20, pp. 249–52 and P. Tomka and G. Hernández, *supra* at note 20, pp. 1780–1.

22 See, e.g., *M/V "Louisa"*, *supra* at note 19, at p. 69, para. 69; *"Arctic Sunrise"*, *supra* at note 19, at p. 246, para. 69; and *"ARA Libertad"*, *supra* at note 19, at p. 343, para. 60.

23 *Gulf of Guinea*, *supra* at note 19, at p. 158, paras. 57–58. For a critique of the somewhat ambiguous meaning of the term, see *Certain Activities Carried Out by Nicaragua in the Border Area* (*Costa Rica* v. *Nicaragua*), *Provisional Measures, Order of 8 March 2011, I.C.J. Reports 2011*, p. 6, at p. 29 (*Separate Opinion of Judge Koroma*).

24 *"Enrica Lexie" Incident*, *supra* at note 19, pp. 196–197, paras. 75–85.

25 See, e.g., *Questions relating to the Seizure and Detention of Certain Documents and Data* (*Timor-Leste* v. *Australia*), *Provisional Measures, Order of 3 March 2014, I.C.J. Reports 2014*, p. 147, at p. 152, para. 22.

26 *Questions relating to the Obligation to Prosecute or Extradite* (*Belgium* v. *Senegal*), *Provisional Measures, Order of 28 May 2009, I.C.J. Reports 2009*, p. 139, at p. 151, para. 57.

27 See in this respect the overviews and arguments in *Passage through the Great Belt* (*Finland* v. *Denmark*), *Provisional Measures, Order of 29 July 1991, I.C.J. Reports 1991*, p. 12, at p. 28 (*Separate Opinion of Judge Shahabuddeen*) and *Pulp Mills on the River Uruguay* (*Argentina* v. *Uruguay*), *Provisional Measures, Order of 13 July 2006, I.C.J. Reports 2006*, p. 113, at p. 137 (*Separate Opinion of Judge Abraham*).

28 Y. Lee-Iwamoto, "The Repercussions of the LaGrand Judgment: Recent ICJ Jurisprudence on Provisional Measures" 55 *Japanese Yearbook of International Law* (2012), p. 247.

of *fumus boni juris*,[29] and it can be seen to serve the purpose of discouraging and distinguishing requests for provisional measures which are clearly without foundation or even "frivolous".[30] On the other hand, this purpose must be balanced against the justified consideration that the Court should not prejudge or even appear to prejudge the merits of the case and should thus abstain from a degree of scrutiny at the provisional measures stage of the proceedings.[31]

It is noted that the question whether the rights claimed by the parties are plausible *in law* under the Convention may be linked to the question whether there exists a dispute concerning the interpretation and application of the Convention, which is a question of *prima facie* jurisdiction.[32] Therefore, while the introduction of the criterion of "plausibility" does not necessarily constitute a significant shift in the jurisprudence of the Tribunal,[33] it does recognize that the existence of rights can be a distinct issue from the existence of jurisdiction by treating the two separately, the approach that has also been taken in recent ICJ case law. This can notably be the case when the Tribunal's jurisdiction is based on a special agreement between the parties, which is the case in *Gulf of Guinea*.

---

29 *Ibid.*

30 Judge Koroma, *supra* at note 23, p. 33, para. 17.

31 See Judge Shahabuddeen, *supra* at note 27 and Judge Abraham, *supra* at note 27, as well as C. Miles, *supra* note 20, pp. 240–1. The question of prejudging the merits is of heightened importance in cases brought before the Tribunal under article 290, para. 5, of the Convention, where the Tribunal itself does not have jurisdiction over the merits of the case. See P. Tomka and G. Hernández, *supra* at note 20, p. 1784 and *"ARA Libertad"*, *supra* at note 19 (*Separate Opinion of Judges Wolfrum and Cot*), p. 364, para 5. To be sure, provisional measures orders are technically not prejudicial. See, e.g., *M/V "Louisa"*, *supra* at note 19, at p. 70, para. 80.

32 See, e.g., *"ARA Libertad"*, *supra* at note 19, at pp. 343–344, paras. 60–67. See also D. Müller and A.B. Mansour, "Procedural Developments at the International Court of Justice" 8 *The Law and Practice of International Courts and Tribunals* (2009), pp. 499–500.

33 *Cf.* C. Miles, *supra* at note 20, p. 243 (writing before the decisions in *Gulf of Guinea, supra* at note 19, and the *"Enrica Lexie" Incident* (*Italy* v. *India*), *Provisional Measures, supra* at note 19): "dispute resolution bodies under [the Convention] are following the same broad strokes established by the ICJ, although they have not yet shown an inclination to examine the strength of the claimant's case on the merits as part of this calculation. Such a discussion was expressly discarded – at least in the sense that such an inquiry must be definitive – as necessary by [the Tribunal] in [*Louisa, supra* at note 19, *at* p. 69, para 69]. It is worth noting, however, that the Tribunal did not say that *no* inquiry was required into the plausibility of the rights on which an application was based. Whether this means that *some* inquiry is required is a matter, however, for a future case."

Secondly, the *Gulf of Guinea* case is interesting for the reason that the Special Chamber elaborated on the jurisdiction of the Tribunal to prescribe provisional measures to "prevent serious harm to the marine environment" under article 290, paragraph 1, of the Convention. While the conditions of *prima facie* jurisdiction, "plausibility of rights" and "urgency" are shared by the Tribunal with the ICJ,[34] this is a distinct option for the Tribunal. Notably, it is an alternative condition to the preservation of the rights of the parties,[35] potentially providing the Tribunal with further discretion to prescribe provisional measures for the protection of the environment,[36] even if it seems likely that such an interest will in most cases overlap with the interests of the parties.[37]

In *Gulf of Guinea*, Côte d'Ivoire explicitly requested provisional measures "to prevent serious harm to the marine environment" allegedly arising from "the oil-related activities being carried out [...] on behalf of and in the name of Ghana."[38] The Special Chamber considered that Côte d'Ivoire had not "adduced sufficient evidence to support its allegations", but noted that "the risk of serious harm to the marine environment is of great concern to the Special Chamber".[39] The Special Chamber then pointed to the obligation of States under the Convention "to protect and preserve the marine environment",[40] and referred to the relevant jurisprudence of the Tribunal and the ICJ for further contextual support.[41] Noting further how "the duty to cooperate is a fundamental

34 See, e.g., *Certain Documents and Data, supra* at note 25, p. 154, paras. 31–2.

35 Article 290, para. 1, of the Convention clearly distinguishes this purpose from the purpose of preserving the right of the parties by the use of the disjunctive.

36 See C. Miles, *supra* at note 20, pp. 226 and 244; P. Tomka and G. Hernández, *supra* at note 20, pp. 1783–4.

37 In *Gulf of Guinea*, the Tribunal decided not to prescribe a measure requested by Côte d'Ivoire, namely the suspension of all Ghanaian exploration or exploitation activities in the disputed area. While the Tribunal considered that such an order would "cause prejudice to the rights claimed by Ghana and create an undue burden on it", it was further noted that the order "could also cause harm to the marine environment": *Gulf of Guinea, supra* at note 19, pp. 164–165, paras. 100–101. Thus, the common environmental interest implicitly overlapped with the interests of Ghana but contrasted with the interests of Côte d'Ivoire.

38 *Ibid.*, at p. 159, paras. 64–65.

39 *Ibid.*, at pp. 159–160, paras. 67–68.

40 *Ibid.*, at p. 160, paras. 69–70, referring to articles 192 and 193 of the Convention.

41 *Ibid.*, at p. 160, paras. 71–72. The Tribunal referred, *inter alia*, to *Legality of the Threat or Use of Nuclear Weapons, Advisory Opinion, I.C.J. Reports 1996*, p. 226, at pp. 241–242, para. 29: "The existence of the general obligation of States to ensure that activities within their jurisdiction and control respect the environment of other States or of areas beyond national control is now part of the corpus of international law relating to the environment."

principle in the prevention of pollution of the marine environment",[42] the Tribunal unanimously ordered, *inter alia*, that Ghana "shall carry out strict and continuous monitoring of all activities [...] in the disputed area with a view to ensuring the prevention of serious harm to the marine environment",[43] and that the parties "shall take all necessary steps to prevent serious harm to the marine environment, including the continental shelf and its superjacent waters, in the disputed area and shall cooperate to that end".[44] These measures specified, and to an extent went beyond, the relevant request by Côte d'Ivoire.[45]

On the whole, the two very recent provisional measures cases neatly illustrate the contribution of the Tribunal to both the harmonized application and development of international law governing provisional measures,[46] as well as highlighting its concern for environmental matters.

III Prompt Release of Vessels and Crews

This environmental theme is also apparent in prompt release cases,[47] which are certainly not insignificant in the Tribunal's jurisprudence.[48] So far, all prompt release cases before the Tribunal have been concerned with the rights of coastal States under article 73 of the Convention, according to which the

42 *Gulf of Guinea, supra* at note 19, at p. 160, para. 73, referring, *inter alia*, to *MOX Plant, supra* at note 19, para. 82, and *Land Reclamation, supra* at note 19, para. 92.

43 *Gulf of Guinea, supra* at note 19, at p. 166, para. 108(1)(c).

44 *Ibid.*, para. 108(1)(d).

45 In its final submissions, Côte d'Ivoire requested the Special Chamber to prescribe provisional measures requiring Ghana *inter alia* to "take all necessary steps to preserve the continental shelf, its superjacent waters and its subsoil": *ibid.*, at p. 152, para. 25.

46 *Cf.* C. Miles, *supra* at note 20, p. 270: "It is encouraging, therefore, that within [ICJ, the dispute settlement bodies of UNCLOS, ICSID and the ECtHR] a relatively uniform and unfragmented law of provisional measures appears to be in effect."

47 For general overviews of the prompt release cases, see, e.g., J. Akl, "Jurisprudence of the International Tribunal for the Law of the Sea in Prompt Release Proceedings" in H.P. Hestermeyer et al. (eds), *Coexistence, Cooperation and Solidarity: Liber Amicorum Rüdiger Wolfrum* (Martinus Nijhoff, 2012) p. 1591; D.H. Anderson, "Prompt Release of Vessels and Crews" in *MPEPIL Online* (updated in 2008); N. Klein, *supra* at note 1, pp. 85–119.

48 *Cf.* N. Klein, *supra* at note 1, pp. 118–9: "[a]lthough Article 292 only applies to limited situations, those situations reflect the most fundamental tensions existing between States in the exercise of rights in the EEZ. The role of ITLOS under Article 292 is to reconcile States' competing interests and to preserve a workable balance as States exercise their respective rights under the Convention."

coastal State may take necessary measures – including the arrest and detention of vessels and crews – to ensure compliance with its laws and regulations applicable in its EEZ.[49] It is the essential purpose of prompt release proceedings to provide a procedural safeguard for flag States against the potentially overzealous exercise of this extended jurisdiction by coastal States.[50] Nonetheless, prompt release cases are also often related to the sustainable management of fisheries. As approximately 90% of fish stocks are captured in the EEZ,[51] the rights or responsibilities of the coastal State are essential in this respect.[52] While the Tribunal has also had opportunities in prompt release cases to consider some general rules of international law, such as the question of nationality of claims,[53] and the binding nature of a protocol of an intergovernmental commission,[54] it is particularly noteworthy in this context how the Tribunal has recognized, on the one hand, the need to reconcile the interests of particular States and, on the other hand, the relevance of prompt release situations to

---

49 Article 73, para. 1, of the Convention. The procedure of prompt release is also applicable in cases of pollution of the marine environment (articles 220 and 226 of the Convention). See D. Anderson, *supra* at note 47, paras. 14–20, and J. Akl, *supra* at note 47, p. 1596.

50 See D. Anderson, *supra* at note 47, para. 3, and N. Klein, *supra* at note 1, p. 86.

51 V.A.M.F. Ventura, "Tackling Illegal, Unregulated and Unreported Fishing: The ITLOS Advisory Opinion on Flag State Responsibility for IUU Fishing and the Principle of Due Diligence" 12 *Brazilian Journal of International Law* 1 (2015), p. 51: "approximately 90 percent of all fish stocks are captured within 200 miles of shore, the traditional limit of the [EEZ], and therefore under coastal states resources sovereignty."

52 It is interesting to note that a number of prompt release cases have been related to the illegal fishing of Patagonian toothfish (also known as Mero or Chilean Seabass). For further information regarding the IUU fishing of toothfish, see generally the webpage of the Coalition of Legal Toothfish Operators at http://www.colto.org/, especially the "Toothfish Fact Sheet: IUU Fishing" at http://www.colto.org/toothfish-fisheries/iuu/ (noting how IUU fishing for toothfish "has been reduced by over 95% since peak levels in the 1990s") (visited on 15 November 2016). The cases related to the illegal fishing of Patagonian toothfish are "*Camouco*" (*Panama* v. *France*), *Prompt Release, Judgment, ITLOS Reports 2000*, p. 10; "*Monte Confurco*" (*Seychelles* v. *France*), *Prompt Release, Judgment, ITLOS Reports 2000*, p. 86; "*Grand Prince*" (*Belize* v. *France*), *Prompt Release, Judgment, ITLOS Reports 2001*, p. 17; "*Volga*" (*Russian Federation* v. *Australia*), *Prompt Release, Judgment, ITLOS Reports 2002*, p. 10.

53 See "*Grand Prince*", *supra* at note 52, at pp. 38–44, paras. 66–93.

54 See "*Hoshinmaru*" (*Japan* v. *Russian Federation*), *Prompt Release, Judgment, ITLOS Reports 2005–2007*, p. 18, at pp. 45–7, paras 83–87. The Tribunal refers to the jurisprudence of the ICJ in the cases of *Maritime Delimitation and Territorial Questions between Qatar and Bahrain* (*Qatar* v. *Bahrain*), *Jurisdiction and Admissibility, Judgment, I.C.J. Reports 1994*, p. 112, and *Case Concerning the Temple of Preah Vihear* (*Cambodia* v. *Thailand*), *Merits, Judgment of 15 June 1962, I.C.J. Reports 1962*, p. 6.

the sustainable management of fisheries – this is reflected in its assessments of what constitutes "a reasonable bond" for the purposes of promptly releasing the vessels in question.[55]

The term "a reasonable bond" is not defined in the Convention, and the methodology developed by the Tribunal represents a salient contribution to the interpretation and application of the Convention.[56] Developing its criteria for the assessment of "reasonable" bonds, the Tribunal has constantly refined its approach, seeking an appropriate balance between the interests of flag and coastal States.[57] Principal criteria were established already in the *"Camouco" Case (Panama* v. *France), Prompt Release*, where it was held that relevant factors include, *inter alia*, "the gravity of the alleged offences [and] the penalties imposed or imposable under the laws of the detaining State".[58] In its jurisprudence, the Tribunal has therefore taken note of the arguments of respondents which point to "international concerns" about illegal fishing and justify high penalties[59] and, consequently, higher bonds.[60] Moreover, the Tribunal has considered it important to note that prompt release cases are not only about the rights of the coastal State, but also about the coastal State's obligation under article 61, paragraph 2, of the Convention to ensure "that the maintenance

55 The term is provided in articles 73 and 292 of the Convention. See generally V. Golitsyn, *supra* note 5, p. 232; J. Akl, *supra* at note 47, pp. 1606–10; D. Anderson, *supra* at note 47, paras. 33 ff; and N. Klein, *supra* at note 1, pp. 108–18.

56 *Cf.* N. Klein, *supra* at note 1, p. 119: "[t]he availability of an international mechanism to deal with the question of prompt release of vessels and crews undoubtedly impacts on the substantive rules of the Convention. The main effect on coastal State authority to be discerned so far has been through the assessment of the reasonableness of bonds set by domestic courts."

57 In the words of the Tribunal, "[t]he balance of interests emerging from articles 73 and 292 of the Convention provides the guiding criterion for the Tribunal in its assessment of the reasonableness of the bond": *"Monte Confurco", supra* at note 52, at p. 108, para. 72.

58 *"Camouco", supra* at note 52, at p. 31, para. 67. As the Tribunal explained in the *"Monte Confurco" Case*, "[t]his is by no means a complete list of factors" and it is not the purpose of the Tribunal "to lay down rigid rules as to the exact weight to be attached to each of them": *"Monte Confurco", supra* at note 52, at p. 109, para. 76.

59 *"Volga", supra* at note 52, at p. 33, para. 68. Indeed, the Tribunal has stated that "[i]t is by reference to these penalties that the Tribunal may evaluate the gravity of the alleged offences": *ibid.*, p. 33, para. 69. See also *"Juno Trader" (Saint Vincent and the Grenadines* v. *Guinea-Bissau), Prompt Release, Judgment, ITLOS Reports 2004*, p. 17, at p. 41, para. 89.

60 For early support from the bench of the Tribunal, see *"Camouco", supra* at note 52 (*Dissenting Opinion of Judge Wolfrum*), p. 72, para. 17, and *"Monte Confurco", supra* at note 52 (*Dissenting Opinion of Judge Anderson*), p. 127 ff.

of the living resources in the [EEZ] is not endangered by over-exploitation".[61] On the other hand, the Tribunal has also emphasized that it is the purpose of prompt release proceedings to "secure the prompt release of the vessel and crew upon the posting of a reasonable bond"[62] and it is therefore inherently appropriate to limit the discretion of coastal States in these matters.[63]

On the whole, the Tribunal has acknowledged in its jurisprudence that prompt release cases involve considerations beyond those of particular flag and coastal States. It is clearly not easy to find an appropriate balance between the competing interests, especially in the abstract, but the Tribunal has developed generally applicable criteria which are flexible enough to accommodate a variety of cases. It is also worthy of note in this respect that in the last two prompt release cases in which "reasonable bonds" were determined by the Tribunal,[64] this was done without dissent on the amount of the bond.

IV Advisory Opinions

Finally, environmental considerations have also been prominent in the two advisory opinions issued by the Tribunal.[65] In these opinions, the Tribunal has again taken note of the jurisprudence of the ICJ and clarified the character of important obligations under the Convention.

In its first Advisory Opinion on *Responsibilities and obligations of States sponsoring persons and entities with respect to activities in the Area (Request for Advisory Opinion submitted to the Seabed Disputes Chamber)*, issued in 2011,[66] the Tribunal's Chamber referred to the *Pulp Mills on the River Uruguay (Argentina* v. *Uruguay)* case argued before the ICJ[67] in clarifying the nature

61 *"Hoshinmaru", supra* at note 54, at p. 50, para. 99.

62 *"Volga", supra* at note 52, at p. 33, para. 69.

63 See *"Monte Confurco", supra* at note 52 (*Separate Opinion of Vice-President Nelson*), p. 124.

64 *"Juno Trader", supra* at note 59, and *"Hoshinmaru", supra* at note 54.

65 See also V. Ventura, *supra* at note 51 (discussing, *inter alia*, how the Tribunal has contributed to the interaction between the law of the sea and international environmental law).

66 *Responsibilities and obligations of States with respect to activities in the Area, Advisory Opinion, 1 February 2011, ITLOS Reports 2011*, p. 10 ("*Activities in the Area*").

67 In that case, the ICJ characterized certain obligations related to the protection and preservation of the environment as obligations of conduct or due diligence. The Court also noted how due diligence obligations entail or imply a "certain level of vigilance" when it comes to the enforcement of the particular measures that have been taken in performance of the obligation: *Pulp Mills on the River Uruguay (Argentina* v. *Uruguay), Judgment, I.C.J. Reports 2010*, p. 14, at p. 77, para. 187, and p. 79, para. 197. Similarly to the matrix of

of obligations of States sponsoring activities in the Area.[68] The Chamber considered that such States are generally obliged "to ensure" that "activities" undertaken in the Area are "in conformity" or "in compliance" with the relevant obligations under the Convention and related instruments.[69] With respect to the character of this "obligation to ensure", the Chamber suggested that it is not an obligation of result but an obligation of conduct and due diligence, which means that the sponsoring State is only liable when it has not taken "all necessary and appropriate measures to secure effective compliance".[70] In addition, the Chamber suggested that the applicable standard by which to assess compliance with the due diligence obligation is that measures taken are "reasonably appropriate".[71]

In the second Advisory Opinion, in which the question of illegal fishing in the EEZ was again prominent, the Tribunal considered (in broad terms) that flag States were obliged under the Convention "to ensure" through appropriate measures that their vessels complied with the applicable national and international rules for fishing and for the protection of the marine environment.[72] Referring to its previous Advisory Opinion and again to the case of *Pulp Mills on the River Uruguay* (*Argentina* v. *Uruguay*), the Tribunal affirmed that the relevant specific obligations were due diligence obligations.[73] To add specific content to the obligations, the Tribunal suggested that the relevant measures must include sufficient sanctions "to deter violations and to deprive offenders of the benefits accruing from their [illegal, unreported and unregulated]

interests in provisional measures cases before the Tribunal, the *Pulp Mills* case was also about seeking a balance between the interests of individual States and common interests in the protection and preservation of the environment: see *ibid.*, at p. 74, para. 177.

68 *Activities in the Area, supra* at note 66, at pp. 41–42, paras. 111 and 115.

69 *Ibid.*, at p. 40, para. 103.

70 *Ibid.*, at p. 41, para. 110 and pp. 76–7, para. 242(4). It is also worthy of note that the Tribunal considered that: "[t]he liability of the sponsoring State for failure to comply with its due diligence obligations requires that a causal link be established between such failure and damage. Such liability is triggered by a damage caused by a failure of the sponsored contractor to comply with its obligations. The existence of a causal link between the sponsoring State's failure and the damage is required and cannot be presumed": *ibid.*, at pp. 76–77, para. 242(4). See also V. Golitsyn, *supra* at note 5, pp. 233–234.

71 *Activities in the Area, supra* at note 62, at pp. 74–75, para. 242(3).

72 *Request for Advisory Opinion submitted by the Sub-Regional Fisheries Commission, Advisory Opinion, 2 April 2015, ITLOS Reports 2015*, p. 4, at p. 63, para. 219(3). Although the conduct of their vessels is not *per se* attributable to flag States, they can still be held responsible for violations of their due diligence obligations under the Convention: *ibid*, at p. 44, para. 146.

73 *Ibid.*, at p. 63, para. 219(3) and pp. 38–40, paras. 125 and 129.

fishing activities".[74] Concerning the obligations of coastal States in relation to fisheries management, the Tribunal furthermore considered that their particular obligations of consultation and cooperation were also obligations of due diligence.[75]

Conclusion

This paper has briefly demonstrated how, during the 20 years of its existence, the Tribunal has contributed to the progressive development of international law through the interpretation and application of the Convention. These contributions, in which environmental considerations have often been prominent, are manifest in the decisions of the Tribunal on maritime delimitation, in provisional measures proceedings, in prompt release cases, and in advisory opinions. With respect to concerns about fragmentation, it is gratifying that the ICJ and the Tribunal appear to be taking consistent views on certain important matters of international law. Indeed, as President Yanai has observed:

> [The] option given to States to choose one or more international courts or tribunals has sometimes given rise to fears of a fragmentation of international law and of conflicting judgments being delivered by different international courts and tribunals. This concern has proved to be unfounded. The Tribunal has regularly referred to judgments of the [ICJ] and its predecessor, the [PCIJ], and to decisions by other courts and tribunals, both on substantive issues and on procedural points.[76]

---

74 *Ibid.*, at p. 42, para. 138. It can also be noted that the Tribunal stated that "the frequency of [illegal, unreported and unregulated] fishing activities by vessels in [the EEZ] is not relevant to the issue as to whether there is a breach of 'due diligence' obligations by the flag State": *ibid*, at p. 45, para. 150.

75 *Ibid.*, at pp. 65–68, para. 219(6).

76 S. Yanai, *supra* at note 2, para 6. Judge Greenwood has similarly considered that: "when the Convention was adopted, a number of commentators expressed concern that the choice of different methods of dispute settlement in article 287 [...] might lead to a fragmentation of this area of international law and even to competing lines of jurisprudence from different courts and tribunals. In fact, there has been a remarkable harmony between the pronouncements of the [ICJ], [ITLOS] and the Annex VII arbitration tribunals": C. Greenwood, *supra* at note 1, para. 7. *Cf.* also P. Gautier, *supra* at note 1, pp. 211–2: "[a]t the time of the entry into force of the Convention, concerns were expressed vis-à-vis the risk of conflicting decisions which could be pronounced by the different courts and tribunals provided for by Part XV. In light of the judicial practice generated by Part XV

Both bodies are thus able to make an important contribution to the development of the law of the sea. In retrospect, in view of the accumulated experience, one may wonder whether the negotiators of Part XV of the Convention in the seventies and early eighties have not committed a mistake when they have not endowed either the Tribunal or the ICJ with default jurisdiction, rather than an Annex VII tribunal. According to the Preamble of the Convention, States Parties "recogniz[e] the desirability of establishing through [the] Convention [...] a legal order for the seas and oceans".[77] As a standing judicial body, the Tribunal is better equipped to contribute to this noble goal than an *ad hoc* tribunal. The ICJ however remains, in accordance with article 92 of the Charter, the principal judicial organ of the United Nations.

---

of the Convention, it may be stated that this risk did not materialize. On the contrary, it seems that the arbitral and judicial bodies which have been dealing with issues concerning the law of the sea were particularly keen in taking into account the existing international jurisprudence."

77 Preamble of the Convention.

PART 3 / PARTIE 3

The Contribution of the Tribunal to the Rule of Law: The Point of View of Practitioners

La contribution du Tribunal à l'état de droit : Le point de vue des praticiens

The Tribunal and the Rule of Law

Alan Boyle

Let me begin with a quotation from the Mexican submission to the ICJ in the *Nuclear Weapons Advisory Opinion* in 1996: "The law is almost the defence par excellence for the weak. Precisely because small countries cannot use force to protect themselves, it is to their advantage to see that an international legal order is established with care and applied on a compulsory basis".[1] When the Philippines found itself confronted by a superpower in a dispute focused on the South China Sea it turned to Part XV of the Convention, and it won.[2]

The *South China Sea Arbitration* (*The Republic of Philippines v. The People's Republic of China*) and other Convention cases since 1996 promote the rule of law in various ways, but first and most obviously through the Convention's provision for binding compulsory jurisdiction. Since 1996, and including prompt release applications, there have been nearly fifty cases across all the various dispute settlement fora dealing with the Convention or the customary international law of the sea – the second largest category of inter-State cases outside the WTO. For practitioners this has been a wonderful opportunity to test the efficacy and limitations of the dispute settlement system designed in a Swiss hotel some 35 years ago.

Klein argues that "[l]iberal states will be the most inclined to turn to international courts and tribunals to resolve their disputes."[3] This may be true for Australia, but Klein's conclusion is contradicted by the record of the UK, US, Canada, France, and Japan.[4] A more persuasive argument is that inter-State litigation is most likely to be initiated by weaker States that have only limited diplomatic leverage over their bigger and more powerful opponents. Nicaragua, Iran, Ecuador and Georgia are obvious examples in the ICJ, but the same is

1 Oral Statement of Mr Sergio González Gálvez, Friday 3 November 1995, CR95/25, pp. 50, 55 in *Legality of the Threat or Use of Nuclear Weapons, Advisory Opinion*, ICJ.

2 *The South China Sea Arbitration* (*The Republic of Philippines* v. *The People's Republic of China*), PCA Case No. 2013–19, 25 October 2015; 12 July 2016. (The author was one of those who represented the Philippines, but the views expressed here are his own).

3 N. Klein, "Who Litigates and Why?" in C. Romano et al. (eds.), *The Oxford Handbook of International Adjudication* (Oxford University Press, 2013), Ch. 26 at p. 572.

4 In the past twenty years, the only developed liberal democracies to initiate ICJ proceedings or Convention proceedings have been Germany, Italy, Ireland, Spain, the Netherlands, Belgium, Australia, and New Zealand. The large majority of cases have come from developing States in Asia, Africa, and Latin America.

© 2018, BY INTERNATIONAL TRIBUNAL FOR THE LAW OF THE SEA | DOI 10.1163/9789004356832_017

true in the Convention cases. Litigation may be the only way to make the respondent state take notice of its neighbour's complaints: the *MOX Plant Case (Ireland v. United Kingdom), Provisional Measures*, the *Chagos Marine Protected Area Arbitration (Mauritius v. United Kingdom)*, and the *Bay of Bengal Maritime Boundary Arbitration between Bangladesh and India* fit this pattern. In others, including the *South China Sea Arbitration (The Republic of Philippines v. The People's Republic of China)*, the applicant has tried negotiation but lacks the diplomatic or military muscle to compel its far more powerful neighbour to settle on reasonable terms. In such cases an authoritative judgment may facilitate a settlement of some kind, whether directly, or by further negotiation, or simply by legitimising the *status quo*.[5] Litigation does not always work for these States, but it succeeds often enough to make it a real option. That is the most obvious lesson for a practitioner. Defending the weak against the strong is what a system of justice is supposed to do. For them, the Convention's proceedings may be the only option. That is why Part XV exists.

Foreign ministry practitioners will be just as familiar with the cases that don't come to court. These are the disputes where Part XV has exercised what the late Judge Park once referred to as the Convention's contraceptive effect. It is never in the interests of any legal system to promote disputes, and if they can be avoided or minimised then the rule of law will be enhanced. From that perspective, Part XV has worked well. Compared to the position prior to the Convention, the threat of litigation has in most cases deterred or derailed unilateral attempts to extend coastal State jurisdiction. The few attempts to extend coastal State fisheries jurisdiction beyond 200 nm have not succeeded.[6] There have been some instances of unilateralism within the EEZ, including the imposition of compulsory pilotage,[7] and the creation of no-take marine protected

5 For a subtle and compelling exposition of these points see A.V. Lowe, "Interplay between negotiation and litigation in international dispute settlement" in T.M. Ndiaye and R. Wolfrum (eds.) *Law of the Sea, Environmental law and Settlement of Disputes* (M. Nijhoff, 2007) pp. 235–47.

6 On the EU/Chile dispute see *Conservation and Sustainable Exploitation of Swordfish Stocks (Chile/European Community), Order of 20 December 2000, ITLOS Reports 2000*, p. 148, and *Conservation and Sustainable Exploitation of Swordfish Stocks (Chile/European Union), Order of 16 December 2009, ITLOS Reports 2008–2010*, p. 13. On Canada's dispute with the EU see "Agreed Minute on the Conservation and Management of Fish Stocks", 34 *International Legal Materials* 1260; P. Davies, "EC–Canada Fisheries Dispute", 44 *ICLQ* (1995), p. 927.

7 By Australia in the Torres Strait: see J. Harrison, *Making the Law of the Sea* (CUP, 2011), pp. 193–6.

areas,[8] but none of these developments have been successfully challenged.[9] The *South China Sea Arbitration* (*The Republic of Philippines v. The People's Republic of China*) is notable mainly because China did not get the point about unilateral claims going well beyond the terms of the Convention.[10] Part XV has thus served to protect the consensus-package deal character of the Convention while allowing for further development within agreed parameters.[11]

These developments could be interpreted in various ways. I would argue that they point to the success of the Convention in helping to promote the rule of law in international relations. This is not the same as saying that there is no disorder in the oceans, or that law affords solutions to the many problems facing modern international relations in the post-Cold War era. But what I do want to suggest is something more than the simple proposition that "rules rule". Rather, by rule of law I mean the assurance and expectation of procedural and substantive justice for all the participants in international society, whether these be economically advanced Western States, or the major developing economies of Brazil, China and India, or the tiny island states of the Pacific, to take only three possible groupings. In the specific context of the modern law of the sea we can observe a legal system for the oceans which is no longer an expression of the interests of its most powerful constituents. Whether we look at the law-making process, or the allocation of rights and responsibilities to States, or the accountability of the principal actors to judicial control, it has acquired a genuine and relatively new sense of its own universality. In this sense there is the foundation for a rule of law in ocean affairs that did not exist before the 1982 Convention came into force.

---

8 Large-scale examples that ban or restrict fishing within the EEZ include the British Indian Ocean Territory (UK), Coral Sea (Australia), Phoenix Islands (Kiribati), Marianas Trench (US), Sala y Gomez (Chile), Pacific Islands National Monument (US), Prince Edward Island (South Africa) and South Orkneys (UK). Decision VII/5 adopted by the parties to the Convention on Biological Diversity also envisages the adoption of MPAs for the purposes of that convention.

9 See *Chagos Marine Protected Area Arbitration* (*Mauritius* v. *United Kingdom*), PCA Case No. 2011–03, 18 March 2015.

10 See PCA Case No. 2013–19, 12 July 2016, paras. 261–2, 270–5.

11 Most obviously this is true of the *Delimitation of the maritime boundary in the Bay of Bengal (Bangladesh/Myanmar), Judgment, ITLOS Reports 2012*, p. 4, the *Chagos Marine Protected Area Arbitration* (*Mauritius* v. *United Kingdom*), and the *South China Sea Arbitration* (*The Republic of Philippines* v. *The People's Republic of China*). See M. Nordquist (ed.), *UNCLOS: A Commentary*, vol. V (Nijhoff, 1989), p. 5; B. Oxman, "Commentary" in: A. Soons (ed.) *Implementation of the Law of the Sea Convention through International Institutions*, 23 Law of the Sea Institute Proceedings 772 (1990), p. 648.

Where then does the Tribunal fit into this picture? What, if anything, makes it special? It is of course only one of the four options for compulsory dispute settlement referred to in article 287 of the Convention; it is not the default option, nor is it the most frequently used. Only four of its 25 cases have been heard on the merits: three involve arrest of ships and one is a maritime boundary case.[12] A further maritime boundary case and a case on jurisdiction over ships are pending.[13] This is not a notably impressive record for a permanent court celebrating its 20th anniversary, although in contrast the ICJ has had no cases specifically under Part XV of the Convention, and only seven Annex VII arbitrations have been heard on the merits.

However, three features give the Tribunal a unique character within the framework of Part XV as a whole. First, alone among the Convention dispute settlement options, the Tribunal has the most comprehensive range of functions. It has jurisdiction over inter-State disputes, it can give advisory opinions, the Seabed Disputes Chamber exercises exclusive jurisdiction over seabed mining, including seabed operators and the Authority, and only the Tribunal can order prompt release of certain categories of detained vessels. Within its special field, the Tribunal has a wider jurisdiction *ratione personae* and *ratione materiae* than the ICJ.

Second, we should not judge the Tribunal only by the number of cases it has heard. Though few in number, its judgments and advisory opinions have been significant: the *Dispute concerning delimitation of the maritime boundary between Bangladesh and Myanmar in the Bay of Bengal* (*Bangladesh/Myanmar*) Judgment is the most important maritime boundary case since the *North Sea Continental Shelf* cases. The *Responsibilities and obligations of States sponsoring persons and entities with respect to activities in the Area* (*Request for Advisory Opinion submitted to the Seabed Disputes Chamber*) is not just an important articulation of environmental obligations of States pursuant to Part XI of the Convention; it is also one of the leading cases on international environmental law. These cases, and the Advisory Opinion on coastal State fisheries, show the importance of a representative tribunal with the authority to interpret and

12 *M/V "SAIGA" (No. 2)* (*Saint Vincent and the Grenadines* v. *Guinea*), *ITLOS Reports 1999*, p. 10; *M/V "Virginia G"* (*Panama/Guinea-Bissau*), *Judgment, ITLOS Reports 2014*, p. 4; *M/V "Louisa"* (*Saint Vincent and the Grenadines* v. *Kingdom of Spain*), *Judgment, ITLOS Reports 2013*, p. 4; *Delimitation of the maritime boundary in the Bay of Bengal* (*Bangladesh/Myanmar*), *Judgment, ITLOS Reports 2012*, p. 4.

13 *Delimitation of the maritime boundary in the Atlantic Ocean* (*Ghana/Côte d'Ivoire*), *Order of 15 December 2016, ITLOS Reports 2016*, p. 18, and *M/V "Norstar"* (*Panama* v. *Italy*), *Preliminary Objections, Judgment, ITLOS Reports 2016*, p. 44.

develop the law of the sea in a coherent way, integrating both the corpus of the Convention-related conventions, related soft law and general international law. Like other international courts and tribunals, the Tribunal's jurisprudence favours coherence over fragmentation.[14] This is perhaps the most important contribution the Tribunal can make to promoting the rule of law.

In general, but with some exceptions, the Convention's different dispute settlement fora have applied the Convention consistently and coherently. For example, in their treatment of the continental shelf beyond 200 nm both the Annex VII arbitral tribunal in *Bay of Bengal Maritime Boundary Arbitration between Bangladesh and India* and the ICJ in *Territorial and Maritime Dispute* (*Nicaragua* v. *Colombia*) refer to and follow the precedent set by the Tribunal's Judgment in the *Dispute concerning delimitation of the maritime boundary between Bangladesh and Myanmar in the Bay of Bengal* (*Bangladesh/Myanmar*). *Bangladesh/Myanmar* is the first case to delimit a maritime boundary beyond 200 nm and in doing so it has given us an authoritative and sensible interpretation of article 76. It establishes in particular that such disputes are not excluded from compulsory jurisdiction pending delineation of the outer limit of the continental shelf by the CLCS, provided there is appropriate evidence of the existence of an extended shelf. The two Bangladesh cases apply the ICJ jurisprudence on coastal concavity as a special circumstance, and more generally they both follow the three stage delimitation process elaborated by the ICJ and applied in arbitral awards. The *Bay of Bengal Maritime Boundary Arbitration between Bangladesh and India* might have established a precedent for applying the angle bisector method to unstable coasts,[15] but the judgment firmly rejects any temptation to create new law on this or any other question. There is no evidence from any of these cases that maritime boundary cases may be decided differently by different fora.

The *Responsibilities and obligations of States sponsoring persons and entities with respect to activities in the Area* (*Request for Advisory Opinion submitted to the Seabed Disputes Chamber*) does not break new ground to the same extent as the *Dispute concerning delimitation of the maritime boundary between*

---

14 See B. Simma, "Universality of International Law from the Perspective of a Practitioner" 20 *EJIL* 2 (2009), p. 265.

15 As argued by Bangladesh. See *Territorial and Maritime Dispute between Nicaragua and Honduras in the Caribbean Sea* (*Nicaragua* v. *Honduras*), *I.C.J. Reports* 2007, p. 741, para. 287; *Delimitation of the Maritime Boundary in the Gulf of Maine Area* (*Canada* v. *United States of America*), *I.C.J. Reports* 1984, p. 329, para. 213; *Delimitation of the Maritime Boundary between Guinea and Guinea-Bissau*, 14 February 1985, *RIAA* Vol. XIX, p. 149, paras. 95–97 and 103.

Bangladesh and Myanmar in the Bay of Bengal (*Bangladesh/Myanmar*),[16] but it illustrates cross-fertilisation between international courts and tribunals even when they are formally applying different bodies of law. The Seabed Disputes Chamber relied extensively on the ICJ's Judgment in *Pulp Mills on the River Uruguay* (*Argentina* v. *Uruguay*) when interpreting the Convention and the Rules and Regulations adopted by the Authority.[17] It seems clear from these cases that the Tribunal, like other international courts and tribunals, prefers coherence over fragmentation.

In the *"Arctic Sunrise" Case* (*Kingdom of the Netherlands* v. *Russian Federation*), *Provisional Measures*, the Tribunal also followed ICJ precedents holding that non-appearance by the respondent does not deprive the court of jurisdiction or otherwise bar the proceedings.[18] The same problem arose in the *South China Sea Arbitration* (*The Republic of Philippines v. The People's Republic of China*) and was dealt with in the same way. Failure to appear has never been beneficial to the absent party. The respondent can then make its case only by sending memoranda to the tribunal, paying academics to write books and articles, or through public statements. This is no way to ensure a hearing of its case. Non-appearance is not helpful to the tribunal, it disadvantages the applicant, and it undermines the commitment of parties to judicial settlement of disputes in accordance with Part XV. It would represent an obvious threat to the rule of law if respondent States were allowed to subvert compulsory jurisdiction under Part XV, but this has not happened, thanks to the firmness and good sense of the Tribunal and the PCA.

Lastly, I would draw attention to an important structural evolution in the role of the Tribunal: the increasing involvement of experienced Tribunal judges as Annex VII arbitrators. Some Annex VII panels look more like a chamber of the Tribunal, to the point where Ghana and Côte d'Ivoire have drawn the obvious conclusion for their maritime boundary case by transferring it to a

16 *Responsibilities and obligations of States with respect to activities in the Area, Advisory Opinion, 1 February 2011, ITLOS Reports 2011*, p. 10; See D. French, "From the Depths: the Seabed Disputes Chamber's 2011 Advisory Opinion", 26 *IJMCL* 4 (2011), p. 525.

17 *Responsibilities and obligations of States with respect to activities in the Area, Advisory Opinion, supra* at note 71, paras. 111 (due diligence), 135 (precautionary approach), and 147 (environmental impact assessment).

18 *"Arctic Sunrise"* (*Kingdom of the Netherlands* v. *Russian Federation*), *Provisional Measures, Order of 22 November 2013, ITLOS Reports 2013*, p. 230, applying article 28 of the Statute. On non-appearance before the ICJ see article 53 of the Statute of the ICJ, and *Fisheries Jurisdiction Case* (*Germany* v. *Iceland*), *I.C.J. Reports 1974*, p. 175, paras. 15–18; *Military and Paramilitary Activities in and against Nicaragua* (*Nicaragua* v. *United States of America*), *I.C.J. Reports* 1986, p. 14, paras. 26–29.

chamber of the Tribunal. This developing interaction between the Tribunal and Annex VII arbitration promotes coherence and consistency in the jurisprudence; it strengthens the legitimacy of the Tribunal and arbitral panels; and it enhances the role of the Tribunal even when a case is formally brought under Annex VII. Not all States agree that Ghana and Côte d'Ivoire have drawn the right conclusion but, especially where the respondent refuses to participate in Annex VII proceedings, it is important to retain the option of selecting the Tribunal's judges as arbitrators. The *South China Sea Arbitration* (*The Republic of Philippines v. The People's Republic of China*) benefitted from the judicial experience of its members.[19] The arbitrators were not intimidated by the absence of the respondent State or the tactics it employed, but nor did they give the applicant State an easy ride. They ensured that all relevant points were fully addressed in two rounds of written pleadings and appointed experts to test the accuracy and adequacy of the evidence. The applicant State was required to justify their claims in oral argument. All the right questions were asked. Finally, in their award the arbitrators upheld the Convention as agreed by the parties. From a practitioner's perspective there are few better ways to promote the rule of law – or to reassure clients that they will get the outcome they deserve.

If Annex VII arbitration is a success – and it is – why would States wish to transfer cases to the Tribunal? In 2009 Bangladesh and Myanmar transferred the first *Bay of Bengal* case to the Tribunal. Why did they do so? First, like the *North Sea Continental Shelf* cases, the case raised novel questions of law of general importance. The parties did not regard an *ad hoc* arbitral tribunal as the right forum for the job in hand – and the case was indeed a landmark because of the way it dealt with the delimitation of the outer continental shelf, the relationship with the CLCS, and the continued relevance of coastal concavity as a relevant circumstance for delimitation purposes.

Secondly, the Tribunal was able to hear the case quickly, and it duly gave judgment in 2012, a mere three years after the case started. This is remarkable. But it was also important: the Judgment could then be relied on when pleading the *Bay of Bengal Maritime Boundary Arbitration between Bangladesh and India*; three of the arbitrators were the Tribunal's judges who sat in the earlier case, and of course they were likely to follow their own Judgment when the

19 The four judges of the Tribunal who sat as arbitrators in the *South China Sea Arbitration* (*The Republic of Philippines* v. *The People's Republic of China*) also sat in the *"Arctic Sunrise" Case* (*Kingdom of the Netherlands* v. *Russian Federation*), *Provisional Measures* hearing; Russia did not participate. The fifth arbitrator, Professor Soons, had previously served as an arbitrator in the *Arctic Sunrise Arbitration* (*Netherlands* v. *Russia*); Russia again failed to participate.

arbitral case was heard in late 2013. From Bangladesh's perspective this was a successful strategy. Quite what the outcome of the arbitration with India would have been had the Tribunal's Judgment in the *Dispute concerning delimitation of the maritime boundary between Bangladesh and Myanmar in the Bay of Bengal* been less favourable I cannot possibly say. The actual outcome of the Annex VII arbitration shows the value of getting the first judgment from a permanent court with an authority that few arbitral tribunals can match.

Finally, courts have an institutional commitment to being perceived by States as doing a good job. Their decisions may come back to haunt them. Taking the easy way out is not usually an option, whereas arbitrators need only decide the case before them. The *Southern Bluefin Tuna Case* might well have gone the other way in a judicial forum. This was a case that required a coherent vision of how the Convention relates to regional agreements and to the dispute settlement provisions (or lack of them) in those agreements.[20] Neither the Tribunal nor the ICJ could easily have evaded that question in the way the arbitrators chose to evade it. Judge Lauterpacht's observations on the drawbacks of arbitration are still relevant: "[t]here was no assurance that the decisions of the arbitrators chosen from the panel of the Court of Arbitration would serve a purpose other than that of disposing of the dispute between the parties. They could not invariably be relied upon to develop and clarify international law."[21] He gave this as one of the principal reasons for creating the PCIJ in 1920, and he saw the development and clarification of the law as one of the main tasks of international courts. That is still true today.

Taken together, all these elements have given the Tribunal a significant role in promoting the rule of law within the framework of the Convention.

---

20 See B. Oxman, "Complementary Agreements and Compulsory Jurisdiction", 95 *AJIL* 2 (2001), p. 277; A. Boyle, "Southern Bluefin Tuna Cases", in R. Wolfrum (ed.) *op. cit.* at note 5.

21 H. Lauterpacht, *The Development of International Law by the International Court*, 2nd ed. (Stevens, 1958), p. 6.

La contribution du Tribunal international du droit de la mer au développement du droit international général – les dix dernières années

Alain Pellet[1]

Monsieur le Président, Madame et Messieurs les Juges – une formule que j'ai eu plaisir à utiliser plusieurs fois dans cette belle salle de Justice, même si j'eusse préféré que le féminin fût aussi au pluriel, Excellences, Mesdames et Messieurs, Chers Collègues,

Quand on célèbre un anniversaire, on cherche plutôt à dire des choses aimables sur le fêté qu'à le critiquer. D'un autre côté, dans une table ronde, un vilain petit canard, qui prend le contrepied des positions des collègues est toujours utile pour mettre un peu d'ambiance et d'animation dans les débats. J'avoue que le rôle ne me déplairait pas, mais j'ai eu beau m'y essayer, mis à part le déséquilibre des « genres », dont les Etats membres, et non le Tribunal, portent la responsabilité, je ne vois pas quelle critique majeure on pourrait adresser à la juridiction de Hambourg. Loin de donner raison à ceux qui vilipendent la « prolifération » des tribunaux internationaux, son existence et sa pratique témoignent des bienfaits de leur multiplication. Et je précise, en zélateur de la Cour internationale de Justice que je suis aussi, que le Tribunal ne porte aucunement ombrage à la grande sœur de La Haye : dans le cadre de sa compétence d'attribution – mais qui couvre un large et important domaine – il en complète et en enrichit l'action.

Ceci est très apparent lorsque l'on s'interroge sur la contribution du Tribunal au développement et à l'affermissement du droit international général – thème que j'ai choisi pour ces brefs propos introductifs, étant entendu que je ne puis que survoler ce vaste sujet dans les quelques minutes qui me sont imparties. Je centrerai ces propos sur les dix dernières années – et c'est bien suffisant puisque, il y a dix ans, à l'occasion du dixième anniversaire, Sir Michael s'était, avec la sagacité qu'il a parfois, interrogé sur le thème, encore plus général, « *The International Tribunal for the Law of the Sea and General International Law* »[2], même si sa perspective était un peu différente de celle que j'ai choisie.

---

1 Remerciements à Benjamin Samson, chercheur, CEDIN, Université Paris Ouest, Nanterre La Défense, consultant en droit international, pour son aide dans la préparation de cet exposé.

2 Sir M. Wood, « The Tribunal and General International Law », *The International Journal of Marine and Coastal Law*, vol. 22, 2007, nº 3, pp. 351-367.

© 2018, BY INTERNATIONAL TRIBUNAL FOR THE LAW OF THE SEA | DOI 10.1163/9789004356832_018

Avec beaucoup de sagesse, le Tribunal, loin de se poser en rival de la CIJ, ce qui n'eût guère eu de sens et aurait affaibli l'autorité de l'un comme de l'autre, a voulu inscrire sa jurisprudence dans le sillage de celle de la Cour qu'il a enrichie en la complétant et en la clarifiant sur certains points car, la Convention, pour être l'instrument de référence et le phare du Tribunal, ne saurait être interprétée et appliquée « en isolation clinique »[3]. Et ce qu'a rappelé le Tribunal dans l'*Incident de l'« Enrica Lexie »* à propos des considérations d'humanité qui, a-til dit, « doivent s'appliquer dans le droit de la mer, comme dans les autres domaines du droit international »,[4] vaut également s'agissant de maints autres chapitres du droit international. Comme il faut choisir, j'ai retenu, à titre d'exemple un domaine – central – du droit international public dans lequel la jurisprudence récente du Tribunal a joué – et joue – un rôle important et utile : le droit de la responsabilité (*lato sensu*).

Dans son très remarquable (et audacieux[5]) avis de 2011 sur les *Responsabilités et obligations des Etats dans le cadre d'activités menées dans la Zone*, le Tribunal a clarifié la définition même de la responsabilité ou plutôt *les* définitions de ce concept protéiforme et d'autant plus difficile à saisir en français que notre belle langue ignore l'utile distinction que fait l'anglais entre *responsibility* d'une part et *liability* d'autre part[6]. Du reste cet avis a aussi le grand mérite de clarifier les relations entre ces deux notions – comme le fait aussi l'avis de 2015 sur la pêche illicite[7] – en même temps d'ailleurs qu'il finit par écarter l'une et l'autre dès lors qu'il s'agit de définir le mot « responsabilité » dans l'article 139 de la Convention[8].

Dans ces deux avis, qui sont une mine de considérations d'importance sur le droit de la responsabilité, le Tribunal a également apporté des éclairages utiles sur la portée des obligations de comportement (par comparaison avec

3 Rapport de l'Organe d'appel, *Etats-Unis – Normes concernant l'essence nouvelle et ancienne*, WT/DS2/AB/R, 29 avril 1996, par. 76.

4 *L'incident de l'« Enrica Lexie » (Italie c. Inde), mesures conservatoires, ordonnance du 24 août 2015, TIDM Recueil 2015*, par. 133 faisant référence à *Navire « SAIGA » (No. 2) (Saint-Vincent-et-les Grenadines c. Guinée), arrêt, TIDM Recueil 1999*, p. 62, par. 155.

5 V.C. Esposito, « Advisory Opinions and Jurisdiction of the International Tribunal for the Law of the Sea », in *Regions, Institutions, and Law of the Sea: Studies in Ocean Governance*, Leiden/Boston, Nijhoff, 2013, pp. 58-68.

6 *Responsabilités et obligations des Etats dans le cadre d'activités menées dans la Zone, avis consultatif, 1er février 2011, TIDM Recueil 2011*, p. 10, pars. 64-71.

7 *Demande d'avis consultatif soumise par la Commission sous-régionale des pêches, avis consultatif, 2 avril 2015, TIDM Recueil 2015*, p. 4, par. 145.

8 *Responsabilités et obligations des Etats dans le cadre d'activités menées dans la Zone, avis consultatif, 1er février 2011, op. cit*, par. 71.

des obligations de résultat) et sur les conséquences possibles d'un manquement. Grâce au Tribunal, on sait maintenant mieux ce qu'une obligation de « veiller à », de « prendre toutes les mesures nécessaires » – une obligation de *due diligence* signifie[9]. Pour ce faire, il n'hésite pas à s'appuyer sur la jurisprudence de la CIJ (notamment dans l'affaire des *Usines de pâte à papier sur le fleuve Uruguay* (*Argentine c. Uruguay*) et, bien sûr, sur les Articles de la CDI sur la responsabilité de l'Etat dont l'avis de la Chambre pour le règlement des différends relatifs aux fonds marins constitue une sorte de revue et illustration systématiques ; mais elle va plus loin et aborde parfois des rivages inexplorés. Je ne crois pas, par exemple, avoir vu auparavant une cour ou un tribunal aborder si clairement la question de la responsabilité conjointe et solidaire[10]. De même, le Tribunal s'est montré moins timide que bien d'autres pour consacrer et appliquer le principe de précaution[11]. Quant à l'avis de 2015, il constitue un apport notable au droit de la responsabilité des organisations internationales[12] et il n'hésite pas à invoquer (et, du même coup, à consacrer) à la fois la notion d'obligations *erga omnes* et l'important (et parfois controversé) article 48 des Articles de 2001[13].

La contribution du Tribunal à la clarification et au développement des règles applicables à la responsabilité sans manquement est encore plus éclatante. Je note par exemple trois affaires jugées par le Tribunal qui ont inspiré la rédaction de la directive 7 sur la protection de l'atmosphère adoptée à titre provisoire en juillet dernier par la CDI[14]. Celle-ci a retenu des affaires du *Thon à nageoire bleue*[15], de l'*Usine MOX*[16] et de celle relative aux *Travaux de poldérisation*[17], la

---

9 *Ibid.*, pars. 111-120, 123-124, 131-132, 136 et 142 et *Demande d'avis consultatif soumise par la Commission sous-régionale des pêches, avis consultatif, 2 avril 2015*, p. 4, pars. 125 et 129-132.

10 *Responsabilités et obligations des Etats dans le cadre d'activités menées dans la Zone, avis consultatif, 1er février 2011*, not. pars. 192 et 201, et point 4 du dispositif.

11 *Ibid.*, pars. 122 et 125-135.

12 *Demande d'avis consultatif soumise par la Commission sous-régionale des pêches, avis consultatif, 2 avril 2015*, p. 4, v. les pars. 156-174, et, en particulier, les pars. 168-174.

13 *Responsabilités et obligations des Etats dans le cadre d'activités menées dans la Zone, avis consultatif, 1er février 2011*, p. 10, par. 180.

14 V. le paragraphe 9 du commentaire de la Directive 7, Rapport CDI 2016, doc. A/71/10, p. 310.

15 *Thon à nageoire bleue* (*Nouvelle-Zélande c. Japon ; Australie c. Japon*), *mesures conservatoires, ordonnance, 27 août 1999, TIDM Recueil 1999*, p. 280, par. 77.

16 *Usine MOX* (*Irlande c. Royaume-Uni*), *mesures conservatoires, ordonnance, 3 décembre 2001, TIDM Recueil 2001*, p. 95, par. 84.

17 *Travaux de poldérisation à l'intérieur et à proximité du détroit de Johor* (*Malaisie c. Singapour*), *mesures conservatoires, ordonnance du 8 octobre 2003, TIDM Recueil 2003*, p. 10, par. 99.

formule, appelée à un bel avenir, selon laquelle les activités susceptibles d'être nocives pour l'environnement (en l'espèce pour l'environnement) devraient « être menées avec prudence et précaution ». La récente ordonnance de la Chambre spéciale prescrivant des mesures conservatoires dans le *Différend relatif à la délimitation de la frontière maritime dans l'océan Atlantique* (*Ghana/Côte d'Ivoire*) ouvre également des perspectives nouvelles en la matière[18] en ce qui concerne notamment la notion de risque de dommage irréparable causé à l'environnement[19].

Toujours s'agissant de la *liability*, le Tribunal a relevé que les efforts de codification de la CDI « n'ont pas, jusqu'à présent, abouti à l'élaboration des règles régissant la responsabilité de l'Etat pour acte licites »[20] ; mais, se référant à l'article 304 de la Convention, il a aussi conclu que « [l]e régime international de la responsabilité n'est, par conséquent, pas considéré comme immuable » et, en particulier que « [d]e nouvelles règles du droit international peuvent voir le jour dans le cadre du régime des activités minières relatives aux grands fonds marins ou en droit international conventionnel ou coutumier »[21]. J'aime à voir dans ces considérations une sorte d'« offre de service » du Tribunal pour participer au développement du droit de la responsabilité si l'occasion s'en présente (et je suis de ceux qui considèrent que, s'ils agissent avec prudence et sagesse, les juridictions internationales peuvent contribuer utilement et puissamment à l'affermissement et à la complétude du droit international)[22].

Il va de soi que les apports jurisprudentiels du Tribunal ne se bornent pas au droit de la responsabilité – *responsibility* et *liability* confondues. En eussé-je eu le temps, j'aurais pu mentionner aussi le droit des sources[23] ou celui de la procédure[24]. Et c'est évidemment encore plus vrai dans le domaine de prédi-

---

18 *Différend relatif à la délimitation de la frontière maritime dans l'océan Atlantique* (*Ghana/Côte d'Ivoire*), *mesures conservatoires, ordonnance du 25 avril 2015, TIDM Recueil 2015*, p. 146, pars. 67-73. V. aussi, en ce qui concerne l'obligation de procéder à une EIA, *ibid.*, paragraphes 1 et 2 du commentaire de la directive 4, Rapport CDI 2016, doc. A/71/10, p. 303.

19 V. *ibid.*, pars. 88-92.

20 *Responsabilités et obligations des Etats dans le cadre d'activités menées dans la Zone, avis consultatif, 1er février 2011, TIDM Recueil 2011*, p. 10, par. 209.

21 *Ibid.*, par. 211.

22 V. not. A. Pellet, « L'adaptation du droit international aux besoins changeants de la société internationale », *R.C.A.D.I.* 2007, tome 329, Nijhoff, Leiden/Boston 2008, pp. 43-47.

23 V. par exemple : *Responsabilités et obligations des Etats dans le cadre d'activités menées dans la Zone, avis consultatif, 1er février 2011, TIDM Recueil 2011*, p. 10, pars. 57-60, concernant l'application des règles relatives à l'interprétation des traités.

24 La pratique des délibérations initiales (v. e.g., *Responsabilités et obligations des Etats dans le cadre d'activités menées dans la Zone, avis consultatif, 1er février 2011, TIDM Recueil 2011*,

lection du Tribunal, le droit de la mer, dans lequel il donne le « la » et je pense tout spécialement à la position de principe qu'il a prise dans *Bangladesh/ Myanmar* en ce qui concerne la délimitation du plateau continental ; il me semble que le *dictum* du paragraphe 379 peut être comparé aux formules jurisprudentielles de la CPJI qui, en quelques lignes avaient réalisé une sorte de codification instantanée du droit international : « De même que les fonctions de la Commission ne préjugent pas de la question de la délimitation du plateau continental entre des Etats dont les côtes sont adjacentes ou se font face, de même, l'exercice par les cours et tribunaux internationaux de leur compétence en matière de délimitation de frontières maritimes, y compris sur le plateau continental, ne préjuge pas davantage de l'exercice par la Commission de ses fonctions relatives au tracé de la limite extérieure du plateau continental »[25]. C'est simple, logique, et ça ne laisse place à aucune incertitude – après une période d'incertitude, le droit est dit.

Juste un mot pour finir : pourquoi tout ceci est-il important pour le praticien ? Parce que la jurisprudence, quand elle s'acquitte de sa mission de « dire le droit » avec clarté et autorité est importante ; parce que cela accroit la prévisibilité du droit et nous permet de conseiller plus efficacement nos clients ; et parce que nous sommes, je crois, tous reconnaissants au Tribunal de sa contribution au développement prudent et progressif, et, en même temps, ferme et clair.

HAPPY ANNIVERSARY ITLOS !

---

p. 10, par. 18) et des questions pré-audiences (v. *Délimitation de la frontière maritime dans le golfe du Bengale (Bangladesh/Myanmar), arrêt, TIDM Recueil 2012*, p. 4, par. 21).

25 *Délimitation de la frontière maritime dans le golfe du Bengale* (*Bangladesh/Myanmar*), *arrêt*, TIDM *Recueil 2012*, p. 4, par. 379.

The Indispensable Contributions of the Tribunal: A Practitioner's View

Paul S. Reichler

It is a great honor for me to address the conference convened to celebrate the Tribunal's 20th anniversary, and to present remarks, from my perspective as a practitioner before the Tribunal, on its contributions to the development and enrichment of the law of the sea, and the peaceful and just resolution of disputes.

In my view, the remarkable contributions of the Tribunal cannot fully be appreciated by looking only at the more than 20 specific cases it has successfully resolved. Rather, to more fully appreciate the Tribunal's immense contribution, it is necessary to keep in mind the Tribunal's unique and intimate connection to the peaceful settlement of disputes through arbitration under Part XV and Annex VII of the Convention. This is a role that is exclusive to the Tribunal, and is not shared with the ICJ. I would like to highlight four points about the important relationship between the Tribunal and Annex VII arbitration, and six points that favorably distinguish the Tribunal from Annex VII arbitration.

The first point about this relationship concerns the fluidity of the transition from arbitration under Annex VII to litigation before the Tribunal. Both of the maritime delimitation cases that have come to the Tribunal – the *Dispute concerning delimitation of the maritime boundary between Bangladesh and Myanmar in the Bay of Bengal* (*Bangladesh/Myanmar*) in 2009 and the *Dispute concerning delimitation of the maritime boundary between Ghana and Côte d'Ivoire in the Atlantic Ocean* (*Ghana/Cote d'Ivoire*) in 2014 – were initiated as Annex VII arbitrations but, after compulsory dispute settlement was assured, were shortly thereafter brought to the Tribunal in lieu of an arbitral tribunal.

This was done in both cases by mutual agreement of the parties. In my opinion, especially as a counsel who more often than not represents claimant States in inter-State disputes, this represents the beginning of a pattern. In the future, we are likely to see more cases in which a claimant State, lacking other alternatives to secure jurisdiction over a respondent, invokes Part XV and Annex VII in order to secure a compulsory dispute settlement process in which the fallback vehicle is Annex VII arbitration. After arbitral jurisdiction is thus assured, other options emerge, such as litigation before the Tribunal (or the ICJ) if the parties can agree. Upon the respondent State's recognition of the

© 2018, BY INTERNATIONAL TRIBUNAL FOR THE LAW OF THE SEA | DOI 10.1163/9789004356832_019

inevitable – that compulsory dispute settlement cannot be avoided – healthy discussions can then begin about more favorable alternatives than Annex VII arbitration.

The second point about the relationship between the Tribunal and Annex VII arbitration is that, even where the case remains subject to the arbitral process, the Tribunal has the jurisdiction to indicate provisional measures pending the constitution of the Annex VII arbitral tribunal. This is a power that has been exercised by the Tribunal very effectively, not only to preserve the rights of the parties, but also to facilitate the final settlement of disputes without having to proceed to the merits. The case of the "*ARA Libertad*" (*Argentina* v. *Ghana*), *Provisional Measures*, is an example.

The third point about the relationship between the Tribunal and Annex VII arbitration is the appointment of arbitrators by the Presidents of the Tribunal. Annex VII does not say how this is to be done, and, as a consequence, the Presidents of the Tribunal have had to develop their own procedures. In the three particular cases in which I have been fortunate to be counsel, I have observed how efficiently and effectively this difficult task – which requires both legal acumen and diplomatic skill – has been performed. These cases include President Jesus's appointment of arbitrators in *Bangladesh v. India*; President Yanai's arbitral appointments in *Mauritius v. United Kingdom*; and President Golitsyn's appointment of members of the Special Chamber in *Ghana/Côte d'Ivoire*. In all three cases, the process conducted by the President produced an agreement by the parties on the arbitrators or judges who were appointed – an achievement that required a great deal of skill, patience and diplomacy on the President's part. There has not been a case where a President of the Tribunal has had to appoint anyone against the will of either of the two parties.

The fourth and last point on the relationship between the Tribunal and Annex VII arbitration is the tendency of the Presidents of the Tribunal to favor its judges in the appointment of arbitrators. As a consequence, in *Bangladesh v. India* there were two judges of the Tribunal plus one former judge on the arbitral tribunal, including party-appointed arbitrators. In *Mauritius v. United Kingdom,* there were three serving judges of the Tribunal. In *Philippines v. China,* there were three serving judges of the Tribunal plus one former judge. I consider this a very positive practice. First, it encourages harmony in the interpretation and application of the law. Second, the appointment of such eminent and highly qualified experts as arbitrators enhances the prestige, authority and stature of the arbitral tribunal in a way that encourages the parties toward greater acceptance of the award. And third, it underscores the importance – indeed, the indispensability – of the Tribunal in the resolution of disputes under the Convention, even in cases that are resolved by arbitration.

In my view, these positive effects are all readily apparent in the *Philippines v. China* case. The appointment by President Yanai of four giants of international law – two judges of the Tribunal and one former judge, plus a highly-distinguished academic expert – all of whom are among the world's most highly respected authorities on law of the sea and international law generally, produced a tribunal of such eminence and impeccable integrity that the prospects for eventual acceptance of its unanimously-rendered Award by both parties and the international community were immeasurably enhanced.

I next turn to what I consider the six advantages of coming to the Tribunal as opposed to remaining in Annex VII arbitration. One is the factor that I have already mentioned: prestige. Many States would normally consider it more prestigious to litigate their case before a sitting permanent court established under the UN system of 21 judges from around the world than they would an arbitral tribunal. There is also the aspect of openness and transparency of proceedings before the Tribunal, which is extremely important to the parties in most cases.

This leads to the second advantage. Partly because of the prestige, the stature and the authority of the Tribunal, the prospects of compliance with its judgments are enhanced, especially as compared with Annex VII arbitration. Of course, the legal obligations to comply are the same, but politically, based on my experience representing States, it is not only the party that expects to win that is concerned about eventual compliance with the judgment or award, but even the party that is concerned that the result might be difficult for it politically to accept. It, too, will likely prefer to have the judgment rendered by the Tribunal, because it may be less difficult to convince disappointed elements in the country that the decision must be respected, than if it were rendered by an arbitral tribunal. In this manner, the extra weight of a judgment by the Tribunal (or by the ICJ) facilitates compliance in challenging circumstances.

The third advantage of the Tribunal is cost. Arbitration is usually more expensive, because the parties are required to bear the burden of both arbitrators' fees and expenses, and administrative charges by the host forum. Coming to the Tribunal avoids all of the arbitrators' costs and administrative charges.

The fourth advantage is the excellence of the facilities. The Tribunal's building, and the courtroom in particular, are modern, spacious and commodious. And the Registry, staff and services are outstanding.

The fifth advantage of the Tribunal is efficiency: the reduced time it takes from the beginning of a case to the end. As counsel in the *Bangladesh/Myanmar* case, I can attest that we were skeptical that we could complete the case in what we considered a short time frame proposed by President Jesus. But we did it, and both parties were better off for it. From beginning to end,

Bangladesh/Myanmar took just a little over 2.5 years, perhaps an international record equivalent to running a mile in less than four minutes. Yet, nothing was lost, either in case preparation or presentation by the parties, or the erudition or eloquence of the Tribunal's Judgment. Following this example, it appears possible that *Ghana/Cote d'Ivoire* will be also completed in under three years, thanks to the efforts of Vice-President Bouguetaia who is President of the Special Chamber.

A sixth advantage of adjudication by the Tribunal, and perhaps its most important, is the innovativeness of the Tribunal in finding practical solutions to disputes under existing legal frameworks that advance the rule of law. Two significant examples stand out. The first is the decision to delimit the maritime boundary beyond 200 nm in *Bangladesh/Myanmar*.

That case presented a situation, unfortunately not uncommon, where the parties had objected to each other's submissions before the CLCS. Bangladesh asked the Tribunal to delimit the entire length of the boundary, including in the area beyond 200 nm. Myanmar opposed, on the grounds that the Tribunal should not delimit in that area unless and until the CLCS confirmed the existence of a shelf beyond 200 nm and issued recommendations on its outer limit. If the Tribunal had decided that it was without jurisdiction to address the delimitation dispute until after the CLCS had performed its functions, the result would have been a classic Catch 22. The CLCS would not have acted while there was a delimitation dispute, but the delimitation dispute would not be resolved until after the Commission had acted. Had this argument been accepted, it would have been a formula not only for permanent deadlock, but also for instability because it would have frozen in place many boundary disputes around the world without hope or possibility of third party resolution.

In its wisdom, the Tribunal decided to avoid such a problem by agreeing to delimit beyond 200 nm notwithstanding the absence of CLCS action, and both parties have accepted the result. The Tribunal's Judgment and reasoning were so persuasive that, in July 2016, the ICJ followed its example and decided, in a case between Nicaragua and Colombia, that it, too, should delimit the boundary beyond 200 nm in advance of CLCS action, where, as in the case between Bangladesh and Myanmar, the CLCS was blocked from acting by the objection of one of the parties.

Another important innovation by the Tribunal was its approach to provisional measures in *Ghana/Côte d'Ivoire*. Previously, it had been the norm to prohibit or discourage the drilling of oil or gas wells in a disputed area pending the final drawing of a boundary by the international court or tribunal. But the case between Ghana and Côte d'Ivoire presented unique circumstances. There were a number of wells where Ghana had commenced, but not completed, drilling before the commencement of the case. It would have been prejudicial to Ghana, and potentially to the marine environment, for Ghana to terminate its activities at those wells in mid-construction. Taking note of this, the Special Chamber granted provisional measures preventing Ghana from initiating any new wells in the disputed area, but allowing it to complete the wells where drilling had already commenced. The Special Chamber also ordered strong measures to protect the marine environment. As a result, the interests of both parties were protected pending the final delimitation of the boundary.

By way of conclusion of these remarks on the occasion of the Tribunal's 20th anniversary, I shall refer back to its origins in the 1982 Convention, and, in particular, to these words from the Preamble:

> The Parties to this Convention … recognizing the desirability of establishing through this Convention, with due regard for the sovereignty of all States, a legal order for the seas and oceans which will facilitate international communication, and will promote the peaceful uses of the seas and oceans, the equitable and efficient utilization of their resources, the conservation of their living resources, and the study, protection and preservation of the marine environment.

I submit that, measured by these standards, the Convention might not yet have fully achieved its loftiest goals, but, as agreed by the overwhelming majority of informed commentators, it has been a very successful international agreement in moving the world toward these objectives. The Convention has even been called, deservedly so in my view, one of the most successful multilateral conventions in international law. In no small regard, the success of the Convention is attributable to the work of the Tribunal, in promoting and advancing the rule of law in regard to the world's seas and oceans, and in bringing about the peaceful resolution of many maritime disputes.

So, it is with admiration and gratitude, and profound respect, that I join others in celebrating the Tribunal's 20th anniversary, and in looking forward to even greater achievement from it in the years ahead.

Understanding the Advisory Jurisdiction of the International Tribunal for the Law of the Sea

Sir Michael Wood

> an opportunity has been missed. The Tribunal has taken a remarkable action by affirming its advisory jurisdiction on the basis of unpersuasive reasoning. Yet it could have demonstrated imagination and established a coherent system guaranteeing the rights of members of the international community in judicial proceedings.[1]

The advisory jurisdiction of the Tribunal is a potential avenue that practitioners (including those working for the Authority and other international organizations) may wish to consider when advising clients. In doing so, they need to be able to understand the scope of the Tribunal's jurisdiction to give advisory opinions, the limitations thereon, and applicable procedures.

The Tribunal has two distinct advisory jurisdictions: first, the advisory jurisdiction of the Tribunal's Seabed Disputes Chamber, which is expressly provided for in the Convention; and second, the advisory jurisdiction of the full Tribunal, which, it has been said, "was essentially created out of the blue by the Tribunal itself through the introduction of Article 138 of the Rules, 15 years after the signing ceremony in Montego Bay."[2] In considering the issues from the point of view of the practitioner, I shall focus on the latter, that is on advisory opinions which may be given by the full Tribunal, under article 21 of its Statute combined with other agreements.

The two Advisory Opinions given so far by the Tribunal relate in turn to each of these two distinct heads of jurisdiction: *Responsibilities and obligations of States sponsoring persons and entities with respect to activities in the Area (Request for Advisory Opinion submitted to the Seabed Disputes Chamber)*,[3]

---

1 *Request for Advisory Opinion submitted by the Sub-Regional Fisheries Commission, Advisory Opinion, 2 April 2015, Declaration of Judge Cot, ITLOS Reports 2015*, p. 4, at p. 75, para. 13.

2 T. Ruys & A. Soete, "'Creeping' Advisory Jurisdiction of International Courts and Tribunals? The case of the International Tribunal for the Law of the Sea", 29 *Leiden Journal of International Law* 1 (2016) pp. 155–176, at p. 173.

3 *Responsibilities and obligations of States with respect to activities in the Area, Advisory Opinion, 1 February 2011, ITLOS Reports 2011*. p. 10 (hereafter "*Responsibilities and obligations of States Opinion*").

© 2018, BY INTERNATIONAL TRIBUNAL FOR THE LAW OF THE SEA | DOI 10.1163/9789004356832_020

and *Request for an Advisory Opinion submitted by the Sub-Regional Fisheries Commission* (SRFC).[4] They offer only limited guidance as regards the advisory jurisdiction of the full Tribunal.

The Secretary-General of the United Nations has written, of advisory proceedings in general, that they "carry great weight and moral authority, often serving as an instrument of preventive diplomacy and contributing to the clarification of the state of international law."[5]

Advisory opinions, as such, have no binding force, though they may be binding under a separate agreement. But in any event, they carry considerable authority; they most certainly have legal effects. Advisory opinions undoubtedly have the potential to contribute to the rule of law. Their role in the settlement of disputes may be indirect,[6] yet by clarifying the law they promote legal certainty, an important aspect of the rule of law.

There remain real concerns about how appropriate advisory proceedings may be in some circumstances. Distinguished authors have referred to the "current health"[7] or "uses and abuses"[8] of advisory opinions. The report of the 1943/44 Informal Inter-Allied Committee that considered the establishment of the ICJ (the London Committee) makes interesting reading.[9] Some members of the Committee:

4 *Request for Advisory Opinion submitted by the Sub-Regional Fisheries Commission, Advisory Opinion, 2 April 2015, ITLOS Reports 2015*, p. 4 (hereafter "*SRFC Opinion*").

5 "Strengthening and coordinating United Nations rule of law activities" Report of the Secretary-General, 20 August 2010, UN Doc. A/65/318, para. 25.

6 As the ICJ has said, "[t]he purpose of the advisory function is not to settle – at least directly – disputes between States, but to offer legal advice to the organs and institutions requesting the opinion", *Legality of the Threat or Use of Nuclear Weapons, Advisory Opinion, I.C.J. Reports 1996*, p. 226, at p. 236, para. 15.

7 R. Higgins, "A Comment on the Current Health of Advisory Proceedings", in V. Lowe & M. Fitzmaurice (eds.), *Fifty Years of the International Court of Justice: Essays in Honour of Sir Robert Jennings* (Cambridge University Press, 1996), pp. 567–581, reprinted in R. Higgins, *Themes and Theories. Selected Essays, Speeches, and Writings in International Law* (Oxford University Press, 2009), pp. 1043–1055.

8 F. Berman, "The Uses and Abuses of Advisory Opinions", in N. Ando et al. (eds.), *Liber Amicorum Judge Shigeru Oda* (2002), pp. 809–828. See also A. Aust, "Advisory Opinions", 1 *Journal of International Dispute Settlement* (2010), pp. 123–151.

9 Report of the Informal Inter-Allied Committee on the Future of the Permanent Court of International Justice, February 10, 1944, 39 *AJIL* 1 (1945) Supplement, pp. 1–42.

> were inclined to think at first that the Court's jurisdiction to give advisory opinions was anomalous and ought to be abolished, mainly on the ground that it was incompatible with the true function of a court of law, which was to hear and decide disputes. It was urged that the existence of this jurisdiction tended to encourage the use of the Court as an instrument for settling issues which were essentially of a political rather than of a legal character and that this was undesirable. Attention was drawn to instances of this which had occurred in the past. Subsidiary objections were that the existence of this jurisdiction might promote a tendency to avoid the final settlement of disputes by seeking opinions, and might lead to general pronouncements of law by the Court not (or not sufficiently) related to a particular issue or set of facts.[10]

However, the Committee also saw "no objection to allowing two or more States, acting in concert, to apply direct to the Court for an advisory opinion"[11] and stated:

> [w]e are also agreed that, provided the necessary safeguards can be instituted, there would, for the reasons given in paragraph 68, be considerable advantage in permitting references on the part of two or more States acting in concert. Applications by an individual State ex parte could not be permitted, for, given the authoritative nature of the Court's pronouncements, ex parte applications would afford a means whereby the State concerned could indirectly impose a species of compulsory jurisdiction on the rest of the world. In addition, the Court must have an agreed basis of fact on which to give its opinion.[12]

The procedure for advisory proceedings raises serious questions. On one view, the fact that their purpose is to advise, not to decide a dispute, and the frequent absence of disputed facts, mean that the court or tribunal is able to be more ambitious in its abstract statements of the law, which might be less appropriate in a contentious case; yet that is not the real purpose of advisory opinions. Another view is that the absence of a dispute rooted in tested facts, and the absence of genuine adversarial pleadings, reduces the ability of the court or tribunal to give a well-considered and focused view of the law. This can to some extent be mitigated through procedural arrangements, as was

10 *Ibid.*, p. 20, para 65.

11 *Ibid.*, p. 22, para 71.

12 *Ibid.*, p. 23, para 74. This suggestion was not accepted at San Francisco.

done in *Accordance with International Law of the Unilateral Declaration of Independence in Respect of Kosovo*.[13]

Requests for advisory opinions often seem abstract; the court or tribunal does not have the benefit of seeing a legal question through the prism of concrete facts. Or, conversely, in some cases where there are real facts before the Tribunal, the advisory procedure may not allow their proper consideration, or be appropriate for addressing any underlying dispute. Then there is the inappropriateness, to put it no higher, of addressing a dispute between States without each party's consent. At the very least, these matters require careful attention to the procedure in advisory proceedings, and a readiness to tailor it to the particular circumstances of the case. For example, there is the almost random order of presentation at the oral hearing, dictated by the alphabet, often the French alphabet. In the *Responsibilities and obligations of States* case this meant that the main protagonists came way down the batting order.

There is, unfortunately, not much guidance on the Tribunal's advisory jurisdiction. There are the provisions of the Convention: articles 159, paragraph 10, 191 and, it now appears, Annex VI, article 21, which reads: "[t]he jurisdiction of the Tribunal comprises all disputes and all applications submitted to it in accordance with this Convention and all matters ("*toutes les fois que cela*" in French) specifically provided for in any other agreement which confers jurisdiction on the Tribunal."

Article 138 of the Rules of the Tribunal provides as follows:

1. The Tribunal may give an advisory opinion on a legal question if an international agreement related to the purposes of the Convention specifically provides for the submission to the Tribunal of a request for such an opinion.
2. A request for an advisory opinion shall be transmitted to the Tribunal by whatever body is authorized by or in accordance with the agreement to make the request to the Tribunal.
3. The Tribunal shall apply mutatis mutandis articles 130 to 137.[14]

---

13 *Accordance with International Law of the Unilateral Declaration of Independence in Respect of Kosovo, Advisory Opinion, I.C.J. Reports 2010*, p. 403. In *Kosovo* there were two rounds of written pleadings, and the main protagonists – Serbia and Kosovo – addressed the Court at the outset of the oral hearing, and were given significantly more speaking time.

14 Judge Cot seemed to regard the adoption of this rule, and the absence of objection thereto by States, as conclusive for the jurisdiction of the Tribunal to give advisory opinions (*Declaration of Judge Cot, ITLOS Reports 2015*, p. 73, para. 4). That rather overlooks diplomatic and legal realities. States may well not react to such a rule in the abstract, on the

The reasons for including article 138 in the Rules adopted in 1997 are unknown,[15] and its legal basis was unspecified. It might simply have been that the judges wanted to expand the work of the Tribunal at a time when there seemed little immediate prospect of contentious cases, or even just to make the Tribunal more competitive with the ICJ, which had a relatively thriving advisory practice.[16]

Regard may be had, within limits, to the practice of other international courts and tribunals. But caution is required. Each court and tribunal and its advisory jurisdiction (if any) is distinct, with its own context, characteristics and statutory provisions. Even the Tribunal's Seabed Disputes Chamber and the full Tribunal are very different. It cannot simply be assumed that the case-law and experience of, say, the ICJ can be transposed to the Tribunal.

There are also extensive writings on advisory proceedings, though again this mostly concerns courts other than the Tribunal and needs to be treated with prudence.

The full Tribunal's power to give advisory opinions remains controversial.[17] Faced with the Tribunal's *SRFC Opinion*, "it is difficult to suppress a feeling of unease"[18] and it is hard not to share the view that the Advisory Opinion, and particularly its paragraph 56, is "not fully convincing".[19]

The issue eventually turned on the interpretation of article 21 of the Statute. Paragraph 56 of the Advisory Opinion reads:

---

assumption that they can question its validity if and when it is sought to be applied in practice.

15 There is an almost complete lack of transparency in the adoption of the Rules of the Tribunal, which may be regretted. The same is true of the Rules of the ICJ (by contrast with the Rules of the PCIJ).

16 As was hinted by Judge Wolfrum at a conference in 2010: R. Wolfrum, "Final Remarks and Conclusions" in R. Wolfrum & I. Gätzschmann (eds.), *International Dispute Settlement: Room for Innovations?* (Springer 2013), p. 445.

17 Even within the EU: In Case C-73/14, the CJEU (Grand Chamber) noted that the neutral position expressed in the European Commission's Written Statement to the Tribunal concerning the issue of the Tribunal's jurisdiction to give the Advisory Opinion sought in Case No. 21 "was dictated by its concern to take into account, in the spirit of sincere co-operation, the divergent views on that issue expressed by the Member States within the Council." Judgment of Grand Chamber of 6 October 2015 – *Council of the European Union v. European Commission*, para. 88.

18 T Ruys & A.Soete, *supra* at note 2, at p. 162.

19 M. Lando, "The Advisory Jurisdiction of the International Tribunal for the Law of the Sea: Comments on the *Request for Advisory Opinion submitted by the Sub-Regional Fisheries Commission*", 29 *Leiden Journal of International Law* 2 (2016), pp. 441–461, at p. 442.

> The words all "matters" ("toutes les fois que cela" in French) should not be interpreted as covering only "disputes", for, if that were to be the case, article 21 of the Statute would simply have used the word "disputes". Consequently, it must mean something more than only "disputes". That something more must include advisory opinions, if specifically provided for in "any other agreement which confers jurisdiction on the Tribunal".

It is difficult not to agree with Judge Cot's view of the weakness of the Tribunal's "convoluted reasoning".[20] The Tribunal's affirmation of its advisory jurisdiction has been described as "regrettably succinct".[21] Nevertheless, on jurisdiction the Opinion was unanimous, and it would be a brave advocate who sought to persuade the Tribunal to change its mind.

The Tribunal offered little guidance on the circumstances in which it would be prepared to assert a jurisdiction to give advisory opinions, though it was encouraged to do so by many of those participating in the proceedings. It said:

> In terms of article 21 of the Statute, it is the "other agreement" which confers such jurisdiction on the Tribunal. When the "other agreement" confers advisory jurisdiction on the Tribunal, the Tribunal then is rendered competent to exercise such jurisdiction with regard to "all matters" specifically provided for in the "other agreement". Article 21 and the "other agreement" conferring jurisdiction on the Tribunal are interconnected

20 *Declaration of Judge Cot, ITLOS Reports 2015*, p. 73, para. 2. As Judge Cot explained at para. 3: "The Tribunal considers its advisory jurisdiction to be founded on the combined provisions of an international agreement, the MCA Convention, and article 21 of its Statute. In my view this interpretation is misguided, as it is contrary to the rules codified in the 1969 Vienna Convention on the Law of Treaties. It presupposes that there is a plain meaning which can be ascribed to the article and that the term 'matters' is more precise than it actually is. Quite a number of States participating in the proceedings skilfully advocated an opposite and equally plausible interpretation. The ambiguity of the provision is blindingly obvious. Reference should have been made to the *travaux préparatoires* for the Convention, which in no way confirm the interpretation adopted by the Tribunal. I would add that that interpretation does not allow the different language versions to be reconciled. The French version does not refer to 'matters' and does not translate that term by '*matières*', which would have been the case had the Convention drafters intended to confer upon the term the special meaning encompassing a reference to advisory jurisdiction." However, Judge Cot's own reasons for accepting the Tribunal's jurisdiction are if anything even less convincing (*Declaration of Judge Cot, ITLOS Reports 2015*, p. 73, para. 4).

21 T. Ruys & A. Soete, *supra* at note 2, p. 173.

> and constitute the substantive legal basis of the advisory jurisdiction of the Tribunal.[22]

Yet it is important for practitioners to be able to understand the scope of and "prerequisites" for the jurisdiction of the full Tribunal referred to in article 138. The Tribunal has only set out these prerequisites in the most formal terms, in a single paragraph (para. 60) of its 2015 Advisory Opinion:

> These prerequisites are: an international agreement related to the purposes of the Convention specifically provides for the submission to the Tribunal of a request for an advisory opinion; the request must be transmitted to the Tribunal by a body authorized by or in accordance with the agreement mentioned above; and such an opinion may be given on "a legal question".

It would have been helpful if in its Opinion the Tribunal had given more explanation of these prerequisites and the limits of its advisory jurisdiction. These matters were discussed extensively in many of the written and oral pleadings in the case. Judge Cot's words of caution are well founded:

> The dangers of abuse and manipulation, if the Tribunal does not provide a procedural framework by exercising its discretionary power, are evident. States could, through bilateral or multilateral agreement, seek to gain an advantage over third States and thereby place the Tribunal in an awkward position.[23]

And then there is the question of discretion. "The Tribunal *may* give an advisory opinion", as article 138 of the Rules says. In the 2014 Advisory Opinion, the Tribunal "[took] refuge behind the jurisprudence of the International Court of Justice and [stated] that it is well settled that a request for an advisory opinion should not in principle be refused except for 'compelling reasons' (para. 71)."[24] Yet it is not obvious that the approach of the ICJ would be appropriate, given the great differences between the ICJ and the Tribunal.[25]

---

22 SRFC *Opinion*, para. 58.

23 *Declaration of Judge Cot, ITLOS Reports 2015*, p. 74, para. 9.

24 *Ibid.*, para. 5.

25 *Ibid.*, para. 7: "The Tribunal's position in advisory proceedings is very different from that of the Court. The advisory procedure in the International Court of Justice is governed by a tight framework. An opinion may be requested only by the General Assembly or the

I have tried to highlight the potential importance of the Tribunal's advisory jurisdiction, and some possible difficulties. As you may have gathered, and as I have indicated in the *Festschrift Wolfrum*,[26] I am in two minds about the value of advisory opinions. At the very least, they need to be approached with "prudence and caution".

Security Council or with their authorization. The request is the subject of a preliminary discussion within a body in which all interested parties are represented. Each State concerned is thus involved in drafting the questions asked."

26 M. Wood, "Advisory Jurisdiction: Lessons from Recent Practice" in Hestermeier et al. (eds.), *Coexistence, Cooperation and Solidarity. Liber Amicorum Rüdiger Wolfrum* (Brill, 2012), pp. 1833–1849.

PART 4 / PARTIE 4

Improving Working Methods in International Adjudication

L'amélioration des méthodes de travail de la justice internationale

L'amélioration des méthodes de travail de la justice internationale – Le point de vue de la Cour internationale de Justice

Ronny Abraham

Excellences,
Mesdames et Messieurs les Juges,
Chers collègues et amis,

C'est pour moi à la fois un grand plaisir et un grand honneur d'être aujourd'hui devant vous, à l'occasion des célébrations entourant le vingtième anniversaire du Tribunal international du droit de la mer. Je vais vous dire quelques mots des méthodes de travail à la Cour internationale de Justice.

Les méthodes de travail de la Cour, et je donne à ces termes un sens large, ont sans conteste beaucoup évolué depuis sa création. Je me propose aujourd'hui d'aborder deux points qui pour moi sont emblématiques de l'adaptation des méthodes de travail de la Cour aux besoins des procédures devant elle. Il s'agit, d'abord, des changements ayant marqué la pratique interne de la Cour en matière de délibération intervenus en réponse au double défi né de l'accroissement de sa charge de travail et du caractère limité de ses ressources. En second lieu, je parlerai du travail de la Cour dans le cadre des demandes en indication de mesures conservatoires et de la façon dont la Cour a pu améliorer ses pratiques à cet égard. Parce qu'elles ont un caractère urgent et prioritaire, les mesures conservatoires requièrent une réaction dans des délais particulièrement brefs et leur traitement illustre concrètement les efforts faits par la Cour pour optimiser ses méthodes de travail et accroître son efficacité.

S'agissant du premier point, je commencerai par quelques observations relatives au contexte historique ayant amené la Cour à faire évoluer certaines de ses pratiques administratives et internes.

Alors que dans les années soixante-dix le rôle de la Cour ne comptait en moyenne qu'une ou deux affaires en même temps, la Cour a vu le nombre d'affaires lui étant soumises se multiplier à partir du début des années quatre-vingt. Cette progression a continué tout au long des années quatre-vingt-dix, ce qui, statistiquement parlant, fit de cette décennie la plus chargée pour la Cour avec au total 35 requêtes dans le cadre d'affaires contentieuses et 3 demandes d'avis consultatifs déposées. Cela représente plus du double du nombre d'affaires

© 2018, BY INTERNATIONAL TRIBUNAL FOR THE LAW OF THE SEA | DOI 10.1163/9789004356832_021

soumises au cours de la décennie des années quatre-vingt, et le triple si l'on compare aux années soixante-dix.

Durant cette même période, la Cour a dû subir des coupes budgétaires résultant des difficultés financières au sein de l'ONU. Nous nous sommes donc retrouvés dans une situation où la Cour devait fonctionner sous le coup de restrictions budgétaires alors même qu'elle était de plus en plus occupée.

Face à cette situation, la Cour s'est montrée déterminée à gérer cette charge accrue de travail avec un maximum d'efficacité. Cela l'a conduite à prendre plusieurs mesures de réorganisation du travail au sein du Greffe, mais elle a également chargé son comité du Règlement de mettre au point des propositions visant à optimiser l'efficacité de ses travaux. C'est de l'un des aspects les plus intéressants de cette réforme que je souhaite vous parler ce matin, à savoir la modification de la pratique interne de la Cour en matière judiciaire.

Afin de comprendre la réforme qui fut opérée, il importe tout d'abord d'expliquer les grandes lignes du processus de délibération. La pratique exige depuis longtemps que chaque juge, dès la clôture de la procédure orale d'une affaire, rédige une note écrite dans laquelle sont analysés les points essentiels de l'affaire. Ces notes, qui revêtent bien sûr un caractère strictement confidentiel, sont traduites et distribuées pour être examinées par les juges avant qu'ils se réunissent pour délibérer dans une affaire. Cette pratique, qui est codifiée dans le document intitulé Résolution visant la pratique interne de la Cour en matière judiciaire, adopté en 1976, a l'avantage de permettre aux juges d'anticiper la direction que prendront les délibérations dans une affaire donnée et de se concentrer, le cas échéant, sur les points de l'affaire qui sont les plus controversés lors des délibérations elles-mêmes. Elle a donc vocation à rendre le processus de délibération plus ciblé et plus efficace. Toutefois, elle nécessite de donner un certain délai aux juges pour rédiger leur note, délai ayant pour conséquence de retarder dans une certaine mesure la tenue des délibérations proprement dites. Elle impose en outre de mobiliser des ressources importantes aux fins de la traduction des textes diffusés.

Pour optimiser le processus de production des arrêts, la Cour décida en 1998, conformément à la recommandation de son comité du Règlement, qu'elle pourrait dorénavant procéder sans notes écrites des juges lorsqu'elle l'estimerait nécessaire, dans des affaires qui s'y prêtent et qui concernent des phases préliminaires à la procédure sur le fond.[1] Il est à noter que cette pratique allégée s'était déjà développée à la Cour dans le cas des demandes en indication de mesures conservatoires.[2]

1 http://www.icj-cij.org/presscom/index.php?pr=618&pt=&p1=6&p2=1.

2 http://www.icj-cij.org/presscom/index.php?pr=618&pt=&p1=6&p2=1.

En 1998, la Cour avait souligné que cette modification de sa pratique se ferait sur une base « expérimentale ».[3] L'expérience se révéla fructueuse et la Cour confirma en 2002 qu'elle avait décidé, selon les termes du communiqué qu'elle a rendu public à cette occasion, « de s'en tenir à la pratique traditionnelle des notes écrites dans les affaires pour lesquelles elle est appelée à rendre une décision au fond » mais qu'elle « [continuerait] à recourir à la pratique ... consistant à se prononcer au cas par cas sur la nécessité ou non de se passer des notes écrites au cours de la phase préliminaire d'une affaire »[4]. Dans la pratique récente, l'absence de notes dans la phase préliminaire apparaît désormais comme la règle générale, à moins que la nature particulière d'une affaire justifie qu'il en soit autrement. Dans les cas où des notes sont utilisées, celles-ci peuvent couramment atteindre plusieurs dizaines de pages, en fonction de la complexité et la difficulté des affaires. Pour accélérer ses travaux, la Cour a cependant rappelé que, je cite le même communiqué: « les notes écrites devraient être aussi concises que possible et que le temps imparti à leur préparation devrait être réduit »[5].

Grâce à ces changements, la Cour semble être parvenue à un délicat équilibre qui lui permet de mieux ajuster son processus de délibération à la nature de la cause qu'elle entend. D'ailleurs, bien que motivée par la situation particulière prévalant au tournant du siècle, cette nouvelle façon de fonctionner continue de jouer un rôle crucial à un moment où la Cour demeure activement sollicitée. Cela est d'autant plus vrai lorsqu'on considère l'importance qu'occupent les procédures incidentes dans le travail de la Cour depuis les dix dernières années. En effet, environ le quart des arrêts rendus par la Cour depuis dix ans dans des procédures contentieuses ont porté sur des exceptions préliminaires.

Je note d'ailleurs que pendant cette même période, malgré un volume d'affaires parmi les plus élevés de son histoire récente et la complexité grandissante des affaires, le délai entre la clôture de la procédure orale et la lecture de l'arrêt par la Cour a été en moyenne inférieur à six mois. On peut donc constater dans les faits les conséquences pratiques positives des mesures que la Cour a prises pour accroître son efficacité et faire face à l'augmentation régulière de sa charge de travail.[6]

3 http://www.icj-cij.org/presscom/index.php?pr=618&pt=&p1=6&p2=1.

4 http://www.icj-cij.org/presscom/index.php?pr=1026&pt=&p1=6&p2=1.

5 http://www.icj-cij.org/presscom/index.php?pr=1026&pt=&p1=6&p2=1.

6 Voir notamment Rapport annuel de la Cour 2010-2011; 2011-2012; 2012-2013; 2013-2014; 2014-2015.

J'en viens au deuxième point que je souhaite aborder ce matin, à savoir la pratique de la Cour dans le cadre des demandes en indication de mesures conservatoires. Il s'agit en effet d'un domaine où l'on peut constater les efforts concrets de la Cour en vue de moderniser ses méthodes de travail pour répondre aux demandes des Parties et aux exigences d'une bonne administration de la justice.

Comme vous le savez certainement, l'article 41 du Statut de la Cour, complété par les articles 73 à 78 du Règlement de la Cour, permet à la Cour d'indiquer des mesures conservatoires pour protéger les droits des Parties à une affaire devant elle en attendant l'arrêt final lorsque les droits en cause sont susceptibles d'être affectés.

A travers ses décisions, la Cour a clarifié les conditions présidant à l'indication des mesures conservatoires :

- Tout d'abord, la Cour doit être convaincue qu'elle a compétence *prima facie* sur le fond du litige ;
- Ensuite, la Cour doit estimer que les droits invoqués par la partie qui sollicite les mesures conservatoires sont au moins plausibles ;
- La Cour doit également s'assurer qu'il existe un lien suffisant entre les droits qui font l'objet de l'instance pendante devant elle sur le fond de l'affaire et les mesures conservatoires sollicitées ;
- Enfin, il doit exister un risque réel et imminent qu'un préjudice irréparable soit causé aux droits en litige avant que la Cour ne rende sa décision définitive – c'est le critère de l'urgence.

Il est évident que le caractère urgent et prioritaire des demandes en indication de mesures conservatoires constitue un défi important pour le travail de la Cour. Notons à cet égard le paragraphe 1 de l'Article 74 du Règlement qui lui impose d'agir avec célérité en prévoyant que « la demande en indication de mesures conservatoires a priorité sur toutes autres affaires ».

Ainsi, lorsque cela est apparu nécessaire, la Cour a dû par exemple interrompre des audiences dans une affaire afin de pouvoir procéder à l'examen d'une demande de mesures conservatoires présentée dans une autre affaire. Ce fut le cas notamment durant les audiences d'avril 1984 dans l'affaire de la *Délimitation de la frontière maritime dans la région du golfe du Maine* (*Canada/Etats-Unis d'Amérique*), qui furent temporairement interrompues après le premier tour afin que la Cour puisse connaitre de la demande de mesures conservatoires présentée le 9 avril dans l'affaire des *Activités militaires et paramilitaires au Nicaragua et contre celui-ci* (*Nicaragua c. Etats-Unis d'Amérique*).

Du point de vue interne, la Cour doit également ajuster son processus de délibération et son calendrier afin de pouvoir donner priorité aux mesures conservatoires. Pensons par exemple aux demandes en indication de mesures conservatoires qui furent présentées de part et d'autre par le Costa Rica et le Nicaragua à l'automne 2013 dans les affaires jointes les opposant, relatives, d'une part, à *Certaines activités menées par le Nicaragua dans la région frontalière* et, d'autre part, à la *Construction d'une route au Costa Rica le long du fleuve San Juan*, alors que les délibérations étaient en cours dans les affaires relatives à la *Chasse à la baleine dans l'Antarctique* (*Australie c. Japon ; Nouvelle-Zélande* (*intervenant*)) et au *Différend maritime* (*Pérou c. Chili*). De même, la Cour a été saisie tout récemment d'une demande en indication de mesures conservatoires dans l'affaire des *Immunités et procédures pénales* (*Guinée équatoriale c. France*) alors que l'affaire de la *Délimitation maritime dans l'océan Indien* (*Somalie c. Kenya*) est en délibération relativement aux exceptions préliminaires.

De façon générale, les mesures conservatoires représentent désormais une partie substantielle du travail de la Cour. Depuis sa création, la Cour a été saisie d'une cinquantaine de demandes en indication de mesures conservatoires, et plus du quart de ces demandes ont été soumises au cours de la dernière décennie. Ceci s'explique sûrement par les circonstances propres aux affaires concernées, mais on peut également signaler que cette période coïncide avec l'arrêt *LaGrand* rendu en 2001, dans lequel la Cour a affirmé pour la première fois le caractère obligatoire de ces mesures.[7]

Malgré la pression qu'exercent ces demandes en mesures conservatoires sur les ressources de la Cour, et en dépit de l'augmentation de sa charge de travail, la Cour a toujours affirmé sa capacité à intervenir promptement lorsqu'il est fait appel à elle pour protéger les droits des parties avant que n'intervienne l'arrêt final.

Elle a ainsi systématiquement fait preuve de célérité dans l'examen des demandes en indication de mesures conservatoires. L'exemple le plus célèbre est celui de l'affaire *LaGrand*, où la Cour rendit une ordonnance en indication de mesures conservatoires 24 heures seulement après le dépôt de la demande qui accompagnait la requête introductive d'instance. A l'autre bout du spectre, le délai le plus long qui se soit écoulé entre le dépôt d'une demande et le prononcé de l'ordonnance a été d'un peu moins de quatre mois dans l'affaire relative à *Certaines activités menées par le Nicaragua dans la région frontalière* (*Costa Rica c. Nicaragua*). Ces extrêmes représentent évidemment des exceptions, liées aux circonstances particulières de chaque affaire, et la moyenne du

7 *LaGrand* (*Allemagne c. Etats-Unis d'Amérique*), *arrêt, C.I.J. Recueil 2001*, p. 502-03, par. 102.

délai entre le dépôt d'une demande en indication de mesures conservatoires et le prononcé de l'ordonnance tourne plutôt aux alentours de six semaines.

Dans l'optique de rationaliser sa pratique relative aux mesures conservatoires, la Cour a adopté en 2006 une instruction de procédure afin de réduire le temps nécessaire à la procédure orale. A cette fin, il est rappelé aux parties qu'elles « devraient limiter leurs exposés oraux … aux questions touchant aux conditions à remplir aux fins de l'indication de mesures conservatoires, telles qu'elles ressortent du Statut, du Règlement et de la jurisprudence de la Cour »[8]. Les Parties sont également averties qu'elles « ne devraient pas aborder le fond de l'affaire au-delà de ce qui est strictement nécessaire aux fins de la demande. »[9]

L'insistance de la Cour sur la brièveté de la procédure orale a porté ses fruits puisqu'on a constaté un raccourcissement notable des exposés oraux dans le cadre de demandes en indication de mesures conservatoires dans la période qui a suivi la publication de l'instruction de procédure.[10] La procédure orale se déroule aujourd'hui en règle générale sur deux ou trois jours.

En guise de conclusion, je souhaite ajouter que bien qu'on puisse se féliciter de l'amélioration des méthodes de travail à la Cour depuis sa création, il n'en demeure pas moins qu'il s'agit là d'un exercice continuel pour la Cour et qu'il ne faut donc jamais cesser d'être vigilants pour identifier les changements qui pourraient devenir nécessaires au fil du temps. Cette réalité est d'ailleurs bien illustrée par l'utilisation par la Cour des instructions de procédures. Adoptées pour la première fois en 2001, elles furent amendées en 2002, 2004, 2005 et 2009. Ces instructions sont, selon les termes de la Cour, « le fruit du réexamen constant … de ses méthodes de travail ». Ce réexamen est continuellement pertinent afin de s'adapter à de nouvelles réalités. Je note d'ailleurs que la Cour a récemment eu la chance de se pencher sur le sujet lors du séminaire qu'elle a organisé à l'occasion de son 70ème anniversaire en avril dernier. L'un des quatre thèmes abordés lors du séminaire portait spécifiquement sur les méthodes de travail de la Cour, ce qui donna l'occasion aux juges de réfléchir avec les praticiens (avocats, conseils et agents des parties) aux domaines dans lesquels celle-ci pourrait améliorer ces méthodes.

---

8 http://www.icj-cij.org/presscom/index.php?pr=94&pt=&p1=6&p2=1.

9 http://www.icj-cij.org/presscom/index.php?pr=94&pt=&p1=6&p2=1.

10 Shabtai Rosenne, *Law and Practice of the International Court: 1920-2005* (Martinus Nijhoff, 2006), à la p. 1416.

Voilà qui conclut mon intervention. Je ne doute pas que les remarques des autres intervenants qui bénéficient chacun de l'expérience d'une autre juridiction seront tout à fait utiles dans le processus de réflexion et de réexamen permanent des méthodes de travail de la justice internationale.

Je ne voudrais pas terminer sans souhaiter, au nom de tous les membres de la Cour, un heureux anniversaire et une longue vie au Tribunal.

Je vous remercie.

L'amélioration des méthodes de travail du Tribunal international du droit de la mer

Joseph Akl

C'est pour moi un honneur d'avoir été invité à présenter, devant ce distingué auditoire, l'expérience du Tribunal touchant l'amélioration de ses méthodes de travail après vingt années d'exercice de ses fonctions en matière judiciaire.

La tâche principale que le Tribunal s'est assignée au cours des quatre sessions tenues durant la première année de son établissement, était d'élaborer et d'approuver les documents de base, nécessaires pour son organisation interne et ses méthodes de travail relatives aux procédures contentieuses et consultatives qui lui seront soumises.

Ces documents comprennent le Règlement du Tribunal et les Lignes directrices pour la préparation et la présentation des affaires dont le Tribunal est saisi, adoptés le même jour le 28 octobre 1997, ainsi que la Résolution sur la pratique interne du Tribunal en matière judiciaire, adoptée le 31 octobre 1997. Les juges Treves, Chandrasekhara Rao et Anderson avaient préparé, respectivement, les projets de ces documents.

Le Tribunal avait devant lui le projet de Règlement établi par la Commission préparatoire de l'Autorité internationale des fonds marins et du Tribunal international du droit de la mer, qui s'inspirait largement du Règlement de la Cour internationale de Justice, tout en tenant compte des aspects spécifiques de l'organisation et des compétences du Tribunal.

Les membres du Tribunal avaient également pris en considération les observations et propositions constructives présentées au colloque CIJ/UNITAR, organisé à l'occasion de la célébration du cinquantième anniversaire de la Cour.

Je me propose de présenter les méthodes de travail du Tribunal, telles qu'elles ressortent du Règlement de 1997 et des documents de base, ainsi que les amendements et décisions adoptés ultérieurement et leur incidence sur l'amélioration des méthodes de travail du Tribunal en matière judiciaire.

Il importe de souligner, de prime abord, que la Réunion des Etats Parties qui s'est tenue à New York en mai 1995 a approuvé les dispositions administratives et financières à prendre quant à la création du Tribunal et a également décidé « que le principe de coût-efficacité serait applicable à tous les aspects des travaux du Tribunal ».[1]

---

1 Rapport de la Réunion des Etats Parties SPLOS/4, 26 juillet 1995, par. 25-e.

© 2018, BY INTERNATIONAL TRIBUNAL FOR THE LAW OF THE SEA | DOI 10.1163/9789004356832_022

L'article 16 du Statut du Tribunal stipule que le « Tribunal détermine par un règlement le mode suivant lequel il exerce ses fonctions. Il règle notamment sa procédure ». Le Tribunal a adopté une politique compatible avec le principe de coût-efficacité, concrétisé dans l'article 49 du Règlement suivant lequel « la procédure devant le Tribunal est conduite sans retard et sans dépenses inutiles ».

De nombreuses dispositions du Règlement et de la Résolution constituent une application de l'article 49 du Règlement aux différentes étapes de la procédure. Elles fixent des délais stricts pour la conduite de la procédure tant écrite qu'orale, ainsi qu'en ce qui concerne les délibérations du Tribunal, à moins que celui-ci en décide autrement eu égard aux circonstances particulières de chaque affaire.

Aux termes de l'article 59, paragraphe 1, du Règlement, les délais pour le dépôt de chaque pièce de procédure n'excèdent pas six mois. De même, conformément à l'article 69 du Règlement, le Tribunal fixe la date de la procédure orale au cours d'une période de six mois suivant la clôture de la procédure écrite.

En ce qui concerne les délibérations du Tribunal, l'article 2 de la Résolution dispose qu'après la clôture de la procédure écrite, chaque juge peut dans un délai de cinq semaines préparer une brève note se limitant à exposer les principales questions appelant une décision et tout point qu'il faudrait clarifier au cours de la procédure orale.

S'agissant des méthodes de travail du comité de rédaction, conformément à l'article 7, paragraphe 1, de la Résolution, le comité de rédaction se réunit immédiatement après sa création afin de préparer un avant-projet d'arrêt qui doit être achevé en principe dans un délai de trois semaines. Le paragraphe 3 du même article, dispose qu'après la distribution de l'avant-projet d'arrêt, tout juge qui souhaite présenter des amendements les soumet par écrit au comité de rédaction dans les trois semaines qui suivent la distribution de l'avant-projet.

L'article 8, paragraphe 1, de la Résolution, précise que les délibérations sur le projet d'arrêt ont lieu dès que possible après sa distribution et, en principe, trois mois au plus tard après la clôture de la procédure orale.

L'article 12 de la Résolution stipule que ses dispositions sont applicables aussi bien en matière contentieuse qu'en matière consultative.

Le Règlement prévoit d'autres méthodes de travail applicables aux deux procédures urgentes introduites, soit conformément à l'article 292 de la Convention relatif aux demandes de prompte mainlevée de l'immobilisation du navire ou la prompte libération de son équipage, soit conformément à l'article 290 relatif aux demandes de prescription de mesures conservatoires. Pour ces deux procédures, les délais sont très courts. En effet, en ce qui concerne la procédure de prompte mainlevée, en vertu de l'article 112, paragraphe 3, du Règlement, le Tribunal fixe le plus tôt possible et au plus tard 15 jours à compter de la date de la réception de la demande la date de l'audience à laquelle chaque partie a droit à un jour pour présenter ses preuves et arguments. En outre, conformément à l'article 112, paragraphe 4, « l'arrêt est adopté le plus rapidement possible et est lu en audience publique du Tribunal au plus tard 14 jours après la clôture des débats ».

Il convient de noter, qu'en pratique, le Tribunal a statué sur les affaires urgentes qui lui ont été soumises dans un délai d'un mois après l'introduction de chaque instance. A ce propos, je voudrais mentionner que le Japon a déposé, le même jour, le 6 juillet 2007, deux demandes fondées sur l'article 292 de la Convention, concernant la mainlevée de l'immobilisation de deux navires battant son pavillon (*cf.* « *Hoshinmaru* » (*Japon c. Fédération de Russie*), *prompte mainlevée, arrêt, TIDM Recueil 2005-2007*, p. 18 ; « *Tomimaru* » (*Japon c. Fédération de Russie*), *prompte mainlevée, arrêt, TIDM Recueil 2005-2007*, p. 74).

Le Tribunal a rendu ses deux arrêts le 6 août 2007, soit dans le même temps que celui qui est imparti pour statuer sur une seule affaire de prompte mainlevée. Ce résultat a nécessité un travail intensif des juges, des membres du comité de rédaction et du Greffe, impliquant des réunions au cours du week-end.

Un des aspects particuliers des méthodes de travail du Tribunal se rapportant à ses délibérations judiciaires, est la préférence de celui-ci pour la brièveté des notes écrites que peuvent préparer les juges.

En vertu de l'article 2, paragraphe 1, de la Résolution, chaque juge peut, après la clôture de la procédure écrite, préparer une brève note écrite se limitant à exposer les principales questions appelant une décision au vu des pièces écrites, et tout point qu'il faudrait clarifier au cours de la procédure orale.

Par ailleurs, l'article 5, paragraphe 1, de la Résolution dispose qu'après la clôture de la procédure orale, les juges disposent de quatre jours pour étudier les arguments présentés au Tribunal en l'espèce et peuvent résumer leurs opinions provisoires par écrit sous forme d'aide-mémoire.

Au cours des délibérations qui suivent, les juges procèdent à un échange de vues sur les questions appelant une décision et expriment leurs opinions provisoires sur ces questions ainsi que sur la solution à donner à l'affaire.

Le Tribunal a choisi d'adopter, à tous les stades de ses délibérations, la méthode de délibérations en plénière, plutôt que la multiplicité de longues notes écrites.

Toutefois, dans le cas d'affaires présentant des questions complexes, le Tribunal peut décider que chaque juge préparera une note écrite qui sera distribuée aux autres juges, dans laquelle il exprime son opinion provisoire sur ces questions. Cette décision a été prise dans de le cadre de l'*Affaire du navire « SAIGA » (No. 2)* (*Saint-Vincent-et-les Grenadines c. Guinée*).

A la lumière de son expérience, le Tribunal a considéré nécessaire d'amender certains articles du Règlement afin d'améliorer ses méthodes de travail, particulièrement celles relatives à la procédure de prompte mainlevée de l'immobilisation du navire ou de prompte libération de son équipage.

L'article 111, paragraphe 4, du Règlement tel qu'adopté en 1997 énonce qu'une demande de prompte mainlevée faite par l'Etat du pavillon est immédiatement transmise à l'Etat qui a procédé à l'immobilisation ou l'arrestation, lequel peut en réponse présenter un exposé « au plus tard 24 heures avant l'audience ».

Il s'est avéré que ce court délai portait préjudice au demandeur et ne lui permettait pas, en ce court laps de temps, d'étudier les arguments du défendeur et de préparer son exposé oral à l'audience, qui se tient le lendemain.

De même, ce délai pose une certaine difficulté aux juges lors de leur délibération avant la procédure orale, le jour même de la réception de la réponse du défendeur.

D'autre part, les délais pour la fixation de la date de l'audience et de la date de la lecture de l'arrêt, imposaient un rythme de travail trop accéléré aux parties, aux membres du Tribunal et au Greffe.

Le 16 mars 2001, le Tribunal a amendé les articles 111, paragraphe 4, l'article 112, paragraphes 3 et 4, du Règlement du 28 octobre 1997.[2]

En vertu de ces amendements, l'Etat qui a procédé à l'immobilisation ou l'arrestation peut présenter un exposé, au plus tard 96 heures avant l'audience, au lieu de 24 heures. La date de l'audience est fixée le plus tôt possible et au plus tard dans un délai de 15 jours, à compter du premier jour ouvrable qui suit de la date de la réception de la demande. L'arrêt est lu en audience publique qui a lieu au plus tard 14 jours après la clôture des débats. Ces délais étaient auparavant de 10 jours.

Dans une procédure au titre de l'article 292 de la Convention, si le Tribunal décide que l'allégation du demandeur est bien fondée, il détermine, conformément à l'article 113, paragraphe 2, du Règlement, le montant, la nature et la forme de la caution ou autre garantie financière à déposer pour obtenir la mainlevée de l'immobilisation du navire ou la libération de son équipage.

---

2 (i) à l'article 111, paragraphe 4, les termes et le nombre « le plus tôt possible, mais au plus tard 96 heures » remplacent les termes et le nombre « au plus tard 24 heures ».
(ii) à l'article 112, paragraphe 3, les termes et le nombre « dans un délai de 15 jours à compter du premier jour ouvrable qui suit la date » remplacent les termes et le nombre « et au plus tard 10 jours à compter de la date ».
(iii) à l'article 112, paragraphe 4, le nombre « 14 » remplace le nombre « 10 ».

Le paragraphe 3 du même article stipule que la caution ou la garantie financière sera déposée auprès de l'Etat qui a immobilisé le navire, à moins que les parties en décident autrement.

Il est arrivé que dans certains cas, des positions divergentes entre les deux parties retardent l'exécution de l'arrêt du Tribunal. Pour remédier à cette situation, le Tribunal a adopté, le 17 mars 2009, des amendements aux articles 113, paragraphe 3, 114, paragraphes 1 et 4, du Règlement adopté le 28 octobre 1997.[3]

Ces amendements prévoient, qu'à moins que les parties n'en décident autrement, le Tribunal détermine si la caution ou autre garantie financière doit être déposée auprès du Greffier ou auprès de l'Etat qui a procédé à l'immobilisation du navire. Ils spécifient également la procédure à suivre dans le cas où la caution ou la garantie financière est déposée auprès du Greffier ainsi que son rôle à cet égard. A cet effet, le Tribunal a établi des lignes directrices concernant le dépôt d'une caution ou garantie financière auprès du Greffier.

Outre les amendements précités, le Tribunal a pris des décisions pour clarifier certains articles du Règlement. Ainsi, l'article 76, paragraphe 1, du Règlement prévoit que le Tribunal peut à tout moment, avant ou durant les débats, indiquer les points ou les problèmes qu'il voudrait voir spécialement étudier par les parties. Le Tribunal peut également durant les débats poser des questions aux agents, conseils et avocats et leur demander des éclaircissements (Règlement, article 76, paragraphe 2). La même faculté appartient à chaque juge qui, pour l'exercer, fait connaître son intention au Président du Tribunal (Règlement, article 76, paragraphe 3). Les agents, conseil et avocats peuvent répondre immédiatement ou dans un délai fixé par le Tribunal (Règlement, article 76, paragraphe 4).

Le Tribunal et les juges ont plusieurs fois eu recours à l'article 76 dans des affaires contentieuses ou consultatives. Dans certaines de ces affaires, les

---

3 (i) Amender comme suit l'article 113, paragraphe 3 :
« A moins que les parties n'en décident autrement, le Tribunal détermine si la caution ou autre garantie financière doit être déposée auprès du Greffier ou auprès de l'Etat qui a procédé à l'immobilisation du navire. ».
(ii) Amender comme suit l'article 114, paragraphe 1 :
« Si la caution ou autre garantie financière a été déposée auprès du Greffier, l'Etat qui a procédé à l'immobilisation du navire en est informé promptement. ».
(iii) Amender comme suit l'article 114, paragraphe 3 :
« La caution ou autre garantie financière, pour autant qu'elle n'est pas requise pour qu'il soit donné suite à tout arrêt, sentence ou décision définitive, est endossée ou transmise à la partie à la demande de laquelle il est émis une caution ou garantie financière ».

représentants des parties ont répondu oralement à l'audience, et dans d'autres, ils ont répondu par écrit aux questions posées ou pour compléter leurs réponses orales.

Je voudrais mentionner une évolution de la pratique du Tribunal en ce qui concerne la publication sur le site internet du Tribunal des réponses écrites des parties aux questions posées par les Tribunal ou par les juges. En effet, jusqu' à une époque récente, cette pratique n'était pas uniforme.

En ce qui concerne les procédures consultatives, le Tribunal et la Chambre pour le règlement des différends relatifs aux fonds marins (ci-après « la Chambre ») ont suivi la même pratique.

Dans l'affaire No 17 (*Responsabilités et obligations des Etats qui patronnent des personnes et des entités dans le cadre d'activités menées dans la zone* (*Demande d'avis consultatif soumise à la Chambre pour le règlement des différends relatifs aux fonds marins*)), la Chambre a adressé à l'Autorité des questions avant et après l'audience. L'Autorité a répondu partiellement à l'audience et a complété sa réponse par deux lettres écrites après la clôture de la procédure orale. Ces deux lettres ont été publiées sur le site internet du Tribunal.

Dans l'affaire No 21 (*Demande d'avis consultatif soumise par la Commission sous-régionale des pêches* (CRSP) (*Demande d'avis consultatif soumise au Tribunal*)), certains juges ont posé des questions à la Commission. Celle-ci a adressé des réponses écrites au Tribunal. La lettre de la Commission a été publiée sur le site internet du Tribunal.

En ce qui concerne les affaires contentieuses, la pratique du Tribunal a varié. Dans deux affaires, les réponses écrites aux questions posées par le Tribunal et par les juges, ont été publiées sur le site internet du Tribunal, tandis que, dans deux autres affaires, elles n'ont pas été publiées sur le site internet.

Pour harmoniser la pratique du Tribunal au titre de l'article 76 du Règlement, le Tribunal a adopté le 17 mars 2016, sur recommandation du Comité du Règlement et de la pratique en matière judiciaire la décision suivante :

> Lorsque des parties répondent par écrit aux questions qui leur ont été posées à l'audience ou qui sont reproduites dans l'ordonnance ou l'arrêt concerné, le texte de ces réponses est publié sur le site internet dans la rubrique contenant la documentation de l'affaire ayant trait à la procédure orale, à moins que la partie soumettant le document demande qu'il en soit autrement, que les parties ou le Tribunal conviennent qu'il en soit autrement.

J'aborderai également un autre point sur lequel la pratique du Tribunal a dû évoluer.

Dans deux procédures consultatives et une procédure contentieuse, des organisations non gouvernementales ont demandé l'autorisation de déposer des mémoires en qualité d'*amicus curiae*, dans le cadre des procédures dont sont saisies le Tribunal ou la Chambre.

Le Statut et le Règlement ne contiennent pas des dispositions concernant l'*amicus curiae*. Par conséquent, le Tribunal et la Chambre ont dû adopter des décisions à l'égard des demandes de participation aux procédures en qualité d'*amicus curiae*.

Dans l'affaire No 17 (*Responsabilités et obligations des Etats qui patronnent des personnes et des entités dans le cadre d'activité menées dans la zone* (*Demande d'avis consultatif soumise à la Chambre de règlement des différends relatifs aux fonds marins*)), le Greffe a reçu le 17 août 2010, un exposé présenté conjointement par le Stichting Greenpeace Council (Greenpeace International) et par le Fonds Mondial pour la Nature ainsi qu'une requête sollicitant l'autorisation de participer à la procédure consultative en qualité d'*amicus curiae*. A la demande du Président de la Chambre, le Greffier a fait savoir à chacune de ces organisations, par lettre en date du 27 août 2010, que leur exposé ne constituerait pas une pièce du dossier puisqu'il n'avait pas été soumis en vertu de l'article 133 du Règlement. En revanche, il serait communiqué aux Etats Parties, à l'Autorité et aux organisations internationales ayant présenté des exposés écrits. Ces derniers ont été informés, par une communication datée 27 août 2010, que l'exposé ne constituait pas une pièce du dossier et serait publié dans une section séparée du site internet du Tribunal. La Chambre a décidé de ne pas faire droit à la requête des deux organisations susmentionnées, sollicitant l'autorisation de participer à la procédure consultative en qualité d'*amicus curiae*.

Dans l'affaire No 21 (*Demande d'avis consultatif soumise par la Commission sous-régionale des pêches*), le Greffier a reçu le 29 novembre 2013 une lettre du Fonds Mondial pour la Nature demandant l'autorisation de déposer un mémoire en qualité d'*amicus curiae* dans le cadre de la procédure. Le Tribunal a appliqué la même pratique que celle de la Chambre.

Les Etats Parties, la CSRP et les organisations internationales ayant présenté des exposés écrits, ont également été informés que le WWF avait soumis un exposé.

Le Greffier a fait savoir au WWF que son mémoire ne serait pas versé au dossier de l'affaire parce qu'il n'avait pas été soumis au titre de l'article 133 du Règlement, mais qu'il serait néanmoins communiqué aux Etats Parties, à la CSRP et aux organisations inter-gouvernementales ayant présenté des exposés écrits et placé sur le site internet du Tribunal dans une section distincte comprenant les documents relatifs à l'affaire.

Il convient en outre de mentionner que dans cette affaire, le Greffier a reçu, le 20 novembre 2013, un exposé écrit des Etats-Unis d'Amérique, Etat non partie à la Convention des Nations Unies sur le droit de la mer.

Le Greffier a fait savoir aux Etats Parties, à la CSRP et aux organisations internationales qui avait présenté des exposés écrits que les Etats Unis d'Amérique avaient soumis un exposé, que celui-ci serait publié sur le site internet du Tribunal dans une section distincte des documents relatifs à l'affaire et que son statut serait examiné ultérieurement par le Tribunal.

Le 1er avril 2014, le Tribunal a décidé que l'exposé soumis par les Etats-Unis d'Amérique devrait être considéré comme faisant partie de l'affaire et publié sur le site internet du Tribunal, sous une rubrique distincte intitulée « Etats Parties à l'Accord de 1995 sur les stocks chevauchants ».

Dans l'*Affaire de l'« Arctic Sunrise »* (*Royaume des Pays-Bas c. Fédération de Russie*), Greenpeace International a sollicité du Tribunal, le 30 octobre 2013, l'autorisation de présenter un exposé écrit en qualité d'*amicus curiae*.

Le 31 octobre 2013, Le Greffier a invité les parties à lui communiquer leurs observations sur la demande de Greenpeace International.

Le 1er novembre 2013, le co-agent des Pays-Bas a informé le Tribunal que le Royaume des Pays-Bas a fait savoir officieusement à Greenpeace International qu'il n'élèverait pas d'objection à sa demande.

Le 5 novembre 2013, le Tribunal a décidé qu'il ne serait pas fait droit à la demande de Greenpeace International et que l'exposé écrit de Greenpeace International ne serait pas versé au dossier de l'affaire.

Par communication du 6 novembre 2013, l'ambassadeur de la Fédération de Russie auprès de la République fédérale d'Allemagne a informé le Tribunal que « compte tenu du caractère non gouvernemental de Greenpeace International, la partie russe ne voit pas de raison d'accorder à cette organisation la possibilité de communiquer des informations au Tribunal dans l'*Affaire de l'« Arctic Sunrise »*.

Je voudrais mentionner pour finir un récent développement ayant trait au lieu où le Tribunal peut siéger.

L'article premier du Statut prévoit que le Tribunal a son siège dans la Ville libre et hanséatique de Hambourg en République fédérale d'Allemagne. Il peut toutefois siéger et exercer ses fonctions ailleurs lorsqu'il le juge souhaitable. L'article 70 du Règlement prévoit la même possibilité.

Le 31 août 2015, une déclaration conjointe a été signée par le Secrétaire permanent du ministère du droit de la République de Singapour et le Président du Tribunal. Cette déclaration conjointe prévoit que Singapour sera le lieu en Asie où pourront siéger une chambre spéciale du Tribunal, ou le Tribunal lui-même, dans le cadre du règlement des différends en matière de droit de la mer.

La déclaration conjointe exprime l'engagement de deux parties de préserver la légalité internationale dans la région.

Conformément à cet engagement, le Gouvernement de Singapour mettra les locaux appropriés à la disposition du Tribunal dès qu'une chambre spéciale, ou le Tribunal lui-même, jugeront souhaitable de siéger ou d'exercer leurs fonctions à Singapour.

Cette Déclaration conjointe nécessite pour son application la conclusion d'accords complémentaires, notamment au sujet des personnes appelées à bénéficier de privilèges, immunités ou facilités en vertu du Statut et des accords pertinents. A cet effet, les consultations entre les deux parties sont en cours.

L'application par le Tribunal des méthodes de travail sur la base des dispositions du Règlement de 1997 et de ses amendements, ainsi que celles de la Résolution, dans les affaires contentieuses et consultatives qui lui ont été soumises, au cours des vingt années écoulées, a permis au Tribunal d'atteindre des résultats conformes au principe énoncé au paragraphe 49 du Règlement selon lequel « la procédure devant le Tribunal est conduite sans retard ni dépenses inutiles ».

L'appui des Etats Parties à la Convention et la confiance dont témoignent à l'égard du Tribunal, les représentants des Etats Parties à des procédures devant le Tribunal, sont indispensables pour l'accomplissement de la mission du Tribunal.

Je souhaiterais à cet égard citer le passage suivant du rapport de la vingt-sixième Réunion des Etats Parties tenue à New York du 20 au 24 juin 2016.

> Plusieurs délégations ont souligné la charge de travail du Tribunal, la portée de ses activités, l'efficacité avec laquelle il rendait ses décisions, sa contribution croissante à l'interprétation de la Convention et du droit international et au développement progressif du droit de la mer, ainsi que son rôle dans le règlement pacifique des différends et le maintien de l'ordre en vertu de la Convention.[4]

Par ailleurs, l'Assemblée générale des Nations Unies, dans sa Résolution 70/235 du 23 décembre 2015, relative à son point d'ordre du jour, les Océans et le droit de la mer, « note avec satisfaction que le Tribunal continue d'apporter une contribution notable au règlement pacifique des différends conformément aux dispositions de la partie XV de la Convention, et souligne qu'il joue un rôle

4 Document SPLOS/333, par. 23.

important et fait autorité dans l'interprétation et l'application de la Convention et de l'Accord relatif à la partie XI ».[5]

Je voudrais finalement citer un extrait d'un discours prononcé par le Professeur Philippe Sands le 17 mars 2005 à une conférence sur le thème Current Maritime Environmental Issues and the International Tribunal for the Law of the Sea.

> It is noteworthy that the Tribunal has already faced a broad range of substantive issues. Generally, it has handed down judgments which are clear, which are reasonably decisive, which have been prepared and delivered expeditiously, and which have generally attracted sufficient majorities to endow them with appropriate authority.

Je vous remercie par votre aimable attention.

---

5 Document A/RES/70/235, par. 49.

The EFTA Court's Working Methods

Carl Baudenbacher

I The EEA Agreement

A *General*

The Agreement on the European Economic Area ("EEA Agreement") consists of an extension of the EU Single Market to the three European Free Trade Association ("EFTA") States Iceland, Liechtenstein and Norway. It is based on two pillars. The law in the two pillars is essentially identical in substance. But each side has own institutions, the European Commission and the Court of Justice of the European Union ("ECJ") in the EU pillar and the EFTA Surveillance Authority ("ESA") and the EFTA Court in the EFTA pillar. The three main procedures are the infringement procedure, the nullity procedure, and the preliminary reference procedure.

B *Homogeneity*

It is said in the EEA Agreement and in the Surveillance and Court Agreement of the EFTA States ("SCA") that the EFTA Court shall follow respectively take into due account relevant case law of the ECJ.[1] This is, in the language of legal realism,[2] the law on the books. In action, this one-sided rule has developed in quite an interesting way. First of all, in the majority of its cases the EFTA Court decides as the first European court in the EEA (so-called going first constellation). We are faced with legal questions where there is no case law by the ECJ. Former ECJ President Vassilios Skouris has stated in that regard:

> The long-lasting dialogue between the EFTA Court and the CJEU has allowed the flow of information in both directions. Ignoring EFTA Court precedents would simply be incompatible with the overriding objective of the EEA Agreement, which is homogeneity. [....] The symbiotic nature of the relationship has contributed to the successful development of the EEA Single Market. Both courts stand as examples for each other thus depicting mutual respect, strengthening the rules of homogeneity and

1 Articles 6 EEA and 3 II SCA.

2 See R. Pound, "Law in Books and Law in Action", 44 *American Law Review* 1 (1910), p. 12 ff.

© 2018, BY INTERNATIONAL TRIBUNAL FOR THE LAW OF THE SEA | DOI 10.1163/9789004356832_023

> representing a high level of appreciation. Cooperation between the two was built on strong foundations which have stood the test of time.[3]

In fact, the EFTA Court has given input into the case law of the EU courts in some 126 cases.[4]

If there is ECJ case law, the EFTA Court would, as a rule, follow it. Homogeneity has been taken seriously from the beginning.[5] But judging is not an exact science. And a mature court is gaining self-confidence. The EFTA Court is not a tribunal of lower instance. It has recently emphasized that it is an independent court of law, that means, it must be convinced by what its sister court has decided. As the EEA Contracting Parties have emphasised in Recital 15 of the preamble to the EEA Agreement, the objective to arrive at, and maintain, homogeneity must be pursued "in full deference to the independence of the courts." One may speak of "creative homogeneity."[6] Professor Shotaro Hamamoto from the University of Kyoto said that there seems to be a certain parallel between the EFTA Court's relationship with the ECJ and the relationship of the Tribunal with the ICJ.

C *Reciprocity*

The second backbone is reciprocity. It is said in the preamble of the EEA Agreement that a dynamic and homogeneous European Economic Area must be achieved on the basis of equality and reciprocity. The law of the EFTA pillar impinges on sovereignty less than the law in the EU pillar. There is no direct effect and no primacy of EEA law. There is, however, an obligation of result. The EFTA Court has also acknowledged full State liability against the resistance of the European Commission and the Nordic governments. Still, the EEA/EFTA States enjoy more freedom than the EU States.

There is, moreover, no written obligation to make a reference to the EFTA Court on any national court. But the EFTA Court said in the *Irish Bank* case that a national supreme court will take into due account its duty of loyalty and the

3 "The Role of the Court of Justice of the European Union in the Development of the EEA Single Market: Advancement trough Collaboration between the EFTA Court and the CJEU", in EFTA Court (ed.), *The EEA and the EFTA Court. Decentred Integration*, (Hart, 2014), p. 12.

4 See C. Baudenbacher, "The Relationship Between the EFTA Court and the Court of Justice of the European Union", in C. Baudenbacher (ed.), *The Handbook of EEA Law* (Springer, 2016), p. 179 ff.

5 See the EFTA Court's very first case E-1/94 *Restamark*, [1994–1995] EFTA Ct. Rep., 15, paras. 32 ff.

6 C. Timmermans, "Creative Homogeneity", in M. Johansson, N. Wahl, & U. Bernitz (eds.), *A European for all seasons: Liber Amicorum in Honour of Sven Norberg* (Bruylant, 2006), p. 471 ff.

principle of reciprocity.[7] That means at the end of the day, that although the EFTA Court's relationship with the national courts of last resort of the EEA/EFTA States is "more partner-like" than the ECJ's relationship with the courts of last resort of the EU States, they are not fully free to choose whether they want to make a reference or not. The preliminary rulings of the EFTA Court are also not legally binding in a formal way, but at the same time, there is the principle of homogeneity. If national courts disregard such a ruling by the EFTA Court, they may bring their country into a state of breach of their duties under the EEA Agreement. That means on balance that the national supreme courts have not retained full sovereignty in the fields in question, but they have retained more sovereignty than their counterparts in the EU Member States. Whether there is an obligation to refer and an obligation to follow must be assessed on a case by case basis. These obligations are not easy to enforce by the ESA.[8]

That the judicial constitution of the EFTA pillar impinges on the sovereignty of the EEA/EFTA States less than the EU system on the EU States has been noted with great interest in the UK after Brexit.

II The Court's Structure

A *Composition*

The EFTA Court is a permanent court which, since 1995, has consisted of three judges and six *ad hoc* judges. At the EFTA Court, *ad hoc* judges play a different role than in the case of the Tribunal. They are only called upon to sit if one of the three regular judges is prevented from participating due to bias or illness. Our experience with the *ad hoc* judges is a mixed one. First, the governments do not pay enough attention to selecting them carefully. Second, they live in their Member States and have sometimes difficulties to understand the spirit of EEA law. The EFTA Court does not work with an Advocate General. The question has been asked by certain governments, as to whether three judges are enough. Is this court not too small? My answer has always been, the WTO Appellate Body sits in a three members' formation, the US Federal Appellate Courts decide most of the cases in three judge panels and Lord Denning allegedly stated after having moved back from the House of Lords to the Court of Appeals, when he was asked, how on earth can you make such a step, "in the Court of Appeals I only have to convince one." Having said that, I must add

7 Case E-18/11 *Irish Bank* [2011] EFTA Ct. Rep. 592, para. 58.

8 See Case E-2/11 *STX Norway Offshore and Others v. Staten v/Tariffnemnda* [2012] EFTA Ct. Rep. 4; Supreme Court of Norway's judgment in Rt. 2013 p. 258 STX; ESA Case No 74557.

that a three member court can only function if all the three judges are fully independent and impartial. That means, in particular, the governments cannot make a reappointment dependant on whether the judge concerned has fulfilled their expectations to take into account their interests.

Having only three judges, the Court always sits *in plenum* and all judges are involved. This results in some sort of "judicial nationalism", even if it is not intended. Appointment and re-appointment is for six years, like in the EU, but there is no equivalent to Article 255 of the Treaty on the Functioning of the European Union ("TFEU") panel. There is a case currently pending in Norway: the Norwegian government has not renewed its judge on the EFTA Court although this gentleman had only been sitting for one term. Certain circles in Norway have claimed that the new judge should be friendlier to its own government. I said in an interview, this would undermine the country's reputation and at the same time, this judge would lose any credibility in the court.

B *Secrecy of the Vote*

The EFTA Court works under a system of secrecy of the vote, no dissents are made public. That is very continental European. There was one critical case in which a judge was seeking reappointment and criticised a seminal judgment of the EFTA Court in public, in order to show his government that he was not the culprit.[9] It didn't help him. He was not renewed anyway.

C *Cabinet System and Manning Table*

The EFTA Court works under a cabinet system as opposed to a pool system, and the cabinet is the judge's little empire. A cabinet consist of one judge, two legal secretaries, and one personal assistant. A cabinet system gives the judges more influence on the judgments than a pool system where the judge works with different lawyers. The EFTA Court does have a registry which is, however, strictly limited to logistics, finances, human resources and procedure. A lot of procedural issues are being dealt with by my Head of Cabinet, Michael-James Clifton.

Our manning table is small, we are 19 persons, three Judges and seven lawyers dealing with the cases. We will have a budget of five million euros in 2017.

D *Case Load*

In the early years of the EFTA Court, my friends from the ECJ used to greet me with the sentence, how many cases do you have? Now, in the meantime, if they

9 Forhandlingene ved Det 35. nordiske juristmøtet i Oslo, 18.-20. August 1999, Del 2, Utgitt av Det norske lokalstyret, 1005 ff.

still ask this question, I say, more cases than you. Because if you think that we are only five and a half million people, then this is true. In 2015, we registered 36 new cases and the average handling time in preliminary reference cases is 8 months. So far, the EFTA Court has registered 276 cases.

E *Language Regime*

The EFTA Court works under a different language regime than the ECJ. English is the working language. It is not real English, it is EFTA English, but still. And I may remind you of what Karl Kraus, the famous Austrian author, has said, "[l] anguage is the mother of thought, not its handmaiden"[10] That means that we may have less French civil law influence in our way of thinking and probably more common law influence. Our judgments in direct actions are given only in English, preliminary rulings are rendered in English and in the language of the referring court. Both versions are authentic although the non-English version is only a translation. As far as I can see, we had one problem in that respect, a big problem, which has not been remedied. In the *Pedicel* case, which was about the ban of advertising alcohol in beverages in Norway, there was a severe mistake in the operative part of the Norwegian version of the judgment, which allowed the Norwegian Supreme Court to rule in favour of the State, although we had meant that the Norwegian State should lose.[11] It is a fundamental problem that final responsibility for the German, the Icelandic, and the Norwegian version of the judgment lays with the judge from the respective country. By now, I would be able to verify the Norwegian version, although not the Icelandic version, but at that time, my Norwegian was not good enough.

III A Word on the Methods of Interpretation

In its famous, and some say infamous Opinion 1/91, the ECJ said that EEA law is simply public international law, and the methods of interpretation of the Vienna Convention on the Law of Treaties will apply.[12] This was inaccurate. In the case law of the EFTA Court it is stated that the EEA law is international law *sui generis*. We apply essentially the same methods of interpretation as the ECJ, including *effet utile*, including dynamic interpretation, also in cases in which

10 "Die Sprache ist die Mutter, nicht die Magd des Gedankens", K. Kraus, "Aphorismen" 288 *Die Fackel* (1909), p. 14.

11 Case E-04/04 *Pedicel AS v Sosial- og helsedirektoratet* [2005] EFTA Ct. Rep. 1; See H.H. Fredriksen & G. Mathisen, *EØS-rett* (Fagbokforl, 2012).

12 Opinion 1/91 [1991] ECR I-6079.

we go first.[13] As far as the underlying image of man is concerned, I think it is fair to say that in essential questions we have been rather market-oriented and we have upheld EFTA values. I may mention a case in which we had to answer the question of whether an insurance company may hand out the insurance contract not as a hard copy but just by way of installing a section on its website. We implicitly found that the consumer can be expected to make a download or to print out this contract from the website whereas our sister court based itself on the idea that the consumer cannot even be expected to make a mouse click, that is already too much.[14] In other words, our judgment was founded on the image of the man on the Clapham *omnibus*, whereas our sister court must have been under the influence of the old German theory about the dozy Jane Blocks. The EFTA Court tends to decide based on facts. It is reluctant to accept presumptions and fictions, e.g. the fiction that every in-house attorney is not independent or the fiction that every attorney that is not in-house is independent.[15]

I may point to another important issue – if there is case law by the European Court of Human Rights in Strasbourg, which conflicts with ECJ case law, that gives us more leeway.[16] The EFTA Court has used this leeway in a fundamental question of competition law, namely, the issue of the scope of judicial review. Should the Commission – or in our setup, the EFTA Surveillance Authority – be given a margin of appreciation when dealing with so-called complex economic questions? The EFTA Court said no, whereas the ECJ has a tendency to grant this margin.[17] This is a serious issue and more and more companies are complaining that they have to pay fines in the millions and even billions without there being full control on the merits by a court of law.

IV Procedure

The more important part in the procedure is the written part. When the case has come in, it is published in the EEA section of the Official Journal. Then the

13 See C. Baudenbacher, *The EFTA Court in Action: Five Lectures* (German Law Publishers, 2010), p. 47 ff.

14 Case C-49/11 [2012] EU:C:2012:419.

15 Case E-08/13 *Abelia v EFTA Surveillance Authority* [2014] EFTA Ct. Rep. 638.

16 C. Baudenbacher, "Swiss Economic Law Facing the Challenges of International and European Law" 131 *Zeitschrift für Schweizerisches Recht* II (2012), pp. 419–538 f.

17 Case E-15/10 *Posten Norge AS v EFTA Surveillance Authority* [2012] EFTA Ct. Rep. 246; e.g. Case C-389/10 P [2011] *KME Germany and Others v Commission*, ECR 2011 I-13125, para. 121; L.M. Baudenbacher, "Aspects of Competition Law Enforcement in Selected European Jurisdictions", 37 *European Competition Law Review* 9 (2016), pp. 343–364.

President assigns the case to a Judge Rapporteur, this may be the President himself. The judges are in control of the cases. Legal secretaries are important, but they are not decision-makers. Written submissions may be made by the parties, by the EEA/EFTA States, the EU States, the ESA and the Commission. But there is a limit on pages and this is strictly enforced. It has happened that a lawyer sent in 53 pages instead of 50 pages, and this submission was returned.

The Judge Rapporteur draws up a preliminary report and then a report for the hearing. The report for the hearing has been abolished in the ECJ. In our setup, it is an important means of transparency. But it has also certain disadvantages: it is often too long, and in a preliminary ruling case, the national court may be tempted to pick and choose, to look up in the report for the hearing what, for example, the Commission has said and then to state that the solution of the EFTA Court does not convince us, we will follow the Commission.

In preliminary ruling cases, the report for the hearing is translated into the language of the referring court. Applications for intervention and also interim measures are decided by the President. The oral part of the procedure is relatively short. In a pre-hearing meeting we tell the parties and participants that they should focus on points of contention and not repeat what has been stated in the written observations. Many of our lawyers are repeat players, they now know how to play the game. Parties and participants are typically granted 15–30 minutes for pleadings, in a big case it may be more, and there is a right to reply. Questions are often sent in advance so that people can prepare for the oral hearing. The EFTA Court has a habit of interrupting the pleaders and of asking questions during the hearing.

V Resolving the Case

After the hearing, the first deliberation takes place immediately. The Judge Rapporteur may be asked to draft the judgment, or to present the pre-draft before a decision is taken. After the presentation of the case – that is an important point – deliberation takes place mainly by written exchange via email. Now, if there is a politically sensitive case, the EFTA Court would not use email, it would exchange USB sticks in order to prevent foreign intelligence services from intercepting communications. In the first *Icesave* case,[18] the regular Norwegian judge was prevented from acting due to bias and we had to sit with the participation of a professor from Oslo. It was before the Snowdon scandal broke, but the EFTA Court felt that it was risky to use email for deliberation

18 Case E-16/11 *EFTA Surveillance Authority v Iceland* [2013] EFTA Ct. Rep. 4.

given the fact that the United Kingdom had a substantial interest in the outcome of the case.

As to the rest, deliberation takes place in a collegiate atmosphere. There may be clashes from time to time, but the EFTA Court tries, as far as possible, to include the views of the minority judge because there is no right to dissent. A problem may arise if the Judge Rapporteur finds himself in the minority. In one case, the minority judge had so strong feelings that after the oral hearing I decided to take the case away from him and to assign it to a judge in the majority.[19]

If at least a majority is satisfied, the case is decided. Further steps are then the external language revision, in preliminary ruling cases the translation, and very importantly, a couple of years ago we have started to read out the judgment aloud to each other. That leads to the detection of mistakes and inconsistencies and to last corrections. Sometimes even substantial changes are made at the very last moment. The judgment is handed down in open court. The judgment is binding from the date of delivery. It is then published on the EFTA Court's website, in the Official Journal, and in the EFTA Court's annual report.

VI A Word on the Court's Judicial Style

The EFTA Court is a small court and, as I said, it does not work with an Advocate General. It therefore tries to be comprehensive, more comprehensive than its sister court, but at the same time it wants to be succinct in its reasoning. As a small court the EFTA Court cannot decree, it cannot make an important ruling on four pages. Nobody will buy that – it must convince its audiences.

The EFTA Court amply cites its sister court's case law, but it also refers to Advocates General, to EU General Court and to the European Court of Human Rights. It occasionally references national supreme courts, probably also in order to make them inclined to refer cases. Occasionally it cites academic literature. The International Justice Project of Brandeis University has written about the *Icesave* judgment in this context: "[t]he so-called *Icesave* judgment is notable in being the first in the history of a European court of regional integration to reference academic literature."[20] The judgment was not only notable because of that but in fact we made reference to the American Nobel Prize

19 Compare the names in the report for the hearing and in the judgment in Case E-10/04 *Paolo Piazza*, [2005] EFTA Ct. Rep. 76.

20 See "International Justice in the News", http://www.brandeis.edu/ethics/international justice/inthenews/2013/Feb2013.html, visited 14 December 2016.

laureate Joseph Stiglitz when dealing with the concept of moral hazard.[21] Most judges don't know what moral hazard is, but I have an advantage here because my wife has dealt with moral hazard in her PhD thesis.[22] In *Icesave*, when stating that the reservation set out in recital 24 in the preamble to the Deposit Guarantee Directive aims expressly to preclude an excessive shifting to the State of the costs arising from a major banking failure we also cited Belgian law professor Michel Tison.[23]

VII End

After delivery, there may be a need for rectification, in case of clerical mistakes or errors in calculation, or obvious slips. And finally, an application for interpretation may be made if a party thinks that something is not clear. Decision is given in the form of a judgment.

21 *Op. cit.* at note 19, para. 167.

22 D. Baudenbacher-Tandler, *Schutz vor neuen Anlegerrisiken* (WIV Wissen-schaftlicher Verlag, 1988).

23 *Op. cit.* at note 19, para. 176.

L'amélioration des méthodes de travail de la justice internationale

Jean-Pierre Cot

Monsieur le Président, Excellences, Mesdames et Messieurs,

Après la savante analyse qui a été faite ce matin par le juge Joseph Akl, je puis être bref. Au demeurant, c'est bientôt le déjeuner et je ne voudrais pas le retarder.

Nous avons été très sensibles, nous, les juges du Tribunal, aux éloges dont vous avez couvert le Tribunal, bien entendu. Il est temps cependant de jeter un coup d'œil à l'envers du décor de notre petite boutique car nous sommes une petite boutique.

Les descriptions qui ont été faites des méthodes de travail de la Cour internationale de Justice ou de la Cour de justice de l'Association européenne de libre-échange sont des descriptions qui nous ont fait, si je puis dire familièrement, saliver d'envie. Ce n'est pas du tout de cela qu'il s'agit ici. Notre petite boutique, est certes animée par 21 juges de grande qualité mais des juges à mi-temps et je dirais même, quand le rôle n'est pas très fourni, un petit mi-temps. Des juges travaillant seuls, sans assistant, sans « clerk » pour utiliser l'expression anglo-saxonne. Une secrétaire pour cinq ou six juges c'est tout ! Pour la plupart nous tapons nos textes à la machine nous-même, heureusement nous avons un excellent Greffier. Je tiens à lui rendre hommage ainsi qu'à notre Greffe qui fait tourner la machine, secondé par une toute petite équipe, cinq ou six juristes opérationnels et je ne parle pas des congés et des maladies qui réduisent d'autant ses effectifs.

Voilà la réalité à partir de laquelle il nous faut raisonner pour essayer de rendre notre affaire plus efficace. L'ambition de notre Tribunal tel qu'il s'était exprimé lors de la création du Tribunal par certains des pères du Tribunal était d'en faire une institution plus leste, plus rapide, plus efficace que la Cour. Qu'en est-il ? Nous avons, je crois, montré notre efficacité dans les procédures d'urgence, dans les mesures conservatoires, dans les procédures de prompte mainlevée nous savons travailler vite et bien. Mais pour les procédures portant sur le fond des affaires nos délais de procédure et nos délais de délibération sont très comparables à ceux de la Cour et si le règlement des différends est plus rapide à dater de la saisine du juge c'est parce que le rôle du Tribunal est beaucoup moins fourni que celui de la Cour !

© 2018, BY INTERNATIONAL TRIBUNAL FOR THE LAW OF THE SEA | DOI 10.1163/9789004356832_024

Alors comment améliorer ces méthodes de travail ? Car on peut toujours faire mieux et c'est cela le thème de notre réunion de ce matin. Je propose quelques pistes pour améliorer ces méthodes de travail, les suivantes :

> Premièrement, je crois qu'il serait important d'obliger tous les juges de préparer une note écrite avant la délibération orale, le juge Akl l'a indiqué tout à l'heure, c'est une faculté qui est ouverte aux juges, certains en usent d'autres n'en usent pas et l'obligation de rédiger une note avait du reste été écartée lors de la préparation des textes de base du Tribunal et notamment de la Résolution sur la pratique interne du Tribunal en matière judiciaire, l'argument étant que la rédaction d'une note fige la position du juge, l'engage et de ce point de vue-là, complique la délibération du Tribunal ensuite puisque les juges ne peuvent pas changer de position. Tel était l'argument qui avait été avancé à ce moment-là. L'argument ne tient pas d'après ma petite expérience avec la Cour comme juge *ad hoc*. Les juges changent volontiers de position à partir du moment où le délibéré commence et ne se trouve pas bloqués, figés par la note préalable. En revanche les exigences d'une note préalable me semblent avoir l'avantage de permettre de mieux cerner le débat, de pointer les difficultés, d'éviter bavardages et répétitions puisque l'obligation de rédiger une note s'accompagne de la circulation de toutes ces notes entre les juges or cet échange de note avant la délibération me paraît être très utile parce qu'il permet à ce moment-là de voir un peu où l'on va et d'éviter par ailleurs dans le délibéré la litanie des répétitions orales de ce qui aura été communiqué par écrit.

Autre amélioration, qui à mon avis pourrait être souhaitable, le tour de table systématique lors de la première délibération du Tribunal afin que chaque juge précise sa position initiale ou précise d'ailleurs son absence de position, ses doutes mais afin se faisant de préparer la délibération et de la centrer davantage que si les interventions se font spontanément et dans un certain désordre.

Autre proposition, la rédaction du document de travail du Président du Tribunal. Nous avons nous ici dans le cadre de nos méthodes de travail l'habitude de travailler à partir d'un document de travail du Président. Tel n'est pas le cas si je me souviens bien à la Cour. C'est un document qui est fort bien fait qui fait le tour des différentes questions qui rassemble les déclarations des parties aussi bien dans le cadre de la procédure écrite que la procédure orale et qui permet ainsi dans le délibéré aux juges, de savoir sur tel ou tel point ce qui a pu être présenté par telle ou telle parties. Cela dit, ce document est un document si bien fait qu'il préjuge très largement la suite, la structure certainement et le contenu de l'arrêt final. Et c'est ici que je vois une difficulté car ce document est mis en place sous la responsabilité du Président et du Greffier. Je pense qu'il serait utile que dans le cadre du Tribunal nous ayons une délibération préalable à la rédaction du document afin que, par une discussion libre, les juges faisant valoir leurs premières impressions donnent une orientation au Président et au Greffier pour établir ensuite cet excellent document de travail qui est la base de notre délibération, de notre méthode de travail. Le Président du Tribunal n'est probablement pas d'accord avec moi parce que l'avantage du système actuel c'est que c'est lui qui tient la main, mais ceci permettrait peut-être aux juges de mieux participer au premier cadrage de la délibération qui est souvent le cadrage décisif.

Enfin dernière proposition, la réduction du nombre de membres du comité de rédaction, qui pour le moment est de six ou de sept, qui en fait est généralement conçu de manière à refléter un peu la répartition géographique des juges, chaque grande région estimant devoir quand même pouvoir tenir la plume. Je trouve que ces comités de rédaction à six ou à sept ne sont pas une bonne chose. Un comité de rédaction, c'est fait pour rédiger et une petite structure est nécessairement beaucoup plus efficace pour rédiger le projet qui est ensuite soumis aux juges. Il ne s'agit pas de nouveau ici de représentation géographique équilibrée dans le cadre d'un comité de rédaction, mais de choisir trois collègues qui peuvent effectivement participer de manière plus resserrée à la rédaction du projet d'arrêt.

Voilà donc les quelques observations qui m'ont été inspirées par la question qui m'avait été attribuée sur l'amélioration de nos méthodes de travail. Elles valent ce qu'elles valent. Je ne me fais pas d'illusion sur la possibilité de les faire passer car j'ai déjà essayé sans grand succès, mais je pense que cela peut peut-être alimenter notre colloque d'aujourd'hui.

Improving Working Methods in International Adjudication

Albert J. Hoffmann

It is imperative that international courts and tribunals pay particular attention to procedural issues, including the expenditure of time, because these are all important elements that contribute to the efficacy of proceedings and ensure the overall effective functioning of the institution. Where necessary, efforts should be made to improve the rules and procedures for case management to enable the court or tribunal and the parties involved to proceed with greater confidence and efficiency.

I have no doubt that international courts and tribunals pay due attention to procedural issues as well as their own working methods and would not hesitate to introduce, where necessary and as circumstances require, changes and improvements to enhance their effectiveness.

In this regard attention could be drawn to the standing Committee on Rules and Judicial Practice of the Tribunal, which is entrusted with the function of reviewing the Rules, the Resolution on the Internal Judicial Practice of the Tribunal, as well as the Guidelines.[1]

The ICJ has a standing Rules Committee to advise the Court on procedural issues, practice directives and working methods.[2] Similar mechanisms exist within the PCA and other adjudicative bodies for the purpose of developing and reviewing procedural rules and judicial practice relevant to their mandate and functions. Initiatives are also periodically taken by bodies external to the abovementioned institutions to examine their procedures and working methods and to make recommendations.[3]

1 See "Committees", available on the website of the Tribunal at www.itlos.org/the-tribunal/committees.

2 See "Chambers and Committees", available on the website of ICJ at http://www.icj-cij.org/court/index.php?p1=1&p2=4.

3 See "Report of the Study Group established by the British Institute of International and Comparative Law to examine the efficiency of procedures and working methods of the International Court of Justice" 45 *ICLQ* s1 (1996), pp. 1–32. The International Law Association ("ILA") at its Biennial Conference in Johannesburg, South Africa in 2016, mandated its Committee on the Procedure of International Courts and Tribunals to identify and analyse issues arising in the practice of select international courts and tribunals such as the ICJ, the

© 2018, BY INTERNATIONAL TRIBUNAL FOR THE LAW OF THE SEA | DOI 10.1163/9789004356832_025

It is common knowledge that the practice and procedure of this Tribunal and that of the ICJ are very similar. The Rules[4] and the Resolution on the Internal Judicial Practice of the Tribunal[5] are largely based on the Rules of Court[6] and the Resolution concerning the Internal Judicial Practice of the Court,[7] as well as the Practice Directions adopted by the ICJ to supplement the Rules of Court.[8]

Even in inter-State arbitration where the process is to a large extent determined by the wishes of the parties to the dispute and reflected in the rules of procedure adopted by the parties, they nevertheless tend to follow the rules and practice of the ICJ. This can be ascribed to the fact that they have become the tried and tested recipe in international adjudication, as well as to the certainty and predictability it brings to the process, but perhaps also because the counsel who appear in inter-State arbitration and who have a big say in how these cases are conducted also regularly appear before the ICJ and the Tribunal.

It is therefore to be expected that many of the practical and procedural problems encountered by the ICJ are also faced by the Tribunal and to some extent by inter-State arbitral tribunals. I am nevertheless of the view that it would not serve any useful purpose to analyse and compare the working methods of the ICJ with that of this Tribunal and to attempt to develop some generic guidelines on, for instance, individual case management or even management of the case-load.

Regarding the latter it is obvious that the ICJ attracts more cases and this is likely to remain so. This is due to the ICJ's primary status as the only international judicial body with general jurisdiction regarding inter-State disputes including the jurisdiction it shares with this Tribunal over all matters regarding the interpretation and application of the Convention. The burden of a heavy case-load and possible backlog in cases may result in the ICJ having to review its working methods. The same cannot be said of the work of this Tribunal

Tribunal, the PCA and the WTO and to come up with specific recommendations addressed to each of these institutions.

4 Rules of the Tribunal, ITLOS/8, adopted by the Tribunal on 28 October 1997 and amended on 15 March 2001, 21 September 2001 and 17 March 2009.

5 Resolution on the Internal Judicial Practice of the Tribunal, ITLOS/10, adopted by the Tribunal on 27 April 2005.

6 Rules of Court, adopted by the ICJ on 14 April 1978.

7 Resolution concerning the Internal Judicial Practice of the Court, adopted by the ICJ on 12 April 1976.

8 Practice Directions, adopted by the Court in October 2001 and amended on 20 January 2009 and 21 March 2013.

where there is a paucity of cases. The situation will hopefully change in time to come when State Parties make full use of the Tribunal to settle their disputes.

The point that I wish to make is that any attempt to review or improve working methods should best be addressed in the context of a specific institution and given the circumstances of a particular situation.

I Length of Proceedings

My personal experience of the working methods of this Tribunal is very positive. There is a general feeling that the Tribunal is efficient in the discharge of its functions and more specifically in managing and disposing of the cases submitted to it for adjudication.[9]

By looking at the List of Cases that the Tribunal has dealt with over the 20 years of its existence, it is noticeable that all the cases were disposed of expeditiously and in an efficient manner. Of the 25 cases submitted (two cases on the merits are still pending), nine cases dealt with prompt release of vessels and crews under article 292 of the Convention, and in all but one (which was discontinued) the Tribunal handed down its judgment within 30 days (mostly within 21 days) after the application was made and even disposed of two applications simultaneously. In all ten cases regarding the prescription of provisional measures under article 290 of the Convention, the Tribunal issued orders in less than two months (but mostly within 30 days) after the request was made and in two provisional measures cases proceedings were joined.

Cases on the merits were disposed of within the following time periods: the *M/V "SAIGA" (No. 2) Case* (*Saint Vincent and the Grenadines* v. *Guinea*) – 16 months; the *Dispute concerning delimitation of the maritime boundary between Bangladesh and Myanmar in the Bay of Bengal* (*Bangladesh/Myanmar*) – two years and three months; the *M/V "Louisa" Case* (*Saint Vincent and the Grenadines* v. *Kingdom of Spain*) – two years and six months (it should be noted that the process was interrupted by the applicant's request for provisional measures); the *M/V "Virginia G"* (*Panama/Guinea-Bissau*) – two years and nine months (here also the Tribunal had to deal with a counter-claim during the proceedings).

---

9 The comments by a number of States during the twenty-sixth Meeting of States Parties held at the UN Headquarters in New York from 20–24 June 2016 as well as the interventions made during the Symposium held at the premises of the Tribunal in Hamburg from 5–6 October 2016 bear testimony to the effective disposal of cases.

The Advisory Opinion given by the Seabed Disputes Chamber at the request of the Authority was given within eight and a half months.[10] The Advisory Opinion given by the Tribunal as a whole at the request of SRFC was given within two years.

The challenge for any court or tribunal involved in international adjudication is to deal with cases fairly and expeditiously. The confidence that parties have in the fairness and soundness with which the court or tribunal gives judgment is strengthened by the time it takes for the judicial body to dispose of the case. This by no means implies "hurried judgments". The Rules make it clear that proceedings shall be conducted without unnecessary delay or expense.[11] Time-limits are set for each written pleading (memorial, counter-memorial, etc.) which shall not exceed six months[12] so as to avoid causing delay in bringing cases to hearing. The oral proceedings shall as a general rule open within six months from closure of the written proceedings.[13] Extensions of these time-limits are allowed only if there is adequate justification.[14]

II Length of Oral Arguments

One of the complaints that have been raised in the context of the oral proceedings concerns the length of oral arguments during the hearing. It is well understood that the purpose of the written pleadings is to give each party the opportunity to state its case by putting forward all the relevant facts, statements of law, arguments and submissions and for the other party to refute these contentions.[15] The parties usually respond to this opportunity in impressive style by submitting comprehensive and well prepared pleadings.

With the ensuing oral proceedings the parties are expected to keep the oral arguments brief and avoid a repetition of all the contentions and material covered in the written pleadings. The Rules make it clear that the oral statements of each party shall be as succinct as possible within the limits of what is requisite for the adequate presentation of its contentions.[16] Accordingly, such

10 Article 191 of the Convention requires the Chamber to give advisory opinions "as a matter of urgency".
11 Article 49 of the Rules of the Tribunal.
12 Article 59 of the Rules of the Tribunal.
13 Article 69 of the Rules of the Tribunal.
14 *Ibid.*
15 Article 62 of the Rules of the Tribunal.
16 Article 75 of the Rules of the Tribunal.

statements shall be directed at the issues that still divide the parties and shall not go over the whole ground covered by the pleadings or merely repeat the facts and arguments contained therein.[17]

Although it may be argued that it is up to the parties and their counsel to decide how best to present their case within the time allocated and the strategy they wish to employ, the appeal for restraint seemed to be warranted by the tendency for unduly lengthy and repetitive oral arguments. As a result, a suggestion has been made that after the closure of the written proceedings and before the oral proceedings, the court or tribunal should establish the practice of indicating to the parties' points which would benefit from further elaboration or development in oral argument. It is felt that this would allow for a more focused hearing and could curtail the length of the oral presentations.

An immediate response to this suggestion is that it is based on the assumption that all judges have carefully studied and considered the written pleadings in advance of the oral proceedings and are able to identify the key areas that would require further elaboration during the hearing. An added difficulty stems from the fact that international judges are representative of different legal traditions and may not attach the same weight to written and oral proceedings.

The intention, as I understand it, is not to replace the practice of judges putting questions to the parties before or during the hearing but to have the parties focus on the more important and specific issues the court or tribunal is seized with and which needs further elucidation.

This is certainly a matter to be looked into by the Rules Committee of each judicial body. Whether it would make any significant difference in the length of oral arguments or the duration of oral proceedings, and for that matter improving the efficiency of disposing with a case, remains to be seen.

III Deliberations and Written Notes

I wish to say something about the deliberations and the preparation of written notes by the Judges which my colleagues have already referred to during their presentations. After the closure of the written proceedings, each Judge may within five weeks prepare a brief written note identifying the principal issues for decision and points to be clarified during the oral proceedings.[18] It is on

17 *Ibid.* See also paras. 14 and 15 of the Guidelines concerning the Preparation and Presentation of Cases before the Tribunal.

18 Article 2(1) of the Resolution on the Internal Judicial Practice of the Tribunal.

the basis of the written pleadings and the Judges' notes that the President's working paper (list of issues) is prepared.[19] Judges have a further opportunity after the closure of the oral proceedings to study the oral arguments of the parties and to summarize their tentative opinions in the form of speaking notes.[20] The preparation of such notes are not mandatory and are not expected to be lengthy but are meant to serve as an aid during Judges' deliberations. The Tribunal's practice of making the preparation of written notes optional differs from that of the ICJ where each Judge is required to prepare a written note setting out his/her views on the case.[21] Subject to further revision after the oral proceedings, the President's working paper forms the basis of the Judges' deliberations upon which the President will seek to determine the majority view on each of the issues on the list.[22] During the deliberations and before establishing majority opinions there is another opportunity, if the Tribunal so decides, for each Judge to express in a brief written note his or her tentative opinion on the issues and the correct disposal of the case, for circulation to other Judges before resuming the deliberations.[23]

Like the colleagues who have spoken before me, I am in favour of Judges being encouraged to prepare a short note on the issues raised and presented by the parties. Not only does this help Judges to prepare for the case and to articulate and share their views with their colleagues but it can be of great help in preparing the President's working paper and can also facilitate the deliberations by reducing the time Judges may take to explain their positions and undoubtedly will assist the Drafting Committee when preparing the first draft of the Judgment.

One problem from a purely practical perspective is the management of such written notes. If all 21 Judges of the Tribunal (or more, when *ad hoc* Judges have been appointed) would simultaneously prepare written notes which all needed to be translated into an official language, other than the one in which they were prepared, before they could be circulated and be ready prior to the President drawing up the working paper in advance of the initial deliberations, this could provide a major challenge for the Registry of the Tribunal.

A further possible disadvantage, especially when the Judge's note is lengthy and well prepared, is that it tends to become an entrenched position and may very well become the basis for a separate or dissenting opinion. Instead

19 Article 2(3) of the Resolution on the Internal Judicial Practice of the Tribunal.
20 Article 5(1) of the Resolution on the Internal Judicial Practice of the Tribunal.
21 Article 4 of the Resolution concerning the Internal Judicial Practice of the Court.
22 Article 5(2), (6) of the Resolution on the Internal Judicial Practice of the Tribunal.
23 Article 5(7) of the Resolution on the Internal Judicial Practice of the Tribunal.

of circulating their written notes and thus benefit from the comments of colleagues, some Judges prefer to use it, depending on the trend during deliberations, to write a dissenting or separate opinion.

Although entitled to hold and express an opinion which may either concur with or differ from the rest of the collegiate body, each Judge has an active role to play in formulating the judgment and to ensure that it fully reflects the collective wisdom of the court or tribunal. During the deliberations every effort should be made (in particular by the President) to attain the opinion of the largest majority possible. The Drafting Committee, composed of Judges belonging to the majority opinion,[24] should prepare a draft judgment which not only states the opinion of the majority as it then appears to exist but which may also attract wider support.[25] It is only after the first reading that those Judges whose positions differ from the majority and who wish to write a separate or dissenting opinion are called upon to provide an outline of their opinion.[26] It is noted that these opinions remain provisional while Judges continue to participate in the examination of the draft judgment and it is expected that the draft judgment may well be amended at the second reading taking cognizance of such opinions.[27] During this process Judges should also be prepared to adjust their own positions and only once all efforts have been exhausted and some positions still differ from the majority should those Judges have the freedom to prepare final dissenting or separate opinions that are directed to the points on which there remain differences with the judgment or that need further clarification or elaboration.[28]

I wish to emphasize that I am not in any way discouraging dissenting or separate opinions. Although not part of the formal judgment these opinions remain an important part of the judicial process and undoubtedly enrich the jurisprudence of an international court or tribunal.

These are only a few remarks for further discussion and reflection.

---

24 Article 6(1) of the Resolution on the Internal Judicial Practice of the Tribunal.

25 Article 7(2) of the Resolution on the Internal Judicial Practice of the Tribunal.

26 Article 8(4) of the Resolution on the Internal Judicial Practice of the Tribunal.

27 *Ibid.*

28 Article 8(6) of the Resolution on the Internal Judicial Practice of the Tribunal.

L'amélioration des méthodes de travail de la justice internationale

Tafsir Malick Ndiaye

Monsieur le Président,
Excellences, Madame et Messieurs les Juges,
Distingués invités

C'est pour moi un grand plaisir de prendre la parole à l'occasion de cette manifestation marquant le 20ème Anniversaire du Tribunal international du droit de la mer. J'interviens aujourd'hui comme père fondateur, comme rescapé du premier « Bench » avec mes collègues Chandrasekhara Rao, Akl et Wolfrum.

Je me réjouis de la présence de mes anciens collègues et amis : MM. les Juges Yankov, Eiriksson, Anderson, Treves et Türk.

Les anniversaires sont une occasion pour célébrer les institutions et leurs réalisations. Ils peuvent aussi permettre non seulement d'évaluer leur contribution, et servir ainsi à faire le point, mais également de réfléchir à l'évaluation pour améliorer l'existant, pour mieux servir.

Je suis persuadé que le Tribunal saura tirer profit de la réflexion commune des juges, des conseils et de la doctrine, en particulier dans le domaine qui nous occupe aujourd'hui : l'amélioration des méthodes de travail de la justice internationale. Cette réflexion peut s'avérer un aiguillon pour s'améliorer, mieux servir et informer l'organisation et le fonctionnement du Tribunal.

Mon propos s'articulera autour de quatre points : les instruments juridiques, la logistique, l'instruction d'une affaire et les nouveaux défis.

Après avoir entendu mes collègues, je peux être bref sur les trois premiers points. J'insisterai donc sur les nouveaux défis qui me paraissent être de la plus grande importance pour les juridictions permanentes.

I Instruments juridiques

L'amélioration des méthodes de travail doit être une des préoccupations majeures des juridictions internationales. Cette nécessité traduit l'importance des instruments juridiques que sont le Règlement de procédure, la Résolution sur la pratique interne en matière judiciaire et les Lignes directrices relatives à

© 2018, BY INTERNATIONAL TRIBUNAL FOR THE LAW OF THE SEA | DOI 10.1163/9789004356832_026

la préparation et la présentation des affaires dont le Tribunal est saisi. Ces trois instruments gouvernent l'ensemble de la procédure devant le Tribunal.

C'est dire l'importance du Comité du Règlement et de la pratique en matière judiciaire. Le Comité veille à l'application et à la révision du Règlement, de la Résolution et des Lignes directrices. Il est chargé de proposer au Tribunal toute modification qu'il pourrait juger souhaitable ou nécessaire d'apporter à ces dispositions. Le Comité est aujourd'hui composé de douze membres. A ce jour, quatre amendements au Règlement de procédure sont intervenus. En revanche, la Résolution et les Lignes directrices n'ont pas encore été amendées.

L'on pourrait penser à l'article 2 de la Résolution relative à la « documentation préparatoire ». Aux termes de ce texte, après la clôture de la procédure écrite, chaque juge peut dans un délai de cinq semaines préparer une brève note écrite se limitant à explorer a) les principales questions appelant une décision au vu des pièces écrites ; b) tout point qu'il faudrait éventuellement clarifier au cours de la procédure orale.

Je dois vous avouer que l'amendement de cette disposition me paraît inopportun, car la faculté laissée aux juges me paraît convenir. Le système actuel tel qu'il fonctionne au Tribunal permet de remplir les missions de façon satisfaisante. L'on n'a pas besoin de copier ce qui se fait à La Haye d'autant plus que cette prestigieuse juridiction, instruite par l'expérience, a réformé le système de la « note écrite obligatoire » en ce qui concerne les demandes en indication de mesures conservatoires comme le Président de la Cour, M. Abraham, nous l'a rappelé il y a un instant. Qui plus est, à la Cour, il y a quinze juges tandis qu'au Tribunal, nous sommes vingt et un juges, avec tous les problèmes qui s'y attachent : lenteur dans le temps de lecture des notes, problèmes liés à la traduction etc. L'expérience acquise dans l'*Affaire du navire « SAIGA »* ne m'incite pas à chérir ce système de la note écrite obligatoire laquelle n'a guère ma faveur.

II La logistique

Doter le Tribunal des outils nécessaires au bon accomplissement de ses missions me paraît être l'objectif principal à atteindre.

Le Tribunal donne l'impression d'être une structure fonctionnelle dont les rouages sont bien huilés lorsqu'il n'a pas d'affaires à instruire. Cependant, on y observe un manque manifeste d'effectif dès qu'il est occupé à connaître d'une affaire. Il faut donc un soutien logistique très efficace pour faire face aux besoins.

Il faut surtout le renforcement du Greffe en personnel, un service juridique digne de ce nom et des « law-clerks » pour assister les juges. En 20 ans, je n'ai pas eu recours aux services du Greffe me disant que les juristes doivent être écrasés de travail et qu'il ne faudrait pas leur en rajouter. Le service juridique du Tribunal se compose en effet de 6 personnes. Le Tribunal doit en outre être doté de moyens informatiques et de technologie du « vingt-troisième siècle » pour lui permettre de s'acquitter efficacement de ses tâches. Evidemment, ces nouveaux moyens vont nécessiter une augmentation singulière des ressources financières. L'on sait que la « religion » des Etats Parties est plutôt l'indigence budgétaire et que par conséquent les ressources financières nécessaires seront indisponibles.

Peut-être qu'il faut mener une campagne de sensibilisation à New York auprès des délégués des Etats Parties et de leurs groupes régionaux pour les rendre conscients de ce que l'on endure dans les institutions comme les nôtres. Il est frappant d'observer que les juridictions internationales sont obligées de recourir à des financements extra-budgétaires pour organiser quelque manifestation que ce soit. Par exemple, notre vingtième anniversaire est financé par le gouvernement japonais. Le « side-event » de New York en juin dernier a été financé par les coréens de la Korea Maritime Institute tandis que les stages sont financés par la Nippon Foundation. Rappelons que le Tribunal n'organise plus ses ateliers régionaux faute de ressources financières disponibles. Autrement dit, les ressources propres du Tribunal sont insuffisantes et son budget est sensiblement réduit à chaque exercice. Il faut une imagination très fertile pour faire face à ces problèmes budgétaires dont la mutabilité va plutôt dans le sens de la réduction systématique ; c'est un signe des temps. Ainsi, la question des ressources à la disposition du Tribunal est une question récurrente, en particulier, avec le problème de la traduction.

III L'instruction des affaires

Le problème de l'instruction des affaires réside pour l'essentiel dans sa durée parfois perçue comme de la lenteur. Cela s'apparente cependant à un mauvais procès fait aux juridictions internationales. Il est vrai qu'il faut entre trente et quarante mois pour le règlement d'une affaire ; mais il ne faut pas se méprendre sur le fait que la fonction judiciaire a ses exigences propres. Le juge international traite avec des Etats souverains décidés à défendre leur cause dans une procédure où le principe fondamental est l'égalité des parties. C'est le fondement commun des dispositions de procédure dans tous les systèmes juridiques et c'est une conséquence du caractère judiciaire du Tribunal.

C'est le souci d'assurer une égalité complète entre les parties qui fonde les décisions prises quant à : l'ordre de production des pièces de la procédure ; la charge de la preuve ; l'audition des parties et leur droit de réponse en application du principe *auditur et altera pars* (voir l'affaire *Nottebohm* (*Liechtenstein c. Guatemala*) ; l'allocation du temps de préparation des dossiers (mémoire / contre-mémoire etc.…) ; et le temps de parole. A dire vrai, ce sont les pièces de la procédure qui prennent du temps. La production du mémoire, du contre-mémoire, de la réplique et de la duplique peut prendre jusqu'à deux années. Si l'on y rajoute la procédure orale, on a une idée du temps nécessaire aux litigants dans une affaire donnée.

En revanche, dès que l'on parvient au stade du délibéré, les choses vont relativement vite. En effet, entre la fin de la procédure orale et le rendu, le prononcé de la décision, il se passe très peu de temps. Autrement dit, le travail proprement dit de la juridiction est assez rapide. Le système fonctionne à peu près correctement. Il faudrait peut-être, en outre, offrir aux Etats Parties l'option de la phase unique en modifiant ou en ajoutant un alinéa à l'article 44 du Règlement pour faire face à la question des délais pour la production des pièces écrites et leur volume. Les écritures volumineuses des parties apparaissent comme une contrainte pour le Tribunal lequel doit en assurer la traduction vers l'autre langue officielle. C'est pourquoi la question qui se pose est celle de savoir si le Tribunal tel qu'il fonctionne aujourd'hui, pourra-t-il faire face à un rôle des affaires très fourni lequel augmenterait singulièrement sa charge de travail ? Cette situation n'affecterait-elle pas la qualité des décisions du Tribunal ? Faudrait-il revoir la question des délais pour la production de pièces écrites et leur volume ? L'on se souvient que dans l'affaire du *Thon à nageoire bleue* – procédure d'urgence – le volume des pièces écrites était tel que l'on frisait le surmenage en termes de charge de travail, sans parler des problèmes presque insurmontables soulevés par la traduction des documents de l'affaire. Et que dire de la pratique consistant à ne traiter que d'une seule affaire à la fois ?

En définitive, toutes ces préoccupations posent la question des ressources à la disposition du Tribunal et en particulier celles nécessaires pour faire face au problème de la traduction. En effet, il s'agit là du problème fondamental du Tribunal comme – du reste – de toute juridiction internationale. Cela requiert sans nul doute la compréhension et l'action des Etats Parties à la Convention.

Les litigants peuvent aussi aider en se conformant strictement aux ordonnances rendues par le Tribunal pour fixer le nombre et l'ordre des pièces de procédure ainsi que les délais pour leur présentation. Les parties peuvent également s'abstenir de présenter une demande tendant à proroger un délai ou à obtenir une décision de considérer comme valable un acte de procédure fait après l'expiration du délai fixé.

En ce qui concerne la procédure orale, les conseils des Etats aideraient singulièrement le Tribunal s'ils pouvaient éviter de répéter à l'audience les arguments déjà développés dans les exposés écrits que les juges sont censés avoir déjà lu.

La question de la pratique consistant à ne traiter que d'une affaire à la fois procède d'une vision assez sage en l'état actuel des choses en ce qu'elle tient compte de l'état réel des ressources financières à la disposition de la juridiction. Un rôle fourni révèlerait immédiatement le poids de la traduction et son importance pour le Tribunal et mettrait à nu les insuffisances observables au niveau de la juridiction. Je me souviens de nombre d'affaires où le Tribunal a dû recourir à des services extérieurs pour assurer la traduction.

C'est dire que le Tribunal hésitera, dans les circonstances du moment, à mettre en œuvre les dispositions du Règlement relatives à la jonction d'instances aux termes desquelles le Tribunal peut à tout moment ordonner que les instances dans deux ou plusieurs affaires soient jointes. Il peut ordonner aussi que les procédures écrites ou orales, y compris la présentation de témoins, aient un caractère commun ; ou il peut, sans opérer de jonction formelle, ordonner une action commune au regard d'un ou plusieurs éléments de ces procédures.

Il convient de noter, par ailleurs, que les procédures d'urgence – la prompte mainlevée et les demandes en prescription de mesures conservatoires – peuvent affecter l'emploi du temps du Tribunal et entraîner des reports dans les affaires. Ce, parce qu'aux termes du paragraphe premier de l'article 112 du Règlement, le Tribunal donne priorité aux demandes de mainlevée de l'immobilisation de navires ou de libération de leur équipage sur toutes autres procédures devant le Tribunal. Toutefois, lorsqu'il est saisi d'une demande de mainlevée de l'immobilisation d'un navire ou de libération de son équipage et d'une demande en prescription de mesures conservatoires, le Tribunal prend les dispositions voulues pour se prononcer promptement sur l'une et l'autre demande. Ceci traduit le fait que le facteur temps est essentiel dans la vie du Tribunal.

Mesdames, Messieurs, j'en arrive maintenant au dernier point que je voudrais examiner devant vous : les nouveaux défis.

IV Les nouveaux défis

Mesdames et Messieurs, les avancées et les développements du droit international doivent faire l'objet d'une attention particulière des juges qui doivent être au fait des problèmes, être à la hauteur, parce que la vocation du Tribunal est de dire le droit. Le droit de la mer est un domaine en mutation rapide et de plus en plus complexe. Le dispositif normatif est très riche et varié. C'est pourquoi ce système juridique doit faire face à des défis multiples inhérents à l'approche retenue par la Convention elle-même, et qui consiste à partager l'océan entre les Etats du monde. La grande faiblesse de l'approche dite zonale réside dans la divergence entre la nature et le droit. L'étendue de la juridiction de l'Etat côtier sur les espaces maritimes est définie selon le critère de la distance compte non tenu de la nature intrinsèque de l'océan et des ressources biologiques ou non biologiques qui y gisent. Le défi principal ici est le parachèvement du partage. Et puisqu'« il n'y a de constant que le changement », de nouveaux problèmes sont apparus qui étaient inconnus au moment de la rédaction de la Convention ou qui ne sauraient être traités sur la seule base de celle-ci. Cette situation a engendré de nouveaux défis qui peuvent ouvrir de nouvelles perspectives pour le droit de la mer : l'on peut y voir la revanche de la nature sur le droit.

Aujourd'hui, la tâche principale que les Etats doivent entreprendre sur la base de la Convention est de parachever le processus de délimitation des espaces maritimes de façon à rendre fonctionnelle la méthode de répartition retenue de la Convention (l'approche zonale).

Ceci engendre quatre formes de délimitation que je vais rappeler : a) la délimitation unilatérale ; b) la délimitation conventionnelle ; c) la délimitation juridictionnelle et d) la délinéation. Ce sont là les défis courants.

D'abord, la délimitation unilatérale concerne la séparation du territoire national d'avec un espace international. Elle s'applique aux espaces relevant de la juridiction de l'Etat côtier : eaux intérieures, mer territoriale, plateau continental et zone économique exclusive. La délimitation de tels espaces relève de la compétence exclusive de l'Etat riverain. Cependant, elle a toujours un aspect international. Comme l'indique la Cour « s'il est vrai que l'acte de délimitation est nécessairement un acte unilatéral parce que l'Etat riverain a seul qualité pour y procéder, en revanche, la validité de la délimitation à l'égard des Etats tiers relève du droit international » (*Pêcheries* (*Royaume-Uni c. Norvège*), *arrêt, C.I.J. Recueil 1951*, p. 132).

Ensuite, la délimitation conventionnelle procède d'une prescription de la Convention laquelle prévoit que toute délimitation de la zone économique exclusive et du plateau continental doit être effectuée par voie d'accord. Il se trouve que de nombreuses frontières maritimes dans notre monde ne sont pas délimitées. Le nombre total de frontières maritimes potentielles est de 420 d'après l'US Department of State et il n'existe qu'environ 200 accords de délimitation à ce jour dont la plupart est entrée en vigueur. C'est dire aussi que le processus n'est pas terminé, d'autant plus que les accords de délimitation existants ne couvrent guère tous les espaces maritimes. Ils ont trait pour la plupart aux plateaux continentaux et laissent indéterminés les autres espaces ; d'où la tendance récente à vouloir asseoir des lignes divisoires uniques qui embrassent toutes les zones sous juridiction nationale. Il s'agit là d'un défi de taille dans les années à venir.

Après, nous avons la délimitation juridictionnelle. La Convention prévoit que s'ils ne parviennent pas à un accord dans un délai raisonnable, les Etats concernés ont recours aux procédures prévues à la partie XV (articles 74, paragraphe 2, et 83, paragraphe 2). La délimitation juridictionnelle procède le plus souvent de l'échec de négociation dans la détermination de la frontière maritime entre deux Etats. De plus, l'existence de ZEE et le développement des technologies relatives à l'exploration et à l'exploitation des ressources minérales ont fait de la délimitation des espaces maritimes un problème majeur des temps modernes. La délimitation a, en effet, engendré plus d'affaires que tout autre sujet de droit international, que ce soit devant les juridictions permanentes ou arbitrales ou de l'annexe VII de la Convention. Depuis 1969, l'on note 23 affaires jugées. De la sorte, il apparaît que le rôle fondamental dans la formulation des règles et principes devant régir le droit de la délimitation maritime revient aux juridictions internationales plus qu'à la pratique interétatique.

Enfin, avec la délinéation, l'on a en vue la détermination de la limite extérieure de plateaux continentaux qui s'étendent au-delà des 200 milles marins. La Convention a institué la Commission des limites du plateau continental, organe scientifique et technique prévu par le paragraphe 8 de l'article 76 et par l'annexe II de la Convention.

Sa tâche consiste à formuler des recommandations sur les demandes présentées par les Etats au titre du plateau continental au-delà de 200 milles marins. L'Etat côtier a seul compétence pour fixer les limites extérieures de son plateau continental au-delà de 200 milles marins. Cependant, il doit le faire sur la base des recommandations de la Commission. Celle-ci comprend 21 membres, experts en matière de géologie, de géographie ou d'hydrographie, élus par les Etats Parties à la Convention parmi leurs ressortissants pour un mandat de cinq ans. A la date du 19 octobre 2016, soixante-dix-sept demandes ont été soumises à la Commission. Elle a eu à faire vingt-quatre recommandations aux Etats côtiers concernés. Il convient de noter que lorsqu'elle examine les demandes à elle soumises, la Commission se prononce sur le bien-fondé de la limite extérieure du plateau continental au-delà de 200 milles marins ; et elle le fait sur le plan scientifique et technique. Elle s'abstient d'interférer dans les différends de délimitation maritime pendants (voir CLCS/L/3, annexe 1).

Les nouveaux défis et perspectives concernent nombre de problèmes apparus après la signature de la Convention et qui n'ont donc pu être couverts par celle-ci. Pour l'essentiel, tout tourne autour de ce que l'on appelle la « gouvernance des mers et des océans » et qui interpelle la communauté des Etats dans son ensemble. Il s'agit de : a) la gestion des ressources biologiques de la haute mer ; b) des changements climatiques ; c) les ressources génétiques ; d) la piraterie ; e) la mise en œuvre de l'article 82 de la Convention ; f) la fonction consultative du Tribunal plénier et g) les violations de la Convention.

A *La gestion et la conservation des ressources biologiques de la haute mer*

La consécration de la notion de ZEE par la Convention censée mettre un terme au conflit d'intérêts entre Etats côtiers et ceux disposant de flottilles à grand rayon d'action ne fit que l'exaspérer. La jouissance par l'Etat côtier de droits souverains aux fins d'exploration et d'exploitation, de conservation et de gestion des ressources naturelles, biologiques ou non biologiques, des eaux surjacentes aux fonds marins dans sa ZEE a eu pour effet de déplacer la flottille de ce qui était considéré comme la haute mer vers les secteurs adjacents au zones économiques exclusives où la proportion des captures s'est amplifiée. Et pour assurer la durabilité des stocks chevauchants et grands migrateurs ainsi que les autres ressources biologiques, les Etats côtiers ont initié des actions diplomatiques qui aboutiront à l'accord relatif aux stocks chevauchants et grands migrateurs du 4 août 1995.

B *Les conséquences des changements climatiques*

Les conséquences des changements climatiques sur les océans sont appelées à figurer pendant longtemps à l'ordre du jour du droit de la mer et risquent d'occuper nombre d'institutions internationales. Le rapport de 2010 du Secrétaire général des Nations Unies sur les océans et le droit de la mer souligne les divers aspects de ces conséquences : l'augmentation du niveau des mers ; la question de l'acidification des océans ; les difficultés de la biodiversité marine ; l'augmentation de la fréquence des événements météorologiques extrêmes et les transferts dans la distribution des espèces biologiques (Doc. NU. A/65/69/Add.1, paragraphe 374).

Etant donné la prolificité des problèmes posés par les changements climatiques et surtout leur différence de nature, plusieurs critères de spécialité devront être mis en œuvre pour faire face à la situation. L'élévation du niveau des mers est susceptible d'affecter nombre d'îles et de hauts-fonds découvrants lesquels risquent de disparaître. Se posera alors le problème des droits sur les zones maritimes qui relevaient de la juridiction desdites îles après leur disparition. De même, la disparition de hauts-fonds découvrants peut avoir des conséquences sur la détermination des lignes de base. Les scientifiques ont révélé que l'élévation du niveau des mers a été plus rapide de 2000 à 2009 que durant les 5000 années précédentes. Le défi immédiat est la protection des archipels menacés et des populations installées sur les littoraux.

C *Les ressources génétiques marines*

La question est examinée par le Groupe de travail spécial officieux à composition non limitée, institué par l'Assemblée générale des Nations Unies en 2004, et chargé d'étudier les questions relatives á la conservation et à l'exploitation durable de la biodiversité marine dans les zones situées au-delà de la juridiction nationale.

La communauté des Etats est doublement consciente de l'abondance et de la diversité des ressources génétiques marines et de leur valeur du point de vue des avantages que l'on peut en retirer ainsi que des biens et services auxquels elles peuvent donner lieu, d'une part. Les Etats sont également conscients de l'importance de la recherche sur les ressources génétiques marines en vue de mieux comprendre les écosystèmes marins ainsi que leurs utilisations et applications potentielles, et de mieux les gérer, de l'autre.

D *La piraterie*

La piraterie remonte aux origines de la navigation maritime. Sa répression est régie par le droit coutumier codifié par la Convention. Le lieu de commission de l'acte de piraterie est la haute mer. Cependant, l'évolution de la piraterie est en porte à faux avec le dispositif normatif. Il se trouve, de nos jours, que les actes de piraterie sont commis dans la mer territoriale voire les eaux intérieures ou même dans les ports. Cette situation engendre un vide juridique qui va nécessiter une interprétation assez singulière des règles existantes pour y faire face.

E *La mise en œuvre de l'article 82 de la Convention*

Il s'agit des contributions en espèces ou en nature au titre de l'exploitation du plateau continental au-delà de 200 milles marins dont la mise en œuvre recèle de véritables défis à relever par l'Autorité. Ce n'est pas un hasard si trente-quatre ans après la signature de la Convention son régime n'est toujours pas fixé. Les enjeux tournent autour des obligations réciproques entre Etats Parties ; la relation entre l'Autorité et l'Etat au plateau continental étendu ; la question de la terminologie ; les fonctions et les tâches à répartir ; la structure et le processus nécessaires pour faciliter la relation administrative entre les Etats et l'Autorité.

F *La fonction consultative du Tribunal plénier*

La clause attributive de compétence consultative du Tribunal plénier se trouve dans le règlement et a fait l'objet de discussion à l'occasion de la demande d'avis consultatif de la Commission sous-régionale des pêches. L'avis consultatif rendu par le Tribunal renforce singulièrement la Convention et jette les bases de futures actions à l'encontre des Etats du pavillon. Il ouvre, en outre, la perspective de soumission de nouvelles questions au Tribunal.

G *La violation systématique de nombre de dispositions de la Convention*

Le nouveau défi, qui risque de mettre en danger – si l'on n'y prend garde – la Convention elle-même, est la violation systématique de nombre de ses dispositions qui peut non seulement affecter *l'ordre juridique des mers* mais surtout *la paix dans le monde*. Cette violation systématique concerne près de 60 Etats c'est à dire plus du tiers des Etats Parties à la Convention (168 Etats Parties). Ces violations doivent favoriser le recours au Tribunal par la mise en œuvre de la partie XV. Il s'agit entre autre des sujets suivants : tracé des lignes de base droites dans des conditions contraire à l'article 7 ; revendication de l'exercice de la juridiction dans les zones contigües pour des raisons de sécurité contraires à l'article 33 ; largeur des mers territoriales excédant 12 mille marins contrairement à l'article 3 ou encore la violation par des Etats du pavillon de l'article 94 de la Convention.

La répugnance des Etats à l'égard du règlement juridictionnel est inhérente à la structure même de la société internationale travaillée par des processus politiques et où les intérêts individualistes des Etats sont omniprésents. Les Etats doivent cependant agir en conformité avec la Convention qu'ils ont mis près d'une décennie à négocier et qu'ils célèbrent à longueur d'années.

Mesdames et Messieurs,

Jean Giraudoux nous offre, dans Electre, ce dialogue :

> LA FEMME NARSES – Oui, explique ! Je ne sais jamais bien vite. Je sens évidement qu'il se passe quelque chose, mais je me rends mal compte. Comment cela s'appelle-t-il, quand le jour se lève, comme aujourd'hui, et que tout est gâché, que tout est saccagé, et que l'air pourtant se respire, et qu'on a tout perdu, que la ville brûle, que les innocents s'entretuent, mais que les coupables agonisent, dans un coin du jour qui se lève ?
>
> ELECTRE – Demande au mendiant. Il le sait.
>
> LE MENDIANT – Cela a un très beau nom, femme NARSES. Cela s'appelle l'aurore.

Je vous remercie de votre aimable attention !

Annexes

Programme of the Symposium 5–6 October 2016

Wednesday, 5 October 2016

9–9:30 a.m. Registration

9:45–10 a.m. *Welcoming remarks*
Vladimir Golitsyn, President of the Tribunal

10–11:30 a.m.

Panel 1:
The Tribunal's jurisprudence and its contribution to the Rule of Law

Panel:
Judge David Anderson, former ITLOS Judge
Judge José Luis Jesus, ITLOS
Judge Elsa Kelly, ITLOS
Judge Jin-Hyun Paik, ITLOS
Judge Tullio Treves, former ITLOS Judge
Chair: President Vladimir Golitsyn

Question and Answer session

11:30 a.m.–noon Coffee break

Noon–1:30 p.m.

Panel 2:
The contribution of the Tribunal to the progressive development of International Law

Panel:
Professor Doris König, Justice, Constitutional Court of the Federal Republic of Germany
Professor Francisco Orrego Vicuña, Heidelberg University Center for Latin America
Professor Bernard H. Oxman, University of Miami School of Law
Professor Tullio Scovazzi, University of Milano-Bicocca
Professor Yoshifumi Tanaka, University of Copenhagen
Judge Peter Tomka, International Court of Justice
Chair: Judge Shunji Yanai, ITLOS

Question and Answer session

© 2018, BY INTERNATIONAL TRIBUNAL FOR THE LAW OF THE SEA | DOI 10.1163/9789004356832_027

1:30–3 p.m. Lunch break

3–4:30 p.m.

Panel 3:
The contribution of the Tribunal to the Rule of Law: the point of view of practitioners

Panel:
Professor Alan Boyle, Edinburgh Law School
Professor Alain Pellet, Emeritus Professor of the University Paris Ouest Nanterre La Défense, former member and former President of the International Law Commission
Mr Paul Reichler, Partner, Co-Chair, International Litigation and Arbitration Department Foley Hoag LLP
Sir Michael Wood, Barrister, Member of the International Law Commission
Chair: Judge Rüdiger Wolfrum, ITLOS

Question and Answer session

5 p.m. Reception

Thursday, 6 October 2016

Panel 4:
Improving working methods in international adjudication

10–10:30 a.m.	*A view from the ICJ* Judge Ronny Abraham, President of the ICJ
10:30–11 a.m.	*The experience of the Tribunal* Judge Joseph Akl, ITLOS
11–11:30 a.m.	*A perspective from the EFTA Court* Judge Carl Baudenbacher, President of the EFTA Court
11:30–noon	Coffee break

Noon–1 p.m. *Panel Discussion*

Panel:
Judge Jean-Pierre Cot, ITLOS
Judge Albert Hoffmann, ITLOS
Judge Tafsir Ndiaye, ITLOS
Chair: Vice-President Boualem Bouguetaia, ITLOS

Question and Answer session

Programme du colloque 5–6 Octobre 2016

Mercredi 5 octobre 2016

9 heures–9 h 30 Inscription

9 h 45–10 heures *Allocution de bienvenue*
M. Vladimir Golitsyn, Président du Tribunal

10 heures–*11 h 30*

Première table ronde :
La jurisprudence du Tribunal et sa contribution à l'état de droit

Participants :
M. David Anderson, ancien juge au TIDM
M. José Luis Jesus, juge au TIDM
Mme Elsa Kelly, juge au TIDM
M. Jin-Hyun Paik, juge au TIDM
M. Tullio Treves, ancien juge au TIDM
Président : M. Vladimir Golitsyn, Président du TIDM

Séance de questions-réponses

11 h 30–midi Pause-café

Midi–13 h 30

Deuxième table ronde :
La contribution du Tribunal au développement progressif du droit international

Participants :
Mme Doris König, professeur d'université, juge à la Cour constitutionnelle fédérale d'Allemagne
M. Francisco Orrego Vicuña, Centre pour l'Amérique latine de l'Université de Heidelberg
M. Bernard H. Oxman, professeur à la Faculté de droit de l'Université de Miami
M. Tullio Scovazzi, professeur à l'Université de Milan-Bicocca
M. Yoshifumi Tanaka, professeur à l'Université de Copenhague

© 2018, BY INTERNATIONAL TRIBUNAL FOR THE LAW OF THE SEA | DOI 10.1163/9789004356832_028

M. Peter Tomka, juge à la Cour internationale de Justice
Président : M. Shunji Yanai, juge au TIDM

Séance de questions-réponses

13 h 30–15 heures Déjeuner

15 heures–16 h 30

Troisième table ronde :
La contribution du Tribunal à l'état de droit :
Le point de vue des praticiens

Participants :
M. Alan Boyle, professeur à la Faculté de droit de l'Université d'Edimbourg
M. Alain Pellet, professeur émérite de l'Université Paris Ouest, Nanterre-La Défense, ancien membre et ancien Président de la Commission du droit international
M. Paul Reichler, associé, codirecteur du service *International Litigation and Arbitration* au cabinet Foley Hoag LLP
Sir Michael Wood, avocat, membre de la Commission du droit international
Président : M. Rüdiger Wolfrum, juge au TIDM

Séance de questions-réponses

17 heures Réception

Jeudi 6 octobre 2016

Quatrième table ronde :
L'amélioration des méthodes de travail de la justice internationale

10 heures–10 h 30 *Le point de vue de la CIJ*
M. Ronny Abraham, Président de la CIJ

10 h 30–11 heures *L'expérience au Tribunal*
M. Joseph Akl, juge au TIDM

11 heures–11 h 30 *Une perspective de la Cour de justice de l'AELE*
M. Carl Baudenbacher, Président de la Cour de justice de l'AELE

11 h 30–midi Pause-café

Midi–13 heures *Table ronde*

Participants :
M. Jean-Pierre Cot, juge au TIDM
M. Albert Hoffmann, juge au TIDM
M. Tafsir Ndiaye, juge au TIDM
Président : M. Boualem Bouguetaia, Vice-Président du TIDM

Séance de questions-réponses

List of Speakers
(in alphabetical order)

Mr Ronny ABRAHAM is the President of the International Court of Justice, of which he became a member in 2005. He is Judge *ad hoc* of the Special Chamber of the Tribunal formed to deal with the *Dispute concerning delimitation of the maritime boundary between Ghana and Côte d'Ivoire in the Atlantic Ocean*. He sits on the Board of the *Société française pour le droit international* and the Board of Editors of the *Annuaire français de droit international*.

Mr Joseph AKL has been a Judge of the International Tribunal for the Law of the Sea since 1996 and served as its Vice-President from 2005 to 2008. From 1997 to 1999 he was President of the Tribunal's Seabed Disputes Chamber.

Mr David ANDERSON was a Judge at the International Tribunal for the Law of the Sea from 1996 until 2005 and has also served as judge *ad hoc* before it. He has been listed as an arbitrator under Annex VII to the United Nations Convention on the Law of the Sea since 2005.

Mr Carl BAUDENBACHER has been a Judge at the EFTA Court since 1995 and has been its President since 2003. He is also the Director of the Competence Center of European and International Law at the University of St. Gallen. From 1993 to 2004, he was a Permanent Visiting Professor at the University of Texas School of Law.

Mr Boualem BOUGUETAIA has been a Judge of the International Tribunal for the Law of the Sea since 2008 and serves as its Vice-President since 2014. He is President of the Special Chamber of the Tribunal formed to deal with the *Dispute concerning delimitation of the maritime boundary between Ghana and Côte d'Ivoire in the Atlantic Ocean.*

Mr Alan BOYLE was Professor of Public International Law at the University of Edinburgh School of Law from 1995 until 2017. He taught international law, international environmental law, and law of the sea. He is a barrister and practises international law from Essex Court Chambers, London.

Mr Jean-Pierre COT has been a Judge of the International Tribunal for the Law of the Sea since 2002 and was President of its Chamber for Marine Environment Disputes from 2008 to 2011. He is also Emeritus Professor at the University of Paris-I and an Associate Research Fellow at the Université Libre de Bruxelles, and has been a member

© 2018, BY INTERNATIONAL TRIBUNAL FOR THE LAW OF THE SEA | DOI 10.1163/9789004356832_029

of several arbitral tribunals and served as judge *ad hoc* before the International Court of Justice.

Mr Vladimir GOLITSYN has been a Judge of the International Tribunal for the Law of the Sea since 2008 and serves as its President since 2014. He was President of the Tribunal's Seabed Disputes Chamber from 2011 to 2014. He is Professor of international law at the Moscow State University and the Vice-President of the Russian Association of International Maritime Law.

Mr Albert HOFFMANN has been a Judge of the International Tribunal for the Law of the Sea since 2005 and served as its Vice-President from 2011 to 2014. He is listed as an arbitrator under Annex VII to the United Nations Convention on the Law of the Sea.

Mr José Luís JESUS has been a Judge of the International Tribunal for the Law of the Sea since 1999 and served as its President from 2008 to 2011. Since 2014, he is President of the Tribunal's Seabed Disputes Chamber.

Ms Elsa KELLY has been a Judge of the International Tribunal for the Law of the Sea since 2011. She was Professor of International Law at the Foreign Service Institute of the Ministry for Foreign Affairs of Argentina and also at the Faculty of Law of the University of Buenos Aires. She presides the Committee of International Environmental Affairs at the Argentine Council for International Relations (CARI).

Ms Doris KÖNIG is Professor of Public Law, European Union Law and International Law at the Bucerius Law School in Hamburg, where she served as Vice-Dean from 2005 to 2007 and as Dean from 2012 to 2014. Since June 2014, she serves as Justice at the German Federal Constitutional Court.

Mr Tafsir M. NDIAYE has been a Judge of the International Tribunal for the Law of the Sea since 1996 and was President of its Chamber for Fisheries Disputes from 2011 to 2014.

Mr Francisco ORREGO VICUÑA is presently a Judge at the International Monetary Fund Administrative Tribunal and Professor of International Law at the University of Heidelberg Centre for Latin America. He has also served as judge *ad hoc* before the International Tribunal for the Law of the Sea.

Mr Bernard H. OXMAN is the Richard A. Hausler Professor of Law at the University of Miami School of Law, where he directs the graduate programme in maritime law. He has served as judge *ad hoc* of the Tribunal and the International Court of Justice as well as arbitrator and counsel in public and private international cases and has advised various governments on international law matters.

Mr Jin-Hyun PAIK has been a Judge of the International Tribunal for the Law of the Sea since 2009 and is member of the Special Chamber of the Tribunal formed to deal with the *Dispute concerning delimitation of the maritime boundary between Ghana and Côte d'Ivoire in the Atlantic Ocean*. He is President of the Asian Society of International Law.

Mr Alain PELLET is Emeritus Professor of the University Paris Nanterre as well as a former member and former Chairperson of the International Law Commission of the United Nations. He was designated to the panel of arbitrators of the International Centre for Settlement of Investment Disputes and to the list of arbitrators under Annex VII of the United Nations Convention on the Law of the Sea. He is President of the *Société française pour le droit international*.

Mr Paul REICHLER is Senior Partner and Chair of the International Litigation and Arbitration Department of Foley Hoag LLP. He has represented States in international litigation and arbitration for over thirty years.

Mr Tullio SCOVAZZI is Professor of International Law at the University of Milano-Bicocca. He occasionally participates, as legal expert, in negotiations and meetings relating to law of the sea, cultural property and human rights.

Mr Yoshifumi TANAKA is Professor of International Law with specific focus on the law of the sea at the Faculty of Law at the University of Copenhagen.

Mr Peter TOMKA has been a Judge at the International Court of Justice since 2003 and served as its Vice-President from 2009 to 2012 and as its President from 2012 to 2015. He is on the list of arbitrators nominated at the International Centre for Settlement of Investment Disputes and under Annex VII to the United Nations Convention on the Law of the Sea.

Mr Tullio TREVES was a Judge of the International Tribunal for the Law of the Sea from 1996 until 2011 and also judge *ad hoc* before the Tribunal. He assists in FAO expert consultations and is listed as an arbitrator under Annex VII of the United Nations Convention on the Law of the Sea. He is arbitrator and counsel in law of the sea cases (ICJ, PCA) and Senior Public International Law Consultant with Curtis, Mallet-Prevost, Colt & Mosle LLP.

Mr Rüdiger WOLFRUM has been a Judge of the International Tribunal for the Law of the Sea since 1996. He served as its Vice-President from 1996 to 1999 and as its President from 2005 to 2008. He was President of the Chamber for Marine Environment Disputes from 1997 to 1999. He is a Member of the Special Chamber of the Tribunal formed to deal with the *Dispute concerning delimitation of the maritime boundary between Ghana and Côte d'Ivoire in the Atlantic Ocean*. He served as Director of the Max Planck Institute for Comparative Public Law and International Law in Heidelberg from 1993 to 2013.

Sir Michael WOOD is a member of the International Law Commission of the United Nations and a Senior Fellow of the Lauterpacht Centre for International Law, University of Cambridge. He is a barrister at 20 Essex Street, London, where he practices in the field of public international law. He was the principal Legal Adviser to the Foreign and Commonwealth Office of the United Kingdom between 1999 and 2006.

Mr Shunji YANAI has been a Judge of the International Tribunal for the Law of the Sea since 2005 and served as its President from 2011 to 2014. He is Professor at Waseda University in Tokyo and President of the Japan branch of the International Law Association.

Liste des intervenants

(par ordre alphabétique)

M. Ronny ABRAHAM est Président de la Cour internationale de Justice, dont il est devenu membre en 2005. Il est juge *ad hoc* de la Chambre spéciale du Tribunal constituée pour connaître du *Différend relatif à la délimitation de la frontière maritime entre le Ghana et la Côte d'Ivoire dans l'océan Atlantique*. Il est également membre du Conseil de la Société française pour le droit international et du comité de rédaction de l'*Annuaire français de droit international*.

M. Joseph AKL est membre du Tribunal international du droit de la mer depuis 1996, et en a été le Vice-Président de 2005 à 2008. De 1997 à 1999 il a été Président de la Chambre pour le règlement des différends relatifs aux fonds marins du Tribunal.

M. David ANDERSON a été juge au Tribunal international du droit de la mer de 1996 à 2005. Il a également siégé en qualité de juge *ad hoc* du Tribunal. Son nom figure depuis 2005 sur la liste des arbitres désignés conformément à l'annexe VII de la Convention des Nations Unies sur le droit de la mer.

M. Carl BAUDENBACHER est Président de la Cour de justice de l'AELE depuis 2003, et juge à cette Cour depuis 1995. Il est le Directeur du Centre de compétences en droit européen et international de l'Université de Saint-Gall. De 1993 à 2004, il a été professeur invité permanent à la faculté de droit de l'Université de Texas.

M. Boualem BOUGUETAIA est Vice-Président du Tribunal international du droit de la mer depuis 2014, et membre du Tribunal depuis 2008. Il est Président de la Chambre spéciale du Tribunal constituée pour connaître du *Différend relatif à la délimitation de la frontière maritime entre le Ghana et la Côte d'Ivoire dans l'océan Atlantique*.

M. Alan BOYLE a été professeur de droit international public à la Faculté de droit de l'Université d'Edimbourg, où il a enseigné le droit international, le droit international de l'environnement et le droit de la mer de 1995 à 2017. Il pratique le droit international en qualité d'avocat du cabinet Essex Court Chambers de Londres.

M. Jean-Pierre COT est membre du Tribunal international du droit de la mer depuis 2002 et a été Président de la Chambre pour le règlement des différends relatifs au milieu marin de 2008 à 2011. Professeur émérite de l'Université Paris 1 et chercheur associé à l'Université libre de Bruxelles, il a été membre de plusieurs tribunaux arbitraux et juge *ad hoc* à la Cour internationale de Justice.

© 2018, BY INTERNATIONAL TRIBUNAL FOR THE LAW OF THE SEA | DOI 10.1163/9789004356832_030

M. Vladimir GOLITSYN est Président du Tribunal international du droit de la mer depuis 2014, et membre du Tribunal depuis 2008. Il a été Président de la Chambre pour le règlement des différends relatifs aux fonds marins du Tribunal de 2011 à 2014. Il est Professeur de droit international à l'Université d'Etat de Moscou et Vice-Président de l'Association russe de droit maritime international.

M. Albert HOFFMANN est membre du Tribunal international du droit de la mer depuis 2005, et en a été le Vice-Président de 2011 à 2014. Il a été nommé sur la liste des arbitres conformément à l'annexe VII de la Convention des Nations Unies sur le droit de la mer.

M. José Luís JESUS est membre du Tribunal international du droit de la mer depuis 1999 et en a été le Président de 2008 à 2011. Depuis 2014, il est Président de la Chambre pour le règlement des différends relatifs aux fonds marins du Tribunal.

Mme Elsa KELLY est membre du Tribunal international du droit de la mer depuis 2011. Elle a été professeur de droit international à l'Institut des affaires étrangères du Ministère des affaires étrangères de l'Argentine et également à la faculté de droit de l'Université de Buenos Aires. Elle préside le Comité des affaires internationales de l'environnement du Conseil argentin des relations internationales (CARI).

Mme Doris KÖNIG est professeur de droit public, de droit de l'Union européenne et de droit international à la Bucerius Law School de Hambourg, dont elle a été la Vice-Doyenne de 2005 à 2007 et la Doyenne de 2012 à 2014. Depuis juin 2014, elle est Juge à la Cour constitutionnelle fédérale d'Allemagne.

M. Tafsir M. NDIAYE est membre du Tribunal international du droit de la mer depuis 1996. Il a été Président de la Chambre pour le règlement des différends relatifs aux pêcheries de 2011 à 2014.

M. Francisco ORREGO VICUÑA est actuellement membre du Tribunal administratif du Fonds monétaire international et professeur de droit international au Centre pour l'Amérique latine de l'Université de Heidelberg. Il a également siégé en qualité de juge *ad hoc* du Tribunal international du droit de la mer.

M. Bernard H. OXMAN est le professeur de droit titulaire de la chaire « Richard A. Hausler » à la faculté de droit de l'Université de Miami, dont il dirige le programme de master en droit maritime. Il a été juge *ad hoc* du Tribunal et de la Cour internationale de Justice ainsi que arbitre ou conseil dans le cadre de diverses affaires de droit international public et de droit international privé, et conseiller de plusieurs gouvernements pour des questions touchant au droit international.

M. Jin-Hyun PAIK est membre du Tribunal international du droit de la mer depuis 2009 et membre de la Chambre spéciale du Tribunal constituée pour connaître du *Différend relatif à la délimitation de la frontière maritime entre le Ghana et la Côte d'Ivoire dans l'océan Atlantique*. Il est Président de la Société asiatique de droit international.

M. Alain PELLET est professeur émérite de l'Université Paris Nanterre et ancien membre et ancien Président de la Commission du droit international des Nations Unies. Il a été nommé sur la liste des arbitres désignés du Centre international pour le règlement des différends relatifs aux investissements et sur celle des arbitres désignés conformément à l'annexe VII de la Convention des Nations Unies sur le droit de la mer. Il est Président de la Société française pour le droit international.

M. Paul REICHLER est associé principal et directeur du service « International Litigation and Arbitration » du cabinet Foley Hoag LLP. Depuis plus de trente ans, il représente des Etats dans des arbitrages et autres procédures de règlement des différends.

M. Tullio SCOVAZZI est professeur de droit international à l'Université de Milan-Bicocca. Il participe occasionnellement en qualité d'expert juridique à des négociations et réunions portant sur le droit de la mer, les biens culturels et les droits de l'homme.

M. Yoshifumi TANAKA est professeur de droit international et spécialiste du droit de la mer à la faculté de droit de l'Université de Copenhague.

M. Peter TOMKA est juge à la Cour internationale de Justice depuis 2003 ; il en a été le Vice-Président de 2009 à 2012 et le Président de 2012 à 2015. Il a été nommé sur la liste des arbitres désignés du Centre international pour le règlement des différends relatifs aux investissements et sur celle des arbitres désignés conformément à l'annexe VII de la Convention des Nations Unies sur le droit de la mer.

M. Tullio TREVES a été membre du Tribunal international du droit de la mer de 1996 à 2011. Il a également siégé en qualité de juge *ad hoc* du Tribunal. Il participe aux consultations d'experts de la FAO et a été nommé sur la liste des arbitres désignés conformément à l'annexe VII de la Convention des Nations Unies sur le droit de la mer. Il est arbitre et conseil dans des affaires relatives au droit de la mer (CIJ, CPA) et consultant principal en droit international public au cabinet juridique Curtis, Mallet-Prevost, Colt & Mosle LLP.

M. Rüdiger WOLFRUM est membre du Tribunal international du droit de la mer depuis 1996, et en a été le Vice-Président de 1996 à 1999 et le Président de 2005 à 2008. De 1997 à 1999, il a été Président de la Chambre pour le règlement des différends relatifs au milieu marin. Il est membre de la Chambre spéciale du Tribunal constituée pour connaître du *Différend relatif à la délimitation de la frontière maritime entre le Ghana et la Côte d'Ivoire dans l'océan Atlantique*. De 1993 à 2013, il a été directeur de l'Institut Max Planck de droit public comparé et de droit international à Heidelberg.

Sir Michael WOOD est membre de la Commission du droit international des Nations Unies et maître de recherche au Centre Lauterpacht de droit international de l'Université de Cambridge. Avocat au cabinet 20 Essex Street de Londres, il y pratique le droit international public. Il a été le Conseiller juridique principal au Bureau des affaires étrangères et du Commonwealth du Royaume-Uni entre 1999 et 2006.

M. Shunji YANAI est membre du Tribunal international du droit de la mer depuis 2005, et en a été le Président de 2011 à 2014. Il est professeur à l'Université Waseda à Tokyo et Président de la section japonaise de l'*International Law Association*.

List of Participants/Liste des participants

Ms Julieta Abgaryan, Lawyer, Juzinflo International Law Firm
M. M'hammed Abidi, Juriste, Ministère des Affaires étrangères et de la Coopération, Direction des Affaires Juridiques et des Traités, Maroc
M. Ronny Abraham, Président, Cour international de Justice
Mr Agarwal Sunil K, Deputy Director, National Security Council Secretariat, India
Mr Mamuka Akhaladze, Director, Maritime Transport Agency of Georgia
M. Joseph Akl, Juge, Tribunal international du droit de la mer
Mr Alejandro Alday González, Legal Advisor, Ministry of Foreign Affairs, Legal Affairs Department, Mexico
Mr Pablo Alonso, Intern, International Tribunal for the Law of the Sea
Mr Ricardo Alves Silva, Lawyer, Miranda alliance
Mr David Anderson, Judge (1996–2005), International Tribunal for the Law of the Sea
Mr Takao Anzawa, Consul General, Consulate-General of Japan, Hamburg
Ms Marietta Brew Appiah-Opong, Attorney General and Minister for Justice, Ministry of Justice, Attorney General's Department, Ghana
Ms Frida Maria Armas-Pfirter, Professor, Austral University
Mr David Joseph Attard, Judge, International Tribunal for the Law of the Sea
Ms Helen Awo Ziwu, Solicitor-General, Attorney General's Department, Ghana
Mr Lawrence Folajimi Awosika, Chairman, Commission on the Limits of the Continental Shelf
Ms Zeinab Ayariga, Ministry of Justice, Attorney General's Department, Ghana
Mr Carl Baudenbacher, President, Court of Justice of the European Free Trade Association States
Ms Inès Bento de Aguiar Branco, Nippon Fellow, International Tribunal for the Law of the Sea
Ms Sonja Boelaert, Senior Legal Adviser, Council of the European Union
M. Boualem Bouguetaia, Vice-Président, Tribunal international du droit de la mer
M. Pierre Boussaroque, Directeur adjoint des affaires juridiques, Ministère des Affaires Etrangères, France
Mr Alan Boyle, Professor, University of Edinburgh, School of Law
Ms Naomi Burke, Associate Legal Officer, International Tribunal for the Law of the Sea
Mr William Campbell, General Counsel (International Law), Attorney General's Chambers, Australia
Mr Friedrich Catoir, Former Ambassador, Member of DiploConsult, Berlin
Ms Neeru Chadha, Former Additional Secretary and Legal Advisor, Ministry of External Affairs, India
Mr P. Chandrasekhara Rao, Judge, International Tribunal for the Law of the Sea

© 2018, BY INTERNATIONAL TRIBUNAL FOR THE LAW OF THE SEA | DOI 10.1163/9789004356832_031

Mr Souchea Chann, Nippon Fellow, International Tribunal for the Law of the Sea

Mr Michael-James Clifton, Head of Cabinet, Court of Justice of the European Free Trade Association States

M. Jean-Pierre Cot, Juge, Tribunal international du droit de la mer

Ms Cymie Payne, Professor, Rutgers University, School of Environmental and Biological Sciences

Ms Akua Dansua, Ambassador, Embassy of Ghana, Germany

Ms Lilian del Castillo, Professor, University of Buenos Aires Law School

M. Abdou Khadir Diakhate, Assistant de programme, Commission sous-régionale des pêches

M. Michel Djimgou Djomeni, Chef de la Cellule des Questions des Frontières et du Droit de la Mer, Ministère des Relations Extérieures, Division des Affaires Juridiques et des Traités, Cameroun

Mr Cuong Do Viet, Intern, International Tribunal for the Law of the Sea

Ms Margareth Domingos Antunes Galho, Legal Counsellor, SONANGOL Shipping

Ms Cleopatra Doumbia-Henry, President, World Maritime University

Mr Jan Dreyer, Lawyer, Dabelstein & Passehl

Mr Gudmundur Eiriksson, Judge (1996–2002), International Tribunal for the Law of the Sea; Jindal Global Law School, Centre for International Legal Studies

Ms Hee jin Eun, Chief Executive Officer, Korwind

Mr Gian Maria Farnelli, Department of Legal Studies, University of Bologna

Mr Raffaele Festa, Legal Division, Ministry for Foreign Affairs, Italy

Mr Stephen Fietta, Principal, Fietta International Law

Mr Matthias Füracker, Legal Officer, International Tribunal for the Law of the Sea

Mr Xiang Gao, Attaché, Ministry of Foreign Affairs, Treaty and Law Department, China

Mr Zhiguo Gao, Judge, International Tribunal for the Law of the Sea

Mr Miguel García García-Revillo, Professor, Universidad de Cordoba, Facultad de Derecho y CCEE

M. Philippe Gautier, Greffier, Tribunal international du droit de la mer

Ms Gabriele Goettsche-Wanli, Director, United Nations, Division for Ocean Affairs and the Law of the Sea

Mr Vladimir Golitsyn, President, International Tribunal for the Law of the Sea

Mr Alonso Gómez-Robledo Verduzco, Judge, International Tribunal for the Law of the Sea

Ms Angeles Gómez-Robledo

Ms Georgina Maria Guillen Grillo, President of the 26th Meeting of States Parties, Permanent Mission of Costa Rica, New York

Ms Eugenia Gutiérrez Ruiz, Deputy Legal Advisor, Ministry of Foreign Affairs of Costa Rica

Mr Shotaro Hamamoto, Professor, Kyoto University, Graduate School of Law

Mr James Harrison, Senior Lecturer, University of Edinburgh, School of Law
Dr Christoph Hasche, Lawyer, Fleet Hamburg LLP
Mr Masamichi Hasebe, Senior Legal Counsel, Japan Association of Maritime Safety
Mr Tomas Heidar, Judge, International Tribunal for the Law of the Sea
Mr Christoph Henrichs, Head of Division International Law, International Organisations, International Jurisdiction, Ministry of Justice, Germany
Ms Ximena Hinrichs, Senior Legal Officer/Head of Legal Office, International Tribunal for the Law of the Sea
Mr Federico Hirsch, Consul Adjunct, Consulate General, Argentina
Mr Albert Hoffmann, Judge, International Tribunal for the Law of the Sea
Mr Kamal Hossain, Judge *ad hoc*, Supreme Court of Bangladesh
Mr Nicolas Howe, Solicitor, Nick Howe Solicitor
Mr Daesong Hyun, Director of Maritime Territory Center, Korea Maritime Institute
Ms Elena Ivanova, PhD Student, University of Luxembourg, MPI Luxembourg
M. Elie Jarmache, Chargé de mission « droit de la mer », Secrétariat général de la mer, France
Mr José Luis Jesus, Judge, International Tribunal for the Law of the Sea
M. Alkaly Kaba, Student, Ecole de droit de la Sorbonne
Mr James Kateka, Judge, International Tribunal for the Law of the Sea
Ms Adolphine Kateka, International Tribunal for the Law of the Sea
Mr Papa Kebe, Ghana/ABNJ Tuna Pilot Project Coordinator, International Seafood Sustainability Foundation
Ms Elsa Kelly, Judge, International Tribunal for the Law of the Sea
Ms Lil Kerhervé, Intern, International Tribunal for the Law of the Sea
Mr Doo-young Kim, Deputy Registrar, International Tribunal for the Law of the Sea
Mr Yasuhiro Kitaura, Director, Law of the Sea Division, International Legal Affairs Bureau, Ministry of Foreign Affairs of Japan
Ms Nathalie Klein, Dean, Macquarie University, Macquarie Law School
Ms Jutta Köhn, Former State Secretary, Kanzlei Jutta Köhn
Mr Jo König, Director, Summer Academy, International Foundation for the Law of the Sea
Ms Doris König, Justice, Constitutional Court of the Federal Republic of Germany, Constitutional Court of the Federal Republic of Germany
Mr Ioannis Konstantinidis, Assistant Professor of International Law, Qatar University, College of Law
Mr David Krivanek, Desk Officer, Division Law of the Sea, Space and Environmental Law, Antarctica, Ministry of Foreign Affairs, Germany
Mr Markiyan Z. Kulyk, Judge, International Tribunal for the Law of the Sea
Mr Rainer Lagoni, Professor, University of Hamburg
Mr Thomas Laker, Presiding Judge, Administrative Court, Hamburg

Ms Ruth Lapidoth, Professor, The Hebrew University of Jerusalem
Mr Rainer Lassig, Head of Division, Division Law of the Sea, Space and Environmental Law, Antarctica, Ministry of Foreign Affairs, Germany
M. Guillaume Le Floch, Professeur, Université de Rennes 1
Mr Anders Leopold, Judge, Department of Justice of the City of Hamburg
Ms Judith Levine, Senior Legal Counsel, Permanent Court of Arbitration
Mr Linlin Li, Deputy Division Director, Ministry of Foreign Affairs, Treaty and Law Department, China
Ms Liesbeth Lijnzaad, Head of the International Law Division, Ministry of Foreign Affairs, International Law division, The Netherlands
Mr Michael Lodge, Legal Counsel and Deputy to the Secretary-General, International Seabed Authority
Mr Anthony Amos Lucky, Judge, International Tribunal for the Law of the Sea
Mr Xinmin Ma, Deputy Director General, Ministry of Foreign Affairs, Treaty and Law Department, China
Ms Sari Mäkelä, Director, Ministry for Foreign Affairs, Finland
Mr Robert A. Makgill, Barrister, Robert Makgill Barrister
Mr José Martín y Pérez de Nanclares, Head of the International Legal Division, Ministry of Foreign Affairs, Spain
Mr Holger F. Martinsen, Consul General, Embassy of Argentina, London
Ms Etta Mensah, Ministry of Justice and Attorney General's Department, Ghana
Mme Alina Miron, Professeur, Université d'Angers
Ms Elzbieta Mizerska-Dyba, Head of Library and Archives, International Tribunal for the Law of the Sea
M. Jean-Jacques Morel, Avocat, Morel Cabinet d'Avocats
Mr Harvey Mpoto, Intern, International Tribunal for the Law of the Sea
Ms Sibusiswe Melody Mutendi, Deputy Director of the Legal Department, Ministry of Foreign Affairs, Zimbabwe
Mr Antoine Mvubu Mabika, Nippon Fellow, International Tribunal for the Law of the Sea
M. Tafsir Malick Ndiaye, Juge, Tribunal international du droit de la mer
Mr Kelve Nobre de Carvalho, Public Prosecutor, Procuradoria-general da República, São Tomé e Príncipe
Ms Cristina Olivos Pascual, Legal Unit of Directorate-General for Maritime Affairs and Fisheries of the European Commission
Ms Gráinne O'Mahony, Deputy Assistant Chief State Solicitor, Chief State Solicitor's Office, Ireland
Mr Francisco Orrego Vicuña, Professor, Heidelberg University Center for Latin America
Ms Orrego Vicuña

Mr Lesther Ortega Lemus, Minister Counsellor, Embassy of Guatemala to the United Kingdom

Mr Bernard H. Oxman, Professor, University of Miami School of Law

Mr Mario Oyarzabal, Legal Adviser, Ministry of Foreign Affairs and Worship, Argentina, Office of the Legal Advisor

Mr Jin-Hyun Paik, Judge, International Tribunal for the Law of the Sea

Mr Dimitri Pampulov, Head of Department, Ministry of Foreign Affairs, Bulgaria, Directorate "International Law"

Mr Stanislaw Pawlak, Judge, International Tribunal for the Law of the Sea

M. Alain Pellet, Professeur, Université Paris Ouest, Nanterre-La Défense

Ms Christine Pichel Medina, PhD Student

M. Michel Pitron, Avocat, Gide Loyrette Nouel

Ms Renate Platzöder, Ludwig-Maximilians-Universität München, Faculty of Law

Mr Naporn Popattanachai, Nippon Fellow, International Tribunal for the Law of the Sea

Mr Paul S. Reichler, Lawyer, Foley Hoag LLP

Ms Elisabeth Rohregger, REC Services SA

Ms Kristina Rzgoeva, Head of Legal Division, Ministry of Economy and Sustainable Development, Georgia, LEPL "Maritime Transport Agency"

Ms Yara Saab, Legal Officer, International Tribunal for the Law of the Sea

Mr Akira Sakota, Professor, Seinan Gakuin University

Mr Benjamin Samson, Ph.D. Candidate, Centre de droit international de Nanterrre (CEDIN), Université Paris Ouest Nanterre La Défense

M. Cletche Sanha, Conseiller juridique, Ministère des Affaires Etrangères, Guinée-Bissau

Mr Arman Sarvarian, Professor, University of Surrey, School of Law

M. Louis Savadogo, Juriste, Tribunal international du droit de la mer

Mr Tulio Scovazzi, Professor, Università degli Studi Milano-Bicocca, Dipartimento delle Scienze Giuridiche Nazionali e Internazionali

Mr Sea Kosal, Under Secretary of State, Ministry of Foreign Affairs and International Cooperation, Cambodia

Mr José Manuel Sérvulo Correia, former Judge *ad hoc*, International Tribunal for the Law of the Sea

Ms Farzaneh Shakeri, former Nippon Fellow, International Tribunal for the Law of the Sea

Mr V.D. Sharma, Joint Secretary, Ministry of External Affairs, India, Legal and Treaties Division

Ms Marie Sheldon, Publishing Director International Law, Brill Martinus Nijhoff Publishers

Mr Yubing Shi, Associate Professor, Xiamen University, South China Sea Institute

Ms Janna Smolkina, Ship Registration Officer, Consulate-General of Panama, Hamburg

Mr Alfred Soons, Professor, Utrecht University School of Law
Ms Suzette Suarez, Professor, Law of the Sea Institute, University of Hamburg
Ms Valeriia Sulima, Intern, International Tribunal for the Law of the Sea
Ms Linlin Sun, Intern, International Tribunal for the Law of the Sea
Ms Yuri Suzuki, Vice-Consul, Consulate-General of Japan in Hamburg
Mr Seiichiro Taguchi, Counsellor, Embassy of Japan, Germany
Ms Ayana Tamaki, Administrative Staff, Consulate-General of Japan, Hamburg
Mr Yoshifumi Tanaka, Professor, University of Copenhagen, Faculty of Law
Ms Oksana Tarasyuk, Consul General, Consulate-General of Ukraine, Hamburg
Ms Diana Tase, First Secretary, Ministry of Foreign Affairs, Directorate for International Law and Treaties, Romania
Ms Virginie Tassin, Avocate, Cabinet d'avocat Tassin
Ms Regine Tchokote Fozet, Nippon Fellow, International Tribunal for the Law of the Sea
Mr Helmut Tichy, Legal Advisor, Federal Ministry for Foreign Affairs, Austria
Mr Peter Tomka, Judge, International Court of Justice
Mr Andrew Townsend, Ministry of Foreign Affairs and Trade, New Zealand
Mr Tullio Treves, Judge (1996–2011), International Tribunal for the Law of the Sea
Mr Fui Tsikata, Legal Practitioner, Reindorf Chambers
Mr Helmut Türk, Judge (2005–2014), International Tribunal for the Law of the Sea
Mr Petr Valek, Legal Advisor, Ministry of Foreign Affairs, Czech Republic
Mr Pieter van Welzen, Lawyer, Clifford Chance LLP
Ms Eva Vazquez Gomez, Law of the Sea Advisor, European Commission, DG Mare
Mr Victor Ventura, Student, University of Hamburg
Ms Silja Vöneky, Professor, Universität Freiburg, Rechtswissenschaftliche Fakultät
Mr Tilo Wallrabenstein, Lawyer and Senior Legal Advisor, Verband Deutscher Reeder, Hamburg
Mr Daniel W. Wambura, Head of Legal Directorate, Ministry of Foreign Affairs, Kenya
Mr Gavin Watson, Legal Counsellor, Foreign and Commonwealth Office, Head of Overseas Territories and Maritime Team, United Kingdom
M. Philippe Weckel, Professeur, Université Nice Sophia Antipolis, Faculté de Droit et de Science Politique
Mr Friedrich Wieland, Head of Unit of the Legal Unit of Directorate-General for Maritime Affairs and Fisheries of the European Commission
Mr Rüdiger Wolfrum, Judge, International Tribunal for the Law of the Sea
Sir Michael Wood, K.C.M.G., 20 Essex Street Chambers, United Kingdom
Mr Sam Wordsworth, QC, Essex Court Chambers
Ms Xiangxing Xu, PhD Student, University of Kiel
Mr Takeshi Yagi, Ambassador, Embassy of Japan, Germany
Mr Shunji Yanai, Judge, International Tribunal for the Law of the Sea
Mr Alexander Yankov, Judge (1996–2011), International Tribunal for the Law of the Sea

Mr Minyou Yu, Professor, Wuhan University, China Institute of Boundary and Ocean Studies

M. Saad Zakhia, Conseiller Juridique, Président du Centre de Conseil juridique et de Recherche, Ministère des Affaires Etrangères et des Emigrés, Liban

Mr Kening Zhang, Professor, Xiamen University South China Sea Institute

Mr Yang Zhang, Vice Consul, Consulate-General of China, Hamburg

Mr Jinxuan Zhang, Third Secretary Ministry of Foreign Affairs, Treaty and Law Department, China

Index

A. International jurisprudence/Jurisprudence internationale

I. ITLOS/TIDM

II. ICJ/CIJ

III. PCIJ/CPJI

IV. Other/Autres

B. International agreements and other instruments Accords internationaux et autres instruments

C. Articles of the Convention/Articles de la Convention

D. Articles of the Rules of the Tribunal
Articles du Règlement du Tribunal